OF SCRIBES AND SCROLLS

Studies on the Hebrew Bible, Intertestamental Judaism, and Christian Origins

presented to

John Strugnell

on the occasion of his sixtieth birthday

Edited by

Harold W. Attridge
John J. Collins
Thomas H. Tobin, S.J.

COLLEGE THEOLOGY SOCIETY RESOURCES IN RELIGION • 5

UNIVERSITY
PRESS OF
AMERICA

Lanham • New York • London

Copyright © 1990 by
The College Theology Society
University Press of America®, Inc.
4720 Boston Way
Lanham, Maryland 20706

3 Henrietta Street
London WC2E 8LU England

Co-published by arrangement with
The College Theology Society

Library of Congress Cataloging-in-Publication Data

Of scribes and scrolls : studies on the Hebrew Bible, intertestamental
Judaism, and Christian origins presented to John Strugnell
on the occasion of his sixtieth birthday / edited by
Harold W. Attridge, John J. Collins, Thomas H. Tobin.
p. cm.
"Co-published by arrangement with the College Theology
Society"—T.p.verso.
Includes bibliographical references.
1. Bible. O.T.—Criticism, Textual. 2. Dead Sea scrolls—
Criticism, interpretation, etc. 3. Christianity—Early church,
ca. 30-600. I. Strugnell, John, 1930- . II. Attridge,
Harold W. III. Collins, John Joseph, 1946- .
IV. Tobin, Thomas H., 1945- .

BS1136.O36 1990 221.4'4—cd20 90-41769 CIP

ISBN 0–8191–7902–7 (alk. paper).
ISBN 0–8191–7903–5 (pbk. : alk. paper).

בעצת תושיה אספר דעת
ובערמת דעת אשוך בעדה גבול סמוך
לשמור אמונים ומשפט

(1QS 10:24-25)

CONTENTS

Foreword vii

I. The Hebrew Bible and its Text

New Qumran Readings For Genesis One
    James R. Davila 3
4QDt^n: Biblical Manuscript or Excerpted Text?
    Sidnie Ann White 13
Early Emendations of the Sribes: The Tiqqun Sopherim in Zechariah 2:12
    Russell Fuller 21
*Orthography and Text in 4QDan^a and 4QDan^b and in the Received
Masoretic Text*
    Eugene Ulrich 29
*Recensional Differences Between the Masoretic Text and the Septuagint of
Proverbs*
    Emanuel Tov 43
Observations on "Wisdom Narratives" in Early Biblical Literature
    Lawrence M. Wills 57
The Beth Essentiae and the Permissive Meaning of the Hiphil (Aphel)
    J. H. Charlesworth 67

II. Second Temple Judaism and Qumran

Ben Sira 48:11 et la Résurrection
    Emile Puech 81
The Meaning of "the End" in the Book of Daniel
    John J. Collins 91
Jason's Gymnasion
    Robert Doran 99
Korah's Rebellion in Pseudo Philo 16
    Frederick J. Murphy 111
*Kenneth Burke Meets the Teacher of Righteousness: Rhetorical Strategies
in the Hodayot and the Serek Ha-Yahad*
    Carol A. Newsom 121
Some Observations on Blessings of God in Texts from Qumran
    Eileen Schuller 133
4Q185 and Jewish Wisdom Literature
    Thomas H. Tobin, S.J. 145
Two Notes on the Aramaic Levi Document
    Jonas C. Greenfield and Michael E. Stone 153

The Gender of Ιαηλ in the Jewish Inscription from Aphrodisias
    Bernadette J. Brooten 163
Tiberius Julius Alexander and the Crisis in Alexandria According to Josephus
    Robert A. Kraft 175

III. Early Christianity and its Environment 185

Daniel 7 and the Historical Jesus
    Adela Yarbro Collins 187
The Mixed Reception of the Gospel: Interpreting the Parables in Matt 13:1-52
    Daniel J. Harrington, S.J. 195
John 10 and the Feast of the Dedication
    James C. VanderKam 203
Curse and Competition in the Ancient Circus
    John G. Gager 215
The Anti-Judaic Polemic of Ephrem Syrus' Hymns on the Nativity
    Kathleen E. McVey 229
The Original Language of the Acts of Thomas
    Harold W. Attridge 241
Two Enochic Manuscripts: Unstudied Evidence for Egyptian Christianity
    George W. E. Nickelsburg 251
Julian's Attempt to Rebuild the Temple: An Inventory of Ancient and Medieval Sources
    David Levenson 261

Abbreviations 281

Notes on Contributors 286

FOREWORD

Those of us who have been privileged to work with John Strugnell know that no scholar of his generation is more learned in the classical and Semitic sources pertinent to the period of Christian origins, and no teacher more generous with his time and expertise. The essays in this volume are dedicated in gratitude to one from whom we have all learned much.

The editors wish to acknowledge the support and assistance of the Foundation for Christian Origins, and to the Departments of Theology at the University of Notre Dame and Loyola University, Chicago, for making this volume possible. Margaret Jasiewicz and her staff at Notre Dame ably supervised the computerization of several of the manuscripts. Susan Myers, a doctoral candidate in the Ph. D. program in Christianity and Judaism in Antiquity at the University of Notre Dame, provided invaluable editorial assistance. Martha Turner, in the same program, provided helpful technical support with computer matters.

March 17, 1990

Harold W. Attridge
John J. Collins
Thomas H. Tobin, S.J.

I. The Hebrew Bible and Its Textual Traditions

NEW QUMRAN READINGS FOR GENESIS ONE

James R. Davila
Tulane University

This paper presents a number of unpublished readings from manuscripts of Genesis discovered at Qumran Cave 4.[1] The treatment is selective: only (and all of the) readings from the manuscripts of Genesis 1 edited in my dissertation (see n. 3 below) which disagree with the MT are included. I have made this choice not because of any intrinsic textual merit or fault of the MT, but simply because variants from the traditional text, which is rather slavishly followed in most translations, are of special exegetical interest.[2] Some of the readings published here are already known from other textual witnesses; others are completely new. Some are secondary variants; others represent a text more original than the MT. It is particularly appropriate that this article is dedicated to Professor John Strugnell, since he sat on

---

[1]The following editions of texts were consulted: for the MT, *BHS*; for the Samaritan Pentateuch, August Freiherr von Gall, *Die Hebräische Pentateuch der Samaritaner* (abbreviated SP) (Giessen: Töpelmann, 1918); for the LXX, Alan E. Brook and Norman McLean, *The Old Testament in Greek* (London: Cambridge University Press, 1911) vol. 1, pt. 1 (Genesis); and John William Wevers, *Septuaginta*, vol. 1: *Genesis* (Göttingen: Vandenhoeck & Ruprecht, 1974) (all superscript abbrevations used herein for the LXX are those of Wevers); for the OL, Bonifatius Fischer et al., *Vetus Latina: Die Reste der altlateinischen Bibel, nach Petrus Sabatier, neu gesammelt und herausgegeben von der Erzabti Beuron*, vol. 1: *Verzeichnis der Sigel für Hand-schriften und Kirchenschriftsteller*; vol. 2: *Genesis* (Freiburg: Herder, 1949, 1951) (all superscript abbreviations used herein for the OL are the ones used in this edition); for the Peshitta, M. D. Koster, *The Old Testament in Syriac* (abbreviated Syr) vol. 1, fasc. 1: *Genesis-Exodus* (Leiden: Brill, 1977); for the Vg, Bonifatius Fischer, Iohanne Gribomont, H. D. F. Sparks, and W. Thiele, *Biblia Sacra: Iuxta vulgatam versionem* 3rd ed., vol. 1: *Genesis-Psalmi* (Stuttgart: Deutsche Bibelgesellschaft, 1983); for *Tg. Onq.*, Alexander Sperber, *The Bible in Aramaic* (Leiden: Brill, 1959) vol. 1; for *Tg. Neof.*, Alejandro Diez Macho, *Neophyti 1: Targum Palestinense MS de la Biblioteca Vaticana*, vol. 1: *Génesis* (Barcelona: Consejo superior de investigaciones cientificas, 1968); for *Tg. Ps.-J.*, E. G. Clarke, W. E. Aufrecht, J. C. Hurd, F. Spitzer, *Targum Pseudo-Jonathan of the Pentateuch: Text and Concordance* (Hoboken, N.J.: Ktav, 1984); for *Fragment Targums P* and *V* (abbreviated *Frg. Tg. P, V*), Michael L. Klein, *The Fragment Targums of the Pentateuch According to Their Extant Sources* (2 vols., Rome: Biblical Institute, 1980).

[2]For a valuable discussion of the appropriate use of the MT for the textual criticism of the Hebrew Bible see P. Kyle McCarter, Jr., *Textual Criticism: Recovering the Text of the Hebrew Bible* (Philadelphia: Fortress, 1986) 13-16.

my dissertation committee and spent many hours helping me work through the difficulties in the Qumran material assigned to me. My thanks go to him for his countless valuable insights, some of which are cited in this article.[3] Any errors that remain are, of course, my responsibility alone.

Five of the manuscripts I was assigned include material from Genesis 1. The texts of two of these manuscripts are not relevant to the main topic of this study, but the manuscripts themselves deserve some mention. 4QGen[b] preserves Gen 1:1-25, 26-27; 2:14-19; and 4:2-11 relatively intact, and has a small fragment of 5:13 or 14 (reading קינן). Its text is identical to the MT except for one orthographic variant: thus it belongs to the same textual family as the MT.[4] As Frank Moore Cross pointed out to me, it is possible that the manuscript did not come from Qumran at all. The leather is coarse and not well prepared, unusual for a Qumran scroll. The manuscript is written in a late Herodian or perhaps even post-Herodian formal hand (ca. 50-68 CE, possibly somewhat later).[5] Most of the scrolls from Cave 4 were

[3]Citations of Strugnell without an accompanying bibliographical reference refer to private communications. I also wish to thank Professor Frank Moore Cross, who assigned me a set of Qumran manuscripts for my doctoral dissertation, "Unpublished Pentateuchal Manuscripts from Cave IV, Qumran: 4QGenEx[a], 4QGen[b-h, j-k]" (Harvard University, 1988), and who acted as chairman of my dissertation committee. A revised version of this thesis will be published in *DJD* 10. I have two other studies of this material forthcoming: "The Name of God at Moriah: An Unpublished Fragment from 4QGenEx[a]" (submitted to *Maarav*, July 1989) and "The Text of Genesis at Qumran" (in progress).

[4]"Textual family" is used here as a technical term, meaning a group of manuscripts that are very closely related but whose genealogy is not necessarily clearly defined. This is the most narrow grouping of manuscripts for the Hebrew Bible. The next largest grouping is the tribe, then the sub-text-type, and finally the text-type. The existence of the last for the Hebrew Bible is still a matter of debate. Regarding textual groupings of manuscripts of the Hebrew Bible see provisionally G. W. Gooding, "An Appeal for a Stricter Terminology in the Textual Criticism of the Old Testament," *JSS* 21 (1976) 15-25. See also my forthcoming study, "The Text of Genesis at Qumran" (n. 3). On the issue of text-types see the latter work as well as William Foxwell Albright, "New Light on Early Recensions of the Hebrew Bible," in Frank Moore Cross and Shemaryahu Talmon, eds., *Qumran and the History of the Biblical Text* (Cambridge: Harvard University Press, 1975) 140-46; Cross, *The Ancient Library of Qumran and Modern Biblical Studies* (2d ed., Grand Rapids: Baker, 1980) 168-94; "The History of the Biblical Text in the Light of Discoveries in the Judean Desert," *Qumran and the History*, 177-95; "The Contribution of the Qumran Discoveries to the Study of the Biblical Text," *Qumran and the History*, 278-92; "The Evolution of a Theory of Local Texts," *Qumran and the History*, 306-20; and Emanuel Tov, *The Text-Critical Use of the Septuagint in Biblical Research* (Jerusalem: Simor, 1981) 253-75.

[5]The technical terminology relating to Hebrew scripts is that of Cross in "The Development of the Jewish Scripts," in G. Ernest Wright, ed., *The Bible and the Ancient Near East: Essays in Honor of William Foxwell Albright* (Garden City: Doubleday, 1965) 170-264. Another important study of the same topic is N. Avigad,

discovered by the Bedouin and removed from their archaeological context. It may be that 4QGen[b] was actually discovered in another Judean Desert cave (perhaps in the Wadi Murabba'ât?) and that the Bedouin accidentally mixed it in with a group of Cave 4 manuscripts. The biblical scrolls discovered in the Murabba'ât caves also conform closely to the text of the MT, and sometimes their palaeographical dates are roughly comparable to that of 4QGen[b].[6]

Some scroll fragments were removed from Cave 4 in controlled excavations. John Strugnell has been kind enough to check all the photographs of these fragments at his disposal, and nothing from 4QGen[b] was among them. I hope to check the rest of the photographs myself in Jerusalem in the near future, but in the meantime the provenance of the manuscript must remain in doubt.

4QGen[d] preserves a damaged text of Gen 1:18-27. It is written in a late Hasmonean formal hand which shows some semiformal influence. It was probably copied ca. 50-25 BCE. Where its text is preserved or can be reconstructed it is identical to the MT, aside from four orthographic variants.

4QGen[g]

This manuscript preserves a fragmentary text of Gen 1:1-11 (frg. 1), 1:13-22 (frg. 2), and a bit of 2:6-7 or 18-19 (frg. 3). Frgs. 1 and 2 probably represent the first two columns of the manuscript, each of which originally contained fourteen lines. 4QGen[g] is written in a late Hasmonean formal hand of about the same date as 4QGen[d]. Aside from minor orthographic differences it has a number of interesting variants from the MT.

In Gen 1:5 the MT, SP, LXX, OL, and Vg read ויקרא אלהים לאור יום, "And God called the light 'day.'" 4QGen[g] however reads יומם, "daytime" for the last word. יומם is an abstract noun (or sometimes an adverb) derived from יום.[7] The reading יומם is reflected in the translations of the Syr, *Tg. Onq.*, *Tg. Neof.*, *Tg. Ps. -J.*, and *Frg. Tg. P.* The Peshitta and these Targumim also have this reading instead of יום in 1:14, 16, 18 (none of these occurrences is preserved on the leather of 4QGen[g]). The reading יומם is clearly secondary in all these passages and seems to be a systematic alteration of יום wherever it is used in an abstract sense in 1:1-2:4a. When the text refers to a specific day, יום is used in all preserved witnesses (1:5 [twice], 8, 13, 19, 23, 31; 2:2, 3). It is possible that the alteration arose from a dittography of *mem* in

"The Palaeography of the Dead Sea Scrolls and Related Documents," in Chaim Rabin and Yigael Yadin, eds., *Aspects of the Dead Sea Scrolls*, (2d ed.; Scripta Hierosolymitana 4; Jerusalem: Magnes, 1965) 56-87.

[6]For example the manuscript of an unidentified psalm from Wadi Murabba'ât, dated by Cross to ca. 75-100 CE in "Development of the Jewish Scripts," 174-81 and figure 2, line 9.

[7]Probably by the addition of the adverbial ending ם-. Cf. GKC 100g and n. 1.

a manuscript whose hand did not distinguish between a medial and final *mem*, that is, in an early manuscript or one written in a palaeo-Hebrew script. Once the error had occurred in a passage that happened to use יום in an abstract sense it could easily have spread to other passages where יום was used in the same way.

In 1:9 4QGenᵍ reads מתחת לשמים, whereas the MT, 4QGenᵇ, LXX, SP, the text of the Leiden edition of the Syr, *Tg. Onq.*, *Tg. Neof.*, *Tg. Ps. -J.*, and *Frg. Tg. P* read מתחת השמים. The apparatus of the Leiden Syr and LXX^DialTA read מתחת הרקיע. (The Vorlagen of the LXX, OL, and Vg cannot be reconstructed here with any certainty.) The original reading is probably מתחת השמים. The others are partial assimilations to the phrase מתחת לרקיע in 1:7. One reading substitutes רקיע for שמים but retains the definite article. The other keeps שמים but substitutes the preposition ל for the article.

In 1:14 4QGenᵍ appears to read [לי]מים against ולימים found in the MT, 4QGenᵏ, SP, LXX, OL, Vg, *Tg. Onq.*, and *Tg. Ps. -J.* The reading of 4QGenᵍ is materially uncertain; it is barely possible that the damaged letter is a *waw*, in which case the text would be identical to the other witnesses. If 4QGenᵍ does have a variant, it is probably secondary. Based on data collected by W. Randall Garr we can say that in epigraphic Hebrew, as well as the epigraphic remains of other Northwest Semitic dialects, a series of coordinated nouns which repeats the preposition before each member of the series always has the conjunction *waw* preceding the preposition for the second and following members of the series.[8] Thus we would expect the conjunction to precede the second, third, and fourth members of the series in Gen 1:14.

In 1:22 4QGenᵍ, along with the SP, reads ירבה, against ירב in the MT and 4QGenᵇ. For the most part it is impossible to determine the Vorlagen of the other witnesses since they do not normally indicate the difference between a jussive and imperfect form. It is also impossible to determine which of the two recoverable readings is original. A jussive makes better sense in the context, but an imperfect is not completely excluded, and it is difficult to explain the presence of the final *he* of 4QGenᵍ and the SP if it was not original. If the *he* was original it is possible that it was accidentally omitted because the eye of the scribe was confused by the two *beth's* on either side, although a haplography normally would be expected to omit one of the *beth's* as well.

There are also three places in 4QGenᵍ where the leather is not preserved, but reconstruction of the damaged lines may indicate that the manuscript had readings different from the MT. Frg. 2, line 2 of 4QGenᵍ is severely damaged, but once contained the first half of the text of Gen 1:14. The right side of the line is

---

[8]*Dialect Geography of Syria-Palestine, 1000-586 B.C.E.* (Philadelphia: University of Pennsylvania Press, 1985) 176-80. This discussion and its implications for the reconstruction of the text of Gen 1:14 were pointed out to me by John Strugnell.

James R. Davila

preserved. It reads [ע]רקי ברקי מארות יהי ויאמר. The word אלהים is written interlinearly above the second and third words. Line 3 of the fragment begins ובין הלילה.... If the line is reconstructed according to the MT, 4QGen[bk], Syr, Vg, *Tg. Onq.*, *Tg. Neof.*, *Tg. Ps. -J.*, and *Frg. Tg. P*, it contains forty-three letter-spaces. The average number of letter-spaces for this column is fifty-one to fifty-two. There are two possible explanations for the discrepancy. It may be that part of the leather of line 2 was unsuitable for writing and was left blank. A similar blank space is found in frg. 1, v 5 between ויקרא and אלהים. Also, in frg. 2 there is stitching on a damaged place on the leather across lines 9-10. The other possibility is that the manuscript read with the SP, LXX, and OL and added the phrase להאיר על הארץ immediately before להבדיל. This phrase is a secondary expansion from v 15. If we reconstruct it in v 14 of 4QGen[g] the line is a little long (fifty-seven letter-spaces), but still within the possible range.

In frg. 2, line 4, Gen 1:16, the line is also too short if reconstructed with the MT, 4QGen[b(fragmentary)], SP, LXX, OL, Syr, *Tg. Onq.*, *Tg. Neof.*, *Tg. Ps. -J.*, and *Frg. Tg. P*. The line is preserved on the right side and reads ברקיע השמים להאיר על הארץ ויהי כ[ן]. Line 5 begins את שני.... If reconstructed according to the other witnesses line 4 would have forty-four letter-spaces. Either a bad patch on the leather was skipped or a longer reading that is no longer attested in any witness was found in this line.

The third possible reconstructed variant is found in frg. 2, lines 13-14, Gen 1:22. Material from roughly the center of each line is preserved. Line 13 reads אלהים [ ] בימי[ם] and line 14 והעוף ירבה ב[ארץ] כי טוב ויבר[ך]. The space from the beginning of [ך]ויבר to the end of ירבה constitutes exactly one line. But the letter-space count is suspiciously long (fifty-nine letter-spaces if reconstructed with the MT, 4QGen[b(d reconstructed)], SP, LXX, OL, *Tg. Onq.*, *Tg. Neof.*, *Tg. Ps. -J.*, and *Frg. Tg. P*). The Vg omits אלהים after ויברך אתם, but because this witness is notorious for its tendency to abbreviate the text, there is no certainty that this variant reflects a Vorlage different from the other witnesses. Nonetheless, it is tempting to reconstruct the text without the אלהים, perhaps lost by haplography with the following אתם (and possibly even restored in an interlinear correction as in frg. 2, line 2, discussed above).

4QGen [h] and 4QGen [k]

The most interesting variants from an exegetical viewpoint appear in these manuscripts. 4QGen[h] is a tiny fragment (2.3 x 1.7 cm) preserving part of the text of Gen 1:8-10. It is written in a late Hasmonean-early Herodian transitional formal script and was probably copied ca. 50-25 BCE. 4QGen[k] partially preserves Gen 1:9 (frg. 1), 1:14-16 (frg. 2), 1:27-28 (frg. 3), 2:1-3 (frg. 4), and 3:1-2 (frg. 5). It is written in a Herodian formal hand, probably from the middle of the period (ca. 1-30 CE).

7

The first variant is found in 4QGen[h]. The full text of the preserved portion reads

שׂ[
ויאמר[
מקוה]
ליבשׂה[

It is line 3 that concerns us. In the MT, 4QGen[b], SP, Syr, Vg, *Tg. Onq.*, *Tg. Neof.*, *Tg. Ps. -J.*, and *Frg. Tg. P* we have the reading מקום, "place" in v 9. The LXX and OL agree with 4QGen[h] in reading מקוה, "gathering." It is particularly fortunate that the leather was preserved here, because 4QGen[h] now gives us the Vorlage of the LXX and OL reading. The LXX reads συναγωγήν. It was generally accepted that מקוה was the proper retroversion,[9] but this retroversion has been disputed. T. L. Fenton has argued that the original reading was מקוים, "gatherings," and he attempts to explain the origin of the other readings by this one.[10] The exegetical issue that prompted his reconstruction has to do with הימים, "the seas" mentioned in v 10. The waters are gathered into "one place" in v 9 and are called the "gathering of the waters" in v 10. But these same waters are called "seas" in v 10 denoting "a plurality of aqueous bodies."[11] In the older consonantal script Fenton's putative original text would have been written מקום, identical to the spelling of the word "place." The reading "place" could have arisen through a misunderstanding of which word was meant. Alternatively, the reading in the MT et al. could have arisen through a haplography of the *waw* and *yod*. The reading מקום in Ps 104:8 may also have contributed to the misreading מקום in Gen 1:9. Once the error was present, a scribe added the word אחד and made the noun singular in order to smooth out the grammar of the text, or perhaps made the changes on the basis of another text that had the reading found in the MT. Fenton also emends the singular מקוה in v 10 of the MT and SP to a plural construct מקוי. This emendation may be supported by the LXX translation συστήματα (plural) "systems," "compounds." Thus, according to Fenton, all references to the waters in vv 9-10 (including the longer text of the LXX,

[9]For example, Hermann Gunkel, *Genesis* (6th ed., HAT; Göttingen: Vandenhoeck & Ruprecht, 1902, 1964) 107; Umberto Cassuto, *A Commentary on the Book of Genesis*, vol. 1: *From Adam to Noah* (Jerusalem: Magnes, 1964) 35; John Skinner, *A Critical and Exegetical Commentary on Genesis* (2d ed.; ICC; Edinburgh: Clark, 1930) 22; E. A. Speiser, *Genesis* (AB; Garden City: Doubleday, 1964) 6; and (with reservations) Claus Westermann, *Genesis 1-11: A Commentary* (Minneapolis: Augsburg, 1984) 78-79.

[10]"'One Place,' Māqôm ʾEḥād in Genesis I 9: Read Miqwîm, 'Gatherings,'" *VT* 34 (1984) 438-45.

[11]Fenton, "One Place," 440.

James R. Davila

to be discussed below) were originally plural, and referred to the various seas known to the Israelites.

The new data from Qumran show that this reconstruction, which was suspiciously complex in the first place, is incorrect. According to Fenton the reading מקוה אחד never existed in a Hebrew manuscript. It was created during the transmission of the LXX when a scribe assimilated the original reading συναγωγάς to the variant מקום אחד. But 4QGen[h] now gives us מקוה in Hebrew.[12] The LXX is translated from a Hebrew Vorlage. Presumably Fenton could still argue that the original Hebrew reading מקוים was altered to מקוה אחד under the influence of the Hebrew variant מקום אחד, but it is difficult to see why a scribe would adopt such a reading, which makes less sense in context than either of the others. It is best to reject the hypothetical original reading מקוים as being unsupported by the evidence.[13]

We are still left with the problem of the "seas" in v 10 versus the "one place" or "one gathering" in v 9. I have little to add to the attempts of previous commentators to grapple with the difficulty. Umberto Cassuto points out that the issue in the passage is that the waters were now limited in their extent; they no longer suffused the primal chaos. Perhaps the point is simply that they were gathered under the firmament (הרקיע) to one place or gathering in the sense that water was now a separate entity, allowing the dry land to appear. In any case, as mentioned by Cassuto,[14] ים sometimes appears in the plural in poetic passages with a singular meaning.[15]

So, thanks to 4QGen[h], we can eliminate מקוים as the original text. This conclusion still does not tell us which reading, מקום or מקוה, is original. The question is tied to the other LXX variant in v 9, and will be addressed in connection with it below.

The other variant in v 9 occurs in 4QGen[k]. The text of frg. 1, which preserves the right margin of the column, reads ותרא היב[שה]. Just enough is preserved to show that this manuscript included the passage found in the LXX, OL[E], and OL[C] in part, but not in the MT, 4QGen[b], SP, Syr, Vg, Tg. Onq., Tg. Neof., Tg. Ps. -J., and Frg. Tg. P. The vital clue is the verb form; it is a converted imperfect niphal, which appears without the he. The passage in the LXX reads καὶ συνήχθη τὸ ὕδωρ τὸ ὑποκάτω τοῦ οὐρανοῦ εἰς τὰς συναγωγὰς αὐτῶν καὶ ὤφθη ἡ ξηρά. Based

[12]It is, of course, impossible to be certain if אחד was actually found in the gap after מקוה since if it were missing the difference would be only four letter-spaces.

[13]The Qumran reading מקוה also allows us to dismiss the retroversion *miqwêm, "[one] gathering of them," a contraction of *miqwêhem suggested by David Noel Freedman, "Notes on Genesis," ZAW 64 (1952) 190-91.

[14]From Adam to Noah, 35.

[15]Cf. also Skinner, Genesis, 22-23.

on this Greek text we can retrovert the Qumran reading approximately as follows:
‏[ויקוו המים מתחת השמים אל מקויהם] ותרא היב[שה]‎.

This fragment proves what should have already been clear on internal grounds: that this LXX reading is based on a Hebrew Vorlage.[16] But the question remains whether the phrase is original or an addition inspired by the structure of the P creation account. The general consensus seems to be that the passage is secondary. Skinner offers no opinion on the matter. Hermann Gunkel takes it to be a harmonizing addition characteristic of the LXX of Genesis 1. Cassuto, E. A. Speiser, and Gerhard von Rad ignore the LXX reading, and so by implication reject it. Claus Westermann accepts the MT as original but gives no reason for his decision.[17]

More recently, Johann Cook has argued in detail that variants between the LXX and MT of Genesis 1 are due to the harmonizing approach of the Greek translator(s), not to a variant Hebrew Vorlage.[18] In the case of the variant in v 9 under consideration here, Cook argues that the translator(s) added the longer reading for one of two reasons. First, the translator(s) may have wished to provide a *Tatbericht* to correspond to the *Wortbericht* in v 9. The other acts of creation in Genesis 1 include both, and the absence of the *Tatbericht* would have been disturbing to the translator(s). Second, there may be a common exegetical tradition behind the LXX and the book of Jubilees. The statement in Jub 2:6 is very similar to the longer reading of the LXX. Both Jubilees and the LXX seem to protest against the ancient myth of the battle between the storm god and the chaos dragon. The translator(s) of the LXX may have expanded v 9 to leave no doubt that the waters were utterly submissive to God at the time of creation.

Frg. 1 of 4QGen[k] shows that Cook's main conclusion is incorrect; the LXX did in fact have a Hebrew Vorlage. But his arguments for the secondary nature of the longer reading could be applied equally well to the Hebrew text, and hence must be considered apart from the harmonizing or nonharmonizing nature of the LXX.

I propose a different and, I believe, much simpler solution for this textual variant in Gen 1:9. I take the reading of the LXX and 4QGen[k] to be original. Thus Gen 1:9

[16]For example, Skinner (*Genesis*, 22) pointed out in 1910 that the plural possessive pronoun αὐτῶν proves that there is a Hebrew original behind the Greek; in Hebrew the plural pronoun suffix refers, of course, to the plural מים, "waters." Fenton fails to understand this grammatical point and cites the plural pronoun as an argument against a Hebrew Vorlage for the passage: "One Place," 443.

[17]Gunkel, *Genesis*, 107-108; Skinner, *Genesis*, 22; Cassuto, *From Adam to Noah*, 35-39; Speiser, *Genesis*, 3, 6; von Rad, *Genesis: A Commentary* (2d ed.; OTL; Philadelphia: Westminster, 1972) 46, 54; Westermann, *Genesis 1-11*, 12.

[18]"Genesis 1 in the Septuagint as an Example of the Problem: Text and Tradition," *Journal of Northwest Semitic Languages* 10 (1982) 25-36. This article follows up Cook's earlier work "Text and Tradition: A Methodological Problem," *Journal of Northwest Semitic Languages* 9 (1981) 3-11.

did contain both a *Wortbericht* and a *Tatbericht*, just as in the other acts of creation. The phrase was lost in the manuscript tradition represented by the MT by haplography. The first Hebrew word of the missing phrase can be retroverted from the Greek as ויקוו, "and [the waters] were gathered." The first word of v 10 is ויקרא, "and [God] called." The scribe's eye skipped from the first letter-cluster ויק- to the second, leaving out the intervening material (homoeoarchton).[19]

Having established the original reading in this case, we can now return to the other variant in v 9, מקום versus מקוה . The most probable solution is that מקום is original. The uncorrupted text of v 9 had the word מקויהם in the second half of the verse. If we assume that מקום was the original reading earlier in the verse, it is easy to see how a harmonizing scribe could have miswritten מקוה instead under the influence of מקויהם. On the other hand, it is very difficult to explain why מקום would have been substituted for an original מקוה.[20]

There is one more variant in Genesis 1 preserved on the leather of 4QGen[k]. It is in v 14 and is found on frg. 2 of the manuscript, line 2 of text, and also appears in the SP and in the Vorlagen of the LXX, OL, and Syr. In the series of coordinated nouns at the end of the verse the final member is given as ולשׁ[נים]. We find ושׁנים in the MT and the Targumim (including both *Frg. Tg. P* and *V*). The Vorlage of the Vg is impossible to reconstruct. Garr has shown that in epigraphic Hebrew (as well as in epigraphic remains of the other Northwest Semitic dialects) the preposition is always repeated before each of a series of nouns that are coordinated (except when a proper noun is found before an appositional noun or a nominal modifier precedes a proper noun).[21] So grammatically it is best to regard the reading ולשׁנים as original.

The most important general implication of the new Qumran material presented in this study is that we must take the LXX of Genesis very seriously as a source for a Hebrew textual tradition alternate to the MT. We have strong reason to believe that the translators of Genesis treated their Vorlage with respect and rendered the Hebrew text before them into Greek with great care and minimal interpretation. A judicious use of the LXX, with careful retroversion, gives the textual critic access to many variant Hebrew readings, some of which are original.[22]

---

[19]Thus Jubilees is probably paraphrasing a Hebrew text identical to 4QGen[k] and the Vorlage of the LXX rather than expanding the text with a midrashic commentary.

[20]It is interesting to note that there is not enough space in line 3 of 4QGen[h] in which to reconstruct the longer original reading in 4QGen[k].

[21]*Dialect Geography of Syria-Palestine*, 176-80.

[22]This conclusion is confirmed by other data discussed in my thesis (n. 3), but which falls outside the scope of this article. Some readings from the Joseph story found in 4QGen[e] and 4QGen[j] confirm that, at least often, the LXX is following a variant Hebrew Vorlage when it differs from the MT.

4QDt^n: BIBLICAL MANUSCRIPT OR EXCERPTED TEXT?*

Sidnie Ann White
Albright Institute, Jerusalem

The Deuteronomy manuscript from Cave 4, Qumran, with which this paper will be concerned, 4QDt^n, (the All Souls Deuteronomy)[1] is an exceptionally well-preserved manuscript. It consists of four complete columns and two partially damaged columns of text. Col. 1 has two sewn edges, and was originally attached to the beginning of col. 2 (they were separated in the process of restoration). Col. 1 contains the text of Deuteronomy 8:5-10. Cols. 2-6 are one continuous sheet of leather, with a sewn edge on col. 2. The text of these columns is Deuteronomy 5:1-6:1. The manuscript was originally reddish brown in color, although now it has faded to beige or grayish brown in places. The surface of the leather was originally smooth and glossy, but with several patches which were unsuitable for writing. The leather is thin, almost transparent in places. There are visible horizontal dry lines on cols. 1-4 and vertical dry lines on col. 1. Points jalons mark the dry lines on col. 2. The writing does not always follow the dry lines carefully.[2]

The measurements for cols. 1 and 2, the order and purpose of which this paper will be concerned, are as follows: Col. 1 is 95 mm in width, and the longest line contains 65 letter spaces. It contains 7 inscribed lines, but 15 dry lines. Col. 2 is 53 mm in width and between 27 and 38 letter spaces long. It contains 12 inscribed lines, but 14 dry lines.

*This article was written in Jerusalem at the W. F. Albright Institute of the American Schools of Oriental Research, during a research leave made possible by a grant from the National Endowment for the Humanities. It gives me great pleasure to dedicate this article to my dear teacher and friend, Professor John Strugnell, on the occasion of his sixtieth birthday.

[1] The purchase of this scroll was made possible by All Souls' Unitarian Church, New York City, hence its name. A photograph and partial translation of the scroll was published by Frank Moore Cross in *Scrolls from the Wilderness of the Dead Sea* (Berkley: University of California Press, 1969). The complete scroll, with photographs, will be published by me in *DJD 10* (Oxford: Oxford University Press, forthcoming).

[2] Dry lines are horizontal lines ruled onto the uninscribed leather with a sharp instrument to guide the scribe as he wrote his text. *Points jalons* are ink marks made at the beginning of each line to aid in the placement of the dry lines.

The paleographical study of 4QDt^n places it in the early Herodian period, ca. 30-31 BCE. The orthography of this manuscript is much fuller than either the orthography of the Masoretic text or of the Samaritan Pentateuch, consistently marking all long vowels (i.e., *aw > ô, *ay > ê, *ī, *ū, and usually *ā > ō), and some short vowels (e.g., כול, החושך).

This paper will investigate the question of the proper categorization of 4QDt^n, whether as a biblical manuscript or as an excerpted text. Following a discussion of that question, a transcription and critical notes of col. 1 will be given.

The question of the categorization of 4QDt^n has been raised by Hartmut Stegemann in a 1967 article. Stegemann asked if it were possible, given the order of the chapters (col. 1 contains Deut 8:5-10, cols. 2-6 contain Deut 5:1-6:1), that 4QDt^n was an excerpted text along the lines of the Nash Papyrus.[3] Stegemann suggests that the order of the chapters, their contents, and the way in which col. 1 was inscribed may lead to the conclusion that 4QDt^n was an excerpted text used for devotional or liturgical purposes. Stegemann finishes his discussion, however, by mentioning the opinion of John Strugnell that this manuscript is a biblical manuscript which was damaged at 8:5-10 and was repaired incorrectly. I will pursue both lines of thought before reaching a conclusion.

The first argument would conclude that 4QDt^n was an excerpted text, possibly used for private devotions or for study. There are several data which support such a conclusion. First, a portion of chapter 8 (in a separate column) precedes the beginning of chapter 5. Col. 1 was sewn onto col. 2, so it is probable that this was deliberate. Col. 1 is also a complete column of text, but it is only partially inscribed; if the scribe had wished to add more text there is still plenty of room on the leather to do so. It is unusual at Qumran not to fill a column of text completely, except at the end of a scroll. This may indicate that this text was excerpted.[4] The

---

[3] H. Stegemann, "Weitere Stücke von 4QpPsalm 37, von 4Q Patriarchal Blessings und Hinweis auf eine unedierte Handschrift aus Höhle 4Q mit Exzerpten aus dem Deuteronomium," *RevQ* 6 (1967) 193–227. The Nash Papyrus is a papyrus manuscript, found in Egypt, which has been dated to the second half of the second century BCE. It contains the entire Decalogue (taken from Exodus) and the Shma^c on a single leaf. It appears to have been a type of lectionary. For further information and bibliography, see W. F. Albright, "A Biblical Fragment from the Maccabaean Age: The Nash Papyrus," *JBL* 56 (1937) 145–76.

[4] Stegemann ("Weitere Stücke," 224) notes that the scribe left empty spaces in the middle of the text (see the transcription and the photograph) and wonders whether special significance should be attached to that fact. While this is true, I do not believe that any special significance can be attached to it; as stated in the introduction, the scribe left several empty spaces on the leather which can only be accounted for by assuming that he encountered bad leather and passed over it while copying his manuscript. Therefore, while it is possible that the empty spaces were left on col. 1 for a particular reason, the physical evidence does not clearly support this conclusion.

column has two sewn edges, indicating that it was placed before col. 1, and that at least one other column preceded it. It was clearly attached to the beginning of col. 1, completely out of the order of the biblical text (the columns which preceded col. 1 were not preserved). In the phylacteries extant at Qumran, we have much evidence for Deut 5:1–6:1 being used separately outside of a biblical manuscript.[5] For example, 4QPhyl[a] contains 5:1-14, then, after a break of six lines, 5:27–6:3. 4QPhyl[b] contains 5:1–6:3; 4QPhyl[g] contains Deut 5:1-21; 4QPhyl[h] contains Deut 5:22–6:5. 4QPhyl[j] contains, on the *recto*, Deut 5:1-24, and, on the *verso*, 5:24–6:3. These appear to be continuous texts, as we have a continuous text of 5:1–6:1 in 4QDt[n]. Unfortunately, there is no other evidence, besides the evidence of 4QDt[n], for 8:5-10 being singled out as a special text at Qumran (in phylacteries, mezuzôt or commentaries). Stegemann, however, notes that in the Samaritan tradition 8:5-10 is set off by empty spaces.[6] This indicates that the text could have been considered as a self-contained unit. Also Moshe Weinfeld, in an unpublished paper, notes, in a mention of 4QDt[n] (not 4QDt[m], which is mistakenly cited), that Deut 8:5-10 is the basis, in the rabbinic tradition, for the duty of blessing after meals, in other words, a text with special significance (see *b. Ber.* 44a).[7] Therefore, there are two traditions, which do, although they are outside of Qumran, set apart Deut 8:5-10 in some way. It is then possible that the Qumran community gave special significance to the text, although 4QDt[n] would be the only extant evidence for that. All this evidence makes clear that the texts from Deuteronomy found in 4QDt[n] were texts that could be singled out for study or devotional purposes.

Finally, the character of the text of 4QDt[n] must be taken into consideration. As I have shown elsewhere,[8] the text of the Decalogue in 4QDt[n] is a harmonizing text. This is most clear in the text of the fourth commandment, the Sabbath commandment, which combines Exod 20:11 with Deut 5:12-15. Harmonizations do occur in biblical manuscripts at Qumran (e.g., 4QpaleoExod[m]), so it cannot be argued on that basis that 4QDt[n] is not a biblical manuscript; however,

---

[5]K. G. Kuhn, *Phylakterien aus Höhle 4 von Qumran* (Heidelberg: Winter, 1957). J. T. Milik, "Tefillin, Mezuzot et Targums (4Q128–4Q157)," *DJD 6* (Oxford: Clarendon, 1977) 33–91.

[6]Stegemann, "Weitere Stücke," 224.

[7]I owe this reference to Dr. Eileen Schuller of McMaster University. This reference should not be taken as an indication that Qumranic and rabbinic practice concerning blessings was the same; it is always risky (given the difference in historical period and the lack of evidence for any direct connection between the two groups) to draw direct parallels between rabbinic literature and the Qumran material.

[8]See my article, "The All Souls Deuteronomy and the Decalogue," forthcoming in *JBL* (1990).

harmonizations are particularly noticeable in the phylactery texts found at Qumran, that is, in specially excerpted texts.[9]

This, then, is the evidence for the argument that this is a collection of excerpted, separate texts: (1) The chapters are out of order. (2) Col. 1 is not completely inscribed. (3) The texts, particularly those of cols. 2-6 (the Decalogue and the Shma[c]) are used elsewhere (both inside and outside of Qumran) as excerpted texts. (4) The type of text contained in 4QDt[n] is of the type most frequently found in excerpted texts.

As mentioned above, John Strugnell has suggested that 4QDt[n] was indeed a biblical manuscript which was damaged at chapter 8 and needed to be repaired. His suggestion would necessitate the following sequence of steps: When the manuscript was repaired, the scribe chose a piece of leather which was too large for the amount of text to be recopied; this would account for the empty lines on col. 1. When the scroll was sewn together, the repair piece was mistakenly added at the beginning of col. 2. This argument is based on a series of events which must be reconstructed: (1) The scroll was damaged (this occurred after the manuscript was inscribed). (2) It was taken for repair. (3) The substitute column (copied by the original scribe) was mistakenly sewn onto the beginning of col. 2. (4) The error was not rectified.

Several problems with this argument exist. First, the argument is based on the assumption that the scroll was damaged in two places, at 8:5-10 *and* at the end of chapter 4 (the section which should have preceded col. 2). There is no evidence for such an assumption, since the beginning and the end of the manuscript have not been preserved. Second, the middle part of the sequence of events proposed above is entirely reconstructed; there is no hard evidence for it. For example, we do not know when or where damaged manuscripts were repaired. Third, there is no other evidence at Qumran for this kind of error, where chapters were mistakenly placed in the wrong order. It is worth noting again that col. 1 is in the same hand as the other columns; it could be argued that the scribe who originally copied the manuscript also repaired it, but it could just as easily be argued that this scribe was actually putting together a collection of excerpted texts. In fact, we know from manuscripts such as 1QIs[a] that corrections were made to manuscripts by different scribes, so that it was not necessarily the same scribe who repaired or corrected the manuscript he originally copied.

Finally, the size of the manuscript should be considered. As the photograph of col. 1 shows, this manuscript is quite small (the photograph is the actual size of the manuscript). Most biblical manuscripts contain twenty-five lines or more per

---

[9]Milik, "Tefillin," 48–79. Many of the phylactery texts at Qumran could be characterized as "mixed" texts. The Nash Papyrus, while not a Qumran text, is also an excerpted text (lectionary) from the 2d century BCE, which contains a harmonizing text of the Decalogue.

column (that is, twice the height of this manuscript);[10] if this manuscript was originally a complete biblical scroll, it would have been quite long (approximately 13 meters long) and thus quite bulky when rolled up. This is a minor point in favor of 4QDt[n] being an excerpted text.

It has been demonstrated that there is evidence elsewhere at Qumran for the use of excerpted texts, and there is also evidence that the particular texts of 4QDt[n] may have been considered as self-contained units. There is very little evidence elsewhere at Qumran for the process of the repair of damaged manuscripts (cf., for example, the Temple Scroll), and the physical evidence of this manuscript, 4QDt[n], is not conclusive, although it can be said that it is physically unlike the typical biblical manuscripts found at Qumran. Therefore, the conclusion of this author is that 4QDt[n] is not a true biblical manuscript, but a text made and used for some devotional and/or study purpose.

The following is an edition of the contents of col. 1, with text-critical notes.

Column 1, 8:5-10

1 וידעת עם לבבך כי כאשר ייסר איש את בנו יהוה אלוהיך מיסרך ושמרתה את
2 מצות יהוה אלוהיך ללכת בדרכיו ולאהבה אותו VACAT
3 כי יהוה אלוהיך מביאך אל ארץ טובה ורחבה ארץ נחלי מים עינות ותהומות
4 יצאים בבקעה ובהר ארץ חטה ושעורה וגפן תאנה ורמון ארץ זית שמן ודבש
5 VACAT
6 ארץ אשר לוא במסכנות תאכל בה לחם ולוא תחסר כול בה ארץ אשר
7 אבניה ברזל ומהריה תחצוב נחושת VAC ואכלת ושבעתה
8 וברכתה את יהוה אלוהיך על הארץ הטובה אשר נתן לך
VACAT

Notes

8:8, line 4 ארץ A medial ṣadê appears in a final position.

---

[10]Cf., for example, 1QIsa[a].

Variants[11]

8:6, line 2 ולאהבה [וליראה M, G, S, Syr., T, V. 4Q preserves a unique variant. It is an anticipation of similar phrases in Deut 11:13, 22, 19:9, and 30:6, 16.

8:7, line 3 טובה ורחבה ארץ G, S] טובה ארץ M, Syr., T, V. The text of M et al. may be the result of haplography owing to homoioteleuton, or the text of 4Q et al. may be expansionistic. There are no parallels to this phrase in Deuteronomy.

8:7, line 3 עינות M, G, S] ܡܒܘܥܐ Syr.: מבועי עינון T: *aquarumque* V. The variants in the daughter versions of M are expansions.

8:7, line 3 ותהומות M, Syr., T] תהומות G, S. עינות ותהומות are functioning as a pair. Therefore, the conjunction is preferable, and the text of G and S is the result of parablepsis.

8:7, line 4 בבקעה ובהר M, S] cf. G, Syr., and T, which have plurals.

8:8, line 4

ורמון   תאנה   וגפן   חטה ושעורה 4Q]
ורמון   ותאנה   וגפן   חטה ושעורה M, Syr., T:
רמון   תאנה   גפן   חטה ושעורה G:
ורמון   תאנה   גפן   חטה ושעורה S.

The problem presented by this list is the presence or absence of the conjunction. All the witnesses agree on the first group of two: חטה ושעורה. The next group of three is a list of fruit products. The text preserved by S is, on the basis of style, preferable, with the conjunction appearing only before the last element in the group, although an argument could be made, on the basis of *lectio brevior*, for G's reading without the conjunction. If the argument made on the basis of style is accepted, the list is reconstructed as:

חטה ושערה גפן תאנה ורמון. Otherwise, the reconstructtion would be:

חטה ושערה גפן תאנה רמון.

8:9, line 6 תאכל בה לחם M, S, Syr., T] תאכל לחמך G, V. The missing בה in G and V may be the result of parablepsis. The suffix may have fallen off of לחם because the suffix is unusual on this noun (it occurs 251 times without a suffix, and only 46 times with a suffix). Therefore, the preferable text would read: תאכל בה לחמך. On the other hand, the suffix may be considered tautologous in Hebrew, and לחם would be preferable.

8:9, line 6 אבניה M, G[A L O], S, Syr., T] cf. G[B C], L, which do not have a suffix. This is acceptable Greek idiom.

8:9, line 6 ולוא G, Syr.] לא M, S, T. On the principle of *lectio brevior*, the conjunction is more likely to be added than deleted, therefore the text of M et al. is preferable.

8:10, line 8 על M, G, S, Syr., T] אל S[B D E a]. The Samaritan manuscripts' reading is the result of the aural confusion of אל-על.[12]

---

[12]Elisha Qimron, in *The Hebrew of the Dead Sea Scrolls* (HSM 29; Atlanta: Scholars, 1986), notes that at Qumran in this period one guttural could be mistakenly written for another because of the weakening of the gutturals. We assume this phenomenon was not limited to Qumran.

Illustration: 4QDt[n]

EARLY EMENDATIONS OF THE SCRIBES:
THE TIQQUN SOPHERIM IN ZECHARIAH 2:12

Russell Fuller
Wellesley College

Most Christian scholars of the Hebrew Bible encounter the siglum *Tiq. Soph.* (= *Tiqqune Sopherim*) only occasionally, usually in the apparatus of the Biblia Hebraica. These readings culled from various lists found in Rabbinic literature indicate emendations made in the text by early Jewish scribes and copyists. The number of such emendations found in the later Masoretic lists is eighteen.[1]

Lists of early emendations for theological or other reasons have been used as one "weapon" in the arsenal of the textual critic. In the battle to establish a "better" form of the received text or even the "original" form of the text, the *Tiqqune Sopherim* traditionally have been used to reach a "pre-Masoretic" or early Masoretic form of the text. Especially before the finds of early biblical and non-biblical manuscripts in the Judean Desert, the *Tiqqune Sopherim* were used in conjunction with the evidence of the versions for text-critical purposes.

As has been shown in a recent study by C. McCarthy,[2] these early "readings" should not be accepted at face value by the textual critic. Rather, each "emendation" must be examined in its own right in order to determine whether the Rabbinic evidence taken in conjunction with all other textual evidence actually indicates an emendation from the perspective of a modern textual critic. As with any other evidence used in the art of textual criticism the data offered by the *Tiqqunim* must first be evaluated in their own context taking account of the history of transmission of the list(s) in which the "emendation" is found. The purpose(s) of the Rabbis in compiling and preserving these lists is also important in determining the worth of each *tiqqun*. Finally and perhaps most importantly, the intention of the original

---

[1]The lists vary in the number of emendations which they record. In general the earliest lists have either eight or eleven. It is only with the later lists that the number stabilizes at eighteen and then not always the same eighteen passages are recorded in every list.

[2]For an excellent treatment of the nature and history of the lists of so-called emendations see C. McCarthy, *The Tiqqune Sopherim and Other Theological Corrections in the Masoretic Text of the Old Testament* (Freiburg: Universitätsverlag; Göttingen: Vandenhoeck & Ruprecht, 1981).

comment in which the *tiqqun* is embedded must be understood so far as this is possible.

Given these methodological necessities, it is clear that the textual critic must be able to locate and evaluate these lists of *Tiqqune Sopherim* to determine whether or not they offer any usable data for the passage under consideration.

Luckily C. McCarthy's recent book on the *Tiqqune Sopherim* provides the textual critic who is not familiar with the lists or Rabbinic literature an easy point of entry into the world of the early Rabbis and their compilations of comments which came to be labeled "emendations."[3] In the discussion which follows this work will be referred to frequently.

This paper is intended as an example of the use of one *tiqqun* for text-critical purposes. The text in question, Zech 2:12, serves as the example to recall all other *tiqqunim* or "emendations" in the earliest of the Rabbinic lists. It is only in the later lists which were arranged to follow the canonical order of biblical books that Zech 2:12 loses its place at the head of the lists of *tiqqunim*. Zech 2:12 was not, however, chosen for this purpose simply because it headed the oldest Rabbinic lists. Zech 2:12 is also preserved on a Hebrew manuscript from Qumran which the writer has had the privilege to edit.[4] This reading from 4Q12[e] is cited by McCarthy in her discussion of Zech 2:12, but, in the writer's opinion, the fragment containing this verse unfortunately was misread. This fact in part motivates this paper.

The MT of Zech 2:12 is:

כִּי כֹה אָמַר יְהוָה צְבָאוֹת אַחַר כָּבוֹד שְׁלָחַנִי אֶל

הַגּוֹיִם הַשֹּׁלְלִים אֶתְכֶם כִּי הַנֹּגֵעַ בָּכֶם נֹגֵעַ בְּבָבַת עֵינוֹ

which the RSV (2:8) renders as: "For thus said the Lord of hosts, after his glory sent me to the nations who plundered you, for he who touches you, touches the apple of his eye."

The earliest rabbinic witnesses to a tradition mentioning Zech 2:12 are found in the Mekhilta of Rabbi Ishmael at Exod 15:7 and in the Siphre on Num 10:35. Both of these compositions record lists of *kinnuyim*, that is, substitutions or euphemisms. I will argue that the distinction between the use of the two rabbinic terms *kinnuy* or "euphemism" and *tiqqun* or "emendation" is significant for the textual critic. In both the Mekhilta and the Siphre on Numbers the logion of Rabbi Judah ben Ilay (ca. 130-160 BCE) on Zech 2:12 is reproduced:

---

[3] McCarthy's discussions of the development of the early lists and of the distinction between the *kinnuyim* or euphemistic substitutions and the *tiqqunim* or emendations are immensely helpful. See McCarthy, *Tiqqune Sopherim*, 25-30; 58-59; 169-71.

[4] 4Q12[e] is a fragmentary manuscript of the Minor Prophets which dates from approximately 75 BCE.

> R. Judah says: It does not say here: "The apple of the eye," but: "The apple of his eye," referring as it were to the One above. Scripture, however, modifies the expression.[5]

There is a variant of this logion found in The Mekhilta of Rabbi Simeon ben Yohai:

> R. Judah says, There is no teaching to be derived from *waw*, but rather from *yodh*, for everyone who does damage to any man of Israel, it is as if he does damage to the One who spoke and the world came into being.[6]

McCarthy understood this later form of the logion to refer to an original reading עֵינִי which was then changed by the early scribes to the MT עֵינוֹ.[7] Her understanding of this particular text echoes that of D. Barthélemy who also argued that the original reading, עֵינִי, was indicated by the logia recording a *tiqqun* for Zech 2:12.[8] He argued that the original reading עֵינִי was changed by the scribes to עֵינוֹ early in the first century of the common era. He supported this line of reasoning with a constellation of evidence based on his work on the Greek Minor Prophets manuscript from the Nahal Hever.[9] As is well known, he argues that the Greek Minor Prophets manuscript represents a first-century revision of the Old Greek/LXX toward the evolving rabbinic recension then current in Palestine. His explanation of the data has been reasonably well accepted. The unique part of Barthélemy's synthesis of the data is his linking of the finalization of the consonantal form of the Hebrew text, which he places in the time of Rabbi Aqiba, with the *tiqqunim*.[10] He sees the *tiqqunim* as a phenomenon related to the stabilization of the Hebrew text. They are the result of the Rabbis' work upon the consonantal text, not some casual collection of Rabbinic comments. Whether or not the evidence supports Barthélemy's reconstruction of the origin and provenience of the *tiqqunim* is not the primary concern of this paper. However, his use of Zech 2:12 as a part of his argument for this reconstruction is of direct interest. I will therefore discuss Barthélemy's theory only indirectly as it bears

---

[5]J. Lauterback, *Mekhilta of Rabbi Ishmael. A Critical Edition on the Basis of the Manuscripts and early Editions with an English Translation* (3 vols., Philadelphia: Jewish Publication Society, 1939) 43.

[6]J. N. Epstein and E. Z. Melamed, *Mekhilta d'Rabbi Simion b. Jochai. Fragmenta in Geniza Cairensi reperta digressit* (Jerusalem: Mekitse Nirdamim, 1955) 2.

[7]McCarthy, *Tiqqune Sopherim*, 62, n. 14.

[8]D. Barthélemy, "Les Tiqqune Sopherim et la critique textuelle de L'Ancien Testament," *VTS* 9 (1963) 289, n. 2.

[9]Still available in *Les devanciers d'Aquila* (VTSup 10; Leiden: Brill, 1963). Forthcoming in DJD edited by E. Tov.

[10]Barthélemy, "Les Tiqqune," 285-304.

on the evidence I wish to present. The view of McCarthy and Barthélemy that the *tiqqun* for Zech 2:12 indicates an original reading עֵינִי as opposed to MT עֵינוֹ is echoed by many biblical scholars. However, the earliest rabbinic lists, those in the Mekhilta of Rabbi Ishmael and the Siphre on Numbers, do not use the term *tiqqun* but rather state that scripture has "used a euphemism," *kinah*, the nominal form for which is *kinnuy*. In other words עֵינוֹ in Zech 2:12 was not considered an emendation by Rabbi Judah, the author of this early logion. Rather, the verse was thought to be euphemistic. It referred to the "One above" indirectly through the use of the third-person masculine singular suffix.

The list itself is found in the sixth chapter of Tractate Shirata, on Exod 15:7-8, which is intended to demonstrate that the enemies of God and the enemies of Israel are identical. The corollary of this argument is that what harms the one also harms the other. It is in the context of this argument that Zech 2:12 is cited. The logion of Rabbi Judah ben Ilay on this verse in Zech and the list of *kinnuyim* follow the citation of Zech 2:12. Following the last *kinnuy* in the list the comment of Rabbi Judah on Zech 2:12 is repeated enclosing the list of *kinnuyim* in an envelope construction or bracket. This repetition of Rabbi Judah's comment on Zech 2:12 to mark off the list of *kinnuyim* clearly indicates that the list is secondary in this context. However the citation of Zech 2:12 is just as clearly *not* secondary since it fits the context of the argument so well. The use of the verbal form *kinah* should be considered alongside the variant form of the logion of R. Judah cited above:

> R. Judah says, There is no *teaching* to be derived from *waw*, but rather
> from *yodh*, for everyone who does damage to any man of Israel, it is as
> if he does damage to the One who spoke and the world came into being
> (emphasis added).[11]

It seems clear that the primary reason that R. Judah cites Zech 2:12 is to support the argument that the enemies of God are those of Israel and vice versa. It seems very likely that the list of *kinnuyim* cited here in the Mekhilta, which is headed by Zech 2:12, was inserted into the chapter because of the use of Zech 2:12 in this passage. The citation of Zech 2:12 served as a "hook" for the insertion of this list of *kinnuyim*. In addition, the wording of this form of the logion makes explicit the *exegetical* interests of the Rabbis. Both Rabbi Judah, the author of the logion, and the transmitters of this text are primarily interested in the "teaching" to be derived from this verse and not in an earlier form of the text or an "emendation" made by earlier tradents. We must take care not to project our contemporary, text-critical interests onto the ancient Rabbis even when they seem clearly to be speaking of "emendations." Another important point to consider in connection with this passage

---

[11]Epstein and Melamed, *Mekhilta d'Rabbi Simion b. Jochai.*

24

is the use of the root *knh* in the verbal form *kinah* which characterizes this list. The early lists, the Melkhilta of Rabbi Ishmael and the Siphre on Numbers, both use *knh*. It is only with the later lists that the term *tiqqun* is introduced.[12] It is also only in the later lists that the "original" reading is also supplied.[13] Depending on the individual case it may be necessary to take seriously this change in terminology.

We turn now to an examination of the evidence for the text of Zech 2:12. McCarthy concluded that the rabbinic evidence taken together with other textual data seemed to indicate the possibility of an early emendation in the text of Zech 2:12.[14] I will first briefly review the evidence from the ancient versions and then integrate a revised understanding of the Qumran evidence. The goal is to draw conclusions concerning the "original" reading of Zech 2:12 and to decide the text-critical worth of the tradition of a *tiqqun* in this case.

The Old Latin is extant only in fragments which were collected by Sabatier.[15] According to his evidence, the Old Latin read *oculi eius*, "his eye", while the Vulgate had *oculi mei*. Interestingly the evidence from the Vulgate is mixed. Some witnesses read *oculi eius*, while others have *oculi mei*. This *may* indicate that an Old Latin tradition lying behind the Vulgate also read *oculi mei*. In addition, Tertullian apparently read *oculi mei* as well, which is usually taken as evidence for the Old Latin reading.[16] We unfortunately still lack a critical edition of all the Old Latin fragments for the Minor Prophets. The editors of the *Biblia Sacra iuxta latinam vulgatam versionem* explain in the prolegomena to their critical edition of the Vulgate with Jerome's commentary that *oculi eius* is the best reading and the one endorsed by Jerome.[17] The conclusion is that the Latin evidence indicates a vague possibility of two readings, but this cannot be substantiated.

The Greek evidence is also not as straightforward as we might hope. Most witnesses read "his eye" in agreement with MT; however Papyrus Washingtonensis (G^w), which dates from the third century of the common era and is thus judged a very important, pre-Hexaplaric witness to the Old Greek text, reads "my eye." Here we might expect help from the Nahal Haver Greek manuscript of the Minor Prophets

---

[12]Compare, for example, Exodus Rabbah 12.1 which records a logion of Rabbi Joshua, "R. Joshua said: This is an emendation of the scribes, for it is written as 'My eye.'" Although the source of this logion is late, Rabbi Joshua was active at the beginning of the third century (ca. 210-240).

[13]McCarthy, *Tiqqune Sopherim*, 58-59; 245-50.

[14]McCarthy, *Tiqqune Sopherim*, 69-70; 247, n. 11.

[15]P. Sabatier, *Bibliorum Sacrorum Latinae Versiones Antique seu Vetus Italica* (2 vols.; Remis, 1743).

[16]See his *Adversus Marcionem* 4.35.1.

[17]*Biblia Sacra iuxta latinam vulgatam versionem ad Codicum Fidem. Liber Duodecim Prophetarum* (vol. 17; Roma: Libreria Editrice Vaticana, 1987) xliv.

published by Barthélemy, but unfortunately Zech 2:12 is not preserved. Barthélemy has maintained that this recension most likely followed G^W to which it seems closely related, but this is arguing from silence and is thus not permissible. The other witness to this recension, which Barthélemy isolated in the Minor Prophets, is Justin Martyr who in this case reads "eye of God."[18] The citation of Justin, however, may not in this case be appropriate. It is possible that Justin may reflect a Rabbinic tradition or understanding of the text of Zech 2:12 which was known to him. Justin's citation of Zech 2:12 is closer to a paraphrase than a quotation. If we compare the exegesis of Judah ben Ilay, cited above, which understands the text to refer to the eye of God, we find an echo of Justin's exegesis and even a certain similarity to the way in which the citation is used in the argument. Justin's familiarity with the Rabbinic exegesis of his day has been well documented.[19] However whether Justin's reading is admitted as evidence or not, it does not allow us to isolate the reading of the Greek recension studied by Barthélemy. If this is true then we cannot, as Barthélemy argued, reconstruct without doubt the reading of the proto-Rabbinic text current in Palestine in the first century of the common era. His argument was based on the incomplete evidence cited above that the Hebrew text in Palestine around the turn of the era would have read "my eye." This would have been changed to "his eye" already by the time of Aqiba.

However, as stated above, one element in the field of evidence was misread. Simply stated the reading of the Qumran fragment, 4Q12ᵉ, is, in the editor's opinion, not עֵינִי as McCarthy states, but rather עֵינוֹ. 4Q12ᵉ is written in a miniscule, semi-formal hand of the mid to late Hasmonean period. Paleographically 4Q12ᵉ should be dated approximately 75 BCE. The text of the relevant line of 4Q12ᵉ is given here in full:

ב
12 [כי הנוגע בכם] נוגע בבת יו

Note that material *within* brackets is not extent on the leather. The surface of the leather is somewhat worn, with some abrasion of the surface and subsequent loss of letters. Note also that the reading which is of greatest importance for our topic here is actually uncertain. It is the editor's *opinion*, based on repeated, close examination of the leather, that the most likely reading is *waw*, that is עֵינוֹ.

If the reading is correct, it changes the text-critical situation of Zech 2:12 and forces us to reevaluate the worth of the other textual witnesses, including the so-

[18]Justin, *Dialogue with Trypho* 137.2. See A. Lukyn Williams, *Justin Martyr: The Dialogue with Trypho* (New York: Macmillan, 1930) 281.

[19]See Williams, *Justin*, 30-34; and Willis A. Shotwell, *The Biblical Exegesis of Justin Martyr* (London: SPCK, 1965) 71-115.

called *tiqqun*. The reading of 4Q12[e] introduced above traces the reading "his eye," preserved in the MT, back to approximately 75 BCE. This is older than any other witness to the text of Zechariah and it establishes the antiquity of the reading "his eye."

A review of the evidence allows us to draw some tentative conclusions. First, as already stated, the reading "his eye," עינו, is far older than the first century of the common era as argued by Barthélemy on the basis of other evidence. Second, the evidence of the Old Latin and the Vulgate suggest the possibility that there was a tradition of two readings in the Old Latin, one of which read "my eye" and the other "his eye." Third, the Greek evidence may also suggest that two readings existed, "my eye" and "his eye." Taken together this seems to indicate that there were two ancient readings for Zech 2:12.

We must now ask what lay behind these two readings. How did two readings arise? In the modern discussions of the *tiqqun* to Zech 2:12 and in the commentaries on this verse the origin of the Rabbis' interest has always been assumed to be because the text was changed by the ancient tradents. The Rabbis compiled and explained the lists of texts which were "emended" by the scribes. However, as we have seen in the case of one of the earliest lists their interest was largely exegetical. In the later lists the term used by the Rabbis to describe the phenomena tabulated in the lists changed. They no longer used the root *knh*, "to use a euphemism," but rather the root *tqn*, "to emend." Usually no significance is attached to this change in terminology. Until McCarthy's recent book not much scholarly attention had been devoted to this subject at all. McCarthy rightly states that each *tiqqun* must be examined individually to determine whether or not the evidence indicates an actual emendation. In the course of this examination it is necessary to carefully examine all the available data. When this is done in the case of one such *tiqqun*, Zech 2:12, we discover that the evidence indicates that there may have been two ancient readings. If there were indeed two ancient readings, and the evidence does not allow for a definite decision, then the final task of the textual critic is to try and decide which reading is preferable if this is possible. In this case the origin of two such readings is easy to postulate. The letters *waw* and *yodh* were frequently confused by scribes in the transmission of a Hebrew manuscript. Such a frequent copyist's error is well documented.[20] In the case of Zech 2:12 a scribe probably confused the two letters at some point. This may have occurred either when a Hebrew manuscript was copied or when a Hebrew manuscript was translated into Greek. It is probably not possible to be certain when the error occurred, although we may make an educated guess. In order to make a judgment as to which reading is preferable, a process which is somewhat subjective, we must take account of the context of the passage. In the

---

[20]Compare, for example, P. Kyle McCarter, *Textual Criticism: Recovering the Text of the Hebrew Bible* (Philadelphia: Fortess, 1986) 47.

immediate context of Zech 2:12, Yahweh is the speaker. If Yahweh is the speaker, as is also the case in v 13, then the reading עֵינִי fits the context best. This does not guarantee, of course, that עֵינִי is the *original* reading, simply that in the judgment of this writer it fits the context best and a good argument can be made for its priority.

In this paper I have tried to accomplish three things. First, I have examined the use of one *Tiqqun Sopherim* for the textual criticism of Zech 2:12 in order to make the point that the existence of a *tiqqun* is no guarantee that an emendation was made in the text by its ancient tradents. Second, I have reexamined the evidence for the text of Zech 2:12 with no unexpected results. Third, I have presented, in revised form, the evidence from a Qumran fragment of a Minor Prophets scroll for the text of Zech 2:12. It is my hope that this presentation reflects the dedication to a field of endeavor which can only be learned by sitting at the feet of one of its masters. I dedicate this essay to John Strugnell in gratitude for his support and shared insight into the intricacies of the textual criticism of the Hebrew Bible.

ORTHOGRAPHY AND TEXT
IN 4QDan[a] AND 4QDan[b] AND
IN THE RECEIVED MASORETIC TEXT

Eugene Ulrich
University of Notre Dame

For certain ancient manuscripts the authors, editors, or scribal copyists had such an acute knowledge of grammar and orthography that it is possible and profitable to describe their orthographic system in detail. If such manuscripts are fragmentary or damaged, letters that are difficult to read can sometimes be more accurately and confidently restored. The Ben Sira scroll from Masada is an example of such a manuscript. Professor John Strugnell was able to describe the system of orthography employed by the scribe and thus gain greater control for determining a number of damaged letters in that scroll.[1]

With regard to the text of the Bible, though the Masoretic Text is used as the common standard text, it has been amply demonstrated for a number of books that the ancient manuscripts discovered at Qumran sometimes provide us with more sound, preferable readings than does the MT, the *textus receptus* from medieval times.

The purpose of this paper is, first, to explore the orthography of the two larger manuscripts of Daniel from Qumran and that of the MT, and secondly, to examine some of the variants in those texts, in order to understand the text of Daniel better than either the Qumran or the Masoretic texts alone would allow. The paper will offer, not an exhaustive study, but a number of highlights from our recently gained vantage point on the Book of Daniel.

Three of the Qumran caves have yielded a total of eight manuscripts of the Book of Daniel from the late Second Temple period, providing us with a good glimpse of the shape of the book at the beginning of the common era. Two manuscripts on leather were found in Cave 1, five in Cave 4, and one on papyrus in Cave 6.[2]

---

[1] John Strugnell, "Notes and Queries on 'The Ben Sira Scroll from Masada,'" in A. Malamat, ed., *Eretz-Israel 9: W. F. Albright Volume* (Jerusalem: Israel Exploration Society, 1969) 109-19. For the publication of the Ben Sira scroll, see Y. Yadin, *The Ben Sira Scroll from Masada* (Jerusalem: Israel Exploration Society and the Shrine of the Book, 1965), Heb., pp. 1-45, Eng., pp. 1-49, and pl. I–IX (anticipatory reprint from *Eretz-Israel* 8 [1967]).

[2] The critical editions of the individual MSS are available in the following sources:

1QDan[a] and 1QDan[b]: D. Barthélemy, *Qumrân Cave I* (DJD 1; Oxford: Clarendon, 1955) 150-52. Because of time factors, these fragments had to be

The Qumran manuscripts, of course, are by no means flawless, but they do demonstrate that the MT of Daniel is also not flawless, and comparison of the Qumran texts with the MT gives us a better perspective on the sound parts of each and the less sound parts of each. Similarly, the Qumran biblical texts in general have exonerated the Old Greek translation of many books, showing that the OG is usually not an erroneous or willfully tendentious translation, but often a faithful translation of what is simply an alternate—sometimes more, sometimes less, preferable—Hebrew text of which in the past we had been simply unaware.

In order to put the present study in a larger context, we can recall some conclusions already generally available from study of the Qumran MSS and the MT concerning the early form of the the text of Daniel. First, with regard to textual variants, there are no major departures from the early Hebrew-Aramaic text which is handed down to us in the Masoretic *textus receptus*. All twelve chapters of the traditional short edition of the book are attested in Cave 4, whereas—at least to date—there appears to be no manuscript evidence[3] of the longer edition attested in the Greek versions.[4] In the five MSS of the Book of Daniel found in Cave 4, the first eleven of the twelve chapters of the book as transmitted in the MT are attested, and the twelfth chapter is quoted in the Florilegium (4Q174).

Secondly, the curious shift from Hebrew to Aramaic at 2:4a in the MT also is confirmed by the ancient MSS 1QDan[a] and 4QDan[a], and the shift from Aramaic back to Hebrew at 8:1 is confirmed by 4QDan[a] and 4QDan[b]; furthermore, all the extant fragments of all the Daniel MSS display the expected distribution of languages.

---

published without photographs; the photographs were subsequently published by J. C. Trever, "Completion of the Publication of Some Fragments from Qumran Cave 1," *RevQ* 5 (1964-66) 323–44.

    4QDan: E. Ulrich, "Daniel Manuscripts from Qumran. Part 1: A Preliminary Edition of 4QDan[a]," *BASOR* 268 (1987) 17-37; idem, "Daniel Manuscripts from Qumran. Part 2: Preliminary Editions of 4QDan[b] and 4QDan[c]," *BASOR* 274 (1989) 3-26. 4QDan[d] and 4QDan[e] survive in only a few small scraps and will be published in the last of the biblical volumes in the DJD series.

    Pap6QDan: M. Baillet, *Les 'Petites Grottes' de Qumrân. 1. Texte. 2. Planches* (DJD 3; Oxford: Clarendon, 1962) 114-16 and pl. XXIII.

    [3]There are, of course, fragments of what can be called a Daniel cycle, plus countless unidentified and "parabiblical" fragments. In this connection we should note that 4QDan[e] has fragments of the Hebrew prayer in Daniel 9, and that 4QTestLevi has, in Hebrew, the prayer which is in Greek in the *Testament of Levi* (Marinus deJonge, ed.; *The Testaments of the Twelve Patriarchs: A Critical Edition of the Greek Text* [Leiden: Brill, 1978] 17, 19). This raises the possibility that some unidentified fragments may have in Aramaic (or Hebrew) the prayers now found only in the Greek versions of Daniel.

    [4]It remains an intriguing question why the Theodotionic text, which was supposedly revised according to the current rabbinic text, contains the longer edition of the book.

Thirdly, though early conjectures suggested otherwise, it is now recognized that the Book of Daniel was considered as a sacred and authoritative book at Qumran, on a level with other books we later consider canonical scripture.[5]

In this paper we will be able to deal only with the two most extensively preserved MSS, 4QDan[a] and 4QDan[b]. 4QDan[a] is inscribed in a formal script of the Hasmonean period or the transition to the Herodian period, and thus may be assigned a date approximately in the middle of the first century BCE, about a century or so after the composition of the book.[6] It has sixteen identifiable fragments preserved, seven of which are from cols. 2-6 of the original scroll. Col. 4 is almost entirely preserved, containing the text of Dan 2:19-33, and it is followed by fragments in the next column from almost every verse of 2:33-46.

4QDan[b] is inscribed in a "developed Herodian formal script" and may be assigned to approximately 20-50 CE,[7] almost a century later than 4QDan[a]. It contains nineteen identifiable fragments, spanning Daniel 5–8, with a large fragment containing generous portions of two columns from Daniel 6.

The following passages from Daniel are extant on the two MSS:[8]

4QDan[a]	4QDan[b]	4QDan[a]	4QDan[b]
1:16-20			6:8-22, 27-29
2:9-11, 19-49		7:5-7	7:1-6, 11?
3:1-2		7:25-28	7:26-28
4:29-30		8:1-5	8:1-8, 13-16
5:5-7	5:10-12	10:16-20	
5:12-14	5:14-16	11:13-16	
5:16-19	5:19-22		

The lack of text shared in common by the two MSS is frustrating; see especially the distribution in chap. 5. Fortunately, however, the two MSS have modestly large fragments from Dan 8:1-5 which overlap, and we will examine these below. With this general perspective on the Daniel MSS we may now center our focus on the orthography of the MT and the two larger MSS found at Qumran.

[5]See the discussion in the 4QDan[a] edition, p. 19. Throughout this paper, see the respective editions for fuller discussion and fuller presentation of the myriad details of each MS.

[6]See the 4QDan[a] edition, p. 20.

[7]Cf. F. M. Cross, "The Development of the Jewish Scripts," in G. E. Wright, ed., *The Bible and the Ancient Near East: Essays in Honor of William Foxwell Albright* (Garden City, NY: Doubleday, 1961) 173-81, and the chart on p. 139, fig. 2, line 6; cf. also the 4QDan[b] edition, p. 5.

[8]For a complete list of all the contents of the published Daniel MSS, see Figure 1 in the 4QDan[a] edition, p. 18.

ORTHOGRAPHY

Although for certain ancient manuscripts the authors, editors, or copyists employed a consistent system of orthography, nonetheless for many manuscripts there is no consistent system. The copyists simply copied the text as they found it, as faithfully as they could (though occasionally adding errors and intentional minor changes). If there was no consistent system on the part of the authors or major editors or scribal editors, then, unless the scribal copyists were both very learned and sufficiently confident to "correct" the spelling,[9] the text reproduced by the copyists will have been as inconsistent as the original. When the orthography of a biblical manuscript is inconsistent, a practical procedure is simply to list the differences between that manuscript and the MT, which usually serves as the standard text for comparison.

As we shall see below, it is necessary to distinguish between using the MT as a standard in the sense of a common, convenient source of reference, and using it with the assumption that it is the standard in the sense of the original or perfect or normative text.[10]

The Orthography of the MT

When we survey the Hebrew-Aramaic manuscripts of the Book of Daniel from Qumran, we notice that there is no consistent system of orthography operative in the form of the book as we meet it. Comparison with the Masoretic *textus receptus* reveals the fact that the MT also lacks a consistent orthographic system.

A thorough analysis of the orthographic practice in the MT of Daniel is surely a desideratum, but that is beyond what we can attempt in the confines of this paper. If it were indeed consistent, then it could be described in short compass, but the greater its inconsistency, the more lengthy and complicated its description necessarily becomes. Thus the lists that follow are meant to be illustrative of the inconsistency in the orthographic practice of those responsible for the MT of Daniel as we receive it. It can be said, of course, that the MT has certain orthographic tendencies: it strikes a moderate balance between a sparse use and a full use of *matres lectionis*. For example, in both the Aramaic section and the Hebrew section, one always finds

---

[9]Consistency in orthography is not, of course, universally regarded as important, as is evident from inspection of sources as diverse as the manuscripts of Shakespeare and the maps and road signs of Jerusalem.

[10]For a discussion of some of the issues involved, see E. Ulrich, "Jewish, Christian, and Empirical Perspectives on the Text of Our Scriptures," in Roger Brooks and John J. Collins, eds., *Hebrew Bible or Old Testament? Studying the Bible in Judaism and Christianity* (Christianity and Judaism in Antiquity 5; Notre Dame: University of Notre Dame, 1990) 69-85.

Eugene Ulrich

כל, never כול, and when long *o* occurs in two successive syllables, usually only one, not both, are marked with *waw*.[11] There are, however, numerous inconsistencies—possibly due to the different hands involved in the composition and editorial history of the book and to the many hands who over the centuries copied the finished book. Again, the lists are not intended to be exhaustive, not all occurrences are listed, and prefixed articles and prepositions are ignored.

(1) MT: The Aramaic Section

גְּלֵא 2:22, 28	גְלֵה 2:47
גֻּב 6:8, 25	גּוב 6:13
רעינהי 5:6	רעיוני 2:29; רעיונך 2:30
רעינהי 5:6	חדוהי ודרעוהי 2:32
כתבא 5:8, 16, 17	כתבה 5:7
פשרא 2:4; 5:8, 17	פשרה 2:5; 5:7, 12, 16[12]
מקרא 5:8, 16; אקרא 5:17	יקרה 5:7; יתקרי 5:12
קיתרס 3:7	קיתרוס 3:5
סבכא 3:5	שׂבכא 3:7
בלאשצר 7:1	בלשׁאצר 5:1, 22, 29, 30
נבכדנצר 5:11	נבוכדנצר 2:28, 46 (cf. Heb.)

(2) MT: The Hebrew Section

עֹמֵד 8:3, 6, 15; 12:1	עוֹמֵד 11:16
נֹגֵעַ 9:21; 10:16	נוֹגֵעַ 8:5
גדלה 9:12; 10:7, 8;	גדולה 8:8, 21
כֹּחַ 1:4; 10:8, 16, 17; 11:15	כוֹחַ 11:6
רצֹנו 8:4	רצוֹנו 11:16, 36
מלאת 10:3	מלאות 9:2
שלֹש 8:14; 12:12	שלוֹש 1:1, 5; 8:1; 10:1
לקרא 2:2; לעמֹד 1:4; 11:15	לבוֹא 11:17
בֵּנוֹ 11:10	לפנָיו 8:4
משמֵם 9:27	משומם 11:31
חֲמֻדות 10:3, 11, 19; 11:38	חמודות 9:23
הָאֵבֶל 8:3, 6	אוּבַל 8:2
נבכדנצר 2:1	נבוכדנאצר 1:1 (cf. Aram.)

---

[11]Note, however, occasional forms such as כרצונו in 11:16, 36 (but כרצֹנו in 8:4).

[12]The (probably medieval) Masoretic vocalization is a secondary effort to make sense of the consonantal orthography, morphology and syntax, and is not necessarily an accurate indication of the original form; see פשרה especially at 5:12, and כתבה at 5:7.

With even such a partial list, one need not continue the quest to describe "the orthographic system of the MT of Daniel."[13] Rather, having seen this illustration of non-systematic usage in the MT, we will now survey the orthographic practice in the scrolls from Qumran.

4QDan^a

The orthographic system[14] of 4QDan^a is also not consistent, but the orthographic practices of 4QDan^a are usually close to those of the MT (in contrast to those of 4QDan^b, as we shall see below); for example, the words כל, לא, and אלהים are never spelled with *waw*. There are, however, eleven orthographic differences between 4QDan^a and the MT. 4QDan^a has *waw* twice where the MT lacks it:

	4QDan^a	MT
5:6	ור̇עינוה̇י	ורעינהי
8:4	כרצו[נו]	כרצנו

has *yod* for <alep in the MT once:

	4QDan^a	MT
2:32	רישה	ראשה

and *he* twice where the MT has <alep

	4QDan^a	MT
2:24	[ופשר]ה	ופשרא
5:17	ופשרה	ופשרא

On the other hand, the MT has *waw* four times where 4QDan^a lacks it:

	4QDan^a	MT
2:20	וגברתא	וגבורתא
2:30	ורעיני	ורעיוני
2:32	ודרע̇י	ודרעוהי
8:5	נגע	נוגע

[13]That quest would be a lengthy and complex undertaking. Perhaps it would lead nowhere. But one imaginable, although unlikely, possibility is that the early author or editor of the Book of Daniel may have employed a consistent orthographic system and that a different consistent system may have been used by later editors or scribes; such a discovery would be of significant value in understanding the composition and editorial history of the book.

[14]These descriptions of the orthography are distilled from those in the editions of 4QDan^a, p. 21, and 4QDan^b, pp. 5-6. See the editions for a number of minor qualifications on the orthography which would be more distracting than necessary in the present paper.

and *yod* twice where 4QDan^a lacks it:

	4QDan^a	*MT*
2:44	אל[ל]ן	אלין
5:17	ונבזבתך	ונבזביתך

Though these are the patterns where 4QDan^a happens to be extant, notice that some of the examples contrast with each other, and for yet others one can find the reverse patterns elsewhere in 4QDan^a and the MT.

4QDan^b

The orthography of 4QDan^b is fuller than that of the MT and of 4QDan^a for both the Hebrew and the Aramaic sections. In 4QDan^b the word כל, e.g., is always spelled with *waw*, and לא is always spelled with *waw* in the Hebrew section. There are twenty-three orthographic[15] differences extant between 4QDan^b and the MT. Six of these are preserved on both 4QDan^b and 4QDan^a, and 4QDan^b is almost always fuller. 4QDan^b has the longer reading five times against the combined 4QDan^a and MT: once using the "cohortative" equivalent of the indicative,[16] and four times adding *waw*. It is only in one instance of *yod* as a *mater lectionis* that 4QDan^b has the shorter reading against the combined 4QDan^a and MT:

	4QDan^b	*4QDan^a = MT*
8:3	ואשאה	ואשא
8:3	עומד	עמד
8:3	באחרונה	באחרנה
8:4	וכול	וכל
8:4	לוא	לא
8:4	[ו]הגדל	והגדיל

In other instances where 4QDan^a is not extant, 4QDan^b never adds *yod* where the MT lacks it but does have *waw* nine times where the MT lacks it, two of which are inserted by the original scribe supralinearly:

	4QDan^b	*MT*
6:9	ותרש'ם	ותרשם
6:13	כול	כל

[15]For the use of longer pronominal suffixes and other minor morphological variants which can be considered together with orthographic differences, see the 4QDan^b edition.

[16]See note 18 below. This is properly a morphological, rather than orthographic, variant.

6:14	קודם	קדם
6:18	ושומת	ושמת
8:7	[ויר]מֹׁסֹהוֹ	וירמסהו
8:7	ולוא	ולא
8:13	וקודש	וקדש
8:14	קודש	קדש
8:15	[בר]אֹותי	בראתי

4QDan[b] has <alep twice where the MT has *he*:

	4QDan[b]	MT
6:11	[ב]עֹליתא	בעליתה
6:19	להיכלא	להיכלה

but it has *he* for the emphatic state once where the MT has<alep:

	4QDan[b]	MT
6:21	[חי]ה	חיא

4QDan[b] has <alep for a III-<alepverb once where the MT has *yod*:

	4QDan[b]	MT
5:12	[?יתקר]א	יתקרי

has *he* for III-weak verbs three times where the MT has <alep:

	4QDan[b]	MT
6:9	[תעד]ה	תעדא
6:15	הוה	הוא
6:18	תשנה	תשנא

and finally, it has <alep for the <Itpe>el once where the MT has a *Hitpa>el* in the Aramaic section:

	4QDan[b]	MT
6:20	ובאתבה[לה]	ובהתבהלה

Thus, 4QDan[b] has twenty-three orthographic (plus minor morphological) differences from the MT. In all six of the instances for which 4QDan[a] is extant, the latter agrees with the MT against 4QDan[b]. For clear perspective, however, we should note that the MT exhibits at other points most of the features of orthographic variation that have been observed in 4QDan[b]. We should also recall that the MT does not have a consistent system of orthography, that neither 4QDan[a] nor 4QDan[b] has a consistent system, and indeed that the inconsistencies in each can often be found exemplified in the other.

Eugene Ulrich

TEXTUAL VARIANTS

When attempting to assess the textual agreement or variation between 4QDan[a] and 4QDan[b] to see the textual relationship between the two Qumran scrolls and then the textual relationship between them and the MT, we find that we do not have much data to work with. We find two interesting passages.

Daniel 8:1-5

The largest overlap of text between 4QDan[a] and 4QDan[b] is at Dan 8:1-5 (see the synopsis on the facing page). But there the two MSS overlap for only fourteen words that are preserved completely on both MSS and seventeen that are preserved only partly on one or both MSS. In order to concentrate on the question of textual variants for 4QDan[a], 4QDan[b], and the MT, let us first note and then eliminate the orthographic differences in this passage. 4QDan[a] has only a single *mater lectionis* that is not found in 4QDan[b]: the *yod* in והגדיל at the end of 8:4 (= MT, see above). The orthographic practice of 4QDan[b], in contrast, is fuller, and in this passage it uses *waw* four times where 4QDan[a] does not: עומד and באחרונה (8:3), וכול and לוא (8:4)—all characteristic of this MS.[17] 4QDan[b] also once has the longer "cohortative" form, ואשאה at 8:3, which at Qumran functions as an alternate form of the indicative.[18] We may recall that 4QDan[a] agrees with the MT against 4QDan[b] in all these minor differences.

When we return to the larger question of the textual content of this passage, we note that there are three significant variants, which are underlined in the following synopsis.[19]

---

[17]In addition, it should be noted, even though the word is not extant in 4QDan[b] at 8:4, that וכול חי[ות] (= MT, without the article) is to be reconstructed, whereas 4QDan[a] has וכל החיות.

[18]E. Qimron (*The Hebrew of the Dead Sea Scrolls* [HSM 29; Atlanta: Scholars, 1986] #310.122, p. 44) describes the form: "It is a well-known feature of DSS Hebrew that cohortative forms ו/אקטלה denote the indicative alongside the forms ו/אקטל, as in the late books of the Bible and the Samaritan Pentateuch." In confirmation, note the "cohortative"-as-indicative וָאֹמְרָה in the MT at 10:19, where 4QDan[a] has the expected "Biblical Hebrew" form ואמר.

[19]The synopsis lists (1) the extant text of 4QDan[a] for the part of its column where it overlaps with 4QDan[b], plus a reconstruction of the destroyed portion of those lines. Then it similarly presents (2) the extant and reconstructed text of 4QDan[b]. The arrangement of the six lines for each MS is dictated by the format of the extant fragments; it is unusually fortunate that the left ends of the lines are extant here for both MSS. The synopsis then presents (3) the MT in an arrangement parallel to the format of the scrolls, for facility of comparison.

Synopsis

The Text of Daniel 8:1-4 for 4QDanᵃ, 4QDanᵇ, and the MT

4QDanᵃ

61	[בשנת שלוש למלכות בלאשצר]המ[לך ד]בר נגלה חזון נראה אלי אני דניא[ל]
60	[אחרי הנראה אלי בתחלה 2]ואראה בחזון ויהי בראתי ואני בשושן הבירה
61	[אשר בעילם המדינה ואראה]בחזון ואני הייתי על אובל אולי 3ואשא עיני
53	[ואראה והנה איל אחד גד]ול עמד לפני האבל ולו קרנים
51	[והקרנים גבהות והאח]ת גבהה מן השנית והגבהה עלה באחרנה
54	[4ראיתי את האיל מנגח י]מה ומזרחה צפונה ונגבה וכל החיות לא

4QDanᵇ

57	[בשנת שלוש למלכות בלאשצר המלך חזון נראה אלי אני ד]ניאל אח[רי]
60	[הנראה אלי בתחלה 2ואראה בחזון ויהי]בר̇אותי ואני בשו[שן הבירה אשר
59	[בעילם המדינה ואראה בח]זון וא̇ני ה̇י̇ית̇י על אובל]אולי 3וא̇שאה עיני
55	[ואראה והנה איל א[ח]ד גדול עמד ל[פני האובל ו]ל̇ו קרנים ק̇ר̇נ̇ים
52	[והקרנים גבהות והאחת גב]הה מן הש̇א̇נית והגב]הה עלה באחרונ̇ה
55	[4ראיתי את האיל מנגח ימה ומזרחה צפונה ונגב]ה וכול [חי]ות לוא

MT

57	בשנת שלוש למלכות בלאשצר המלך חזון נראה אלי אני דניאל אחרי
59	הנראה אלי בתחלה 2ואראה בחזון ויהי בראתי ואני בשושן הבירה אשר
58	בעילם המדינה ואראה בחזון ואני הייתי על אובל אולי 3ואשא עיני
42	ואראה והנה איל אחד עמד לפני האבל ולו קרנים
51	והקרנים גבהות והאחת גבהה מן השנית והגבהה עלה באחרנה
47	4ראיתי את האיל מנגח ימה וצפונה ונגבה וכל חיות לא

From analysis of the foregoing synopsis we can make the following observations:

Line 1. 4QDanᵇ and the MT are identical in text and letter count.[20] The scribe of 4QDanᵃ adds two words probably suggested by the parallel introductory formula of

---

[20]At the left side of each line the number of letters per line is given, serving as one control for the quantitative reconstruction of missing text. Since it is primarily width, not number of letters, that is being measured, spaces between words are counted in the "letter" count, unless two words are written together without space for word division (as, e.g., ואשאעיני in 4QDanᵃ at 8:3, line 3).

chap. 10, recognizes that they are incorrect here, crosses out the two erroneous words,[21] continues with the correct introduction for chap. 8, and writes אחרי on the next line.

Line 2. 4QDan[b] and the MT are identical (except for the assumed fuller spelling of בראותי in 4QDan[b]). 4QDan[a], because of the error in line 1 and the subsequent shift of אחרי to line 2, shifts אשר to line 3.

Line 3. 4QDan[b] and the MT are identical (except for the longer form ואשאה in 4QDan[b]). 4QDan[a] begins with אשר but ends with the same word as in 4QDan[b] and the MT.

Line 4. The longer reading קרנים קרנים is extant in both 4QDan[a] and 4QDan[b], and the longer reading גדול is extant clearly in 4QDan[b] and probably in 4QDan[a]. Thus, our analysis must begin with this evidence. The smaller letter count for 4QDan[a] and 4QDan[b] is partly due to a slightly shorter line in both MSS and partly due to the slightly more spacious script in 4QDan[a] in this line.[22] But the smaller letter count means that 4QDan[a] very probably had all the text that the MT has plus the additions as in 4QDan[b].

Line 5. The three texts are identical (except that 4QDan[b] has the fuller באחרונה). The short letter count means that והקרנים must be reconstructed at the beginning of line 5 in both 4QDan[a] and 4QDan[b] in agreement with the MT. This in turn proves that the second קרנים in line 4 is truly a plus in 4QDan[a] and 4QDan[b], not a shorter variant replacing והקרנים in line 5.

Line 6. 4QDan[a] and 4QDan[b] are identical (except for the fuller spellings וכול and לוא in 4QDan[b], partly counterbalanced by the article in החיות in 4QDan[a]). Again, 4QDan[a] clearly has the addition ומזרחה, and 4QDan[b] probably had it also. If 4QDan[b] did not have ומזרחה, then its line would have contained only forty-eight letters, and that implausibly short count would necessitate some alternate irregularity in this line of the MS.

Thus, 4QDan[a] presents two certain pluses relative to the MT and one probable plus: ‏2° קרנים‎, ‏ומזרחה‎, and ‏גד[ו]ל‎. 4QDan[b] clearly preserves the ‏2° קרנים‎ plus and preserves clearly the plus that is only "probable" in 4QDan[a] (גדול); it must have preserved also the remaining clear plus in 4QDan[a] (ומזרחה)—unless we posit some even less predictable variant. In support, πρὸς ἀνατολάς (= ומזרחה) in the Old Greek translation of the verse, in combination with the occurrence of the plus μέγαν (=גדול) in agreement with 4QDan[b] in the preceding verse, also argues in favor of the likelihood of ומזרחה in 4QDan[b]. Prescinding from the minor and customary orthographic differences in 4QDan[b] and the article in 4QDan[a], the text of the two

---

[21] See the photograph of the fragment of 4QDan[a] and the edition.
[22] See the photograph.

39

Qumran MSS stands in complete mutual agreement against the MT in the three variants which occur, whereas neither Qumran MS preserves an agreement with the MT against the other Qumran MS in this or any of the other Daniel fragments. In fact, let us examine one further example.

Daniel 5:12

At Dan 5:12 4QDan[a] has another variant from the MT. Of the small, four-line fragment, the few words in the first two lines share the same basic text with the MT, though with three minor, single-letter variants. The third line differs completely from the MT, while the fourth line is of little help, having only the top of a *lamed*. The variant in the third line reads וֹכֹתבא יקרא, and it occurs in the place where one would expect the last two words of the MT reading כען דניאל יתקרי ופשרה יהחוה. If, however, the "writing-interpretation" formula is studied for all of chap. 5, the 4QDan[a]-MT variant becomes clear. There are five occurrences in the chapter, at 5:7, 8, 12, 16, and 17. In the MT, the double clause "read the writing and make known the/its[23] interpretation" occurs in four of the five instances, and the exception is here at 5:12, where only the second clause, but not the first, occurs. The scroll should be reconstructed to read:

$$\text{[כען דניאל יתקרא}^{24}\text{]וֹכֹתבא יקרא] ופשרה יהחוה].}$$

Critics, I am sure, will delight in debating whether this was a set formula, part of which was omitted by parablepsis from the MT tradition, or whether the text tradition from which the Qumran MS was copied inadvertently or intentionally filled in a routine expansion in an originally shorter text.[25] Whatever the judgment on the superiority of the reading, 4QDan[a] in fact has]וֹכֹתבא יקרא[at the point where it should follow יתקרי in 5:12.

4QDan[b] has an even smaller fragment, but with equally clear and important results. The two-line fragment has only one complete letter and eight partial letters. Fortunately, all but one of the partial letters can be identified with near certainty, and, though not one letter of line 2 agrees with the MT, the fragment must be placed at 5:12.[26] Line 1 agrees with both 4QDan[a] and the MT. Line 2 reads]אֹ וכֹתֹ[, and,

---

[23]For the ambiguous orthography and Masoretic pointing, see the Aramaic orthography chart above and the orthography and variants in the 4QDan[a] and 4QDan[b] editions.

[24]Or, less likely, יתקרי with the MT; see the text of 4QDan[b] below.

[25]An interesting, but not decisive (because of general orthographic inconsistency), factor is that ופשרה appears incorrect in the MT without כתבא preceding. It could, of course, be argued casuistically that the queen may be speaking elliptically.

[26] For the detailed argument see the 4QDan[b] edition, p. 7.

Eugene Ulrich

based on the spatial controls provided by three other nearby fragments in the same column, its text may be restored as:

[כען דניאל יתקר]א וכֹ[ה]בא יקרא ופשרה יהחוה].

The results of this second pair of overlapping fragments provide confirmation of our earlier finding—that 4QDan[a] and 4QDan[b] share variant readings in common against the MT. Indeed, it may be asserted now that 4QDan[a] and 4QDan[b] stand in agreement against the MT in four readings, all of which are pluses relative to the MT, all (with the quite possible exception of וכתבא יקרא) are secondary additions, and all (with the possible exception of קרנים 2°) are predictable. In contrast, neither of the two Qumran MSS ever agrees with the MT in a textual variant against the other Qumran MS, whereas the Old Greek agrees with 4QDan[a] and 4QDan[b] against the MT in two of the four readings.

CONCLUSION

We have examined the orthography of the Masoretic Text and of the two larger manuscripts of Daniel from Qumran, 4QDan[a] and 4QDan[b], and then inquired into the nature of the interrelationship of these texts at points where all three are extant and able to be compared.

We found that 4QDan[a] and 4QDan[b] each have orthographic tendencies but that they do not have a consistent orthographic system. The examination also revealed that the MT has orthographic tendencies but that it too does not have a consistent orthographic system. Though for an individual reading, comparison with a Qumran manuscript may show the MT as displaying a certain orthographic feature, the MT not infrequently displays in another verse the contrasting feature that marked the Qumran reading. Thus, orthography in both the Qumran manuscripts and the MT of Daniel is partly stable but somewhat fluid. A specific conclusion that emerged is that 4QDan[a] and the MT have similar orthographic practices in common against the generally more liberal use by 4QDan[b] of *matres lectionis*. In all six orthographic differences where both 4QDan[a] and 4QDan[b] are extant, 4QDan[a] agrees with the MT against 4QDan[b].

That pattern of agreement changed dramatically when we moved from orthography to textual interrelationships. Although in orthography 4QDan[a] always agrees with the MT against 4QDan[b], in all four textual variants that occur where the two Qumran manuscripts have extant fragments which overlap, 4QDan[a] and 4QDan[b] always share the same text against the MT. Due to the fragmentary nature of the evidence, only one agreement is fully certain, but strong evidence is extant for the other three and the most cogent interpretation is surely to conclude that 4QDan[a] and 4QDan[b] agree in four longer readings against the MT.

Moreover, since neither Qumran manuscript agrees with the MT in a single reading against the other Qumran manuscript, we can conclude that 4QDan[a] and 4QDan[b] stand in one text family over against that exemplified in the Masoretic *textus receptus*.

We can venture further, now beyond the area of what can be documented, and suggest the following possibility. We have seen that in textual affiliation 4QDan[a] and 4QDan[b] stand in one text family in contrast to the MT, and that 4QDan[b] in both palaeographic script and orthographic profile—including the active insertion of supralinear *matres lectionis* by the scribe—is a later and more developed manuscript than 4QDan[a]. Given this pair of facts, the fertile suggestion arises that 4QDan[b] may have been copied[27] from 4QDan[a] (or at least from a very closely related manuscript)[28] by a scribe who was intent upon reproducing the text in the more contemporary, more full and clear and interpretative orthography of the late Second Temple period.

[27]Though by no means conclusive, it is an additional supporting argument that for the eight lines where the two Qumran MSS overlap in the Dan 8:1-5 passage, five lines actually end with exactly the same word. And if the scribe of 4QDan[a] had not erred by confusing the introduction to chap. 8 with the introduction to chap. 10—an error that the scribe of 4QDan[b] would have immediately recognized and not copied—seven of those eight lines would exactly coincide.

[28]If from "a very closely related manuscript," of course that would add a third, probably Qumran, MS to the 4QDan[a]–4QDan[b] text family.

RECENSIONAL DIFFERENCES BETWEEN THE MASORETIC TEXT AND THE SEPTUAGINT OF PROVERBS[*]

Emanuel Tov
The Hebrew University, Jerusalem

The Septuagint is more than a textual witness to the biblical text. At times it also reflects recensional stages in the development of the biblical books differing from those reflected in the Masoretic Text (MT). As a rule, the LXX reflects an earlier stage than the MT as, for example, in the case of Jeremiah, Joshua, the story of David and Goliath, and Ezekiel.[1] Only the first one is supported by Hebrew evidence from Qumran,[2] while for the others the LXX remains the sole witness. These and other recensional differences between the MT and LXX are discussed at length in the author's *Introduction to Textual Criticism*,[3] where full bibliographical references are provided.

In the previous paragraph two major discrepancies between the LXX and MT have been disregarded for different reasons. The large omissions in the LXX of Job should probably be ascribed to the Greek translator, and hence are less relevant to the textual criticism of the Hebrew Bible,[4] and the status of the major differences in the Greek text of Exod 35-40 (transpositions, omissions) remains undecided.

The LXX of Proverbs has not been discussed extensively in this context, not only because the text is difficult and cannot be assessed easily, but also because scholars tended to ascribe its deviations from the MT to inner-translational factors rather than to its Hebrew *Vorlage*. As long as these deviations are ascribed to the translator's whims, they are irrelevant to the textual criticism of the Hebrew Bible, and their main importance lies in the realm of exegesis. However, if at least some of

[*]I would like to thank Mrs. N. Leiter for helpful comments which improved the article.

[1]For a detailed discussion and bibliography, see the present author's *The Text-Critical Use of the Septuagint in Biblical Research* (Jerusalem Biblical Studies 3; Jerusalem: Simor, 1981) 293-306.

[2]4QJer[b,d], to be published by the present author in 1990.

[3]To be published (1989) in Hebrew by Mossad Bialik.

[4]For an analysis and bibliographical references, see C. Cox, "Elihu's Second Speech according to the Septuagint," in W. E. Aufrecht, *Studies in the Book of Job* (Studies in Religion 16; Waterloo: Wilfred Laurier University Press, 1985) 36-53.

these deviations of the LXX derived from a different Hebrew *Vorlage*, that Hebrew text would have differed recensionally from the MT. This approach is suggested in the present article, but the alternative possibility, that of major exegetical deviations introduced by the translator, will be discussed first.

1. *Translational Factors*

There is considerable evidence in the Greek translation that points to inner-translational factors rather than a different Hebrew text behind the differences between the LXX and MT.

1. Most scholars agree that the translation contains much evidence of contextual exegesis, in both minor and major details.[5]

2. A major divergence between the two texts is the occurrence of scores of doublets, almost all of which seem to be translational doublets of the same verse rather than Greek translations of Hebrew doublets.[6] Indeed, the great number of these doublets in the Greek Proverbs is exceptional within the Greek Bible. These doublets pertain to single words and pairs of words, but more frequently to whole verses. As a rule, the two elements of the doublet are juxtaposed in the same verse (e.g., 1:14; 2:21; 9:6; 15:6), but sometimes they occur in adjacent verses (1:18-19; 14:35-15:1). Usually one of the two members of the pair of doublets is more faithful to the Hebrew text, and the other one is free or even paraphrastic. According to a rule laid down long ago by P. A. de Lagarde,[7] the free rendering reflects the original translation, and the more literal one a revisional rendering. While it is not impossible that the two renderings derived both from the original translator, it is more likely that one of them, the literal one, was added at one of the stages of the textual transmission by a reviser who considered the original translation too free. The nature of these doublets may be exemplified by the following example:

4:10 וירבו לך שנות חיים
καὶ πληθυνθήσεται ἔτη ζωῆς σου
ἵνα σοι γένωνται πολλαὶ ὁδοὶ βίου

---

[5]The evidence is extensive. For a partial discussion, see A. J. Baumgartner, *Étude critique sur l'état du texte du livre des Proverbes d'après les principales traductions anciennes* (Leipzig: Imprimerie Orientale W. Drugulin, 1890); G. Mezzacasa, *Il libro dei Proverbi di Salomone: Studio critico sulle aggiunte greco-alessandrine* (Roma: Instituto Biblico Pontificio, 1913); G. Gerleman, *Studies in the Septuagint* (LUÅ NF 52, 3; Lund: Gleerup, 1956).

[6]For a recent discussion, see Z. Talshir, "Double Translations in the Septuagint," in C. E. Cox, ed., *VI Congress of the International Organization for Septuagint and Cognate Studies* (SCS 23; Atlanta: Scholars, 1987) 21-63.

[7]P. A. de Lagarde, *Anmerkungen zur griechischen Übersetzung der Proverbien* (Leipzig: Brockhaus, 1863) 20.

Emanuel Tov

The individual elements of the Hebrew are thus rendered twice in the following way:

וירבו	καὶ πληθυνθήσεται	ἵνα γένωνται πολλαὶ
לך	σου	σοι
שנות	ἔτη	ὁδοὶ
חיים	ζωῆς	βίου

The first set of translations is more literal than the second.

3. Translational exegesis is visible in the *addition* of stichs or whole verses, to be exemplified by the following verses:

a. 6:11 וּבָא כִמְהַלֵּךְ רֵאשֶׁךָ וּמַחְסֹרְךָ כְּאִישׁ מָגֵן (and your poverty will come like a vagabond, and your want like an armed man) εἶτ᾽ ἐμπαραγίνεταί σοι ὥσπερ κακὸς ὁδοιπόρος ἡ πενία καὶ ἡ ἔνδεια ὥσπερ ἀγαθὸς δρομεύς (then poverty comes upon you as an evil traveller and want like a good runner)

Although the translation of this verse is quite free, most of the elements of the Hebrew can be recognized in the Greek. Of particular interest is the opposition created by the translator between the κακὸς ὁδοιπόρος and the ἀγαθὸς δρομεύς, an opposition which is further developed in a translational plus ("11a" in the edition of Rahlfs):[8]

"6:11a" ἐὰν δὲ ἄοκνος ᾖς ἥξει ὥσπερ πηγὴ ὁ ἀμητός σου, ἡ δὲ ἔνδεια ὥσπερ κακὸς δρομεὺς ἀπαυτομολήσει (but if you are diligent, your harvest will come as a fountain, and poverty will flee away as an evil runner)

This plus at the end of the simile of the ant (vv 6-11) further develops the theme of v 11 from which two elements are repeated: κακὸς δρομεύς and ἔνδεια. The previous verses mention the idle man (ὀκνηρός [vv 6, 9]), and the present one, "11a," continues their idea by referring to the rewards of the opposite character, the ἄοκνος, a word which does not occur elsewhere in the LXX. The use in v "11a" of words occurring in the Greek context makes it likely that the addition has been made

---

[8]In the system of Rahlfs, most added stichs are denoted with a supernumerary notation as "11a," "11b," etc. Some added stichs, however, such as in 16:11 discussed below, are not denoted in a special way.

in Greek rather than Hebrew, and therefore the Hebrew reconstruction of this plus by Lagarde (p. 23), וּבָא כמו הֵלֶךְ רֵישֶׁךָ וּמַחְסֹרְךָ כְּאִישׁ בָּאִישׁ נָמֹג, is unwarranted.[9]

b. A similar impression of composition in Greek is created by the added simile referring to the μέλισσα (bee) earlier in the chapter ("6:8a-c" [not found in MT]), where the ὀκνηρός is told to go to the bee and to learn from its ways. This simile is thus very close to that of the ant found in vv 6-11. The secondary character of this exegetical expansion is suggested by its unusual formulation as "or go to the bee" which is rather awkward in the text after the simile of the ant.

    c. 11:16 אֵשֶׁת חֵן תִּתְמֹךְ כָּבוֹד וְעָרִיצִים יִתְמְכוּ עֹשֶׁר (a gracious woman grasps honor, and violent men grasp wealth)

      α   γυνὴ εὐχάριστος ἐγείρει ἀνδρὶ δόξαν
      β   θρόνος δὲ ἀτιμίας γυνὴ μισοῦσα δίκαια
      γ   πλούτου ὀκνηροὶ ἐνδεεῖς γίνονται
      δ   οἱ δὲ ἀνδρεῖοι ἐρείδονται πλούτῳ
    (α   a gracious wife brings glory to her husband,
      β   but a woman hating righteousness is a throne of dishonor;
      γ   the idle men come to lack wealth,
      δ   but the diligent support themselves with wealth)

In the Hebrew text of 11:16 אֵשֶׁת חֵן (γυνὴ εὐχάριστος in the LXX) is contrasted with עָרִיצִים; both of them "grasp" something different. However, the Greek translator probably did not understand the exact meaning of the first stich— hence his unusual rendering—nor did he realize the exact nature of the parallelism— hence his addition of two stichs. These added stichs (β, γ) provided oppositions to the two stichs representing MT (α, δ). To the γυνὴ εὐχάριστος (α) the LXX added stich β concerning the γυνὴ μισοῦσα. The content of this added stich has close connections with the wordings of the translation elsewhere, so that it was probably added by the original translator himself. For the first phrase in stich β, cf. θρόνος αἰσθήσεως (a throne of knowledge) in 12:23. The "throne of dishonor" is probably meant as the opposite of the "throne of honor" (כִּסֵּא כָבוֹד), mentioned in 1 Sam 2:8; Isa 22:23; Jer 14:21; 17:12. It reminds one also of the θρόνος ἀρχῆς (Prov 16:12) used in connection with δικαιοσύνη (as here), as well as of similar phrases

_____

[9] It should be noted that the Hebrew text of 6:10-11 recurs in 24:33-34 with minor differences, and that the translation of these verses is different although ὥσπερ ἀγαθὸς δρομεύς recurs in 24:34. The translation in chap. 24 is not followed by an addition like "6:11a," but on the other hand 24:34 is preceded by an added ἐὰν δὲ τοῦτο ποιῆς. Thus both the additions in "6:11a" and 24:34 as well as the one in "8:21a" start with ἐάν.

Emanuel Tov

(20:28; 25:5; 29:14). For the last phrase of that stich, cf. 13:5: λόγον ἄδικον μισεῖ δίκαιος.

To stich δ, reflecting the MT, the translator added stich γ as contrast. This stich creates an opposition between πλούτου, not obtained by the idle men, in γ, and πλούτῳ, obtained by the diligent, in δ. At the same time, the wording of this plus is based on the vocabulary of the "canonical" section, 6:6, 11, as well as of the added "6:11a" ἄοκνος...ἔνδεια.[10]

d. 12:11 עבד אדמתו ישבע לחם ומרדף ריקים חסר לב (he who tills his
land will have plenty of bread, but he whose pursuits are empty
has so sense)

11 α ὁ ἐργαζόμενος τὴν ἑαυτοῦ γῆν ἐμπλησθήσεται ἄρτων
β οἱ δὲ διώκοντες μάταια ἐνδεεῖς φρενῶν
"11a" γ ὅς ἐστιν ἡδὺς ἐν οἴνων διατριβαῖς
δ ἐν τοῖς ἑαυτοῦ ὀχυρώμασιν καταλείψει ἀτιμίαν
(α he who tills his land will be satisfied with bread,
β but they that pursue vanities are void of understanding;
γ he who enjoys himself in amusements of wine,
δ will leave dishonor in his own strongholds)

The Hebrew verse presents an opposition between עבד אדמתו and מרדף ריקים; v "11a" of the LXX adds a parallel to the latter.

In the added stich (δ) ὀχυρώμασιν is based on ὀχύρωμα, occurring in v 12. From the fact that it occurs in the next verse, rather than a preceding one, one might conclude that the Greek addition was made on the basis of an already existing translation.

Stichs γδ continue the train of thought of stich β, even though the verse is phrased in the singular. They probably elaborate on the theme of μάταια mentioned in stich β. The addition uses ἀτιμίαν from the context (v 9) and this word also features in the plus in 11:16 (see above). Elsewhere, too, ἀτιμία is a cherished word of the LXX of Proverbs. For the reference to the drinking of wine, cf. also Prov 23:20; 31:4.

e. 17:21 ילד כסיל לתוגה לו ולא ישמח אבי נבל (he who fathers a
stupid son makes sorrow for himself and the father of a fool
has no joy)

[10]As a result, the attempt of some scholars to reconstruct a Hebrew *Vorlage* of this Greek plus seems unwarranted. Note, e.g., BH: וכסא קלון אשה שנאת ישר הון עצלים יחסרו .

47

α καρδία δὲ ἄφρονος ὀδύνη τῷ κεκτημένῳ αὐτήν
β οὐκ εὐφραίνεται πατὴρ ἐπὶ υἱῷ ἀπαιδεύτῳ
γ υἱὸς δὲ φρόνιμος εὐφραίνει μητέρα αὐτοῦ
(α the heart of a fool is grief to its possessor;
β a father rejoices not over an uninstructed son;
γ but a wise son makes his mother happy)

The meaning of the Hebrew verse is lost in Greek, probably because the translator read לב instead of ילד. For the phrase, cf. 12:23, לב כסילים = καρδία δὲ ἀφρόνων, and 15:7 (for a similar change, see the LXX of 17:10). Possibly because of the lack of a good parallelism between stichs α and β, stich γ was added as an antithetical parallel to the second stich. At the same time, stich γ was added because of the association with the Hebrew and Greek text of 10:1 (cf. also 15:20; 23:24), where, incidentally, the same rare תוגה is used as here.

The list of these inner-translational pluses is long. For similar pluses of the LXX, see "4:27a" (note the expansion on the theme of "right" and "left" found in the MT and LXX of v 27; v "27b" contains a double translation of v 26); "7:1a"; "8:21a"; "9:12a-c"; "9:18a-d"; "10:4a"; "12:13a"; "13:13a"; "17:16a"; "18:22a"; 19:7; "22:14a"; "24:22a-e"; "25:10a"; "27:20a"; "27:21a"; "28:17a." This list also includes cases of additions made on the basis of verses from other books:[11]

f. 13:9   אור צדיקים ישמח ונר רשעים ידעך (the light of the righteous shines brightly, but the lamp of the wicked will be put out)
φῶς δικαίοις διὰ παντός
φῶς δὲ ἀσεβῶν σβέννυται (the righteous always have light, but the light of the ungodly is quenched)

To the opposition between δικαίοις and ἀσεβῶν in this verse, v "9a" adds a similar opposition:

"13:9a" ψυχαὶ δόλιαι πλανῶνται ἐν ἁμαρτίαις
δίκαιοι δὲ οἰκτίρουσιν καὶ ἐλεῶσιν (deceitful souls wander in sins, but the righteous have pity and are merciful)

The second part of this addition may be based on Ps 37(36):21 (cf. also 111(112):4):[12]

---

[11]In addition to the below mentioned examples, see 1:7 (cf. Ps 111:10); 3:16 (cf. Isa 45:23 and Prov 31:26 [see below]; "26:11a" (cf. Sir 4:21).

[12]At the same time, the origin of the idea of the wandering souls (of the living or the dead?) as in Proverbs is not clear, although one is reminded of Wis 17:1:

48

Ps 37:21   לוה רשע ולא ישלם וצדיק חונן ונותן (the wicked borrows
             and does not pay back, but the righteous is generous and gives)
36:21   δανείζεται ὁ ἁμαρτωλὸς καὶ οὐκ ἀποτείσει
          ὁ δὲ δίκαιος οἰκτίρει καὶ διδοῖ (the sinner borrows and does
          not pay back, but the righteous has pity and gives)

For a similar addition in the context, see v 11 δίκαιος οἰκτίρει καὶ κιχρᾷ
(the righteous has pity and lends).

2. Differences due to the Vorlage

1. The preceding section provided ample evidence of changes made either by the
translator or in the course of the textual transmission of the translation. From the
outset it thus would seem reasonable to ascribe all major differences between the
translation and the MT to these factors. However, there are indications that beyond
the aforementioned instances there are also major differences between the two texts
deriving from a different Hebrew *Vorlage* used by the translator. This situation thus
makes the text-critical evaluation of the LXX of Proverbs very difficult.

    a. The translation of 3:16, referring to Wisdom, contains several details
beyond the MT. After ארך ימים (long life) it adds καὶ ἔτη ζωῆς (= חיים ושנות [cf.
v 2]), and after πλοῦτος καὶ δόξα, it adds two stichs ("3:16a"):

"3:16a" α   ἐκ τοῦ στόματος αὐτῆς ἐκπορεύεται δικαιοσύνη
     β   νόμον δὲ καὶ ἔλεον ἐπὶ γλώσσης φορεῖ
   (α   out of her mouth proceeds righteousness,
     β   and she carries law and mercy upon her tongue).

    Stich α is based on Isa 45:23, יצא מפי צדקה (from my mouth righteousness
goes forth), where the LXX uses a different verb, ἐξελεύσεται. Stich β provides a
more literal version of Prov 31:26, ותורת חסד על לשונה (and the teaching of
kindness is on her tongue), than the LXX *ad locum*:

    31:25   ...ἐννόμως. καὶ τάξιν ἐστείλατο τῇ γλώσσῃ αὐτῆς
         ([... and lawfully?]. And she commanded order to her tongue).

ἀπαίδευτοι ψυχαὶ ἐπλανήθησαν, and Prov 21:16: ἀνὴρ πλανώμενος ἐξ ὁδοῦ
δικαιοσύνης.

Though inner-Greek activity cannot be excluded, the inner-translational differences between the translations in "3:16a" on the one hand and 31:26 and Isa 45:23 on the other make it likely that the plus in Prov "3:16a" did not derive from inner-Greek activity. Rather this plus is based on an expanded Hebrew text (מפיה תצא צדקה ?תורת חסד על לשונה ?).

b. The plus in "3:22a" is more or less identical with the text of 3:8:

"3:22a" ἔσται δὲ ἴασις ταῖς σαρξί σου
καὶ ἐπιμέλεια τοῖς σοῖς ὀστέοις (it will be healing to your flesh and safety to your bones)

3:8 רפאות תהי לשרך ושקוי לעצמותיך (it will be healing to your flesh and refreshment to your bones)
τότε ἴασις ἔσται τῷ σώματί σου
καὶ ἐπιμέλεια τοῖς ὀστέοις σου

In both cases the Greek text occurs after negative commands (אל תהי 7 = μὴ ἴσθι; 21 אל ילזו = μὴ παραρρυῇς). It is not likely that the text of "3:22a" has been repeated on the inner-Greek level, since the two translations differ. Rather, the discrepancies between the two texts most likely derived from different translations of the same Hebrew text (note the differences between τότε [8] and δὲ ["22a"], the different rendering of לשרך, τῷ σώματί σου [8], ταῖς σαρξί σου ["22a"],[13] and the differences between σου [8] and σοῖς ["22a"]. In that different Hebrew text the verse may have occurred twice, and in both places it suited the context.

c. The same reasoning obtains regarding the repetition of the following verse:

27:1 (אל תתהלל ביום מחר) כי לא תדע מה ילד יום
(for you do not know what a day may bring forth)
οὐ γὰρ γινώσκεις τί τέξεται ἡ ἐπιοῦσα
(for you do not know what the next day will bring forth)

3:28 ... οὐ γὰρ οἶδας τί τέξεται ἡ ἐπιοῦσα

The contexts in which the verse occurs in both places are similar, in both cases after מחר in the preceding stich. In 27:1 the Greek has an equivalent in MT, but it

---

[13]Both Greek words are known as translation equivalents of the same words, even if the exact equivalent in this verse is not clear, בשר or שר = שאר. Elsewhere in the LXX of Proverbs, σῶμα reflects שאר (5:11; 11:17; instead of בשרים in 25:20 the LXX read another text, either בשר or שאר, as well as בשר (4:22; 5:11; 26:10[?]). Elsewhere, σάρξ reflects בשר (passim) and שאר (Mich 3:2, 3).

has none in 3:28. The occurrence of this verse in 3:28 probably does not represent an inner-Greek repetition (note the differences between the verbs in the two Greek versions). Rather, it reflects a Hebrew text in which the verse occurred twice. Since the MT itself contains several instances of recurring verses (see n. 22), it is not surprising that the *Vorlage* of the Greek contains additional instances of recurring verses.

2. Major differences between the two texts are visible in *transpositions* of verses and groups of verses. Rahlfs denoted these verses as supernumerary pluses ("12a," etc.), as in the preceding examples, but actually they represent transpositions, often coupled with pluses and minuses. The mere numbering in the edition of Rahlfs (the only extant critical edition of the Greek Proverbs), thus creates a misleading tool for its investigation.

a. The main example of this phenomenon is found in the verses at the end of chap. 15 and the beginning of chap. 16. The sequence of the verses in the LXX is as follows according to the numbers of MT:

15:1-27	
16:6	(Rahlfs: "15:27a")
15:28	
16:7	(Rahlfs: "15:28a")
15:29	
16:8	(Rahlfs: "15:29a")
16:9	(Rahlfs: "15:29b")
15:30	
15:32, 33	(note omission of v 31)
16:2 (?)[14]	(note omission of v 1)
16:5	(note omission of v 3 and transposition of v 4)
"16:7" first stich of the LXX (note omission of v 6)	
16:7 first stich, represented as the second stich of 16:7 in the LXX	
16:8	(differing from v 8 of the MT)—in other words, the greater part of vv 7-8 of MT lacks in the LXX
16:4	(Rahlfs: 9)
16:10ff.	

[14]It is not certain that the verse which is denoted by Rahlfs as 16:2 indeed represents 16:2 of the MT, as it also presents elements that could be taken as reflecting 16:4.

The reason for these major changes is not connected with the textual transmission, as suggested by Lagarde[15] nor with the disorderly status of the MS(S) from which the translation was made.[16] Rather, the two texts represent **recensionally different** editions. The sequence of most individual sayings in these chapters is loose, and as each saying is more or less independent, two different editorial traditions could have existed concerning their sequence. One notes especially the transposal of several verses of what is now chap. 16 to what is now the end of chap. 15; one also notes the change of place of 16:4. These phenomena are coupled with the omission of 15:31; 16:1, 3, and the replacement of 16:6-8 of MT with two different Greek verses (named 16:7-8 by Rahlfs). One should further note that 15:31 (וגו' שמעת אזן), lacking in the LXX, could have been added secondarily in the edition of MT as an appendix to the previous verse dealing with מאור עינים and שמועה טובה. The first eleven verses of chap. 16 in MT display a certain principle (occurrence of the name of God in all verses except for vv 8 and 10), but this situation does not necessarily render that version preferable to that of the LXX, where such an editorial principle is not visible. Furthermore, the type of parallelism of the verses in the arrangement of MT does not make it a more coherent unit than that of the LXX.

b. The sequence in chap. 20 is as follows in the LXX (according to the verse numbers of MT):

1-9
20-22   (Rahlfs: "9a-c")
10-13
23-30   (note omission of vv 14-19)

As in the preceding case, there is no logical connection between the verses, and both sequences are possible. Editorial rather than scribal factors must have determined the different sequences, as this is also coupled with an omission (vv 14-19). Toy[17] ascribed these different sequences to "accident or scribal caprice."

---

[15]Lagarde, (*Anmerkungen*, 51) suggested that the text of chaps. 15 and 16 was written in adjacent columns and that the translator wrongly read the text horizontally rather than vertically. However, Lagarde took into consideration only the transposition of the verses from chap. 16 to chap. 15, and not the other phenomena in the translation (omissions, additions), and therefore from the outset his solution is less plausible.

[16]Thus Baumgartner, *Étude critique*, 149.

[17]C. H. Toy, *The Book of Proverbs* (ICC; Edinburgh: Clark, 1899) 388.

c. The sequence in chap. 17 is as follows in the LXX (according to the verse numbers of MT):

1-16
19b   (Rahlfs: "16a")
20b   (Rahlfs: "16a")
17-18
19a
20 including a translation of v 20b (also translated in the LXX of v "16a")
21-28

d. The sequence in chap. 31 is as follows in the LXX (according to the verse numbers of MT):

1-24
26   (Rahlfs: 25)
25   (Rahlfs: 26)
27
26a   (Rahlfs: "28a"); a second translation is found in "3:16a"
28-31

e. The same explanation applies to major differences in sequence between the various segments of the book in chapters 24-31. According to their headings, the following eight collections of proverbial material are recognized in the book of Proverbs according to the MT:[18]

I	1:1 - 9:18	("The proverbs of Solomon")
II	10:1 - 22:16	("The proverbs of Solomon")
III	22:17 - 24:22	("The words of the wise")
IV	24:23-24	("Also words of the wise")
V	25 - 29	("These are also proverbs of Solomon which the men of Hezekiah king of Judah copied")
VI	30	("The words of Agur" [and other sayings])
VII	31:1-9	("The words of Lemuel")
VIII	31:10-31	(an acrostichon about the virtuous woman)

[18]Toy (*Proverbs*, vi) subdivides the MT into five consecutive sections. Our own understanding is closer to that of W. Frankenberg (*Die Sprüche* [HAT; Göttingen: Vandenhoeck & Ruprecht, 1898] 2-5), who mentions eight subgroups, and O. Eissfeldt (*The Old Testament: An Introduction* [Oxford: Blackwell, 1965] 472), who speaks about seven sections. Of the commentators, only Frankenberg (*Die Sprüche*, 10-11) paid detailed attention to the sequence of the LXX, the logic of which he tried to explain.

This description of the contents of the MT, it should be remembered, is based on explicit headings in that text, but at least in two cases these headings may be misleading. Chap. 30 is represented as "the words of Agur" (and other sayings) since v 1 contains the only heading in this chapter. However, most commentators doubt whether all of the verses in this chapter should be ascribed to a collection of "the words of Agur." Indeed, the nature of vv 15-33 (numerical sayings) differs from that of the first fourteen verses, and probably the real "words of Agur" comprised even less than fourteen verses. Therefore, when representing here and below "the words of Agur" as one section, this formal approach may be misleading. Likewise, not all of chap. 31 should be ascribed to "the words of Lemuel," and its second part, an acrostichon about the virtuous woman, should be considered a separate unit.

The sequence of the LXX can be described as following according to the sections and numbers of the MT:

I-III	1:1-24:1-22	
VI, part 1	30:1-14	("The words of Agur," first part)
IV	24:23-34	("Also words of the wise")
VI, part 2	30:15-33	("The words of Agur," second part)
VII	31:1-9	("The words of Lemuel," first part)
V	25-29	
VIII	31:10-31	(an acrostichon about the virtuous woman, formally representing "the words of Lemuel," second part)

In other words, the LXX separates between the two parts of section VI ("The words of Agur") and of chap. 31 (VII ["the words of Lemuel"] and VIII [the acrostichon of the virtuous woman]). Furthermore, it reverses the internal order of sections IV, V, VI and VII, part 1.

When turning now to a comparative analysis of the sequence in the MT and LXX we see no reason to favor either one of the two systems. The connection between the sections is such that in principle both can be equally correct.

From the outset the juxtaposition of sections III and IV, as in the MT, is to be preferred to the arrangement of the LXX as III contains "the words of the wise" and IV "also the words of the wise" (thus Frankenberg [n. 18], who considers IV a "Nachtrag" to III). However, one could also argue against the arrangement of the MT. For why should collection IV need a separate heading at all if both it and the previous collection contain "words of the wise"? Therefore, in a way, the arrangement of the LXX has more to be recommended than that of the MT, since the separation of IV from III requires a separate heading for IV, as in the LXX.

The separation in the LXX between the different sections of "the words of Agur" and "the words of Lemuel" is contextually not any better or worse than their juxtaposition as in MT. One should remember that both of these collections are composed of at least two segments whose contents are not necessarily connected. Thus not all the sayings in chap. 30 should be considered as "the words of Agur." In any event, vv 15-33 (various numerical sayings) are set apart, and could certainly be placed elsewhere. Likewise, chap. 31 is composed of different segments; its second part, an acrostichon about the virtuous woman, is not connected with the first part, "the words of Lemuel," and could therefore be placed elsewhere, as it is in the LXX. In the arrangement of the LXX the second part of "the words of Agur" (VI, part 2) has no separate heading, and therefore belongs, as it were, to section IV ("also words of the wise"); contextually this arrangement is equally good as the one of MT. On the other hand, both Agur (VI) and Lemuel (VII) are described as "of Massa" ("the Massaite"), so that their juxtaposition in MT, at the end of the book is preferable to their separation in the LXX. However, even in MT the "words" of Agur" are not really juxtaposed to "the words" of Lemuel," since the second part of chap. 30 actually does not contain sayings of Agur.

In this description the arrangement of the MT has been compared with that of the presumed *Vorlage* of the LXX, beyond the understanding of the translator. For the translator often misunderstood the nature of the headings, as in the following cases:

24:23   גַם אֵלֶּה לַחֲכָמִים הַכֵּר פָּנִים בְּמִשְׁפָּט בַּל טוֹב (These also are words of the wise. Partiality in judgment is not good)
ταῦτα δὲ λέγω ὑμῖν τοῖς σοφοῖς ἐπιγινώσκειν
αἰδεῖσθαι πρόσωπον ἐν κρίσει οὐ καλόν
(and these things I say to you, the wise men, to know: it is not good to respect a face in judgment)

The heading has been taken as an integral part of the sentence.

30:1   דִּבְרֵי אָגוּר בִּן יָקֶה הַמַּשָּׂא
(The words of Agur the son of Jakeh of Massa)
τοὺς ἐμοὺς λόγους υἱέ φοβήθητι καὶ δεξάμενος αὐτοὺς
μετανόει (my son, fear my words, and receive them and repent)

The proper name אָגוּר has been taken as a verbal form, and the first word has been read as דְּבָרַי.

31:1   דִּבְרֵי לְמוּאֵל מֶלֶךְ מַשָּׂא (אֲשֶׁר יִסְּרַתּוּ אִמּוֹ) (The words of Lemuel,
king of Massa [which his mother taught him])
οἱ ἐμοὶ λόγοι εἴρηνται ὑπὸ θεοῦ, βασιλέως χρηματισμός
(My words are spoken by God, an oracle of the king)

As in 30:1, the first word has been read as דִּבְרֵי, and the proper name Lemuel
has been separated into two parts. These changes brought about further changes in
the translation.

3. Another indication of a different *Vorlage* is the fact that in various instances
the text of the LXX is shorter than that of the MT: 8:29a, 33; 11:4, 10b, 11a; 15:31;
16:1, 3; 18:23-24; 9:1-2; 20:14-19; 21:5, 18b; 22:6; 23:23. The number of these
instances is too large for assuming a scribal phenomenon (parablepsis).

3. Conclusion

The upshot of the preceding analysis is that the translator used a Hebrew book of
Proverbs which differed recensionally from that of the MT. These differences
consisted of major and minor differences in sequence as well as differences in pluses
and minuses. If the interpretation of these differences is correct, we have gained
further insights into the history of the growth of the book of Proverbs. At a
relatively late time the different editorial stages of the growth of the book were still
reflected in the texts.

When the book of Proverbs was translated into Greek, presumably in the second
century BCE, a scroll was used that contained an editorial stage of the book differing
from the one now contained in the MT. Such an understanding parallels views
developed previously regarding other biblical book; cf. the first paragraph of this
article and notes 2-4. This view does not imply that the editorial changes were made
as late as the time of the Greek translation, but that at that time, in a geographically
remote center of Judaism, such early scrolls were still available.[19]

---

[19]This view had already been suggested by H. B. Swete (*An Introduction to the
Old Testament in Greek* [Cambridge: Cambridge University Press, 1902; reprinted, New
York: Ktav, 1968] 241), although he still allows for the possibility that the translator
himself may have been involved in the changes. Our own views are more in agreement
with those of G. Mezzacasa, *Il libro dei Proverbi*, 2-3; Eissfeldt, *The Old Testament*,
472, and S. Ahituv, "Proverbs," *Encyclopaedia Biblica* 5 (Jerusalem: Bialik, 1968) 554
(Hebrew). The latter three views mention the possibility of recensional differences
between the MT and LXX, although none goes into detail.

OBSERVATIONS ON "WISDOM NARRATIVES" IN EARLY BIBLICAL LITERATURE

Lawrence M. Wills
Harvard Divinity School

Among John Strugnell's many scholarly interests have been ancient Jewish wisdom traditions and legends of the wise courtier. Despite the importance of court legends in the Old Testament—the Joseph story, Esther, Daniel, and 1 Esdras are all influenced by this genre—this topic has not received its due attention among scholars. Although Professor Strugnell never addressed this topic in print, five of the six authors who have treated the court legend in any depth have studied with him.[1] In this essay, I would like to continue a dialogue with Professor Strugnell on the role of wisdom traditions in court narratives by investigating a few particular narratives and making some preliminary observations about the important methodological issues that are involved.

By the late 1960's, many scholars had sought to isolate wisdom influences on narrative sections of the Bible. The most enduring of these were Gerhard von Rad's study of the Joseph story, Shemaryahu Talmon's on Esther, and that of R. N. Whybray on the Succession Narrative of David and Solomon (2 Samuel 9-20, 1 Kings 1-2), but there were many others as well.[2] Although various formal and

---

[1] The scholars who have written on the court legend are, to my knowledge: George W. E. Nickelsburg, *Resurrection, Immortality and Eternal Life in Intertestamental Judaism* (HTS 26; Cambridge: Harvard University Press; London: Oxford University Press, 1972) 49–57; idem, "The Genre and Function of the Markan Passion Narrative," *HTR* 73 (1980) 153–84, and idem, *Jewish Literature Between the Bible and the Mishnah* (Philadelphia: Fortress, 1981) 19–28; John J. Collins, "The Court-Tales in Daniel and the Development of Apocalyptic," *JBL* 94 (1975) 218–34; Susan Niditch and Robert Doran, "The Success Story of the Wise Courtier," *JBL* 96 (1977) 179–93; William Richard Goodman, Jr., "A Study of 1 Esdras 3:1-5:6" (Diss., Duke Univ., 1972), and W. Lee Humphreys, "A Life-Style for Diaspora: A Study of Esther and Daniel," *JBL* 92 (1973) 211–23. Only Humphreys was not a student of Prof. Strugnell. My own dissertation, "The Jew in the Court of the Foreign King: Ancient Jewish Court Legends," was completed under Prof. Strugnell's supervision, and will be published by Harvard Dissertations in Religion. The present essay treats some of the same issues as my thesis, but here I am pressing certain questions further and addressing methodological concerns that pertain to the study of wisdom narratives.

[2] G. von Rad, "The Joseph Narrative and Ancient Wisdom," in his *The Problem of the Hexateuch and Other Essays* (New York: McGraw-Hill, 1966) 292–300; S. Talmon,

terminological criteria were brought forward, the central methodological approach of these studies was to provide what I would call a "proverbial correlative," that is, to establish that a theme in the narrative was also an overriding concern in the books of Proverbs and Ben Sira.

In 1969 James L. Crenshaw sought to oppose this proliferation of perceived wisdom influence in all parts of the biblical canon by questioning the entire notion of narrative wisdom.[3] Crenshaw's critique is based on a sound principle: discussions of purported wisdom influence on genres not traditionally associated with wisdom should only be advanced when the criteria are clearly spelled out. The assertion of the presence of wisdom elements should include not just a catalogue of wisdom themes or terminology, but also an accounting of the *Sitz-im-Leben* of the document. That is, one must specify under what conditions a tradition was used, by whom, and to whom it was addressed. Crenshaw attempts to clarify the various spheres of activity for the bearers of wisdom traditions in ancient Israel:

> ... one must distinguish between family/clan wisdom, the goal of
> which is the mastering of life, the stance hortatory and style proverbial;
> court wisdom, with the goal of education for a select group, the stance
> secular, and method didactic; and scribal wisdom, the goal being
> education for all, the stance dogmatico-religious, and the method
> dialogico-admonitory. (130)

Crenshaw concludes that the term "wisdom" should be reserved only for those documents which have traditionally been placed within the wisdom canon of Proverbs, Job, Ecclesiastes, Ben Sira, and Wisdom of Solomon, and that scholars who have sought wisdom influence in biblical narratives such as the Joseph story or Esther have failed to provide the necessary accounting of the *Sitz-im-Leben*. Crenshaw's arguments have not persuaded all scholars of biblical wisdom, but I believe he was correct on two points: (1) definitions of wisdom used in narrative analysis are often vague and subjective, and (2) a close inspection of the arguments advanced reveals that they are not as cogent as they at first appear. Von Rad, for example, will have difficulty asserting that Joseph portrays the wise courtier when he has no training in court wisdom, cannot defend himself before his brothers or Pharaoh, and relies for success on divine revelation, a theme conspicuously absent in court wisdom.

"'Wisdom' in the Book of Esther," *VT* 13 (1963) 419–55, and R. N. Whybray, *The Succession Narrative* (Napierville, IL: Allenson, 1968). See also below, nn. 3 and 4.

[3] J. L. Crenshaw, "Method in Determining Wisdom Influence Upon 'Historical Literature,'" *JBL* 88 (1969) 129–42.

Lawrence M. Wills

It is my contention that the role of wisdom in narratives is a fascinating and complex question, which is ripe for new attention and new methods. Crenshaw's article should have been taken as a redefinition of the problem and a goad to renewed investigation, rather than a death knell.[4] What I propose to accomplish here is to investigate one type of biblical narrative with regard to wisdom associations and *Sitz-im-Leben*, not to refute all of Crenshaw's conclusions, but to indicate what the agenda should include for the next stage of research. The limitations of this essay do not permit me to discuss in detail the very definition of wisdom which I am presuming, but I may at least say that wisdom texts reflect an attempt to raise the reader (or hearer) to a higher state of success, happiness, or salutary well-being. I am here, however, more interested in the form than the content of wisdom: one group, aware of its position, *transmits* such teaching to another in what is conceived of as a continuous succession, whether from grandmother to grandchild or teacher to student. It is the institution of transmission, whether oral or written, that is key to defining and identifying wisdom.[5]

There are three very interesting short narrative episodes in the Deuteronomistic history which take place in the court or in the king's presence, and fall into the same pattern: Nathan's "parable" of the poor man's ewe (2 Sam 12:1-14), the petition of the wise woman of Tekoa (2 Sam 14:1-17), and an unnamed prophet's chastisement of Ahab (1 Kgs 20:35-43). In the first, Nathan narrates the account of a rich man who has taken and slaughtered a poor man's beloved ewe lamb. King David angrily condemns the rich man, whereupon Nathan proclaims that the king is actually guilty of the same crime against Uriah the Hittite. In the second, Joab summons a wise woman from Tekoa to create a similar ruse. She pleads with King David to intervene with her family to keep them from executing her only son, who was guilty of killing his brother. When David agrees that the son should not be killed, the wise woman responds that, in the same way, David should be reconciled to Absalom. In the third, a prophet, pretending to be a soldier, approaches Ahab and cries that he has lost the prisoner that was in his charge. When Ahab says that he must die as a result, the

---

[4]On Crenshaw's criticism of von Rad, see "Method," 136–37. It should be noted that several scholars have pursued interesting new studies of wisdom narratives which are less vulnerable to Crenshaw's criticisms: Hans-Peter Müller, "Die weisheitliche Lehrerzählung im Alten Testament und in seiner Umwelt," *Die Welt des Orients* 9 (1977) 77-98, and J. A. Loader, "Jedidiah or: Amadeus. Thoughts on the Succession Narrative and Wisdom," in W. C. van Wyk, ed., *Studies in the Succession Narrative* (publisher and city not given, 1986) 167–201.

[5]Cf. Hartmut Gese, "Wisdom literature in Persian period," in W. D. Davies and Louis Finkelstein, eds., *Cambridge History of Judaism* (Cambridge: Cambridge University Press, 1984) 190, on didactic transmission as the key to the definition of wisdom, and Wills, "Court," chap. 1.

prophet responds that Ahab must also die for failing to execute *his* prisoner, Ben-hadad.

All three episodes describe a similar method that a person may use to criticize the king. The interlocutor enters the presence of the king, presents a scenario which, unbeknownst to the king, is completely fictitious. The scenario elicits a condemning judgment from the king, and the interlocutor points out that the scenario actually applies most of all to the king himself. Faced with his own judgment against himself, the king is forced to recognize the truth of the condemnation, and is powerless—as kings so often are in legend in the face of their own decrees—to punish the interlocutor.

These three narratives have received some scholarly attention which is worth noting. Uriel Simon called these "juridical parables," and gave a preliminary description of this type of narrative.[6] Burke O. Long uses this same term for these narratives in his commentary on 1 Kings, and Joseph Blenkinsopp makes further formal observations, calling these three stories "parables."[7] Rather than use the term juridical parable, which focuses on the notion of the king's verdict on himself, I will use the term "disguised parable." The essence of the narrative is not really juridical. The king does not pronounce a legal judgment against himself (although he *thinks* that he has pronounced a legal judgment against someone else); he is more struck with his own guilt, and the irony that he has judged himself. As we shall see, some of the non-biblical examples are not juridical at all, but concern policy decisions of the king. Parable can also be a troublesome term, in that in modern usage it is generally laden with deeper levels of meaning than these stories afford, but it is commonly used in the scholarly literature, and the Hebrew *mashal* is broad enough to include this usage.[8]

[6]U. Simon, "The Poor Man's Ewe-Lamb. An Example of a Juridical Parable," *Bib* 48 (1967) 207–42.

[7]Burke O. Long, *1 Kings* (FOTL 9; Grand Rapids: Eerdmanns, 1984) 221-22, 252; J. Blenkinsopp, *Wisdom and Law in the Old Testament* (New York: Oxford University Press, 1983) 36.

[8]Cf. *b. B. Bat.* 15b, where Nathan's story of the ewe lamb is called a *mashal* For a discussion of the applicability of the term "parable," see George W. Coats, "Parable, Fable, Anecdote: Storytelling in the Succession Narrative," *Int* 35 (1981) 368–82, and D. M. Gunn, *The Story of King David: Genre and Interpretation* (JSOTSup 6; Sheffield: JSOT, 1978) 40–43. It should be noted that in many ways Genesis 38 also reflects this pattern. Tamar asserts her rights within the law of levirate marriage, not by spinning a fictitious story, but by manipulating events so that Judah unknowingly pronounces judgment on himself. Important differences can also be seen, however: the authority figure here is not a king but a patriarch, the story is longer, covers a much greater period of time, and differs in its "parabolic" operation. In the other three narratives, the fictitious story or "parable" evaporates and disappears as soon as its function is over, and the king's perspective has been altered. Here, however, the

Lawrence M. Wills

The background and history of this form, however, has not been investigated thoroughly, and a short digression at this point into the non-biblical parallels is necessary before we turn again to consider the three disguised parables above. Although it is not broadly attested in world literature, the examples that do survive are very telling. A very interesting use of this story type is found at Herodotus 1.27. Croesus, the king of Lydia, after enjoying great success in defeating all of the cities of Asia Minor, sets his sights on the Greek islands and proceeds to build ships to capture them. Bias of Priene, one of the Greek "Seven Sages," and now a court advisor to Croesus, informs him that the islanders are procuring horses to attack him on land. This comes as good news to Croesus, who is overjoyed that the Greek islanders would attack him on what is now his turf, playing at his game. "In the same way," responds Bias, "they would have *you* at a disadvantage if you attack their islands with ships." Croesus sees the wisdom of Bias' advice and signs a treaty with the islanders.

At this point we may speculate on the *Sitz-im-Leben* of this disguised parable in Herodotus. Herodotus preserves many court legends, most of which deal with courts in Asia Minor and Persia. They are short, anecdotal, probably oral legends which glorified the wise courtier in the court of the king, and they reflect the interests of the courtier class in depicting how one may counsel the king without incurring royal displeasure. We recall at this point that one of Crenshaw's main categories of wisdom was court wisdom, and certain sections of Proverbs and *Aḥikar* can be identified with the court. In Herodotus this same courtly interest is reflected in narratives which were likely recounted within the extended court system that grew up in Asia Minor after the Persian conquest. In two episodes which have been intertwined (3.34-35), we see this dual focus on preserving one's life while advising the king. In one, a group of courtiers tell Cambyses that he is greater than his father Cyrus. Croesus (king of Lydia in the legend above, but now the courtier of Cambyses, king of Persia) disagrees, and says, "Your father was greater." Before Cambyses can erupt into yet another mad rage, Croesus continues, "You have not

"parabolic action"—Tamar's prostitution—rises in prominence to become the main issue at hand. Her pregnancy, however achieved, is the motive of the story and the connection with the rest of the patriarchal narrative. Judah's change of perspective now appears as secondary, and is dispensed with in one verse, v 26. Gary Rendsburg has shown the connection between the family narrative of Genesis 38 and that of David's family in 2 Samuel, which might place the narrative in the same circles as the three disguised parables ("David and his Circle in Genesis XXXVIII," *VT* 36 [1986] 438-46). On the use of deception by Tamar and the wise woman of Tekoa, see Esther Fuchs, "Who is Hiding the Truth? Deceptive Women and Biblical Androcentrism," in Adela Yarbro Collins, ed., *Feminist Perspectives on Biblical Scholarship* (Chico: Scholars, 1985) 137–44. Genesis 38 has undergone a process of literary development which takes it beyond the form-critical observations here, but I hope to pursue the analysis of it in the near future.

produced a great successor, which your father was able to do in you." This, of course, pleases Cambyses and secures Croesus a favored place in the court, but the accompanying story shows the contrasting possibility. When Cambyses asks the court what Persians in general think of him, Prexaspes replies that the Persians admire him greatly, but they have just one small criticism: he drinks too much. Cambyses explodes and says to Prexaspes, "I am sober enough to shoot an arrow right through your son's heart!"—which he then proceeds to do. The directness of Prexaspes leads to endangering himself and his son, while the indirectness and humor of Croesus leads to success.[9] Thus, here and for Herodotus' disguised parable above concerning Bias, we can suggest a *Sitz-im-Leben* specific enough, I think, to meet Crenshaw's criteria: didactic legends of the courtier class. The correlation between the themes of these narratives and the typical teachings of court wisdom in the Ancient Near East provide for a much more specific "proverbial correlative" than is possible in the Joseph story or Esther.[10]

Two other examples in Herodotus, however, alter the pattern of the disguised parable, and do not necessarily allow for the assignment of this same *Sitz-im-Leben*. The first is found at 3.32. Cambyses has just put to death his own brother as a suspected usurper of the throne, and at dinner his sister, after stripping the leaves from a head of lettuce one by one, asks Cambyses whether he prefers the lettuce whole or stripped. He says that he prefers it whole, to which she replies, "What I have done to this lettuce, you have done to the royal family." Cambyses not only does not repent of his past crime, but falls into a rage and kills his sister. Herodotus throughout describes Cambyses as a madman, however, and this unusual development in the disguised parable may perhaps be attributed to his characterization of Cambyses.

The second occurs at 1.159, where a Lydian general, fleeing the Persians, enters Cyme and pleads for sanctuary. The residents consult an oracle at a temple of Apollo, where the god responds that they should turn over the Lydian to the Persians. A certain Aristodicus, however, begins walking around the temple, taking birds from the nests in the surrounding trees. The voice of Apollo comes from the temple, demanding to know how Aristodicus can harm the birds that are under the protection of the temple grounds, to which Aristodicus responds, "Lord Apollo, will you protect your suppliants while ordering the people of Cyme to surrender theirs?" Surprisingly, Apollo says, "Yes, indeed I will!" This story, first, concerns a god and

---

[9]Cf. also 3.31. There are many legends of wise courtiers in Herodotus, on which see Wills, "Court," chap. 2; Richmond Lattimore, "The Wise Adviser in Herodotus," *CP* 34 (1939) 24-35; Heinrich Bischoff, "Der Warner bei Herodot," and Karl Reinhardt, "Die Persergeschichten," both in Walter Marg, ed., *Herodot: Eine Auswahl aus der neueren Forschung* München: Beck, 1965) 302-20 and 320-69 respectively.

[10]In the Hebrew Bible, cf. for instance Prov 16:14-15, 25:2-15.

not a king as the superior figure, but more important, the expected softening of the god's judgment does not occur. Apollo is angry with Aristodicus, and becomes even more rigid in his judgment as a result of Aristodicus' breach of temple laws; he further forbids him from resubmitting the question of suppliants to the god. The god has already given his response, and gods are more difficult to mollify than kings; the technique for appealing a king's judgment backfires with Apollo. Thus, in respect to form, the first Herodotean disguised parable (concerning Bias) lies closer to the biblical examples than do the latter two. They vary from the first in the following ways: both involve a parabolic action rather than a fictitious scenario, both fail to alter the judgment of the superior—in fact the parabolic actions only bring on more severe penalties—and neither involves a courtier. We are left with one disguised parable in Herodotus which is associated with court wisdom (the Bias legend), and two others which, though interesting as more distant parallels, are not similar enough to warrant close comparison.[11]

It would also be natural to search for this narrative pattern among oral folk tales, but the folk parallels which are often adduced are not very close. Stith Thompson's index of folk tale motifs lists several entries which contain an unrecognized "parable" which elicits a person's self-judgment,[12] but, on the one hand, many are quite whimsical and do not contain any serious moral import (as do all the examples above), and on the other hand, they do not take as their central dramatic setting the hierarchical and potentially dangerous relationship of king and subject. A motif similar to the disguised parable does occur, however, at the conclusion of "The Goose-Girl" from the Grimm brothers' collection of fairy tales, which is interesting for our purposes.[13] In this story a princess, betrothed to a prince whom she has

[11] The only other examples from ancient literature which I have found are quite distant historically, although they do bear out the connection with court wisdom. The Persian *Shah Nameh (Epic of the Kings)*, written in the medieval period by Firdowsi but containing much older material, also contains a disguised parable. At 29.1 the wise courtier Mazdak wishes to move the king to open the granaries during a famine. He tells the king various stories of hardheartedness toward those in need, and at the conclusion of each the king condemns the perpetrator soundly. The next day Mazdak begins distribution of the food, having recourse to the king's judgments on the previous day. Philostratus, *Apollonius of Tyana* 6:34, has also evidently adapted a disguised parable to a more literary retelling. See also Wills, "Court," chap. 2.

[12] S. Thompson, *Motif-Index of Folk-Literature* (6 vols.; Bloomington/London: Indiana University, 1966). Consider, e.'g., the various examples of "Wisdom learned through parables" in J80–99. Gunn's folk parallels lack the central motif of the inferior addressing the potentially dangerous superior (*David*, 42).

[13] Hermann Gunkel cites this story as a parallel, calling it "the deceitful wife" (*The Folktale in the Old Testament* (Sheffield: Almond, 1987) 145. He also makes the very interesting observation that the core of Nathan's parable may have been a fable about a rich man's cruelty, with no application at all (54-55). This would not affect

never met, sets out with her maidservant for the prince's palace. The wicked maidservant supplants the princess and presents herself at the palace, saying that the real princess is her servant. The real princess now finds herself tending the geese, but the king, upon leaving the palace, sees the goose-girl and discovers the truth about her. When he returns, he places before the deceitful maid a fictitious scenario analogous to the events which have occurred, and asks her judgment. She, of course, recommends the cruelest punishment against the perpetrator. "It is you," says the king, "and you have pronounced your own sentence, and thus shall it be done to you." The ending at first sight seems identical to the disguised parable, but upon closer comparison, we find that there are differences. First, here it is the king who elicits judgment from a subordinate. Second, unlike the Bias legend, there is no attempt to bring the impostor to a change of heart. She is merely naming her own just punishment. This strict justice is typical of folk tales,[14] but is not the main theme of the wisdom legend. The main point of the Bias legend in Herodotus is, how does one *instruct* the king, counseling the wise action, while showing enough restraint to keep one's head attached to one's shoulders. The delicate relationship between courtier and king is central.

At this point we may turn from the speculation about the *Sitz-im-Leben* of the disguised parable in Herodotus and elsewhere to the examples in the Hebrew Bible with which we began. We find that the similarities and differences are both instructive. The Bias legend, a court wisdom product, involved the relationship of king and subject, as did many of the other examples. It was suggested that such disguised parables arose as oral narratives of that class of people who made their living addressing the king, that is, courtiers. Not all of the people addressing the king are courtiers, however. In the Deuteronomistic history the addressee is the king in each case, but the interlocutors vary. To be sure, Nathan is depicted at times as a court prophet,[15] but in 1 Sam 14 it is a "wise woman" who enters before the king (although she was enlisted by David's commander-in-chief, Joab), and in 1 Kgs 20,

my analysis, which pertains to the manner of application of the parable to the king. Coats' use of the term "fable" (in the article "Parable," above) differs from Gunkel's and from most scholarly definitions.

[14]A mirror image of this motif is found at Esth 6:6-11, where Haman thinks he is naming his own reward, but in fact the reward is intended for his nemesis, Mordecai. This begins the process of the reversal of his fortunes and of Mordecai's, as Susan Niditch notes (*Underdogs and Tricksters* [San Francisco: Harper & Row, 1987] 130). Although Haman is not tricked into naming his own punishment, he does create it, in the form of the gallows that he had erected for Mordecai.

[15]There is nothing in the references to Nathan in 2 Samuel 12 to indicate that he is specifically a *court* prophet, but at 1 Kings 1 he clearly is, since he is placed side-by-side in the new reign of Solomon with Zadok, the established priest, Benaiah, the new commander-in-chief and Bathsheba, the established queen-mother. At 2 Samuel 7 Nathan is also by implication the court prophet.

an unnamed prophet who accosts King Ahab. The courtier ideal is thus not evident. Another crucial element of the Bias legend in Herodotus is also lost in the Deuteronomistic work: the clever manipulation of a potentially dangerous king. The Bias legend in Herodotus clearly exults in the wise courtier's ability to move deftly through the minefield of court diplomacy before an autocratic king. Whether Croesus captures the Greek islands or not is not the point of the Herodotus legend; what is the point is that Bias was wise enough as a courtier to orchestrate a change of policy safely. In the background, of course, is also the notion that the courtier is really responsible for good governance, not the strong king. This is a courtier's ideology, but not a king's.

On the other hand, the prophets of the Deuteronomistic history, Nathan and the unnamed prophet, are called by God to denounce the king's action, and they execute their responsibility fearlessly. They trick the king into a self-judgment, but there is no sense that they are acting wisely to avoid the royal displeasure. The story of the unnamed prophet at 1 Kings 20 does not even seek a repentant king or a reformed policy. Such a change of heart on the king's part could conceivably have protected the courtier from retribution, but the prophet merely seeks the poetic justice of having the unregenerate king name his own punishment, much like the ending of "The Goose-Girl." Of the three Deuteronomistic history narratives, only the wise woman is parallel to Herodotus in showing a subordinate trying to influence policy, while at the same time escaping possible retaliation.[16] The Herodotus example of Bias, however, reflects a greater integrity of form and content: the clever and ironic, even playful structure corresponds to the theme of the methods of the wise courtier in counseling the king. It is a short handbook of proper attitude for the courtier. Yet, even where the Deuteronomistic protagonists do not fear the king, the stories presume that a danger is present which the prophet bravely ignores, and they draw from the same underlying tension.

The disguised parable in the Hebrew Bible neatly reflects the difficulties posed by Crenshaw's challenge. One could make a plausible case that by analyzing the Bias

---

[16]This is perhaps the only one of the three that does not derive from prophetic circles. Since the wise woman is playing out Joab's design, and it is ultimately detrimental to the state, this story reflects the redactional point of view of the composer of the Succession Narrative (so P. Kyle McCarter, *II Samuel* [AB; Garden City, NY: Doubleday, 1984] 350–52). 2 Samuel 12, on the other hand, may represent a later, prophetic addition to the Succession Narrative, since 1) Nathan is depicted in a wholly different way in 1 Kings 1, and 2) the text could read quite smoothly if 12:1-15a were removed. Ernst Würthwein (*Die Erzählung von der Thronnachfolge Davids: theologische oder politische Geschichtsschreibung* [Zürich: Theologischer Verlag, 1974] 24-25) and Henry Preserved Smith (*A Critical and Exegetical Commentary on the Books of Samuel* [ICC; Edinburgh: Clark, n.d.] 322), among others, argue this, but see also McCarter, *II Samuel*, 305.

legend in its context in Herodotus, a relatively precise *Sitz-im-Leben* could be assigned to it that can be associated with court wisdom. The parallel narratives in the Deuteronomistic history, however, reflect a shift to a prophetic interest, which calls into question an easy identification with wisdom traditions. It is agreed that courtiers and court schools produced wisdom texts, as did scribes and scribal schools, but what about prophets and prophet "guilds"? Prophetic guilds certainly existed, but did they maintain the same sort of didactic transmission of learning and values which the court schools and scribal schools did? Alexander Rofé has categorized a number of prophet legends as didactic, and paints a picture of the transmission of prophetic values in narrative form.[17] One could argue for the existence of wisdom narratives here on this criterion alone. In regard to the three disguised parables, however, it might have fallen victim to Crenshaw's criticisms, in that a didactic, sapiential narrative form may have been adapted to literary needs which do not directly involve didactic transmission of values.

Following the cross-cultural comparison, several things become clearer. The prophetic disguised parable is associated formally with the courtly disguised parable as preserved in Herodotus, indicating that the form is, first, international, and second, associated (in one context, at least) with wisdom transmission. The wisdom *Sitz* of the Bias legend indicates that the form of the disguised parable can move between the court wisdom setting and the prophetic setting. This further indicates that, on one hand, a broader comparison of narratives is indeed a fruitful way to discern wisdom narratives in the Hebrew Bible, but that on the other hand, the situation calls for a methodological precision that recognizes that wisdom forms can be adapted to various needs, which may or may not have a continuing didactic transmission. Recognizing the cautions of Crenshaw and others,[18] the next stage in the study of wisdom narrative should be both broader and narrower than it has been; it will likely be broader in being more comparative and folkloristic, but it must also specify just who is passing along what to whom.

[17]A. Rofé, "Classes in the Prophetical Stories: Didactic Legenda and Parable," VTSup 26 (1974) 143-64; idem, "The Classification of the Prophetical Stories," *JBL* 89 (1970) 427-40; and idem, *Sippurê Hanebî'îm* (Jerusalem: Magnes, 1982). On prophet guilds, see Frank Moore Cross, *Canaanite Myth and Hebrew Epic* (Cambridge: Harvard University Press, 1973) 223, and John Gray, *I & II Kings* (2d ed.; London: SCM, 1970) 432. It is important to note that whether the transmission was originally oral or written is not crucial for our purposes. They were, however, most likely oral. So Rofé, "Classes," 163; Gray, *Kings,* 431; and McCarter, *II Samuel,* 305-306.

[18]Burke O. Long urges caution, not just in regard to the assigning of a *Sitz-im-Leben* to wisdom forms, but to other forms as well, since similar forms can be adapted to different uses ("Recent Field Studies in Oral Literature and the Question of *Sitz im Leben,*" *Semeia* 5 [1976] 35-49). The thrust of the present essay, however, is that caution should not lead us to pessimism about assigning specific social contexts to some forms, even where that social context may change.

THE *Beth Essentiae* AND THE PERMISSIVE MEANING OF THE HIPHIL (APHEL)*

J. H. Charlesworth
Princeton Theological Seminary

Before the destruction of the Temple by the Roman soldiers in 70 CE the semantic meaning of the *beth* prefixed before Hebrew and Aramaic nouns increased remarkably. A rare, but ancient, meaning was apparently employed in the living, spoken language used by the members of the Qumran community,[1] including, most likely, the *Môrēh Haṣ-ṣédek*. It is the *beth Essentiae*. The Hiphil, and parallel verbal stems in other languages, is almost always defined as the "causative" stem. This definition is inaccurate, because it is incomplete.

The purpose of this essay is to clarify these two dimensions in Semitic philology. It is a distinct honor and pleasure to dedicate these observations to John Strugnell. In 1962 I accepted a Merit Scholarship to Duke Divinity School so that I could study Semitics, especially the texts of the Dead Sea Scrolls. Memories of those days, now long ago, are vivid to me now as I ponder my long and fruitful association with John Strugnell. I recall how he made lasting impressions on me. He was a charming Oxonian, an invaluable resource person who astoundingly corrected the "authoritative" grammar by Gesenius-Kautzsch-Cowley and lexicons such as those by Brown-Driver-Briggs and Koehler-Baumgartner. My appreciation of Semitics and biblical studies increased markedly under his personal tutelage. His intense concentration on details was contagious. Over almost thirty years we have been close. He has been a special confidant and intimate friend. May he like the odists who perceived continue to rise up ܐܬܢܝܚܬ (*Odes of Solomon* 26:12).

* I am grateful to Professors J. J. M. Roberts and C. L. Seow and to my assistant Mark Harding for helping me improve an earlier draft of this paper.

[1] Shelomo Morag ("Qumran Hebrew: Some Typological Observations,"*VT* 38 [1988] 148-64) has demonstrated that aspects of General Qumran Hebrew, such as the morphophonemic and morphological structures caused by variations in accents, result from phonological processes. Hence, Qumran Hebrew results from "a living, spoken, language" (p. 163). Rather than a continuation of Late Biblical Hebrew, Qumran Hebrew is generally caused by "a continuation of an old dialectical variation" (p. 161).

1. The *Beth Essentiae*

As is well known, Hebrew, Aramaic, and Syriac are deficient in prepositions.[2] While Greek, for example, has numerous prepositions,[3] Semitic languages have relatively few, and thus in Hebrew, Aramaic, and Syriac one preposition is employed to denote diverse phenomena. Before a noun, the preposition *beth* ostensibly originally signified (abiding) "in,"[4] and developed to denote more than spatially, temporally, or conditionally "in (of place, or of ideas), into, on, upon, at, among, by, against, for, with, within, together with, besides, near, under, on account of, according to."[5] Besides the instrumental *beth* there are other denotations and connotations, like the *beth* that indicates value (Gen 23:9) or material (1 Kgs 7:14).[6] In the post-exilic era, it appears in texts[7] with an increasing number of verbs to denote the *nota accusativa*,[8] and not only (as earlier) to specify the stricter "connection between verb" and object.[9]

The proclitic *beth* represents a complex, even unparalleled, range of syntactical meanings. It is used, for example, to introduce a temporal infinitive clause (e.g., Gen 2:4, 9:14). Obviously the semantic field contributed to and colored the meaning of a proclitic *beth* . Most of the apparently additional meanings of *beth* in the Second Temple Period are adequately discussed by Y. Thorion[10] and by K. Beyer.[11]

Unfortunately, another significant denotation of proclitic *beth* is seldom mentioned, or inelegantly bypassed in the basic Hebrew grammars, lexicons, or

---

[2] See the discussion of prepositions in B. K. Waltke and M. O'Connor, *An Introduction to Biblical Hebrew Syntax* (Winona Lake, IN: Eisenbrauns, 1990) 187-225. As they state, the "diversity of the senses of ב is remarkable" (p. 196).

[3] And English, obviously and fortunately; otherwise this article could not be written.

[4] Hence from the primitive meaning of "abiding in," יוֹם בְּיוֹם denotes "day by day."

[5] In languages cognate to Hebrew the preposition *beth* has even wider meanings. See, for example, A. F. Rainey, "Some Prepositional Nuances in Ugaritic Administrative Texts," *Proceedings of the International Conference on Semitic Studies Held in Jerusalem, 19-23 July 1965* (Jerusalem: Israel Academy of Sciences and Humanities, 1969) 205-11.

[6] The *beth* can be adverbial, temporal, modal, instrumental, causal, final, circumstantial, and concessive.

[7] It is possible that this frequency appeared earlier than the post-exilic period. We are dependent on texts that survived.

[8] This linguistic phenomenon becomes apparent in the Hebrew of Qumran.

[9] *Pace* KB, 104.

[10] "Die Syntax der Präposition B in der Qumranliteratur," *RevQ* 12 (1985) 17-63.

[11] *Die aramäischen Texte vom Toten Meer* (Göttingen: Vandenhoeck & Ruprecht, 1984).

philological studies.[12] Since it is not included in the lengthy summaries of the meaning of proclitic *beth* by Thorion and Beyer, and is not discussed by Qimron in his grammar of Qumran Hebrew, it would seem to many Semitists that there is no *beth essentiae* in the Hebrew and Aramaic of Jewish writings that antedate the destruction of the Temple in 70 CE. This impression is perhaps strengthened by the comment in Koehler-Baumgartner that some linguistic forms were "früher בְּ essentiae genannten."[13] The comment might imply that there is no *beth essentiae*. Would it not be safe to be skeptical about the existence of *beth essentiae*? Should we not agree with the distinguished Göttingen professor, Georg Heinrich August Ewald, who concluded, "Das oft gemissbrauchte *Beth essentiae* ist im A. T. nirgends wirklich zu finden, und der spätere arab. Gebrauch das בְּ bei dem Prädicat in einigen Fällen kann nicht verglichen werden"?[14]

To conclude that there is no *beth essentiae* in the Semitic languages of pre-70 Jews is to ignore that Semitic studies have grown enormously since 1827 and to miss the emergence and development of historical linguistics, thanks to the indefatigable labors of scholars and especially to the discovery of manuscripts that clearly antedate 70. I shall now attempt to demonstrate what P. Paul Joüon stated long ago, "Au point de vue grammatical le *Beth essentiae* est particulièrement important."[15] The *beth essentiae*—sometimes called the pleonastic *beth* or *beth d'identité*—is the *terminus technicus* for a compounded *beth* prefixed to a predicate (often a predicate nominative or a predicate adjective), and denoting the quality, essence, or characteristic of a thing or person. As Joüon reported, "Ce terme ancien, assez peu clair, veut sans doute dire que le nom introduit par le בְּ fait partie de l'*essence* (au sens large) de la chose dont il est parlé."[16] The *beth essentiae* is succinctly presented in Brown-Driver-Briggs (p. 89): בְּ introduces the *predicate*, denoting it as that *in* which the subj. consists, or *in* which it shows itself (the *Beth essentiae*, —common in Arabic, esp. with a ptcp. or adj. and in a negative sentence..." Waltke and O'Connor succinctly report, "The *beth* of identity (*beth*

---

[12]The *beth essentiae* is noticeably not discussed in: T. O. Lamdin, *Introduction to Biblical Hebrew* (New York: Scribner's, 1971); E. Qimron, *The Hebrew of the Dead Sea Scrolls* (HSS 29: Atlanta: Scholars, 1986); M. Jastrow, *A Dictionary of the Tarqumim, the Talmud Babli and Yerushalmi, and the Midrashic Literature* (2 vols.; New York: Pardes, 1950); K. Beyer, *Die aramäischen Texte vom Toten Meer* (Göttingen: Vandenhoeck & Ruprecht, 1984); Y. Thorion, "Die Syntax der Präposition B."

[13]*Lexicon*, 103.

[14]G.H.A. Ewald, *Kritische Grammatik der hebräischen Sprache* (Leipzig: Hahnschen Buchhandlung, 1827) 607.

[15]P. P. Joüon, *Grammaire de l'Hébreu Biblique* (Rome: Pontifical Biblical Institute, 1923; corrected 1965; reissued 1987) 404.

[16]Joüon, *Grammaire*, 404.

essentiae) marks the capacity in which an actor behaves ('as, serving as, in the capacity of'; ## 27-28)."[17] It is often translated into English by "being" or "as."

Unfortunately, scholars and translators have not comprehended this meaning of proclitic *beth*. The *beth essentiae* is present in biblical Hebrew as the following examples indicate.[18]

A. *To denote the essence or characteristic of God:*[19]

Exod 6:3   God said to Moses, "I appeared unto Abraham, Isaac and Jacob בְּאֵל שַׁדַּי as (or being in the character of) 'El Shaddai' (God Almighty); but by my name YHWH I was not known to them."

B. S. Childs correctly states that the "prepositon is a *beth essentiae*," and points to Exod 3:2.[20]

Exod 18:4   כִּי-אֱלֹהֵי אָבִי בְּעֶזְרִי   "for the God of my father was (in essence) my help..."

R. J. Williams and B. Childs rightly cite this verse as an example of the *beth essentiae.*[21]

Ps 118:7   יְהוָה לִי בְּעֹזְרָי   "YHWH (was) to me (in essence) my helper."[22]

---

[17]Waltke and O'Conner, *An Introduction to Biblical Hebrew Syntax,* 198.

[18]For further examples and discussions, see G. R. Hauschild, "Des En d'identité: semitische Herkunft und bibelsprachliche Entwicklung," *Festschrift zur Einweihung des Goethe-Gymnasiums in Frankfurt a. M.* (7. Januar 1897) 151-74; E. König, *Syntax der Hebräischen Sprache* (Leipzig: Hinrichs, 1897) 431; C. Brockelmann, *Grundriss der vergleichenden Grammatik der semitischen Sprachen* (Berlin: Reuther & Reichard, 1913) 2.368; Joüon, *Grammaire,* 404-405; BDB, 88-89; H. S. Nyberg, *Hebreisk Grammatik* (Uppsala: Almqvist & Wiksells, 1952) 327-28; KB, 103.

[19]Ps 54:6 is not a good example of *beth essentiae* (contrast GKC, § 119 i 379). Ps 68:5 seems corrupt, as indicated by variants, Masora parva (see BHS), and the LXX rendering.

[20]B. S. Childs, *The Book of Exodus* (OTL; Philadelphia: Westminster, 1974) 110.

[21]R. J. Williams, *Hebrew Syntax: An Outline* (Toronto/Buffalo: University of Toronto Press, 1976) 95; Childs, *The Book of Exodus,* 320.

[22]Not: "The Lord taketh my part with them that help me..." Contrast *The Holy Scriptures* (Tel Aviv: "Sinai" Publishing, 1984) 1444. The RSV also misses the point: "The LORD is on my side to help me..." Much better is the translation "With the LORD on my side as my helper..." See *TANAKH: A New Translation of the Holy Scriptures According to the Traditional Hebrew Text* (Philadelphia: The Jewish Publication Society, 5746/1985) 1249.

J. H. Charlesworth

M. Dahood ("Yahweh is for me, my Great Warrior") suggested that the *beth* is emphatic;[23] but A. A. Anderson correctly understood that the *beth* is an example of *beth essentiae*, and cites Gesenius-Kautzsch's discussion.[24]

Job 23:13   Job answers and says about God Almighty: וְהוּא בְאֶחָד   "And
he is (one whose being is) one; and who can turn him?"
The *beth* in the Hebrew phrase should not be ignored, and translated something like "he is alone," or "he is one"; and it should not be emended to בחר.[25] It is a *beth essentiae*, as Cyrus H. Gordon observed in a recent note.[26]   On Job 23:13 F. I. Andersen wisely states that "Israel's highest confession of faith was that the Lord is One (Dt 6:4). Once the preposition is recognized as *beth essentiae*, it is obvious that Job is saying the same thing here."[27] The RSV translation catches the grammatical force of the *beth essentiae*: "But he is unchangeable and who can turn him?" The *beth* is carefully constructed to indicate some of the character or essence of God.

Isa 40:10   הִנֵּה אֲדֹנָי וְהוִה בְּחָזָק יָבוֹא   "Behold, the Lord YHWH shall come as (being) a strong one."
J. N. D. Watts correctly points out that the *beth* here is another example of the *beth essentiae*.[28]
The *beth* in Isaiah 40:10 was understood and rendered adverbially (denoting how the Lord shall come), an acceptable option idiomatically,[29] by the translators of the

[23]M. Dahood, *Psalms III: 101-150* (AB 17a; Garden City: Doubleday, 1970) 157.

[24]A. A. Anderson, *The Book of Psalms* (New Century Bible; London: Oliphants, 1972) 799.

[25]See G. Beer, *Der Text des Buches Hiob* (Marburg: Elwertsche, 1897) 155; and K. Budde, *Das Buches Hiob* (HKAT; Göttingen: Vandenhoeck & Ruprecht, 1896) 132. Also, see the careful work, but disappointing conclusion in favor of emendation, by E. Dhorme, *A Commentary on the Book of Job* (Leiden: Brill; London: Nelson, 1967). See the judicious comments on the *beth essentiae* by S. R. Driver and G. B. Gray, *The Book of Job* (ICC: Edinburgh: Clark, 1921) 2.162.   M. H. Pope also decides in favor of emending באחד to בחר. Two alterations are required and an analogy with Ps 132:13 is (like all analogies) interesting but not conclusive. See Pope's comments in his *Job* (AB 15; Garden City: Doubleday, 1965) 156.

[26]C. H. Gordon, "'In' of Predication or Equivalence," *JBL* 100 (1981) 612-13.

[27]F. I. Andersen, *Job* (Tyndale Old Testament Commentaries; London: Inter-Varsity, 1976) 210.

[28]J. N. D. Watts, *Isaiah 34-66* (Word Biblical Commentary; Waco, TX: Word Books, 1987) 86.

[29]Another option would have been to take חזק as the noun חֵזֶק.

Septuagint (μετὰ ἰσχύος), the Peshitta (ܒܚܝܠܐ), and Targum (בתקוף): "with strength."[30]

The *beth* before חזק in 40:10 is usually—and correctly—understood as a *beth essentiae*.[31] Its rarity in biblical Hebrew and in the Hebrew of the Second Temple Period is indicated, as E.' Y. Kutscher pointed out, by the variant in 1QIsa[a]: בחזק, which begins line 10 on col. 33.[32] Kutscher suggested that the scribe was confused by the grammatical construction; it is not likely that "he knew what to make of" the *beth essentiae* in Isa 40:10. Kutscher concluded, "He therefore altered the pattern of the noun to: חזוק."[33]

The *beth essentiae* is not employed with an adjective. Prima facie חָזָק looks like an adjective in the extant text and pointing of the MT; but Brown-Driver-Briggs (305) take it as substantive: "as, in the character of, a strong one." The scribe of IQIsa[a] changed the apparent adjective to a noun, and thereby removed what was perceived to be a problem.

B. *The* beth essentiae *denotes the character (but not essence) of the human*:[34]
Deut 26:14 "I have not eaten during my mourning from it (i.e., the tithe),
nor have I removed from it בְּטָמֵא (while being) unclean."
The *beth* in Deut 26:14 is probably a *beth essentiae*, as S. R. Driver stated.[35] The rendering of the RSV and TANAKH signal the use of the *beth essentiae*:

> I have not eaten of the tithe while I was mourning,
> or removed any of it while I was unclean... (RSV)
> I have not eaten of it while in mourning;
> I have not cleared out any of it while I was unclean. (TANAKH)

---

[30]And also by Jerome: "in fortitudine veniet."

[31]See BDB, 89; KB, 103; GKC, § 119 i 379; Joüon, *Grammaire*, 404; Kutscher, *The Language and Linguistic Background of the Isaiah Scroll (1QIsa*[a]*)* (Studies on the Texts of the Desert of Judah 6; Leiden: Brill, 1974) 373; Hauschild, "Des En d'identité," 163.

[32]See the color photograph in F. M. Cross, D. N. Freedman, J. A. Sanders, eds., *Scrolls from Qumrân Cave I* [John C. Trever's Photographs] (Jerusalem: Shrine of the Book, 1972).

[33]E. Y. Kutscher, *The Language*, 373. The scribe of 1QIsa[a] worked from a classical Hebrew Scroll which "frequently seemed strange to him, and at times he did not understand it properly. Hence he emended the text which was before him— sometimes aware of what he was doing, but frequently unconsciously—to bring it into closer accord with the language as he knew it" (p. 17).

[34]I am not convinced that Num 13:23 is another example of the *beth essentiae*; but perhaps Joüon (*Grammaire*, 404) and KB (103) are correct.

[35]S. R. Driver, *A Critical and Exegetical Commentary on Deuteronomy* (ICC; Edinburgh; Clark, 1902), esp. 127, 291-92.

72

J. H. Charlesworth

It should now be clear that the *beth* in biblical Hebrew, as a *beth essentiae*, can function to denote the essence or character of God or the human. The use of *beth* in this way is found in Arabic, as was acknowledged long ago.[36] Also, the Egyptian preposition *m*, which usually denotes, like beth, "in," also signifies one who is "in the position of," or "as acquiring a particular quality or "property."[37] The *beth essentiae* is also found in Mishnaic Hebrew.[38]

I now shall try to clarify that the *beth essentiae* is also found in Qumran Hebrew. In 1QH 8:4-5 we are confronted by the following:

או]דכה אדוני כי נ[תתני במקור נוזלים ביבשה

What is the meaning of the *beth* before "overflowing fountain"? Does the author claim that the Lord has placed him "*by* an overflowing fountain in a desert"? If the author is only beside the fountain, what is the force of the opening line of the psalm?

It seems likely that we are confronted with another example of the *beth essentiae*. The opening of the psalm would thus be rendered:

I [praise you, O Lord, because you] placed me
as (in essence) an overflowing fountain in a desert,
and (as) a spring of water in a land of dryness,
and (as) the irrigator of the garden.

This translation is apparently required by a later section of the same psalm, 1QH 8:16:

ואתה אלי שמתה בפי כיורה גשם לכול [
ומבוע מים חיים ולא יכזב
And you, O my God, have put in my mouth as it were early
rain for all [
and a spring of living water; and it shall not fail...

If, in fact, the author sees himself as one whom God has made the source of water, living water, then he is not merely beside the fountain. He is *characteristically* the fountain or spring.

[36]W. Wright, *A Grammar of the Arabic Language* (10 vols.; London: Norgate, 1875) 2.168-76.

[37]See A. Gardiner, *Egyptian Grammar* (London: Oxford University Press, 1957) 124, 140.

[38]See the examples given by M. H. Segal, *A Grammar of Mishnaic Hebrew* (Oxford: Clarendon, 1927) 171-72.

The book of Ezekiel has profoundly influenced the author of 1QH 8; it is especially clear that Ezekiel 31 (the allegory of the trees) and Ezekiel 47 (the river that flows out from the Temple to the East) has shaped the psalm. These literary links lead us to another second-century BCE author who was also profoundly influenced by Ezekiel, and who wrote in Hebrew. The thoughts of Ben Sira increase the possibility that the author of 1QH 8 saw himself as "the fountain." According to Ben Sira 24:30, which is inspired by Ezekiel 47,[39] the author[40] explains that Wisdom found a home in Israel (contrast *1 Enoch* 42). Claiming to be imbued with Wisdom, he explains, *inter alia*, that, he is as a torrent and a canal for the (eternal) garden. Note the extant recensions:

> Hebrew: Also I, as (כ) a torrent from a river
> and as (כ) a canal[41] of water pour forth into a garden..."[42]
>
> Syriac: Also I, (am) as (ܐܝܟ) an irrigation stream
> and as (ܐܝܟ) conduits which descend into a garden.[43]
>
> Greek: And I, as (ὡς) a canal from a river,
> and as (ὡς) a waterway went forth into paradise.[44]

As W. O. E. Oesterley long ago argued, and P. W. Skehan and A. A. Di Lella recently stated, the author—Ben Sira—portrays himself as "an irrigation canal drawn

---

[39]See O. Rickenbacher, *Weisheitsperikopen bei Ben Sira* (OBO 1; Göttingen: Vandenhoeck & Ruprecht, 1973) 168-69, and M. Gilbert, "L'éloge de la Sagesse," *RTL* 5 (1974) 326-48; esp. 340.

[40]Ben Sira 39:27-43:30 was found in a fragment at Masada. Yadin judged it to be "in the original Hebrew version." See the photographs in Y. Yadin, *The Ben Sira Scroll from Masada* (Jerusalem: Israel Exploration Society and the Shrine of the Book, 1965) 1. The oldest portions of Ben Sira—and in Hebrew—were found in Ca. 2 and 11; 11QPsᵃ Sirach contains 51:13-20b(?) and 51:30b. See J. A. Sanders, *The Psalms Scroll of Qumrân Cave 11 (11QPsᵃ)* (DJD 4; Oxford: Clarendon, 1965) 79-85. Of course, portions of Ben Sira were found in five manuscripts in the Cairo Geniza; see esp. A. A. Di Lella, "The Recently Identified Leaves of Sirach in Hebrew," *Bib* 45 (1964) 153-67, and B. G. Wright, "Ben Sira 43:11b—"To What Does the Greek Correspond?" *Textus* 13 (1986) 111-16.

[41]See Jastrow, p. 75.

[42]See the Hebrew text in M. S. Segal, ספר בן סרא השלם (Jerusalem: Mosad Bialik, 1958).

[43]See the Syriac MS published by A. M. Ceriani, *Translatio Syra Pescitto: Veteris Testamenti* (London: Williams and Norgate, 1876) ad loc.

[44]For the Greek, see any edition of the Septuagint.

J. H. Charlesworth

off from the great river of Wisdom,"[45] and as "a rivulet from her stream."[46] Both Ben Sira and the author of 1QH 8 (probably the Righteous Teacher) portray themselves as being possessed by God or Wisdom, and metaphorically portray this understanding by referring to themselves as a source of water for a garden.[47]

The verb נתן is used with the *beth essentiae* in Ps 69:22.[48] In 1QH 8:4 it also has an object: the author is placed "in a desert," and seems himself as "an overflowing fountain." The author is the source of water for "the trees of life," who must be his followers. In contrast to both M. Delcor and G. Jeremias,[49] I understand the *beth* in במקור to be a *beth essentiae*.[50]

2. *The Permissive Hiphil (Aphel)*

Almost without exception Hebrew grammarians tell their readers that the Hiphil is a "causative stem." The major reference grammars on biblical Hebrew, those by Joüon and Gesenius-Kautzsch-Cowley do not give a full and representative meaning of the Hiphil (H *binyan*):

> Le hifil est la conjugaison active de l'action caustive.... Le sens fondamental est celui de *causatif*. (Joüon, 120-22)
> The *meaning* of *Hiphᶜîl* is primarily, and even more frequently than in *Piᶜēl ... causative* of *Qal*. (GKC § 53 c 144)

Neither of these major reference works states that the Hiphil can bring a permissive meaning to a verb.

---

[45]W. O. E. Oesterley, *Ecclesiasticus* (Cambridge: Cambridge University Press, 1912) 162.

[46]P. W. Skehan and A. A. Di Lella, *The Wisdom of Ben Sira* (AB 39; New York: Doubleday, 1987) 337.

[47]For fuller discussion see my "An Allegorical and Autobiographical Poem by the Moreh Haṣ-Ṣedek (1QH 8:4-11)," in the S. Talmon Festschrift, in press.

[48]"... they gave as (in essence) my food (בְּבָרוּתִי), gall..."; see BDB, 678. Dahood did not take the *beth* in Ps 69:22 as an example of the *beth essentiae*. See his *Psalms II: 51-100* (AB 17b; Garden City: Doubleday, 1968) 162.

[49]M. Delcor, *Les Hymnes de Qumran (Hodayot)* (Paris: Letouzey et Ané, 1962) 199; G. Jeremias, *Der Lehrer der Gerechtigkeit* (SUNT 2; Göttingen; Vandenhoeck & Ruprecht, 1963) 249.

[50]I thence agree with the early translation by A. Dupont-Sommer:
Je [te] rends [grâces, ô Adonaï]!
Car tu m'as placé comme une source de fleuves
  dans un lieu desséché...
See his *Les écrits esséniens découverts près de la Mer Morte* (4th ed.; Paris: Payot, 1980) 240.

75

The discussion of this form is also abbreviated and incomplete in Segal's Mishnaic Hebrew grammar. The Aramaic and Syriac grammarians also customarily report that the Aphel is a "causative stem." This is the definition in the major Syriac grammars by Nöldeke, Duval, Staerk, Ungnad, and Brockelmann, and in the Aramaic grammars by Rosenthal, Odeburg, Golomb, and Kutscher. Note these excerpts:

> ... the causative conjugation *Aphel*.... (Nöldeke)[51]
> Aph'el a le sens d'un causatif... (Duval)[52]
> Das ... Aphel ist wie das entsprechende hebr. Hiphil meist kausativ... (Ungnad)[53]
> The basic meaning of the pacᶜẹl is intensive or causative, and that of the haₚᶜẹl, causative. (Rosenthal)[54]

A serious scholar who had memorized everything in Joüon, Gesenius-Kautzsch-Cowley, Nöldeke, Duval, Ungnad, and Rosenthal would have no inkling that the Hiphil and Aphel can add the dimension of permission to a verb. The discussions of the C stem (H *binyan*) in our major grammars are inaccurate because they are incomplete. They fail to report that this verb stem has an allowative or permissive meaning, especially when the *nomen regens*, implicit or explicit, is God. The meaning of many passages has been lost, or distorted, by the failure to comprehend the full meaning of the C stem, the Hiphil and Aphel.

I shall attempt to show that it is no longer acceptable to repeat that Semitic verbs fall into three classes: Simple Stems (Grundstamm, voix simple), Intensive Stems (Intensivstamm, voix intensive), and a Causative Stem (Kausativ, voix causative). The latter stem has more than one meaning; here I wish to stress that it denotes permission, especially when the subject is God.

Fortunately, Lamdin's *Introduction to Biblical Hebrew* indicates that the Hiphil can have a permissive meaning. He presents one example: "God has allowed me to see your children too" (Gen 48:11).[55] This meaning is reflected in the translation of Gen 48:11 by E. A. Speiser: "... God has let me see your progeny..."[56] In the most recent beginning Hebrew grammar, C. L. Seow clarifies that the Hiphil, which he

---

[51]T. Nöldeke, *Compendious Syriac Grammar* (trans. J. A. Crichton; London: Williams & Norgate, 1904) 105.

[52]R. Duval, *Traité de grammaire syriaque* (1881; reprinted, Amsterdam: Philo, 1969) 182.

[53]A. Ungnad, *Syrische Grammatik* (Munich: Beck, 1913) 63.

[54]F. Rosenthal, *A Grammar of Biblical Aramaic* (Wiesbaden: Harrassowitz, 1963) 42.

[55]Lambdin, *Introduction* , 212.

[56]E. A. Speiser, *Genesis* (AB 1; Garden City: Doubleday, 1964) 355.

calls the H *binyan*, has not only a causative but also a permissive sense.[57] He presents two examples, Gen 48:11 and Deut 4:36, which may be translated "from the heavens he allowed you to hear his voice." In the recently published *An Introduction to Biblical Hebrew Syntax*, which appeared after this article was in nearly final draft, Waltke and O'Connor inform the reader that the Hiphil can denote permission; they give two more examples: Gen 41:39 ("Since God *let* you *know* all this...") and Ezek 32:14 ("Then I *will let* her waters *settle*, and her streams *flow* like oil").[58] Another example of the permissive (or allowative) Hiphil, which they place under the Hiphil of toleration, is Ps 89:43 ("You *have allowed* all his enemies *to rejoice*").[59]

Examples of the permissive Hiphil (and Aphel) abound in the voluminous Semitic literature now for us to study. I shall limit my examination here to only three examples of the permissive Hiphil (or Aphel) in one Jewish psalm and in two Jewish prayers. Two of them antedate the destruction of 70 CE.

In Ps 155:11 (*5ApocSyrPs* 3) we find the following:[60]

זכורני ואל רשכחני ואל תביאני בקשות ממני

Remember me and forget me not, and do not allow me to enter into situations too hard for me.

The meaning of the Hiphil imperfect, תביאני, is "you allow me to enter (or come into)." Surprisingly, what is not mentioned in our major reference grammars is noted in BDB (97-99): "בוא... *Hiph*.... *1. cause to come in, bring in... 2. cause to come, bring, bring near ... allow to come...*" The corresponding Syriac is pointed as an Aphel in the manuscript: ܬܥܠܝܢܝ , "you allow me to enter." Of course, both the Hebrew and Syriac verbs are qualified by a preceding negative. The Lord is called upon for help so that the one who prays will not *be allowed to* enter into too difficult situations.

In the Babylonian Talmud, in *Berakoth* 60b, we find a prayer which contains virtually the same formula as in Psalm 155:

ואל תביאני לידי חטא

And do not allow me to enter into..."

---

[57]C. L. Seow, *A Grammar for Biblical Hebrew* (Nashville: Abingdon, 1987) 121.

[58]Waltke and O'Connor, *An Introduction to Biblical Hebrew Syntax*, 445.

[59]Ibid., 446.

[60]For the Hebrew, see Sanders, *Psalms Scroll*, 71; for the Syriac, see W. Baars, "Apocryphal Psalms," in *The Old Testament in Syriac According to the Peshiṭta Version* (Leiden: Brill, 1972) 9-10.

The object is "the grasp of sin." A literal translation, recognizing only the causative force of the *H binyan*, would be inelegant: "And do not cause me to enter into the hands of sin..." The syntax seems clear: "And do not allow me to fall into the grasp of sin..." As J. Jeremias stated, "das Kausativum hat hier eine permissive Nuance."[61]

In the oldest recension of the Old Syriac Gospels, the late fourth-century *Sin. Syr.* 30 discovered 100 years ago by A. S. Lewis (following the advice of J. Rendell Harris), we find the oldest recension in Semitic of the Lord's Prayer.[62] The fifth petition is singularly important for us:

ܪܠܐ ܬܥܠܢ ܠܢܣܝܘܢܐ

And do not allow us to enter into temptation.

As is readily apparent, this rendering is appreciatively different from the grammatically simple but theologically perplexing, and well-known, Greek: "and do not lead us into temptation."[63] The Aphel ܬܥܠ in this petition is impressively similar to the examples surveyed already; it is another example of the permissive Aphel.

Conclusion

These philological observations clarify that the proclitic *beth* and the H *binyan* have a wider range of meanings than indicated in grammars, lexicons, studies, and translations. The semantic range is larger than we had assumed; yet there are boundaries they keep us protected from the realm of speculation. The meaning of a text begins with the intentionality of the author and must be searched for with philological sensitivity, within the parameters of syntax and context, and the contours of sociological ethos.

[61] J. Jeremias, *ABBA: Studien zur neutestamentlichen Theologie und Zeit-geschichte* (Göttingen: Vandenhoeck & Ruprecht, 1966) 169.

[62] I express my indebtedness and appreciation to Archbishop Damianos of St. Catherine's Monastery, the Sinai, for four visits to study Syr. Cod. 30, and to Bruce and Ken Zuckerman, with whom were completed a full rephotographing of the MS, using the most advanced methods, techniques, film, and equipment.

[63] See the excellent discussion on the permissive dimension of the original meaning in J. Carmignac's *Recherches sur le "Notre Père"* (Paris: Letouzey & Ané, 1969) 246-47, 282, 284-90 ("ne souffre pas que nous soyons introduits").

II. Late Second Temple Judaism and Qumran

BEN SIRA 48:11 ET LA RÉSURRECTION

Emile Puech
Ecole Biblique et Archéologique Française, Jérusalem
Centre National de la Recherche Scientifique, Paris

Cette note n'a pas l'intention d'étudier la conception de la vie après la mort dans le livre de Ben Sira, ni son évolution depuis la composition originale jusqu'aux derniers états du texte à travers les diverses étapes de la transmission soumise à l'influence de nouvelles idées théologiques,[1] mais simplement de proposer une nouvelle lecture du texte hébreu, manuscrit B (cité MS B), de Ben Sira 48:11 qui paraît rendre compte des états ultérieurs du verset dans les différentes versions qui nous sont parvenues.

Le verset 48:11 appartient à un ensemble plus vaste, 48:1-12a, concernant Elie, son action, la désignation d'un prophète comme successeur, v 8 (héb., pluriel en grec) et son enlèvement céleste dans un tourbillon et le feu, v 9 ("dans un char aux chevaux de feu" grec, "et avec des troupes de feu [...]" héb.). Ainsi est dépeint l'enlèvement d'Elie comme une mystérieuse exception au sort commun des hommes à la fin de leur vie terrestre. Puis à partir du verset 10, l'auteur s'intéresse à la mission future et eschatologique du prophète.

Grec:

> ὁ καταγραφεὶς ἐν ἐλεγμοῖς εἰς καιρούς
> κοπάσαι ὀργὴν πρὸ θυμοῦ
> ἐπιστρέψαι καρδίαν πατρὸς πρὸς υἱὸν
> καὶ καταστῆναι φυλὰς Ἰακώβ (*id.* syriaque)
>
> "Toi qui fus désigné dans des menaces pour les temps
>   favorables
> pour apaiser la colère avant qu'elle n'éclate,
> pour ramener le cœur des pères vers les fils
> et pour rétablir les tribus de Jacob"

---

[1] Bien qu'il mérite d'être repris et précisé, ce travail d'ensemble a été entrepris dans une thèse manuscrite présentée à la Commission Biblique en 1951 à Rome par Conleth Kearns, "The Expanded Text of Ecclesiasticus. Its Teaching on the Future Life as a Clue to its Origin."

MS B[2]

הכתוב נכון לעת להשבית אף לפנ[י (בא??)יום ייי?]3
להשיב לב אבות על בנים ולהכין שבט[י ישר]אל

"Toi qui fus désigné précisément pour le terme
pour apaiser la colère avant [(que vienne??) le jour de
Yhwh (?)]
pour ramener le cœur des pères vers les fils
et pour rétablir les tribu[s d'Isra]ël"

Le renvoi transparent à Malachie 3:23-24 s'impose puisque dans ce passage il est
écrit que Dieu va envoyer le prophète Elie: הִנֵּה אָנֹכִי שֹׁלֵחַ לָכֶם אֵת אֵלִיָּה הַנָּבִיא
לִפְנֵי בּוֹא יוֹם יְהוָה הַגָּדוֹל וְהַנּוֹרָא: וְהֵשִׁיב לֵב אָבוֹת עַל בָּנִים וְלֵב בָּנִים עַל אֲבוֹתָם
אָבוֹא... פֶּן. L'enseignement du prophète Malachie était donc maintenu bien vivant
dans ce courant de tradition sapientielle et parmi les scribes plus tard (voir Matt
17:10-12; Luc 1:17), même si le deuxième stique (3:24a) porte une variante
importante en étant remplacé par "et pour rétablir les tribus d'Israël." A la dimension
individuelle s'ajoute ainsi la dimension collective du peuple. Sont envisagés pour les
temps à venir non seulement la conversion des individus, "le cœur des pères vers les
fils (et celui des fils vers leurs pères)" mais encore le rétablissement des tribus (cf. Isa
49:6, "de Jacob" soulignant l'espérance messianique). C'est dans un tel contexte que
vient ensuite le macarisme du verset 11 avec de nombreuses variantes dans les
versions.

---

[2]Solomon Schechter, ed., *Facsimiles of the fragments hitherto recovered of the
Book of Ecclesiasticus in Hebrew* (Oxford: Oxford University Press, 1901).
[3]Mal 3:23: לפני בוא יום יהוה est trop long pour la lacune du MS B, et
probablement encore une orthographe défective בא, F. Vattioni, *Ecclesiastico: Testo
ebraico con apparato critico e versioni greca, latina e siriaca* (Napoli, 1968) 263. P.
W. Skehan and A. A. di Lella (*The Wisdom of Ben Sira: A New Translation with Notes,
Introduction and Commentary* [AB 39; Garden City, NY: Doubleday, 1987] 530-31)
propose "the day of the LORD" (= ܡܪܝܐ ܕܝܘܡܗ ܘܗܒܘ), ce qui est
tout à fait acceptable pour la lacune, tandis que la Syrohexaplaire traduit ܠܡܒܛܠ,
ܩܕܡ ܕܢܐܬܐ ܝܘܡܗ voir A. M. Ceriani, *Translatio Syra Pescitto Veteris
Testamenti ex codice Ambrosiano sec. Fere VI photolithographice edita*, (Milan:
Pagliani, 1876) I. fol. 236v., and idem, *Codex Syro Hexaplaris Ambrosianus
photolithographice editus* (Milan, 1874) fol. 96r. R. Smend (*Die Weisheit des Jesus
Sirach hebräisch und deutsch* [Berlin, 1906] 55) propose לפני חרון א[ל avec restes du
ל, invisible sur le facsimilé! M. Ts. Segal (ספר בן סירא השלם [Jérusalem: Mosad
Bialik, 1958] 330ss.) propose לפנ[י חרון].

Emile Puech

Verset 11:

Grec:

μακάριοι οἱ ἰδόντες σε
καὶ οἱ ἐν ἀγαπήσει κεκοσμημένοι (Grec I)
κεκοιμημένοι (Grec II -Syrohexaplaire)[4]
καὶ γὰρ ἡμεῖς ζωῇ ζησόμεθα
"Bienheureux ceux qui t'ont vu
et qui ont été décorés dans l'amour (Gr I)
se sont endormis dans l'amour (Gr II -Syrohexaplaire)
car nous aussi assurément nous vivrons."

Syriaque (Peshitta):

ܗ̇ܘܒܐ ܢܚܙܝܟ ܘܡܐܬ ܕ
ܒܪܝܪ ܠܐ ܡܐܬ ܐܠܐ ܚܝܐ ܢܚܐ

"Heureux celui qui t'a vu et est mort,
en vérité il ne meurt pas mais vraiment il vivra."

Latin:[5]

Beati sunt qui te viderunt
et in amicitia tua decorati sunt
nam nos vita vivimus tantum
post mortem autem non erit tale nomen nostrum.
"Bienheureux ceux qui t'ont vu
et qui dans l'amitié ont été décorés
car nous, nous vivons seulement (notre) vie
mais après la mort notre (re)nom ne sera pas tel."

Le texte hébreu du manuscrit B ne comprend que deux stiques comme le syriaque de la Peshitta mais le manuscrit étant lacuneux, la lecture reste discutée:

אשר ראך ומת[ ] [ ]ה̇[ ]ה[

---

[4]H. B. Swete, *The Old Testament in Greek according to the Septuagint* (2 vols.; Cambridge: Cambridge University Press, 1922) 2.746. La Syrohexaplaire lit:

[5]Voir Vattioni, *Ecclesiastico*, 262; de même Kearns, "The Expanded Text," 181.

83

1. *11a hébreu* :

Les versions et l'emploi de אשר normalement au pluriel en hébreu exigeraient un original אשרי ou une vocalisation conséquente du lexème. Le MS B et le syriaque lisent ensuite un parfait *qal* au singulier ראה-חזך alors que les versions grecques et latine ont le pluriel οἱ ἰδόντες σε = *qui te viderunt*, très vraisemblablement sous l'influence d'une relecture. Le mot suivant ומת[, le troisième du stique en hébreu et le dernier du premier stique en syriaque מבחתיה, a donné lieu à un développement et à la formation d'un stique parallèle dans les versions grecques, la syrohexaplaire et la version latine. L'expansion de ומת appuie bien davantage la lecture κεκοιμημένοι de certaines versions grecques (voir syrohexaplaire et sahidique) que celle κεκοσμημένοι des onciaux, forme due probablement à une corruption dans la copie ou la lecture de κεκοιμημένοι. Il est possible, voire probable, que la traduction d'un original ומת par κεκοιμημένοι (= שכבא en syriaque) beaucoup plus acceptable dans ce contexte de résurrection entrevue lors du retour d'Elie ait entraîné une précision complémentaire. Mais ἐν ἀγαπήσει paraît quelque peu étrange, même avec la correction ἀγαπήσει > ἀγάπῃ ou l'addition de σοῦ de manuscrits grecs, de l'Ethiopien ou du latin *amicitia tua* .[6] D'où la conjecture de R. Smend proposant la correction ἐν ἀναπαύσει de forme assez proche, mais la lecture ἀγαπήσει, qu'elle soit accidentelle ou plus vraisemblablement intentionnelle car l'amour divin est un thème favori de Grec II et n'est pas inconnu de Grec I, aurait entraîné la correction κεκοσμημένοι.[7] Quoi qu'il en soit de l'hébreu original, la lacune du MS B ne permet pas de lire une séquence de quelque longueur après [...]ומת. Une conjecture בנוה, bien qu'unique, pour appuyer ἐν ἀναπαύσει serait elle-même un peu longue et בנחת est sûrement trop long. Il vaut mieux conclure à un texte hébreu du MS B de même type que celui de la *Vorlage* de la Peshitta, sans complément après ומת. Ce sont les versions grecques et d'autres ensuite qui ont interprété le mot dans ce contexte d'après les conceptions théologiques de leurs milieux respectifs, soucieuses de montrer la mort comme un repos, non comme une fin absolue. En effet, comme l'a bien vu Kearns,[8] il ne suffit pas, dans cette conception, d'avoir vu Elie avant de mourir pour être heureux. Il faut encore être mort de la mort du juste, c'est-à-dire "s'être endormi dans le repos." Mais l'original mettait l'accent sur la conversion ou la remise en ordre prônée par Elie lors de son retour.

[6]Voir Swete, *The Old Testament in Greek*, et J. Ziegler, *Sapientia Jesu Filii Sirach* (Göttingen: Vandenhoeck & Ruprecht, 1965) 351.

[7]R. Smend, *Die Weisheit des Jesus Sirach* (Berlin: Reimer, 1906) 462.

[8]Ibid., 183.

Emile Puech

2. *11b hébreu* :

Le deuxième stique très lacuneux en hébreu devait contenir l'explication du macarisme, comme dans le syriaque. La traduction grecque "car nous aussi assurément nous vivrons," bien que fondée sur le pluriel du premier stique, peut difficilement passer pour la motivation attendue. Elle a donc peu de chance de refléter l'original, pas davantage le latin qui glose le grec.

Selon les auteurs, le MS B aurait conservé une lettre à longue hampe, *kaf* (?), puis en fin de stique *he* ou même *yod-he*.[9] Peters[10] notait déjà que le MS B ne portait aucune trace de haste de *lamed*, excluant donc la négation suggérée par le syriaque ... ܟܢ ܚܝܐ ܠܐ ܚܝܐ, mais sans remarquer la lettre à longue hampe. Aussi suggérait-il de comprendre כי גם אנחנו חיה נחיה en s'appuyant sur le grec et refusait-il, pour l'espace, la proposition de Smend [כי חיה] [ו]אֹ[ש]רי נפ[ש]ך תח[יה. Mais il y lisait la résurrection avec le retour d'Elie. Ensuite Smend corrigea quelque peu sa lecture et proposa [כי חיה תח[יה] [ו]אֹשרי[ך,[11] en signalant que le *kaf* pourrait être aussi *pe* final. Le second stique ne serait alors pas une explication du premier, mais un nouveau macarisme se rapportant à Elie: "Et heureux es-tu car assurément tu vivras."[12] Ces restauration et exégèse ont été acceptées par Kearns parce qu'elles tiendraient compte de la paléographie, de traductions (syriaque et arabe) et s'accorderaient parfaitement avec l'eschatologie conservatrice de Sira I, excluant ainsi la possibilité de vie après la mort pour qu'autres qu'Elie.[13] Segal a proposé une autre interprétation fondée sur le grec et le syriaque en lisant: [כי אֹף [הוא היה יחי[ה en notant que la lettre à longue hampe pouvait être *kaf*, *nun* ou *pe* finaux.[14] Il commente ainsi: "Celui qui a vu Elie avant de mourir (re)vivra après sa mort, tout comme Elie. Si cette interprétation est exacte, on peut penser que Ben Sira croit qu'Elie ressuscite des morts même après son enlèvement au ciel, comme il l'a fait pendant sa vie, de même Elisée," et d'ajouter "Evidemment Ben Sira ne croit pas à une résurrection générale mais qu'il existe des hommes particulièrement dignes d'une vie après la mort et c'est à eux qu'Elie se manifeste avant de mourir."

---

[9]C'est encore la lecture acceptée dans Z. Ben Hayyim, ed., *The Book of Ben Sira, Text, Concordance and an Analysis of the Vocabulary* (Jerusalem, 1973) 60.

[10]N. Peters, *Der jüngst wiederaufgefundene hebräische Text des Buches Ecclesiasticus* (Freiburg, 1902) 274.

[11]Smend, *Die Weisheit des Jesus Sirach hebräisch und deutsch*, 55, lecture acceptée par Peters ensuite et bien d'autres auteurs.

[12]Smend, *Die Weisheit des Jesus Sirach*, 462.

[13]Kearns, "The Expanded Text," 183s. On note cependant que le syriaque ne supporte pas (substantially) cette exégèse puisqu'il lit la troisième personne au sing., non la deuxième qu'on attendrait pour se rapporter à Elie!

[14]Segal, ספר, 330, 332.

Dans les notes de sa traduction, Skehan met en doute l'interprétation de Segal envisageant la résurrection de quelques hommes méritants alors que Ben Sira ne croit manifestement pas à la résurrection des morts.[15] Il proposerait comme original hébreu en 11b: כִּי אַף אֲנַחְנוּ נֹחַ נָנוּחַ, "for we too shall certainly come to rest" au sens de נוּחַת עוֹלָם de Sir 30:17b? Puis חָיָה נִחְיָה aurait été un essai d'amélioration à l'époque du petit-fils de Ben Sira. Cette manière de voir n'est pas sans points faibles, les plus importants étant de s'appuyer uniquement sur le grec pour la lecture de la première personne du pluriel, אֲנַחְנוּ et נִחְיָה, et d'introduire le repos, נוּחַ, lesquels sont évidemment étroitement liés à la croyance attribuée à "Ben Sira" sur ce point précis. Les auteurs s'accordent généralement sur les relectures du grec (ou de sa *Vorlage*) introduisant au v 11 l'idée de résurrection et de récompenses pour les justes.[16]

Nouvelle proposition de lecture de 11b

L'examen du facsimilé permet de voir avant la longue hampe de *kaf, nun* ou *pe* finaux, mais pas *qof* ou *sade* final, des traces de lettres avec un retour à gauche, très vraisemblablement deux *taw* consécutifs. Au bord de la cassure au début du deuxième stique, il semble bien y avoir des restes de lettre, au mieux *kaf*. Comme le contexte et les versions exigent une motivation du macarisme précédent, on n'hésite pas à lire כ[י תתן] ˙ [. La deuxième personne du verbe reprend logiquement le suffixe de la deuxième personne du premier stique et doit se rapporter à Elie. Dans ce cas, le dernier verbe devrait logiquement être à la troisième personne du singulier comme au premier stique et en syriaque, et non à la première personne du pluriel comme en grec et latin. L'espace et les traces suggèrent de comprendre au mieux כ[י תתן] ח[יי]ם[וי]חיה ou à défaut כ[י תתן] חיים[וי]ח[יה]. Le mot חיים est *ad sensum*, voir 50:22 pour les dimensions, ζωῆ en grec et la paronomase en syriaque (à la rigueur רוח(ו) ou נפש(ו) mais נשמת serait trop long). Voir figure 1.

La question du temps du verbe en 11a reste posée. Faut-il lire: רָאָךְ "t'a vu" (la forme orthographique du MS B sans *waw* est sûrement celle du parfait comme dans la Peshitta, le latin et la syrohexaplaire, le grec ayant un participe, mais l'original hébreu ראך pouvait se lire רֹאָךְ en *scriptio defectiva* aussi bien que רָאָךְ), ou "te voit/te verra" en comprenant la forme comme un parfait prophétique? Se référant au passé, le singulier renverrait-il à Elisée (v 12ss.) qui a vu Elie disparaître et aurait été assuré de revivre? La tradition n'ayant gardé aucune allusion à une telle interprétation, elle devrait être écartée. Des auteurs pensent que le verset ferait allusion à la félicité de tout contemporain du prophète qui a vu Elie, même s'ils sont

---

[15]Segal, ספר, 532.

[16]Avec Kearns, "The Expanded Text," 184.

morts.[17] Se référant au futur, au retour attendu d'Elie selon Mal 3:23, le v 11a serait à comprendre: heureux celui qui, avant de mourir, te verra venant inaugurer les temps messianiques,[18] mais il y manque la motivation attendue.

Se fondant sur le seul stique 11a, les interprétations ne pouvaient qu'être hésitantes et variées. Il semble qu'une saine exégèse du passage doive suivre la progression de la pensée de l'auteur. Parmi les faits et gestes dans cette eulogie d'Elie, on compte en particulier la réanimation d'un mort (v 5), puis l'enlèvement du prophète au ciel dans un tourbillon. L'auteur passe ensuite à la mission eschatologique d'Elie: préparer la conversion des cœurs et la restauration des tribus avant le jour de Yhwh (v 10). Le verset 11 ne peut se rapporter qu'à cette mission future et attendue. D'où la félicité de celui qui verra le retour d'Elie avant de mourir, car il est (et était) dans le pouvoir d'Elie de ramener des hommes à la vie (1 Kgs 17:17-24), lui qui, d'après la tradition, n'a pas connu la mort (le shéol) mais a été transféré au ciel comme Hénoch. Sans doute, il n'est pas question de résurrection générale, ni de celle de tous les justes, mais de justes qui verront le retour d'Elie et sont ainsi assurés de revivre.

On comprend donc ce verset du MS B, moyennant une ou deux déficiences orthographiques:[19]

אשר(י) ר(ו)אך ומת כ]י [תתן ח]ייֹ[ם [וי]חיה

"Heureux qui te verra avant de mourir
c[ar]tu rendras la v[i]e[et il] (re)viv[ra]."

S'inscrivant dans la tradition de Malachie, cette lecture du v 11 semble bien être à l'origine, ou du moins être le premier témoignage d'une intervention d'Elie pour le

---

[17]G. H. Box and W. O. E. Oesterley, "The Book of Sirach," dans R. H. Charles, ed., *Apocrypha and Pseudepigrapha of the Old Testament in English* (2 vols.; Oxford: Clarendon, 1913) 1.501; V. Ryssel, "Die Spruche Jesus', des Sohnes Sirachs," dans E. Kautzsch, *Die Apokryphen und Pseudepigraphen des Alten Testaments*. Vol. 1, *Die Apokryphen des Alten Testaments* (Tübingen: Mohr [Siebeck], 1900) 463. Se référant à Elisée, voir F. Saracino, "Resurrezione in Ben Sira?" *Henoch* 4 (1982) 185-203, esp. 198s.

[18]Voir Smend, *Die Weisheit des Jesus Sirach*, 461, J. Knabenbauer, *Commentarius in Ecclesiasticum cum appendice: Textus "Ecclesiastici" hebraeus* (Paris: Lethielleux, 1902) 454.

[19]De préférence à un original אשרי אשר ראך, plus difficile pour la langue et les accents, on retient plus volontiers le processus suivant: chute du *yod* de אשרי (à moins d'une vocalisation appropriée) et écriture défective du participe ראך tout à fait normale au début du 2e s. avant J. C., puis la non insertion du *waw* de la *scriptio plena* dans quelque manuscrit à la base de la Peshitta et du MS B. La *Vorlage* hébraïque de Grec I et II a été lue רֹאֶך .

retour à la vie ou la résurrection de justes. Il n'est pas étonnant que la tradition postérieure ait parfois associé Elie à la résurrection des morts: בא המתים והתחיית על ידי אליהו הנביא זכור לטוב אמן, "et la résurrection des morts doit arriver par l'intermédiaire du prophète Elie, sa mémoire soit bénie, amen" (*m. Sota* 9.15). En *Talmud Jerushalmi, Shabbat*, il est dit que la résurrection mène à concevoir la venue d'Elie.[20] Par ailleurs, les Sages ont encore enseigné qu'il existe trois clés non remises par Dieu à un messager, les clés de la naissance, de la pluie et de la résurrection. Cependant il peut arriver que Dieu donne pour un temps l'une ou l'autre clé à un juste; ainsi la clé des tombeaux fut-elle remise à Elie, Elisée et Ezéchiel (*b. Sanh.* 113a, *Midr. Ps.* 78.5).[21] Mais ce cas passé à l'origine d'une des interventions d'Elie lors de son retour eschatologique s'en distingue nettement.

En somme, l'hébreu du MS B comprenant deux stiques balancés peut-il, moyennant quelques corrections orthographiques mineures, revendiquer une antériorité quelconque? Le premier stique est au singulier comme dans la Peshitta qui suppose un hébreu identique. Les versions grecques (Grec I et II) et les latine et syrohexaplaire à leur suite qui ont traduit par un pluriel lisaient peut-être un texte hébreu au pluriel par suite d'une correction ou relecture, mais il est peu probable que leur texte hébreu ait été différent en 11aβ. En effet, il est plus vraisemblable d'envisager un passage au pluriel de la part du traducteur grec qui aurait comme généralisé la félicité à tous les justes mourant dans l'amour (Grec I) ou dans le repos (Grec II) et aurait donc opéré lui-même le changement théologique de ומת > καὶ οἱ κεκοιμημένοι ἐν ἀναπαύσει (> ἀγαπήσει) devenant ensuite καὶ οἱ κεκοσμημένοι ἐν ἀγαπήσει (σου = latin) pour l'adapter sans doute à sa propre conception. En conséquence, pour 11a, il n'est aucunement nécessaire de présupposer un Hébreu I ou II différent de celui du MS B (avec אשרי) et de la *Vorlage* de la Peshitta mais avec le כְּתִיב רָאך / קְרִי: רָאֶך.

Le deuxième stique est un peu plus délicat. Le grec appuie ou nécessite la présence de כי, du substantif חיים et du verbe חיה à l'inaccompli, ce que la Peshitta laisse aussi entendre à moins d'une paronomase hébraïque. La présence de ἡμεῖς peut s'expliquer de plusieurs manières: soit comme une adaptation théologique pure et simple dans la ligne du pluriel précédent, le traducteur espérant bien être compté parmi ces bienheureux, soit par un substrat hébreu dans le texte à traduire, mais la graphie assez proche de תתן et de נחנו(א) aurait pu être cause d'une erreur de lecture et/ou faciliter le glissement de sens et l'adaptation théologique par le traducteur lui-même. Il est aussi possible que le mot entre כי et חיים ait été corrompu, car la Peshitta porte dans ce cas une lecture divergente, mais on ne peut être certain que sa *Vorlage* ait été différente. La *Vorlage* ou le traducteur syriaque lui-même a pu adapter

[20]M. Schwab, *Le talmud de Jérusalem* (Paris: Maisonneuve, 1881) 4.16s.

[21]W. G. Braude, trans., *The Midrash on Psalms translated from the Hebrew and Aramaic* (Yale Judaica Series 13.2; New Haven: Yale University Press, 1959) 25s.

Emile Puech

le texte selon sa propre conception de la mort: 11aβ # bα. Quoi qu'il en soit de l'orthographe ou de la lecture vocalisée de l'original et des changements du MS B, ce dernier, avec son opposition 3e personne - 2e personne (11a) et 2e personne - 3e personne (11b), reflète certainement au mieux le texte hébreu original. La version latine a paraphrasé le grec en ajoutant *tantum* et un stique supplémentaire (comparer 41:12-13 et 11:28) mais la croyance en la vie future de cette addition sans appui textuel semble revenir à celle des temps anciens. De fait, l'interprétation de 11a se rapporte au passé et ne fait aucune allusion à l'avenir. On se demande ce que signifie alors *beati ...* dans le contexte du retour d'Elie, v 10.

En définitive, l'hébreu du MS B, certainement du type pré-Grec I-II et de la *Vorlage* de la Peshitta en 11a et très vraisemblablement aussi en 11b semble bien avoir reproduit dans ce verset l'hébreu original de l'auteur Ben Sira lui-même, moyennant les corrections orthographiques signalées, (י)אשר et ר(ו)אך (*scriptio defectiva* normale en Ben Sira mais *plena* attendue en MS B). Une croyance en la résurrection de justes, sans contradiction avec 7:17; 14:16-17; 38:21, ne saurait surprendre dans la formulation hébraïque, très certainement pré-danièlique et donc pré-qumrânienne,[22] de ce verset directement lié à la mission eschatologique d'Elie. Bien évidemment, il ne pouvait être question de résurrection générale, tout comme d'ailleurs en Daniel 12 un peu plus tard.[23] Cette résurrection de justes n'est pas directement liée aux récompenses et punitions, mais à la conversion de justes lors du retour d'Elie (Mal 3:23; Ben Sira 48:11; Matt 17:11; Luc 1:17), "Heureux celui qui te voit avant de mourir, car tu rendras la vie et il revivra." L'hébreu de Ben Sira devait donc se lire:

אשרי ראך ומת   כי תתן חיים ויחיה

Il m'est agréable d'apporter cette modeste contribution à l'hommage offert à Mr. le Professeur John Strugnell qui a consacré de longues années à scruter des textes hébreux plus ou moins bien conservés, y compris le manuscrit hébreu de Ben Sira trouvé à Masada.

---

[22]Voir J. Strugnell et D. Dimant, "4Q Second Ezechiel," *RevQ* 13 (1988) 45-58. Les fragments 2-3 de 4Q385 commentant Ezek 37 (vision des ossements desséchés) attestent sûrement la croyance en la résurrection comme récompense des justes. L'abondance des copies retrouvées à Qumrân (4Q385-390) posent le problème de l'origine de la composition, qumrânienne ou pré-qumrânienne. Il est certain que le livre était au moins lu et recopié dans la communauté dès l'époque hasmonéenne, mais le texte pourrait être plus ancien, les éléments de vocabulaire ne permettant pas de trancher avec assurance.

[23]B. J. Alfrink, "L'idée de résurrection d'après Dan., XII,1.2," *Bib* 40 (1959) 355-71.

Appendice: Figure 1

Ben Sira 48:10-12a MS B
Dimension (1:1)

THE MEANING OF "THE END" IN THE BOOK OF DANIEL

John J. Collins
University of Notre Dame

Eschatology, discussion of "the end," is a topic of central importance in biblical studies, which continues to play a vital part in modern theology. Already in the eighth century BCE Amos declared, "The end has come upon my people Israel" (Amos 8:2). For Amos, the end in question was the end of Israel as an independent nation. Similarly, Ezekiel spoke of the "end" of Judah. While the classical prophets entertained expectations of definitive change, they did not expect an end of this world or of the historical process. Such ideas emerge in the apocalyptic literature, beginning in the early second century BCE, where we are told that "the world will be written down for destruction," and "the first heaven will vanish and pass away, and a new heaven will appear."[1] By the end of the first century CE expectation of an end of this world was widespread. The new heaven and new earth of Revelation entailed the passing away of the first heaven and earth (Rev 21:1). According to *4 Ezra* 7:30 this world would be returned to primeval silence for seven days.

The place of the Book of Daniel in this development is disputed. On the one hand, it is often regarded as the first instance of "true and explicit eschatology" in the Hebrew Bible.[2] On the other hand, it never speaks of an end of this world, and one scholar has even suggested that its eschatology is no different from that of the Enthronement Psalms or of earlier prophecy.[3] Yet the later chapters of Daniel are dominated by the expectation of an "end" to a degree that has no parallel in the Psalms or earlier Prophets. Daniel is also exceptional, even among the ancient apocalypses, in attempting to calculate the exact time until that "end" would come. It is true that the more elaborate scenarios of later apocalypses such as *4 Ezra* should

---

[1] *1 Enoch* 91:14, 16 (the *Apocalypse of Weeks*). Even here the historical process does not come to an end, since "after this there will be many weeks without number for ever . . ." (91:17).

[2] J. P. M. van der Ploeg, "Eschatology in the Old Testament," *OTS* 17 (1972) 92.

[3] Rex A. Mason, "The Treatment of Earlier Biblical Themes in the Book of Daniel," in James L. Crenshaw, ed., *Perspectives on the Hebrew Bible: Essays in Honor of Walter J. Harrelson* (Macon, GA: Mercer University Press, 1988) 99.

not be read back into Daniel,[4] but neither should the distinctivenes of Daniel over against the earlier Prophets be ignored. There is, moreover, evidence of development in the expectation of the end within Daniel 7-12, and it is important that all the evidence be taken into account.

The word קץ, end, occurs 14 times in Daniel 8–12.[5] Some of these occurrences are not immediately relevant to our discussion. In 9:26 and 11:45 "his end" refers to the death of Antiochus Epiphanes. In 11:6, 13 the reference is to the end of a period of years in the history of the Ptolemies and Seleucids. In the other instances, however, a more definitive end is in view. In four instances, 8:17, 19; 11:27, 35 there is an allusion to Hab 2:3, where קץ is linked with מועד, appointed time. In 8:17; 11:35, 40; 12:4, 9 the expression is עת קץ, time of the end. In 12:6 the end is specified as "the end of the wonders" and in 12:13 as "the end of the days." The word קץ is also used without qualification in 9:26 and 12:13. The idea of an end is tied to the calculation of time in 12:6-7 where the "end of the wonders" is expected after "a time, times and half a time."

The end and the kingdom

The first attempt to calculate a definite period of time in Daniel is found in 7:25, which says that "the most high holy ones"[6] will be given into the power of the little horn for "a time, times and half a time." In this case, the period of time in question is clearly the length of the persecution. At the end of this period the little horn will be condemned "to destruction and perdition until the end" (עד סופא). "Until the end" here seems to mean that the destruction is final, not that it will terminate at a certain point, and so the Aramaic word does not have the quasi-technical force that קץ

---

[4]The tendency of older handbooks to produce a synthetic view of apocalyptic eschatology, based especially on *4 Ezra* and *2 Baruch*, is found occasionally in recent scholarship (e.g., the "Systematic Presentation" of Messianism in Emil Schürer, *The History of the Jewish People in the age of Jesus Christ* [rev. and ed. Geza Vermes, Fergus Millar and Matthew Black; Edinburgh: Clark, 1979] 2.514-47) but has been generally rejected in work of the last two decades. See my attempt to differentiate between the different apocalypses in "The Jewish Apocalypses," *Semeia* 14 (1979) 21-59 and in *The Apocalyptic Imagination* (New York: Crossroad, 1984) passim; also Michael E. Stone, "Apocalyptic Literature" in M. E. Stone, ed., *Jewish Literature of the Second Temple Period* (CRINT 2/2; Philadelphia: Fortress, 1984) 383–441. Even Schürer balances the systematic presentation with a historical survey which attempts to treat the material in chronological order (pp. 497-513).

[5]The Aramaic equivalent, סופא, occurs twice in chap. 7. In v 28 it indicates the end of the revelation. In v 26 the beast is not condemned to be destroyed "until the end."

[6]Usually taken as "the holy ones of the Most High." See André Lacocque, *The Book of Daniel* (Atlanta: Knox, 1979) 131; John Goldingay, "'Holy Ones on High' in Daniel 7:18," *JBL* 107 (1988) 495-97.

John J. Collins

acquires in the later chapters. The decisive point in Chapter 7 is expressed as a judgment scene. Thereafter the kingdom of the beast will be destroyed and the people of the holy ones will receive an everlasting kingdom. The motif of kingdoms in chap. 7 is taken over from chaps. 1-6, which deal with the succession of Near Eastern kingdoms, and, in 2:44 with a final kingdom set up by God. In chap. 7 the kingdom is initially given to the holy ones, or angels (7:18),[7] but also to "the people of the holy ones" (7:27) who will presumably rule on earth. Nothing is said of the nature of this kingdom. The essential point is that Israel will enjoy sovereignty over the other nations, and the visionary has simply not sketched out any details. Taken in isolation, this eschatological kingdom is compatible with the expectations of the older Prophets, although it could be filled out in various ways. Chap. 7 is probably the oldest part of Daniel 7-12, since it is written in Aramaic (like the older tales) and makes no clear reference to the profanation of the temple, which figures prominently in chaps. 8-12.

The end and the temple
In Chapter 8, the angel Gabriel explains to Daniel that "the vision is for the end-time" (8:17) or for "the appointed time of the end" (8:19). Both phrases echo Hab 2:3: כי עוד למועד ויפח לקץ ולא יכזב "for the vision awaits its time; it hastens to the end, it will not lie."[8] The allusion to Habakkuk lends authority to the view that a vision has an appointed time for its fulfilment. The "end" in Habakkuk was the goal of the vision. In Daniel it is the עת קץ, a distinct chronological period. The end-time here embraces the sequence of events described in Daniel's vision, and so is a period rather than the end-point of that period. In 8:19 the time of the vision's fulfillment, "the appointed time of the end," is also called "the latter time of the wrath" (אחרית הזעם). Similarly in the Qumran scrolls we find references to the קץ האחרון (1QpHab 7:7, 12; compare the last generation in CD 1:12; 1QpHab 7:2) and to the קץ חרון, the age of wrath (CD 1:5; 1QH 3:28). In all of these cases the קץ refers to the period of tribulation before the definitive divine intervention.

Daniel 8 also addresses the duration of this period. One holy one asks another in 8:13: "for how long is the vision?" and specifies it with reference to "the daily offering, the desolating transgression and the sanctuary and the host given over to be

---

[7]For the angelic interpretation of the holy ones see my *The Apocalyptic Vision of the Book of Daniel* (HSM 16; Missoula: Scholars, 1977) 123-47, and the forthcoming commentary on Daniel in the Hermeneia series.

[8]See however J. Gerald Janzen, "Habakkuk 2:2-4," *HTR* 73 (1980) 53-78, who reads ^{c}ed, "witness," for $^{c}\hat{o}d$, and understands the root פוה as testify: "For the vision is a witness to a rendezvous, a testifier to the end--it does not lie."

trampled."[9] The answer is given in terms of the daily offering: "for two thousand three hundred evenings and mornings until the sanctuary is set right." The actual interpretation of the vision ends with the breaking of the little horn (i.e., the death of Antiochus Epiphanes) and describes neither the rededication of the temple nor anything that comes after it. The number of days given, 1,150, is problematic, since it is less than the three and a half years of Daniel 7, but greater than the three years for which the temple was actually desecrated (1 Macc 4:52-54). It is undoubtedly a real prediction, made before the rededication of the temple. The divergence from the three and a half years may be explained by the fact that it refers to a different, and shorter period than chap. 7. The earlier reference was to the duration of the persecution; the calculation in chap. 8 begins from the desecration of the temple some months later.[10]

In chap. 8, then, the end of the period of wrath coincides with the end of the desecration of the temple. The ensuing state is not described.

The most elaborate account of Daniel's eschatological chronology is found in chap. 9 in the prophecy of the seventy weeks of years. The three and a half years of Daniel 7 (and again of chap. 12) correspond to the last half-week of Daniel 9, when the desolator "will suppress sacrifice and offering and the desolating abomination will be in their place, until the pre-determined destruction is poured out" (9:27). Here again the dominant concern is with the profanation of the temple. Little is said about what is to follow this last half-week, except for the introductory statement in 9:24: "Seventy weeks are determined for your people and for your holy city, to finish the transgression, to bring sins to completion and to cancel iniquity, to bring in everlasting righteousness, to seal vision and prophet and to anoint a most holy place." The clearest point in this list is the last: the rededication of the temple. We cannot conclude from this that Daniel's only aspiration was the restoration of the cult. "To bring in everlasting righteousness" suggests a more far-reaching transformation. There is no doubt, however, that the desecrated temple dominates both chaps. 8 and 9 and that its restoration was the primary focus of the author's hopes in these chapters.

---

[9]On the textual problems of this passage see James A. Montgomery, *Daniel* (ICC 19; New York: Scribners, 1927) 340-45.

[10]Hans Burgmann ("Die vier Endzeittermine im Danielbuch," *ZAW* 86 [1974] 544) suggests that this figure was a compromise between the three and a half years of Daniel 7 and the three years that the temple was desecrated according to 1 Maccabees. It is not apparent why such a compromise should be found in Daniel, especially since other, contradictory figures are also given.

John J. Collins

The end and resurrection

In chap. 11, in the review of Hellenistic history in the guise of prophecy, we are twice reminded that "there is still an end at the appointed time" (11:27, compare 35, again alluding to Habakkuk). The "time of the end" is defined somewhat differently here from chap. 8. In 11:35, the persecution of the "wise" is not yet in the "time of the end." In 11:40 that phrase introduces the real prediction of the last compaign and death of the Syrian king. This is followed in 12:1 by the account of the resurrection of the dead "at that time." The focal point of the end in this section is no longer the rededication of the temple, but the judgment of the dead.

The observation that the rededication of the temple is not the final "end" envisaged in the Book of Daniel is corroborated in the Epilogue in 12:5-13. In a manner reminiscent of chap. 8 an angelic figure asks "how long until the end of the wonders?" The root פלא, wonder, is used in different forms for the actions of Antiochus Epiphanes in 8:24 and 11:26. The wonders certainly include the desecration of the temple, but the reference here is broader than in chap. 8. The angel's answer repeats the "time, times and a half" of chap. 7. The duration is further specified in 12:11: "From the time when the continual offering is taken away and the desolating abomination is set up is one thousand two hundred and ninety days." This figure is a possible calculation of three and a half years,[11] but it is obviously higher than the 1,150 days of chap. 8, although both calculations start from the disruption of the temple cult. Dan 12:12 adds a further 45 days, to reach 1,335.[12]

By far the simplest explanation of this variation is that the date was recalculated when the first number of days had passed, and then again when the second number elapsed.[13] It is a well-known fact that groups who make exact predictions do not just give up when the prediction fails to be fulfilled. Instead they find ways to

---

[11]Karl Marti (*Das Buch Daniel* [HKAT 18; Tübingen: Mohr, 1901] 92) breaks it down as 42 months of 30 days each, plus an intercalated month of 30 days. Burgmann ("Die vier Endzeittermine," 547) offers a more complicated calculation based on a 364 day year and also involving intercalary days.

[12]Thomas Fischer, *Seleukiden und Makkabäer* (Bochum: Brockmeyer, 1980) 143-44 attempts to treat the figures in Dan 12:11-12 as prophecies after the fact. The 1,290 days would then refer to Judas' capture of the temple, 1,335 to the re-dedication. By counting back from the date of the re-dedication in December, 164, he arrives at a starting point in mid-167, and suggests that the daily offering was disrupted some six months before the installation of the desolating abomination. Dan 12:11, however, clearly takes both the disruption of the cult and the installation of the abomination together as the starting-point, and so Fischer's proposal is unsatisfactory.

[13]This explanation was proposed by Hermann Gunkel, *Schöpfung und Chaos in Urzeit und Endzeit* (Göttingen: Vandenhoeck & Ruprecht, 1895) 269, and has been widely accepted.

explain the delay.[14] One such way was to make a revised (presumably more precise) calculation. The re-calculation, however, had to be elicited by something, most probably by the passing of the date originally predicted. It is interesting to note that Dan 12:12 uses the verb הכה, waits, which is also used in Hab 2:3, a passage to which Daniel has frequently alluded: "if it tarries wait for it, for it will surely come and it will not be late." The *Pesher on Habakkuk* from Qumran applies this passage to the "men of truth ... when the last end-time is drawn out for them" (1QpHab 7:9-12). A similar situation is envisaged in Daniel. The "end" which was envisaged after 1,150 days, and then again after 1,290 days, is drawn out, and the faithful must "wait" for the later date.

If this interpretation is correct, however, both figures in chap. 12 were added after the actual rededication of the temple, which took place exactly three years after its desecration. For the author of this section of Daniel, the "end" is not constituted by the restoration of the temple cult. Rather it is marked by the resurrection. It is the "end of days" (קץ הימין) when Daniel too will rise to his destiny (12:13).

Obviously, the final date predicted by Daniel also came and went. Daniel's prophecy was not discredited. Indeed Josephus, more than two centuries later, claimed that Daniel was distinguished from the other prophets because he not only prophesied future things but also fixed the time at which they would come to pass (*Ant.* 10.11.7 § 267). The exact figures took on symbolic significance, just as Jeremiah's prophecy of 70 years had been re-interpreted in Daniel. For Josephus, Daniel's prophecy extended to the destruction of Jerusalem by the Romans. For Hippolytus and Jerome it referred to the time of the Antichrist and the end of the world. These, of course, were later adaptations of Daniel's prophecy, but it is clear from 12:5-13 that the Hebrew writer already looked beyond the restoration of the temple for an "end" that involved the transcendence of death.

---

[14]See the classic study by Leon Festinger et al., *When Prophecy Fails: A Social and Psychological Study of a Modern Group that Predicted the Destruction of the World* (New York: Harper & Row, 1956). Festinger's theory is applied to OT prophetic texts, but not to Daniel, by Robert P. Carroll, *When Prophecy Failed. Cognitive Dissonance in the Prophetic Traditions of the Old Testament* (New York: Seabury, 1979).

John J. Collins

Interpreting the variety
There is, then, some variety in the meaning of "the end" within Daniel 7-12. One way to explain this is to suppose that these chapters were composed over a few years and that the thought of the author or authors was modified in the process. We have already seen some reason to think that chap. 7 is slightly older than 8-12, if only by a few months, since it is in Aramaic and does not reflect the desecration of the temple. The end it envisages is the end of the persecution, to be followed by a Kingdom of the people of the holy ones. Chaps. 8 and 9 appear to have been written shortly after that event and are dominated by the shock it engendered. Accordingly, in these chapters, the primary focus of "the end" is the restoration of the temple cult. Chaps. 10–12, however, give a more comprehensive account of the period of wrath, and focus their hopes not on the restoration of the temple but on the resurrection of the dead. The epilogue in Dan 12:5-13 was apparently written after the rededication of the temple, but still awaits the coming of "the end of the wonders." It may be, then, that "the end" took on new meanings in the light of new circumstances, and that the focus on the resurrection of the dead only emerged in the composition of the final major section, chaps. 10–12. While this conclusion is plausible, however, it is less than certain. Chaps. 7-9 are all very elliptical in what they say about the salvation that is to come, and it would be rash to conclude that each gives a complete account of the author's beliefs at a given time.

As the book stands, in any case, the visions in chaps. 7–12 must be read as complementary, and not as independent compositions. The juxtaposition of complementary accounts is a typical feature of dream reports from antiquity (cf. the dreams of Gilgamesh and of Joseph) and is very typical of apocalyptic literature (compare the *Similitudes of Enoch, 4 Ezra, 2 Baruch* , Revelation).[15] From the viewpoint of the final editor, the removal of the desolating abomination and the restoration of the temple cult are preconditions of the end, but do not in themselves constitute the state of salvation. That state is described somewhat vaguely as a kingdom in chap. 7. Its most distinctive feature is specified in chap. 12 in the resurrection of the dead and the exaltation of the *maskilim* to the stars. Whether or not this latter belief was held by the author when chap. 7 was composed, the association of the righteous with the stars or angels is highly congruent with the close association of the faithful Jews with the most high holy ones in the earlier chapter.[16]

As the vast majority of commentators have recognized, the eschatology of these visions differs from that of the earlier Prophets and the Psalms in several significant

---

[15]Adela Yarbro Collins, *The Combat Myth in the Book of Revelation* (HDR 9; Missoula: Scholars, 1976) 33-44.
[16]For the equivalence of stars and angels in Dan 12:3, see Collins, *The Apocalyptic Vision*, 136-37. Compare *1 Enoch* 104:1-6.

respects. They are pervaded by a sense of determinism, since the whole course of post-exilic history is purportedly foretold in the time of the exile, and all is written in the "book of truth" (Dan 10:21). The idea of an end at an appointed time is part of that scenario. In this respect Daniel is much closer to the Enochic *Apocalypse of Weeks* and *Animal Apocalypse* than to anything else in the Hebrew Bible. The most significant difference over against the Hebrew Scriptures, however, lies in the hope of resurrection.[17] This is not a minor modification of prophetic eschatology but entails a profound shift in world-view.[18] For the prophets, the goal of salvation was long life in the land and to see one's children's children.[19] For the *maskilim* of Daniel, as for the righteous of *1 Enoch* 104, it is to become companions to the host of heaven. There is, of course, continuity with prophetic eschatology too. Daniel still thinks collectively of the people, and the judgment of the dead is not individualized as it is in later apocalypses. Daniel still entertains the hope for a kingdom on earth, in which the restored temple will surely have its place. The resurrection, however, adds a new ingredient to biblical eschatology, which would lend itself to more otherworldly tendencies in some strands of Judaism and in Christianity. Despite the communal emphasis in Daniel 12, the hope of the *maskilim* is radically different from that of a prophet such as Jeremiah. Only those who are committed, for theological reasons, to harmonizing the Hebrew Scriptures could fail to recognize the distinctiveness of Daniel on this point, or to appreciate its affinity with the pseudepigraphic apocalypses.

[17]Some scholars find a belief in individual resurrection already in Isa 26:19 (e.g., Robert Martin-Achard, *From Death to Life: A Study of the Development of the Doctrine of the Resurrection in the Old Testament* (Edinburgh: Oliver & Boyd, 1960) 130-38; Gerhard F. Hasel, "Resurrection in the Theology of Old Testament Apocalyptic," *ZAW* 92 (1980) 267-84; Leonard J. Greenspoon, "The Origin of the Idea of Resurrection," in Baruch Halpern and Jon D. Levenson, eds., *Traditions in Transformation* (Winona Lake, IN: Eisenbrauns, 1981) 247-321. That passage, however, can be read more naturally, like Ezekiel 37, as a metaphor for the restoration of the Jewish nation.

[18]See my essay, "Apocalyptic Eschatology as the Transcendence of Death," *CBQ* 36 (1974) 21-43; reprinted in Paul D. Hanson, ed., *Visionaries and Their Apocalypses* (Philadelphia: Fortress, 1983) 61-84.

[19]This is still the case even in Isa 65:17-25, which speaks of a new heaven and a new earth.

JASON'S GYMNASION

Robert Doran
Amherst College

Discussion of the background of the Maccabean revolt often quickly moves into misty territory where at times the actors seem to play mythic roles—good vs. evil, poor vs. rich, lovers of Torah vs. Hellenizers. The authors of 1 and 2 Maccabees should be proud of how their propaganda has shaped and determined attitudes "even up to this day." One particular facet of that propaganda has been the emphasis on the building of a gymnasion in Jerusalem as the first step in the turning away from God's covenant.

> [The king] gave them power to follow the practices of the gentiles. Thereupon they built a gymnasium in Jerusalem according to the customs of the gentiles (κατὰ τὰ νόμιμα τῶν ἐθνῶν) (1 Macc 1:13-14).

The author of 2 Maccabees emphasizes that Jason was undoing ancestral customs (2 Macc 4:11: τὰς μὲν νομίμους καταλύων πολιτείας παρανόμους ἐθισμοὺς ἐκαινίζεν), but the example he produces to prove his case is the building of the gymnasium and participation in it (2 Macc 4:12-15). Tarn and Griffith wrote that it was an anti-climax that the two definite charges against the hellenizing Jews were that "they favoured Greek athletic exercises (which involved nudity) and wore Greek hats."[1] Without discussing nudity and head-gear for the moment, is it an anti-climax? Why did so much fuss surround Jason's building a gymnasion and an ephebia (2 Macc 4:9)? For Tcherikover, the answer was a constitutional one: "for in every Greek city the gymnastic education, and especially the ephebate, was a prerequisite for the reception of the young man into the citizen corporation."[2] Jason, in Tcherikover's view, set in motion a constitutional change and new rules for admittance to citizenship in the newly constituted *polis*. But are such constitutional changes implicit in building a gymnasion and an ephebia? To answer this question one must look more closely at this institution.

---

[1]W. W. Tarn and G. T. Griffith, *Hellenistic Civilisation* (3rd ed.; London: St. Martins, 1952) 213.
[2]V. Tcherikover, *Hellenistic Civilization and the Jews* (Philadelphia: Jewish Publication Society, 1959) 163.

The Gymnasion and Citizenship

No self-respecting city could be without a gymnasion (Strabo 5.4.7; Pausanias 10.4). Here children, youths, men, and seniors could gather to exercise and converse. It was primarily the place where males could get away from homes, although occasional references to female participation in the gymnasia are found.[3] During the centuries and throughout the regions of antiquity the gymnasia had different functions and rules. One must take seriously Marrou's caution: "The Hellenistic cities could not even agree on a common calendar; it is therefore hardly likely that they would be able to pursue a uniform educational policy."[4]

Jean Delorme has well shown that the gymnasion was a public building. It was usually municipally owned and controlled and the man in charge, often titled the gymnasiarch, was a public official.[5] One notes, however, that there could be privately-owned gymnasia such as that at Samareia in the Fayum.[6] Gymnasia founded by individuals such as the Ptolemaieion and the Antiocheion of Iasos were often handed over to the city-state and they certainly came within the purview of the state.[7] Education remained very much a state concern.

The stages of Greek education varied. Till seven the child stayed at home and then was sent to school where physical and literary education went hand in hand.[8] The next major stage was entrance into the ephebia. The origins of this organization are disputed, but it was widespread in the Hellenistic world.[9] G. Cohen has emphasized how the gymnasium was the means whereby Greco-Macedonian colonists kept themselves separate from the native populace.[10] Knowledge about this

---

[3]Clarence A. Forbes, *Greek Physical Education* (New York: Century, 1929) 230-31, for women at Smyrna, Pergamum, and Magnesia ad Maeander; H. I. Marrou, *A History of Education in Antiquity* (New York: Sheed and Ward, 1956) 117. See the bibliography in Nigel B. Crowther, "Studies in Greek Athletics," *Classical World* 79 (1985/86) 124-25.

[4]Marrou, *A History of Education*, 104. Note also the various uses to which gymnasia could be put as outlined by Clarence A. Forbes, "Expanded Uses of the Greek Gymnasium," *CP* 40 (1945) 32-42.

[5]Jean Delorme, *Gymnasion. Etude sur les monuments consacrés à l'éducation en Grèce* (Paris: Boccard, 1960) 254-55. Cf. Forbes, "Expanded Uses of the Greek Gymnasium," 32-33.

[6]P. Jouquet, "Une nouvelle requête de Magdola," *Raccolta di Scritti in onore di Felice Ramorino* (Milan: Vita e Pensiero, 1927) 381-90.

[7]Delorme, *Gymnasion*, 123 and 257-58.

[8]Forbes, "Expanded Uses," 32-33; Marrou, *History of Education*, 117, 142-59.

[9]For towns where ephebia are found, see F. Poland, *Geschichte des griechischen Vereinswesen* (Leipzig: Teubner, 1909) 90-92, 537-38; and Forbes, *Greek Physical Education*, 263-64.

[10]Getzel M. Cohen, *The Seleucid Colonies: Studies in Founding, Administration and Organization* (Historia Einzelschriften 30; Wiesbaden: Steiner, 1978) 36-37.

institution comes primarily from the ephebia in Athens. Whatever its origins, the Athenian ephebia from 336/5 to 323/22 meant compulsory military service for all about to become citizens. Each year the demes were to draw up a list of young men eighteen years old, and this list was handed over to the *Boule* for checking. Those enrolled spent two years in military service—one year of physical and military instruction, the second in maneuvers and as guards on the frontiers. Later the time of service was reduced to one year, and the numbers of ephebes show it was no longer compulsory: Pélékidis estimates from 334-326 BCE a total of around 650 ephebes per year; for the year 267/66, the total was 33.[11] He suggests that sometime in the 3rd century BCE, possibly because of the Macedonian desire not to have armed people in Athens, the ephebia became no longer obligatory and was to be only for one year.[12] This change correlates somewhat to the growing professionalism of the army which Delorme has suggested was also behind the move of the gymnasia inside the city.[13] Military maneuvers gave way to physical exercises and lectures in philosophy. As Marrou comments: "it remained nevertheless a college to which the gilded youth of Athens and elsewhere came to receive the finishing touches of their education."[14]

Later young men from outside Athens could be ephebes in Athens, and that fact is instructive. O. W. Reinmuth has studied the inscriptions which deal with foreigners in the Athenian ephebia, first attested in an inscription of 119/8 BCE,[15] and has placed this development within the larger context of citizenship in Attica.[16] Reinmuth showed that "the ephebia at Athens, originally a school for citizenship of its own youth, developed into a means of training young men of non-Attic birth as well for citizenship in Attica."[17] Reinmuth marked three stages in the development of the ephebate: the first, when ephebia training was necessary for citizenship; the second, till 119/8, when it was no longer a requirement for full citizenship; the third, from 119/8, when foreigners were admitted. The relationship between citizenship and ephebic training emerges from Reinmuth's analysis: completion of the city's ephebic training was proof of citizenship, but after the first stage of the development of the ephebia, not all citizens went through ephebic training.

---

[11]Chrysis Pélékidis, *Histoire de l'Ephébie attique des origines à 31 avant Jésus-Christ* (Paris: Boccard, 1962) 283-94, 165-66.

[12]Pélékidis, *Histoire*, 159-72.

[13]Delorme, *Gymnasion*, 464.

[14]Marrou, *A History of Education*, 108.

[15]IG. 2.1008.

[16]O. W. Reinmuth, "The Ephebate and Citizenship in Attica," *TAPA* 79 (1948) 211-31. Pélékidis allows for an earlier admittance of foreigners, and makes valuable observations on Reinmuth's work (*Histoire*, 187-96) while basically accepting it.

[17]Reinmuth, "The Ephebate," 230.

Before the introduction of compulsory ephebic training, "citizenship in Attica was obtained by birth or by grant to aliens. The qualifications for admission to the citizen body on the basis of birth were two: both parents must be Attic citizens and the candidate must have reached the age of eighteen."[18] Later, once ephebic training was no longer an added prerequisite for citizenship, one again became a citizen by birth or by grant. Reinmuth has shown that, in the third stage of the development of the ephebia, another method was possible: all foreign ephebes were entitled, by virtue of their ephebic training, to enrollment in an Attic deme and Attic citizenship. All ephebes were citizens, but not all citizens were ephebes. Such a relationship between citizenship and ephebic training is attested from 41 CE in Claudius' rescript to Alexandria,[19] lines 54-57: "All those who have become ephebes up to the time of my principate I confirm and maintain in possession of the Alexandrian citizenship with all the privileges and indulgences enjoyed by the city except those who contrived to become ephebes although born of slaves." Here again ephebic training is presumptive proof of citizenship. Claudius is denying such a claim to citizenship on grounds of a more basic requirement for citizenship, i.e., that one not be born of slaves. Clearly some had hoped to override this requirement by undergoing ephebic training. The rescript of Claudius does not say that to be an Alexandrian citizen one had to be an Alexandrian ephebe. Rather, his rescript allows that an Alexandrian ephebe is normally an Alexandrian citizen but with exceptions, thus making a wedge between citizenship and ephebic training. P. M. Fraser suggested that "the whole principle of admission through the ephebate as a permanent provision suggests an imposed solution intended to alter radically the constitution of a citizen-body suffering from undernourishment, and this ... is much more probable as a measure of Augustus than of a Ptolemy."[20] Fraser notes that in the Ptolemaic period "the normal practice would be for citizenship to be restricted to persons of Greek parentage, of whom the father at least was a citizen."[21] The prerequisite to ephebic training in Alexandria during the Roman period was that one not be of servile origin. As earlier in Athens, Roman Alexandria added ephebic training as a means of obtaining citizenship to the basic prerequisite of citizenship by birth.[22] The same

[18]Reinmuth, "The Ephebate," 211.

[19]P. Lond 1912; *Sel. Pap.* 212; CPJ 153. I have used the text in E. Mary Smallwood, *Documents Illustrating the Principates of Gaius Claudius and Nero* (Cambridge: Cambridge University Press, 1967) 99-102. The translation used here is that of Naphtali Lewis and Meyer Reinhold, *Roman Civilization.* Vol. 2. *The Empire* (New York: Columbia University Press, 1955) 366-69.

[20]P. M. Fraser, *Ptolemaic Alexandria* (3 vols.; Oxford: Clarendon, 1972) 1.77.

[21]Fraser, *Ptolemaic Alexandria*, 1.76.

[22]See Aryeh Kasher, *The Jews in Hellenistic and Roman Egypt* (Tübingen: Mohr [Siebeck], 1985) 313.

situation is found in an inscription from Ptolemais in Egypt of 104 BCE at SEG 8.641 where entrance to the gymnasium and consequently citizenship is being given to fifteen worthy men in exchange for the money required for the making of two statues, one of the king and one of Sarapis. Again, this inscription does not prove that all citizens had to be ephebes but that one mechanism for acquiring citizenship was by completing ephebic training. In Pellene, Pausanias notes as something unusual that no one could be enrolled on the citizen register before he had been an ephebe.[23] Here in this "ancient gymnasion" the old traditions were adhered to, but it is an anomaly. Tcherikover used the above examples from Ptolemais and from Claudius' rescript to support his thesis that Jason was changing the constitution of Jerusalem by redefining admittance to the citizen body through ephebic training.[24] For Tcherikover, one had to enroll in the ephebia to become a citizen of Jerusalem. Presumably he meant that even those born of Jews would no longer be citizens unless they enrolled in the ephebia. The analysis above shows the flaw in this argument. In the second century BCE, ephebic training was not necessarily a prerequisite for citizenship. All those who were ephebes at Jerusalem may have become citizens, but not all citizens had to undergo ephebic training. The requirement for citizenship remained birth as a Jew. Tcherikover goes beyond the evidence in his assumption.

The Gymnasion and the City

In Athens after 119/8 BCE to be an ephebe of the city's gymnasion entitled one to be a citizen. Within this statement one sees the intense pride the community had in its educational experience—such training fitted one to be a citizen. Here one approaches the connection between the gymnasion and the *politeia* of a city. When Aristotle begins to describe the state of the Athenian constitution in his time, he outlines first of all the formation of the ephebia.[25]

When discussing cultures different from their own, Greek authors consistently note how the educational system is an integral part of each culture's *politeia* (on Egypt: Herodotus 2.91, Diodorus Siculus 1.81.7; on Persia: Xenophon, *Cyropaedia* 1.2.2-15[26]). In his witty conversation between Solon and the Scythian Anacharsis, Lucian has Solon defend gymnastic exercises against Anacharsis' ridicule by stressing

[23]Pausanias, 7.25.5

[24]Tcherikover, *Hellenistic Civilization*, 467, n. 23.

[25]Aristotle, *Ath. Pol.* 42.

[26]As Clarence A. Forbes (*Greek Physical Education*, 94) stated about Xenophon's *Cyropaedia*: "as a source book on Persian education it is absolutely valueless.... The education of Cyrus is no more than a slightly altered and idealized sketch of Spartan education." Nevertheless, it is informative to note what terms Xenophon uses in describing "Persian" education.

the connection between civic organization and these, to Anacharsis, silly pursuits (Lucian, *Anach.* 14.40). At Rome, the antipathy of Cato and other conservatives towards the gymnasium is well known. Complaints were made about the unRoman behavior of Scipio (Livy 29.19.12; Plutarch, *Cato Maior* 3.7). Delorme has suggested that the Romans saw the Greek contests not as a principle of civilization, but as relaxation and that this attitude is reflected in the architecture of their palaestrae.[27] Even in the Roman landscape, however, some prominent Romans of the 2nd century BCE were well disposed to Greek athletics.[28]

The strong connection between education and *politeia* is particularly well attested for Sparta. When Solon praises Spartan practices, Anacharsis asks why the Athenians have not imitated them. Solon's reply is interesting: "Because we are content, Anacharsis, with these exercises which are our own; we do not much care to copy foreign customs (τὰ ξενικά)." (Lucian, *Anach.* 39) In every discussion of Greek education, Sparta's system, its ἀγωγή, is given a separate chapter.[29] Sparta had its own way of forming its citizens. Awareness of this deep division between Sparta and other Greek cities is important in understanding what Philopoemen did to Sparta in 188 BCE. Besides demolishing the walls of Sparta, dispersing foreign mercenaries and scattering newly-freed slaves, the Achaeans are said by Livy to have abrogated the laws and customs (*leges moresque*) of Lycurgus and to have forced the Spartans to adopt the laws and institutions (*legibus institutisque*) of the Achaeans: "that so all would become one body, and concord would be established among them.... The state of Lacedaemon having, by these means, lost the sinews of its strength, remained long in subjection to the Achaeans; but nothing did so much damage as the abolition of the discipline of Lycurgus (*disciplina Lycurgi*), in the practice of which they had continued during seven hundred years" (Livy 38.34). In his telling of this abrogation of ancestral laws, Plutarch uses more precise language:

> Now, glutting his anger at the Lacedaemonians and unworthily trampling upon them in their misery, he treated their constitution

[27] Delorme, *Gymnasion*, 432-40. N. B. Crowther ("Rome and the Ancient Olympic Games," *Proceedings of the Fifth Canadian Symposium on the History of Sport and Physical Education* [Toronto: The School of Physical and Health Education, University of Toronto, 1982] 52-58) has also shown Romans were less interested in participating in, than in observation of, the Olympic games.

[28] R. S. Robinson, "Athletic Festivals in Greece and Their Roman Patrons in the Second Century B.C.," *Classical Studies Presented to B. E. Perry* (Urbana: University of Illinois, 1969) 263-71. For a full discussion of Roman education, see S. F. Bonner, *Education in Ancient Rome* (Berkeley/Los Angeles: University of California, 1977).

[29] See Forbes, *Greek Physical Education*, 12-43, as well as the sections in the bibliography compiled by Crowther, "Studies in Greek Athletics," *Classical World* 78 (1984/85) 550; 79 (1985/86) 123.

(τὴν πολιτείαν) in the most cruel (ὠμότατον) and lawless (παρανομώτατον) fashion. For he took away and abolished the system of training which Lycurgus had instituted (τὴν Λυκουργεῖον ἀγωγήν) and compelled their boys and their young men (τοὺς ἐφήβους) to adopt the Achaean in place of their ancestral discipline (τῆς πατρίου παιδείας μεταλαβεῖν) being convinced that while they were under the laws of Lycurgus (ἐν τοῖς Λυκούργου νόμοις) they would never be humble.

For the time being, then, owing to their great calamities, the Spartans suffered Philopoemen to eat away, as it were, the sinews of their city, and became tractable and submissive; but a while afterwards, having obtained permission from the Romans, they abandoned the Achaean polity (τὴν Ἀχαικὴν πολιτείαν) and resumed and reestablished that which had come down from their fathers (τὴν πάτριον), so far as was possible after their many misfortunes and ruin (Plutarch, *Phil.* 16.5-6).[30]

Here one can see that, for Plutarch, to change the education system was to change the πολιτεία. Both were inextricably mixed, and the terms used are νόμοι, ἀγωγή, πάτριος.

The language at 2 Macc 4:10-17 resonates with that used in the preceding discussion by Herodotus, Diodorus Siculus, Xenophon, Lucian, and Plutarch. The contrast of τὰς νομίμους πολιτείας with παρανόμους ἐθισμούς (4:11), the zeal after τὰς ἀγωγάς (4:16), the antithesis between τὰς πατρώους τιμὰς and τὰς Ἑλληνικὰς δόξας—all these terms would be at home in distinguishing two educational systems. Even the author's disparaging image of priests hastening away from temple service at the sound of a gong to take part in the palaestra resembles other put-downs of physical exercises. Anacharsis may be speaking some of Lucian's own thoughts about physical exercises, as Delorme notes.[31] Also, Catullus says in Cicero's *De Oratore*:

> I look at all these things differently, for I consider that the Greeks themselves originally invented their palaestrae, seats and porticoes for the sake of exercise. Gymnasia were invented many centuries before philosophers began to babble in them; and even in our day, although philosophers occupy all the gymnasia, yet their auditors

[30]The use of the same image of sinews in both Livy and Plutarch may point to a common source.

[31]Delorme, *Gymnasion*, 430. Lucian (*Dial. Mort.* 1.1 [329]) also mocks the philosophers wrangling in the Craneum at Corinth.

are more eager to hear the gong (*discum audire*) than the philosopher. As soon as the gong sounds, even though the philosopher is in the middle of speaking about grave and important matters, they all abandon him to take an oil-rub. So they prefer the smallest pleasure to the greatest advantage." (*De Oratore* 2.5.21)

Both Catullus and the author of 2 Maccabees disparage physical exercises, but the different contrasts—philosophy, temple service—reflect the different authorial stances on education.

Naked and Uncircumcised?

What has to be grasped is that the debate envisaged in 2 Macc 4:10-17 is a debate over education. It is not a question of nudity or head-gear. Wearing the Greek *petasos* is a colloquialism. As Harris remarks: "It would be difficult to think of any sport or contest more vigorous than croquet in which competitors could wear such a hat."[32] Nor is it necessary that the Jerusalem athletes exercised naked. Goldstein has rightly stressed that, if they had, the author of 2 Maccabees would not have hesitated to mention the fact.[33] Thucydides had noted earlier that "even today many foreigners, especially in Asia, wear these loincloths for boxing matches and wrestling bouts" (Thucydides 1.6). Nudity need not have been *de rigueur* for participation. J. P. Thuillier has argued that Roman athletes were not naked, and N. Crowther suggested that the Romans probably did not practice naked on a permanent basis until perhaps the time of Augustus.[34]

The sneering jibe at 1 Macc 1:15 about uncircumcision should also not be pressed too hard. It appears within a passage devoted to character assassination of the Maccabean opponents, 1 Macc 1:11-15. The opponents are "base fellows" υἱοὶ παράνομοι (cf. 10:61, 11:21).

It was then that there emerged from Israel base fellows who led many people astray. "Come," (πορευθῶμεν) they said, "let us reach an understanding with the gentiles surrounding us (μετὰ τῶν

[32]H. A. Harris, *Greek Athletics and the Jews* (Cardiff: University of Wales Press, 1976) 31.

[33]Jonathan A. Goldstein, *2 Maccabees* (AB 41A; Garden City, NY: Doubleday, 1983) 230.

[34]J. P. Thuillier, "Denis d'Halicarnasse et les jeux romains" (Antiquités romains, VII, 72-73)," *Melanges d'Archéologie et d'Histoire de l'École Française de Rome* 87 (1975) 563-81; N. B. Crowther, "Nudity and Morality: Athletics in Italy," *CJ* 76 (1980-81) 119-23.

κύκλῳ ἡμῶν) for since we separated ourselves from them many misfortunes have overtaken us." (1 Macc 1:11)

The phrasing echoes Deut 13:12-15:

> If you hear in one of your cities, which the Lord your God gives you to dwell there, that certain base fellows have gone out among you and have drawn away (ἀπέστησαν) the inhabitants of the city, saying, "let us go (πορευθῶμεν) and serve other gods," which you have not known, then you shall inquire and make search and diligently; and behold, if it be true that such an abominable thing has been done among you, you shall surely put the inhabitants of that city to the sword, destroying it utterly, all who are in it and its cattle, with the edge of the sword.

One also recalls how the civil war against the Benjaminites began because "base fellows" attacked the concubine of the Levite in Judg 19:22 and how Abijah, king of Judah, described Jeroboam king of Israel as surrounded by "base fellows" who precipitated the split between Judah and Israel (2 Chr 13:7). Civil strife in Israel is consistently portrayed as the work of such "base fellows." The theme of being like the other nations is also one associated with wrongdoing as at 1 Sam 8:4-8, at Exod 34:15, Deut 7:2-4, and particularly at 2 Kgs 17:7-18. In this long reflection over the downfall of Samaria, the author stresses how Israel "had feared other gods and walked in the customs of the nations (ἐπορεύθησαν τοῖς δικαιώμασιν τῶν ἐθνῶν).... They went after (ἐπορεύθησαν) false idols and became false, and they followed the nations round about them (ὀπίσω τῶν ἐθνῶν τῶν περικύκλῳ αὐτῶν)."[35]

After such a thoroughly negative characterization in 1:11-13 comes the statement that they built a gymnasium, a statement again coloured by the negative "according to the customs of the gentiles." 1:15 also abounds in biblical imagery of movement, agriculture and slavery. The opponents distance themselves from the holy covenant, and the Greek ἀφίστημι is found frequently with this sense of apostasy as at Deut 13:10, 13; 32:15; Josh 22:18, 19, 23, 29. The image of yoking oneself to the nations echoes the phrase of Num 25:3 (Aquila and Theodotion translate צמד at Num 25:3 by ἐζευγίσθη) and Ps 106:28 when Israel yoked itself to Baal of Peor. Selling oneself to do evil is what is said of the Israelites at 2 Kgs 17:17 and also of the exceedingly wicked Ahab (1 Kgs 21:20, 25; LXX 3 Kgs 20:20, 25).

It is within this concentrated mass of biblical allusions that the reference to uncircumcision takes place. One notes first of all the awkwardness of the phrase—

---

[35] 2 Kgs 17:7-8, 15. For further biblical resonances, see Jonathan A. Goldstein, *1 Maccabees* (AB 41A; Garden City, NY: Doubleday, 1976) 199-210.

they made for themselves foreskins. The language most associated with such an operation is ἐπισπάω as at 1 Cor 7:18: μὴ ἐπισπάσθω—"let him not become uncircumcised." The Hebrew is מָשַׁך, as in the examples in Strack-Billerbeck 4.133-34. These verbs, whose root meaning is "to draw over," also lie behind the Latin *inducere* at *Test. Mos.* 8:3.[36] All of these examples are of course later than 1 Macc 1:15, but they suggest that if one wants to declare the technical medical act of uncircumcision, one would not use the poetical "made foreskins for themselves." Some Jews may have undergone the physical operation but, as Goldstein properly notes, no other contemporary witness mentions it.[37] I would suggest that the author has used the image of all the Hasmonean opponents making foreskins to wear in order to invoke consciously how they have rejected God's covenant (cf. Gen 17:14). He has wrought a new metaphor in response to the Greeks' pride in their uncircumcision, a metaphor which mocks the aping of Greek ways.

In conclusion, the physical exercises were part of a whole educational packet, a packet which, to mix in Livy's and Plutarch's metaphor, struck at the very sinews of a city. To tamper with the education system was to tamper with the *politeia* of a nation, its own feature and stamp, its χαρακτήρ.[38] What the author of 2 Maccabees sees at stake, then, is not whether one exercised or not, but what kind of a nation was being formed.

Conclusion

Education at an ephebia was not necessarily a prerequisite for citizenship and so the building of a gymnasium and ephebia did not imply a change in who were citizens, but it would have had profound impact on the power relationships within that body. Being part of the men's club would have meant exercising not only physical but also social power and Jason's position would no doubt have been strengthened. Secondly, the language of 2 Macc 4:10-17 finds its proper context in a debate over educational systems. The attack on the activities in the gymnasion by the author of 2 Maccabees is not anti-climactic nor does it have "a touch of the

---

[36]I am not convinced that *Test. Mos.* 8:1-5 dates from the Antiochan persecution as Nickelsburg ("An Antiochan Date for the Testament of Moses," in G. W. E. Nickelsburg, ed., *Studies in the Testament of Moses* [SCS 4; Cambridge: Society of Biblical Literature, 1973] 34-35) holds. The passage is so wildly inaccurate (see John J. Collins, "The Date and Provenance of the Testament of Moses," *Studies in the Testament of Moses*, 19-20) and reflects the most morbid fears of male fantasies— penis operations and wives given up to prostitution. It is hard to take it seriously as reportage.

[37]Goldstein, *1 Maccabees*, 200.

[38]Polybius (18.34.7-8) bases his use on the image of the χαρακτήρ of a nation on its ἔθη καὶ νόμιμα.

Robert Doran

ridiculous."[39] If he were to be talking about constitutional changes they might be. But the author is talking of educational changes, for him a major crime against Jewish usages. Within this context of educational change, the language of 2 Macc 4:9-17 is coherent and resonates with other non-Jewish descriptions of educational changes. The primary charge levelled at Jason is that of educational reformer, not constitutional reformer. Once one looks at the events of 175-169 BCE from this perspective, one begins to see Jason and the events surrounding his high-priesthood in a different light.

[39]Jonathan A. Goldstein, "Jewish Acceptance and Rejection of Hellenism," in E. P. Sanders with A. I. Baumgarten and Alan Mendelson, eds., *Jewish and Christian Self-Definition* (3 vols.; Philadelphia: Fortress, 1981) 2.77.

KORAH'S REBELLION IN PSEUDO-PHILO 16

Frederick J. Murphy
College of the Holy Cross

It is an honor and a pleasure to contribute to this volume for Professor John Strugnell. I shall always remember his generosity as my dissertation advisor at Harvard. The breadth and depth of his knowledge is truly phenomenal, and those who have studied with him are fortunate indeed. A contribution on the *Biblical Antiquities* (*Liber Antiquitatum Biblicarum*) of Pseudo-Philo is particularly appropriate here because Professor Strugnell wrote the article on that work for the *Encyclopaedia Judaica*.[1] He was also advisor for D. J. Harrington's dissertation on Pseudo-Philo.[2]

This paper analyzes Pseudo-Philo's account of Korah's rebellion.[3] The author of Pseudo-Philo rewrites Numbers 16 for his (or her)[4] own purposes. Pseudo-Philo is remarkably free in its treatment of the biblical text, here and throughout the work. In this respect it has often been compared to the *Genesis Apocryphon*, Josephus' *Antiquities*, and the *Book of Jubilees*.[5] Although Pseudo-Philo does explain some problematic features of the biblical text, its primary purpose is not explanation of the

---

[1] (16 vols.; eds., C. Roth et al.; New York: Macmillan, 1971-72) 13.408–09. See also J. Strugnell, "More Psalms of David," *CBQ* 27 (1965) 207-16, on *Bib. Ant.* 59.

[2] *Text and Biblical Text in Pseudo-Philo's Liber Antiquitatum Biblicarum* (Harvard, 1969). Harrington's critical text of Pseudo-Philo is in the first volume of D. J. Harrington, J. Cazeaux, C. Perrot, P.-M. Bogaert, *Pseudo-Philon, Les Antiquités Bibliques* (SC 229-30; Paris: Cerf, 1976).

[3] For a collection of Korah traditions, see L. Ginzberg, *The Legends of the Jews* (7 vols.; Philadelphia:Jewish Publication Society of America, 1910-1938) 3.286–303. This paper uses traditional biblical names, even when Pseudo-Philo uses other spellings.

[4] The treatment of women in Pseudo-Philo is noteworthy and awaits detailed treatment. Deborah (30-33), Jael (31:3-9) and Seila (Jephthah's daughter, 40) are all prominent in the *Biblical Antiquities*. There are also two striking examples of stock phrases from the Hebrew Bible being recast to include women: Deborah is called a "woman of God" in 33:1, and Seila goes to the "bosom of her mothers" in 40:4.

[5] For a recent review of work on the "rewritten Bible," see D. J. Harrington, "Palestinian Adaptations of Biblical Narratives and Prophecies: I. The Bible Rewritten (Narratives)," in R. A. Kraft and G. W. E. Nickelsburg, eds., *Early Judaism and Its Modern Interpreters* (Atlanta: Scholars, 1986) 239.

biblical text, and so it differs from what is strictly termed "midrash."[6] It is the assumption of this study that the author had before him the text of the Bible, and also had at his disposal current interpretations of the biblical text.[7] He uses the biblical narrative as a framework, but freely omits, adds, and rewrites material. Some of his expansions of the text are traditional, but some may well be his own composition.[8]

Pseudo-Philo sometimes rewrites biblical stories using material from elsewhere in the Bible.[9] The determination of precisely what biblical and traditional materials are alluded to is complicated by two factors. The first is that, although originally composed in Hebrew, the *Biblical Antiquities* survives only in Latin, which itself is a translation from Greek.[10] One is always dealing with the translation of a translation. The second is that Pseudo-Philo is so free with the biblical text (and probably with inherited traditions) that allusions are not always as clear as they might otherwise be.

Nickelsburg does not treat Korah in his article on good and bad leaders in Pseudo-Philo, presumably because Korah was not a ruler of all Israel.[11] Nonetheless, Korah heads a band of 200 men who join in his rebellion.[12] It is the contention of this paper that Korah is indeed one of the bad leaders of Pseudo-Philo.

[6]Harrington, "Palestinian Adaptations," 242–43.

[7]D. J. Harrington has shown that Pseudo-Philo uses a "Palestinian" text type of the Bible ("The Biblical Text of Pseudo-Philo's *Liber Antiquitatum Biblicarum*," *CBQ* 33 [1971] 1–17), using the typology of F. M. Cross ("The History of the Biblical Text in the Light of the Discoveries in the Judaean Desert," *HTR* 57 [1964] 281–99).

[8]For another view, see R. Bauckham, "The Liber Antiquitatum Biblicarum of Pseudo-Philo and the Gospels as 'Midrash,'" in R. T. France and D. Wenham, eds., *Gospel Perspectives, Volume III: Studies in Midrash and Historiography* (Sheffield: JSOT, 1983) 33–76. Bauckham is a strong proponent of the traditional basis of most of what Pseudo-Philo writes, restricting his role to that of "redactor" defined narrowly. He holds that Pseudo-Philo exercises most freedom in speeches and conversations of the characters and in additions of proper names to the text.

[9]Bauckham, 40-59. He makes the point that Pseudo-Philo's use of Scripture to explain Scripture always keeps commentary on the primary passage in the foreground.

[10]This is the view of L. Cohn, "An Apocryphal Work Ascribed to Philo of Alexandria," *JQR* 10 (1898) 277–332, and is generally accepted.

[11]G. W. E. Nickelsburg, "Good and Bad Leaders in Pseudo-Philo's *Liber Antiquitatum Biblicarum*," in G. W. E. Nickelsburg and J. J. Collins, eds., *Ideal Figures in Ancient Judaism* (Chico: Scholars, 1980) 49–65.

[12]Pseudo-Philo is unique in holding that the number was 200. The number is 250 in the MT, the LXX, Josephus and the Vulgate. There seems to be no motivation for this change, so Perrot is probably right when he attributes it to scribal error (*Pseudo-Philon*, 2.122). In later tradition, association with the "assembly of Korah" is paradigmatic for being in opposition to God and liable to punishment (*b. Sanh.* 109b).

In addition to being the leader of a small group within Israel, he is implicitly contrasted with the good leaders. Whereas they are willing to die for the Torah, he is willing to die in opposition to it. The contrast is made more effective by the influence of the martyrdom stories of 2 Maccabees in the retelling of the story.

In Num 15:37-41 God instructs Moses about the tassels to be attached to the corners of the garments of the Israelites. The passage comes at the end of a chapter in which obedience to the Law is paramount. God explains that the tassels are to remind the Israelites of the commandments and of their obligation to obey them all. Numbers 16 tells the story of Korah, but no connection is drawn between the tassels and Korah's rebellion. Pseudo-Philo makes the connection. It summarizes the passage about the tassels in a single sentence, and then tells of Korah's reaction: "In that time he commanded that man (Moses) about the tassels. Then Korah and two hundred men with him rebelled and said, 'Why is an unbearable law imposed upon us?'" (16:1).[13] God reacts angrily, and makes a speech against them.

It is the textual proximity of the rule of the tassels at the end of Numbers 15 to the story of Korah in Numbers 16 that leads to seeing the rule of the tassels as the cause of Korah's rebellion.[14] The connection between the tassels and the rebellion is known in targumic and rabbinic literature.[15] Pseudo-Philo implies that Korah protests not just the rule of the tassels but the Law as a whole, as is made clear by the rest of the chapter.[16] That implication is made explicit and considerably developed in rabbinic literature, which also expands the opposition between Moses and the rebels.[17] In some rabbinic material, Korah's attack on the Law is an attempt to discredit Moses by making the Law look absurd, implying that the Torah is from the hand of Moses and not from God's hand.[18] Korah's opposition to Moses

---

[13]In *Num. Rab.* 16:4 Moses makes Korah shave his body, and it is this that is the unbearable burden. The English translation of Pseudo-Philo is that of D. J. Harrington, in *OTP* 2.297-377.

[14]This is according to the hermeneutical rule of "juxtaposition." See Bauckham, "The Liber Antiquitatum Biblicarum," 38 and 69, n. 17. For further information on Pseudo-Philo's use of this rule he refers to M. Wadsworth, "Making and Interpreting Scripture," *Ways of Reading the Bible* (Brighton: Harvester, 1981) 10-16.

[15]For example, *Num. Rab.* 16:3; *b. Sanh.* 110a. See also *Tg. Yer. I* Num. 16:2.

[16]See 4 Macc 5:20-21: "To transgress the law in matters either small or great is of equal seriousness, for in either case the law is equally despised." This statement is made by Eleazar bearing witness during his trial. 4 Maccabees is a rewriting of the martyrdom stories of 2 Maccabees 6–7.

[17]It is said that Moses and the Torah are true, but Korah and company are liars (*b. Sanh.* 110b; *b. B. Bat.* 74a; *Num. Rab.* 16:20).

[18]*Num. Rab.* 16:3; *b. Sanh.* 110a. There is an interesting parallel to the rabbinic tradition in *Bib. Ant.* 25:13, where Benjaminite sinners question whether God wrote the Torah or Moses invented it.

becomes paradigmatic in rabbinic traditions for wrongful controversy over Torah, and it is contrasted with the lawful controversies of the schools.[19] Josephus does not connect the law of the tassels and the rebellion (*Ant.* 4.2.1–3.4 §§ 11-58). He blames Korah's jealousy of Moses for the rebellion. Korah feels that his birth (of the tribe of Levi and related to Moses) and his wealth qualify him for the post of high priest, given by Moses to Aaron.[20] Josephus' narrative stays on the level of the power struggle between Korah and Moses and does not have Korah attacking the Law itself. In fact, Korah accuses Moses of violating the Law by appointing Aaron. Korah does not openly oppose the Law in Josephus, although Josephus clearly portrays him as acting contrary to God's will.

It is remarkable that *Biblical Antiquities* 16 ignores the power struggle between Moses and Korah, especially since it is so prominent in the biblical narrative, Josephus, and targumic and rabbinic literature. In rabbinic literature, Korah's opposition to the Torah is put in the context of the power struggle between Korah and Moses.[21] In 57:2, the only other mention of Korah in the *Biblical Antiquities*, opposition to the leadership of Moses is suggested (probably as a reflection of Num 16:15), but it is absent from chapter 16.[22] Similarly, all reference to the fact that Korah's rebellion was a Levitical power struggle is suppressed. There is no counterpart to Num 16:8-11 where Moses chides the rebels for being unsatisfied with their Levitical functions and coveting the priesthood. Nor is the more general attack on the priesthood, reflected in the confrontation between Korah and Moses in Num 16:3-7, found in Pseudo-Philo's version.[23] Rather, the focus is entirely on whether Korah is willing to accept God's Law. When Korah rebels against the specific rule of the tassels, it is God who gets angry and makes a speech against him. The element of God reacting directly to Korah's rebellion is typical of Pseudo-Philo.[24] Pseudo-Philo always stresses God's direct participation in the action. There is no direct confrontation between Moses and Korah in chapter 16. Although Moses and Korah

---

[19]*M. ʾAbot* 5:17; *ʾAbot R. Nat.* 46; *b. Sanh.* 110a. The rabbinic expansions of the story are later developments that grow out of the kind of connection between the tassels and Korah made by Pseudo-Philo.

[20]For the issue of wealth, see *b. Sanh.* 110a; *Tg. Yer. I* Num 16:19; *Num. Rab.* 16:15. In *Num. Rab.* 16:7 Moses is especially upset that it is his own kinsman who rebels (cf. *Num. Rab.* 16:2).

[21]In *b. Sanh.* 110a and *Num. Rab.* 16:20 Korah is paradigmatic for one who rebels against his master.

[22]The connection between the words of Moses in Num 16:15 and those of Samuel in 1 Sam 12:3 is made in *Bib. Ant.* 57:2-3 and *Num. Rab.* 16:10.

[23]The attack on Aaron's priesthood is emphasized by Josephus. See also *Num. Rab.* 8; *b. Sanh.* 110a.

[24]See F. J. Murphy, "God in Pseudo-Philo," *JSJ* 19 (1988) 1-18; and "Divine Plan, Human Plan: A Structuring Theme in Pseudo-Philo," *JQR* 77 (1986) 5-14.

stand before the people, as in the Bible, they do not exchange words directly. Moses reports God's words to the people, not to Korah, in 16:4.

In God's speech (16:2-3), the idea that the earth opens its mouth (16:2) connects the Korah story with that of Cain and Abel (Gen 4:11).[25] In *Bib. Ant.* 16:2 God says that when the earth swallowed Abel's blood it was commanded not to swallow blood any more. "And now the thoughts of men are very corrupt; behold I command the earth, and it will swallow up body and soul together" (16:3). The idea seems to be that the sin of Korah and his companions is even more serious than that of Cain. Cain's sin resulted in the earth's swallowing blood, Korah's in swallowing body and soul together. Korah and his cohorts do not die, but "melt away" until God's visitation. Then they will not be "spit back" by hell as will other humans (3:9-10; 19:12-13; 25:7). Instead, they will die at that time, totally separated from the rest of humanity, unremembered. They share this extreme punishment with only the Egyptians and the generation of the flood (16:3). The idea that Korah and his fellow rebels will never rise is one known to rabbinic literature.[26]

In *Bib. Ant.* 16:3 the sin of Korah is generalized so that it is "the thoughts of men (*cogitationes hominum*)" that are corrupt. That seems to be an indictment of the human race as a whole, and indeed Pseudo-Philo is punctuated with such pessimistic statements about humanity (3:4; 15:7; 19:9; 33:3; etc.). One may therefore attribute this generalization to the author. This is supported by the observation that Pseudo-Philo's speeches seem usually to be his own free compositions. However, only Korah and his cohorts receive the extreme punishment of being swallowed body and soul by the earth, never to rise. In fact, the passage stresses that their extreme punishment set them apart from the rest of humankind. The uniqueness of the punishment of Korah and company is present in the biblical text as well. It appears that the indictment of the human race in general is Pseudo-Philo's distinctive contribution.

The narrative in 16:4-6 contains features suggesting that the author was influenced by the martyrdom stories of 2 Maccabees 6–7. In the story of Korah Pseudo-Philo reverses the martyrdom theme of 2 Maccabees. In 2 Maccabees, the old man Eleazar, and the mother and her seven sons are willing to die rather than transgress Torah. They stand face-to-face with their punishment and make the decision to obey God. Korah does precisely the opposite. Faced with his own punishment, he is willing to die rather than to obey Torah.

The parallel between the scenes in 2 Maccabees and *Bib. Ant.* 16 is made clearer by Pseudo-Philo's alteration of the order of events of Numbers 16. In Numbers 16,

---

[25] See *b. Sanh.* 37b.

[26] See *m. Sanh.* 10:3; *ʾAbot R. Nat.* 36:2. In *b. Sanh.* 109b (*j. Sanh.* 10:4) R. Akiba says they will not take part in the world to come, but R. Judah b. Bathyra thinks they will eventually rise.

Korah opposes Moses, and Moses challenges him to a test before God. Korah shows up for the test at the tent of meeting, apparently thinking that he might win God's favorable decision. Of course, God is on Moses' side. Moses intercedes for Israel and succeeds in arranging that God punish only Korah, Dathan, Abiram, and those who belong to them, so the rest of the people are told to separate from them. Moses announces that the unusual fate to be visited on the sinners will prove that he, Moses, acts for God. The earth then swallows them. In contrast to the biblical version, in Pseudo-Philo Korah's punishment is made known to him *before* he makes his final decision not to obey Torah.

Immediately after God's speech announcing the punishment, 16:4 has the following surprising words: "And though Moses was speaking all these words to the people, Korah and his men were still defiant." The words are surprising because up to this point God has been speaking, not Moses. Pseudo-Philo accomplishes two things at once here, in rather abbreviated form. First, it characteristically emphasizes God's participation, so it is originally God who speaks. Second, it wants God's plans to be known to Korah and to all the people so that Korah's decision is made in full awareness of its consequences, and is made in a public setting, paralleling the decision of the martyrs of 2 Maccabees who undergo a public trial.

The absence of Dathan and Abiram from Pseudo-Philo's version of the story is in keeping with Pseudo-Philo's tendency to focus on individuals. It also supports the idea that Pseudo-Philo treats Korah like a bad leader. Nickelsburg notes that Pseudo-Philo's heroes stand out from the crowd and are also differentiated from other prominent characters in the plot.[27] For example, Abraham is set off from the eleven other resisters (chap. 6), and Amram is contrasted with the elders (chap. 9). Further, the actions and words of the leaders frequently take place in public assemblies.[28]

In 16:4-6 there is the following structure.

A. Moses tells the people (and so Korah) of the punishment that awaits Korah and his men if they persist.
B. Korah and his men remain defiant.
C. Korah summons his seven sons.
D. The sons refuse to join Korah. They answer that their father (Korah) has not begotten them, but God has formed them. If they walk in God's ways, they will be God's sons.
E. The earth is opened before Korah and his men.
F. The sons accuse him of madness in his day of destruction.
G. Korah refuses to listen to his sons' appeal.
H. The earth opens its mouth, swallows the rebels and their

27 Nickelsburg, "Good and Bad Leaders," 52–53.
28 Nickelsburg, "Good and Bad Leaders," 60.

households, and Korah and the others cry out until the earth closes again.

The structure of the passage shows it to be a kind of trial scene. Numbers 16 is also a trial before the tent of meeting, and Pseudo-Philo has enhanced the aspects of trial. Later tradition considers the Korah episode a formal trial.[29] Korah and company stand before Moses, God's representative, and are told of the punishment they will incur if they persist in their defiance of the Law. Despite the warning, they do persist. Korah's sons point out to him his foolishness, but he remains steadfast. Finally, the punishment is carried out.

The Bible says the sons of Korah were Levitical singers.[30] That seems to contradict Num 16:31-33 which says that Korah and "all the men that belonged to Korah" perished. There is a qualification of Numbers 16 in Num 26:11, where it says, "Notwithstanding, the sons of Korah did not die." Later tradition explains the survival of Korah's sons by claiming that they repented of their sin.[31] This is quite a different solution to the problem of the biblical text than that of Pseudo-Philo 16 which says that the sons never sinned. In any case, there is no parallel for the interchange between the sons of Korah and their father in *Biblical Antiquities* 16.

The fact that Korah has seven sons in *Biblical Antiquities* 16 invites comparison with the trial of the woman and her seven sons in 2 Maccabees 7. A closer look at the details of *LAB* 16 suggests that the comparison be widened to include Eleazar's trial in 2 Maccabees 6. In 2 Maccabees the two chapters are meant to be read together as examples of those who prefer martyrdom to violation of Torah.[32] *Testament of Moses* 9, the story of Taxo and his seven sons, seems to be a combination of the two stories. It would not be surprising if Pseudo-Philo took elements from each of the two stories to enrich its presentation of Korah's trial.

In all of the passages (2 Maccabees 6, 7, *Biblical Antiquities* 16) the one on trial stands before an authority figure and faces punishment unless he/she retracts his/her position. In each case the person stands firm despite attempts at persuasion to change his/her mind, and so incurs punishment. Eleazar, the sons and the mother die

---

[29]*Mo ʿed Qat.* 16a; *Tg. Yer. I* Num. 16:12.

[30]2 Chr 20:19; Pss 42, 44-49, 84-85, 87-88. They are gatekeepers in 1 Chr 9:19 and 26:1, 19, and bake sacrificial cakes in 9:31.

[31]See *Num. Rab.* 16:8, where it says that Korah foresaw the prominence of his progeny, and on that basis presumed that God would judge in his favor against Moses. For other traditions growing out of Num 26:11 see *b. Meg.* 14a; *b. B. Bat.* 117b; *Num. Rab.* 16:19.

[32]R. Doran, "The Martyr: A Synoptic View of the Mother and Her Seven Sons," in G. W. E. Nickelsburg and J. J. Collins, eds., *Ideal Figures in Ancient Judaism* (Chico: Scholars, 1980) 190–91.

because they refuse to violate Torah and so are heroes. Korah dies because he refuses to obey it and so contrasts with the heroes. Although Korah's 200 men and their households also die, Korah is the focus of attention in the narrative, in keeping with Pseudo-Philo's emphasis on the individual leader.

In the case of Eleazar, figures friendly to him try to persuade him to disobey Torah. He refuses. Then he is brought to the rack, the instrument of his destruction, and his persuaders accuse him of madness. He does not listen to them. When he is just about to die he utters a loud groan. In Pseudo-Philo, Korah's sons explain why they cannot join him in his rebellion, saying that if their father does not relent they must take different paths. This is an implicit appeal to him to change his position. The earth opens its mouth, making the punishment clear, and the sons accuse him of madness and point out his imminent destruction. Just before the earth closes on them, the rebels utter a loud cry.[33] The parallels between the two stories are clear: (a) unsuccessful attempts at persuasion by friends; (b) confrontation with punishment; (c) accusation of madness; (d) refusal of one on trial to listen; (e) a cry before death; (f) death. The big difference is that Eleazar dies in defense of Torah and Korah dies in opposition to it.

The words of the mother and her seven sons in 2 Maccabees contain heroic statements of devotion to God and God's Torah. There may be a subtle allusion to these statements in *Bib. Ant.* 16:5. The mother does not want filial love to distract her sons from devotion to God. She tells them,

> It was not I who gave you life and breath, nor I who set in order the elements within each one of you. Therefore the Creator of the world, who shaped the beginning of man and devised the origin of all things, will in his mercy give life and breath to you again, since you now forget yourselves for the sake of his laws. (7:22b-23)

Antiochus tries to persuade the youngest son to apostasize, and promises "with oaths that he would make him rich and enviable if he would turn from the ways of his fathers" (7:24b). The situation of the woman's sons is reversed for Korah's sons, who must separate themselves from their father if they are to remain loyal to God. They say, "Our father has not begotten us, but the Most Powerful has formed us. And now if we walk in his (God's) ways, we will be his sons. But if you are unbelieving, go your own way." For the sons in 2 Maccabees 7, walking in their fathers' ways is the same as walking in God's ways. For Korah's sons, God's ways and their father's ways are opposites. Korah's sons opt for God's ways, telling their father to go his own way. The idea that God is one's true parent occurs in both 2 Maccabees 7 and *Biblical Antiquities* 16, and in both cases it is used to argue for

---

[33]In *Num. Rab.* 16:20 they are said to cry, "Moses, our master, save us."

obedience to Torah despite family love. However, in 2 Macc 7:22-23 it is the mother who uses the idea to urge her sons to loyalty to God whereas in *Bib. Ant.* 16:5 it is the sons who use the idea against their father to defend their refusal to follow him.

The idea that Korah and company will not rise again (*Bib. Ant.* 16:3) fits the emphasis on resurrection found in 2 Maccabees. The sons of the mother go to their deaths with confidence that they will rise again. The third son warns Antiochus: "For you there will be no resurrection to life" (7:14b). Again Pseudo-Philo reverses crucial elements, for it is the one on trial, Korah, who will not rise, rather than the judge as in 2 Maccabees 7.

After Korah and the others are swallowed by the earth, the people say to Moses, "We cannot stay around this place where Korah and his men are swallowed up." Moses responds, "Take up your tents from round about them; do not be joined in their sins" (16:7). The element of the separation of the people from the rebels serves a different function in Pseudo-Philo than in Numbers. In Numbers 16:24 God tells Moses to order the people away from the swellings of Korah and his fellows lest they be destroyed when God punishes the sinners. The separation takes place before the punishment, and protects the people as a whole from the *effects* of the rebels' sin. In *Bib. Ant.* 16:7 the separation occurs after Korah and the others are gone, and is at the initiative of the people. Moses' answer in Pseudo-Philo makes the separation a symbol of renunciation of the *acts* of the sinners: "Do not be joined in their sins (*nec coniungamini peccatis eorum*)." The language recalls the refusal of Abraham and eleven others to participate in the sinful building of the Tower of Babel: "Nor are we joining in your scheme (*nec coniungimur voluntati vestre*)" (6:4). Separation from the place of Korah's punishment becomes a decision not to follow Korah's ways.

As in Numbers, the selection of Aaron through the flowering rod follows the story of Korah's rebellion in Pseudo-Philo (chap. 17). In Numbers 17, the election of Aaron takes place in the context of the "murmuring" of Israel, and God appoints Aaron to put an end to power struggles in Israel. Pseudo-Philo suppresses any hint of a power struggle.

Korah contrasts starkly with Pseudo-Philo's heroes, Abraham in particular. Nickelsburg (61-62) points out that a trait of many of Israel's good leaders is that they are willing to risk death for God and Israel. Abraham stands trial for his refusal to participate in the building of the Tower of Babel. Korah stands trial for his willingness to challenge Torah. Throughout the *Biblical Antiquities* Israel's heroes are rescued from mortal danger by the God in whom they trust. Korah can expect no such protection from the God against whom he rebels. Korah is a foil for the heroes.

Korah's rebellion in *Biblical Antiquities* 16 is a good example of Pseudo-Philo's recrafting of biblical material for its own purposes. The major changes made in Numbers 16 by Pseudo-Philo are: (a) the suppression of the elements of power struggle between Korah and Moses and the attack on the priesthood by the Levites; (b) increased emphasis on God's participation in the plot, including the insertion of a speech by God conveyed by Moses to all the people; (c) the interchange between Korah and his sons. The suppression of the power struggles is the more remarkable given the prominence of those conflicts in Numbers 16-17, and the extent to which that aspect of the biblical text is emphasized and developed in Josephus, and targumic and rabbinic literature, and its mention in 57:2. Pseudo-Philo seems to sidestep the power struggles within Israel, concentrating on whether people are willing to die obedient to Torah and trusting in God. The portrait of the good leaders who are willing to die, but do not because God protects them, is enhanced by the negative portrayal of Korah, one who defies death because he will not obey Torah, and who dies at God's hand.

KENNETH BURKE MEETS THE TEACHER OF RIGHTEOUSNESS: RHETORICAL STRATEGIES IN THE HODAYOT AND THE SEREK HA-YAHAD*

Carol A. Newsom
Candler School of Theology

One of the Hodayot that many scholars associate with the Teacher of Righteousness concludes with this lively if rather disconcerting self-description: "My bowels heave like a ship in a raging wind, and my heart is in turmoil to the point of destruction. A whirling wind engulfs me because of the devastation caused by their sin" (1QH 7:4-5; Puech 15:7-8).[1] There is no doubt that we are in the presence of a first-class piece of rhetoric here. The speaker defines a character for himself, establishes a social world of at least three parties (himself, his audience, and the sinners who distress him), and implies a world of values. The traditional quality of the imagery and even of the emotional stance assumed by the speaker provides an index of the cultural context within which this particular performance is to be evaluated and to which it responded.

It is curious that so little attention has been paid to the rhetorical dimensions of Qumran literature. Rhetoric, as Kenneth Burke wryly noted, "considers the ways in which individuals are at odds with one another, or become identified with groups more or less at odds with one another,"[2] "the ways in which the symbols of appeal are stolen back and forth by rival camps."[3] To embrace a sectarian existence is to be flung, willy-nilly, into just this sort of symbolic mud-wrestling. To be sure, the rhetorical enterprise also has its more decorous moments. At its broadest reach rhetoric concerns all the ways in which character, community, and culture are

---

*It is with deep appreciation that I offer this essay to John Strugnell, generous teacher and good friend.

[1]Column and line numbers are given according to Sukenik's edition and according to the reconstruction published by Emile Puech, "Quelques aspects de la restauration du Rouleau des Hymnes (1QH)," *JJS* 39 (1988) 38–55. Unless otherwise noted, all translations are my own.

[2]Kenneth Burke, *A Rhetoric of Motives* (Berkeley: University of California Press, 1969) 22.

[3]Kenneth Burke, "Synthetic Freedom," *New Republic* 89 (20 January 1937) 365, quoted in Robert L. Heath, *Realism and Relativism: A Perspective on Kenneth Burke* (Macon, GA: Mercer University Press, 1986) 212.

generated through acts of discourse.[4] In this regard, too, the rhetoric of a sectarian community is of particular interest, since such a community must be rather self-conscious about the creation of the discourse that gives it identity.

In the discussion that follows I want to consider briefly the rhetorical situation of the Hodayot, especially those often associated with the Teacher of Righteousness, and to compare the rhetorical strategies of the Hodayot and the Serek ha-Yaḥad for dealing with a common issue, the problem of disaffection.

It would be nice if the study of the rhetoric of the Hodayot somehow allowed one to bypass the vexed questions of the *Sitz im Leben* of the Hodayot and the identity of the "I" of the compositions. Unfortunately, that is not the case. But it is possible to recast those questions in such a way as to avoid some of the dead ends to which they often seem to lead. We are unlikely ever to know the precise *Sitz im Leben* of the Hodayot. But whether the Hodayot were read privately, recited publicly, or used as part of formal worship, the most important thing is that they were used repeatedly. Over thirty years ago Hans Bardtke stressed the significance of this fact and drew the essential conclusion that the repetition of the various forms and images, and even the emotional patterns of the Hodayot, served to shape the beliefs and religious emotions of those who read them.[5] Unfortunately, the discussion of Bardtke's suggestion that the Hodayot be seen as a sort of "spiritual exercise" tended to become preoccupied with the issue of personal vs. cultic use of the Hodayot, so that there has been little exploration of the specific ways in which the Hodayot persuade their readers to a set of shared meanings, a particular experience of the self, and a distinctive cultural world.

The identification of the "I" of the texts has been an even more contested issue. If there can be said to be any scholarly consensus on the matter, it is this: although most of the compositions present an "I" who could represent the subjectivity of any member of the Qumran community, a few speak in the persona of a leader (2:1-19 [P. 10:3-21]; 4:5-5:4 [P. 12:6-13:6]; 5:5-19 [P. 13:7-21]; 5:20-7:5 [P. 13:22-15:8]; 7:6-25 [P. 15:9-28]; 8:4-9:36 [P. 16:5-17:36]; 14:8-22 [P. 6:19-33]). There is rather less consensus as to whether the "I" of these prayers of the leader represents the Teacher of Righteousness, as many have argued, or one of the institutional leaders of

---

[4]The understanding of rhetoric I am embracing here is broader than classical Aristotelian rhetoric. It is best represented by the various writings of Kenneth Burke but also by writers such as James Boyd White, *When Words Lose Their Meaning: Constitutions and Reconstitutions of Language, Character, and Community* (Chicago and London: University of Chicago Press, 1984) and Richard Harvey Brown, *Society as Text: Essays on Rhetoric, Reason, and Reality* (Chicago and London: University of Chicago Press, 1987). The semiotic theory of culture developed by Clifford Geertz in *The Interpretation of Cultures* (New York: Basic Books, 1974) and *Local Knowledge* (New York: Basic Books, 1983) is closely related.

[5]Hans Bardtke, "Considérations sur les Cantiques de Qumrân," *RB* 68 (1956) 231.

the community (the *mebaqqer* or the *maskil*), as Licht originally suggested.[6] Though there is not space here to discuss the evidence, I am persuaded that there is good reason for concluding that the Qumran community read the compositions listed above (with the possible exception of 14:8-22 [P. 6:19-33]) as referring to the Teacher of Righteousness.[7]

Rhetorical Form and Social Structure

The Hodayot of the Teacher are variously concerned with the problems of the formation and leadership of a sectarian community. Locating the community in a moral world of significant choices and defining the boundaries that articulate sectarian identity are an important part of their work. But there are also inner-community problems of a predictable sort—disaffection and conflict with established leadership. These are chronic problems that the sociology of sectarianism teaches us to expect. Whether or not these Hodayot were written in response to specific, acute situations, their topics would have remained pertinent throughout the life of the sect. To appreciate how the Hodayot of the Teacher functioned to address these perennial issues, it is necessary to take a brief look at the resources provided by their form of speech in the context of the social structure of the community.

Like the older Israelite thanksgiving psalms, which were addressed to God but clearly intended to be "overheard" by members of the psalmist's community, the Hodayot of the Teacher assume a dual audience. Though I would not discount the literal address to God as insignificant, I want to focus here on the way these overheard prayers engage the human audience. There are three features especially worth comment. First of all, no matter how historically distant the actual Teacher of Righteousness became in the chronology of the community, the immediacy of the language of prayer has the effect of contemporizing the Teacher and his experience.

A second resource of the rhetoric of prayer is that it permits a wholly unified point of view. Everything in the world of the text is experienced from the perspective of the speaker. Though occasionally the speech of others is quoted, it is always in a way that allows the primary speaking voice of the text to characterize and control the voice of the other.

Thirdly, and most importantly, the tradition of prayer to which the Hodayot belong is one in which the speaker's subjectivity is to be elaborately displayed: accounts of experiences, social humiliations or triumphs, emotions, hopes, fears, and even physical sensations are all marshalled as part of the discourse of the self at prayer. In its original environment such ego-exhibitionism may have functioned to

---

[6]Jacob Licht, *The Thanksgiving Scroll* (in Hebrew; Jerusalem: Bialik, 1957) 22–26.

[7]See most recently Philip Davies, *Behind the Essenes* (Atlanta: Scholars, 1987) 87–105.

attract the attention of the deity, to rehabilitate the speaker in the view of his fellows, and to witness to the power of the deity. But what would be the uses of such a discourse of the self for negotiating issues of leadership within a sectarian community? The form of speech in prayer rules out direct appeal to the human audience to behave in a certain way or to adopt a certain stance. The speaker has to persuade through indirection. Various kinds of conduct, attitudes, and persons may be praised and blamed in the course of the Hodayot, but these specific arguments are all embedded in an appeal that consists finally in the self-presentation of an individual subjectivity. It is the speaker himself that the audience will accept or reject.

Although the persona projected in these prayers is a strong one, the personal and charismatic form of leadership they embody is not. The leader cannot simply speak and be assured of obedience. Nor, apparently, can he punish those who challenge him. Instead, he must appeal, courting the good will and personal attachment of his followers. This repressed feature of the relationship between leader and followers is ironically disclosed, of course, in the very use of the motifs of the psalm of lament. Implicitly, the audience is being called on to aid the speaker, as God explicitly is in such psalms.

I have been speaking here as though the relationship between leader and followers created in the text matched an actual social reality. But that is not necessarily the case. We don't really know if the Qumran community, even at the time of the Teacher of Righteousness, was truly a sect with a charismatic form of leadership. Perhaps it was. But the Teacher of Righteousness apparently came to an already existing group, about whose social organization we know nothing. What we do know is that for most of its existence the Qumran community did not have an egalitarian structure with personal/charismatic leadership but rather a hierarchical and bureaucratic social structure. Entrance was highly regulated, and property of full members held in common, so that exit would be costly. Leadership roles appear to have been relatively well defined and limited by the authority vested in the community sitting in council. Order of precedence was meticulously defined. Behavior was thoroughly regulated and subject to disciplinary rules. Throughout the texts one finds a deep suspicion and distrust of the individual who resists the authority of the group. Though personalities always matter to some extent, the organization described in the Serek ha-Yahad is designed to limit their influence.

There are some significant advantages for a sect in adopting this kind of organization. Egalitarian sects with charismatic leadership are extremely susceptible to factionalism and schism. Though there are some notable exceptions, the prospects for a lengthy existence of such a group are not good, as the observations of anthropologist Mary Douglas and sociologist Aaron Wildavsky suggest:

> We have noticed that some religious sects are conspicuously more short
> lived and prone to fission than others and that the best survivors tend to

have adopted hierarchical forms of organization.... How did the Shakers survive? Our first explanation is that they held property in common and our second is that they created their own form of hierarchy. Holding property in common in itself is not enough. There is also the will to make compartments and regulations which obscure most political issues and lighten the burdens of deciding on issues too hot to avoid. Some of the communities which broke up early never managed to turn the personal authority of their founders into institutional forms. Others gave over their life decisions to committees. [8]

That last remark suggests that the advantages of bureaucratic organization are not without their costs, one of which is precisely the depersonalizing of the ethos of the community. In times of stress, what will there be to remain loyal to? I would suggest that the Qumran community owed its remarkable longevity in part to its success in combining institutional authority with elements of personal attachment. The Hodayot of the Teacher would have played a crucial role in this balance. Because of their personal language, they provide a focus for loyalty. Their ability to contemporize the tensions and crises described by the speaker provides a context for the practice of certain attitudes and motivations that would help the community negotiate the chronic problems of its own marginality in Jewish society and the disaffection of some of its members. But the signal advantage of making the Teacher of Righteousness the focus of personal motivation is that he is dead and gone. The risks of actual charismatic leadership are thus nicely contained, and the community may enjoy the best of both organizational worlds.

Confronting Disaffection: Two Rhetorical Strategies

To appreciate the way in which the institutionalized, bureaucratic ethos of the Serek ha-Yaḥad and the personal ethos of the Hodayot could work to complement one another, it is useful to compare the way each treats the problem of disaffection among community members. The two texts to be compared are 1QS 7:15-25 and 1QH 5:20-7:5 (Puech 13:22-15:8).

The relevant portion of the Serek ha-Yaḥad reads as follows:

The man who goes about slandering his neighbor shall be excluded from the purity of the many for one year and fined. But a man who goes about slandering the community shall be sent away from them and shall never return.

---

[8]M. Douglas and A. Wildavsky, *Risk and Culture* (Beerkeley: University of California Press, 1982) 113–14. I have reversed the order of the quotations.

The man who makes complaints about the authority of the community shall be sent away and shall not return. But if it is against his neighbor that he makes complaints without cause, he shall be fined for six months. The man whose spirit so deviates from the fundamental principles of the community that he betrays the truth and walks in the stubbornness of his heart, if he returns, he shall be fined for two years. In the first year he shall not touch the purity of the many, and in the second he shall not touch the drink of the many, and he shall sit behind all the men of the community. When he has completed two years, the many shall be asked about his affairs. If they allow him to draw near, he shall be registered in his rank, and afterwards he may be asked about judgement. But no man who has been in the council of the community for ten full years and whose spirit turns back so that he betrays the community, and who leaves the many to walk in the stubbornness of his heart, shall ever return to the council of the community. Anyone from the men of the commun[ity who has any]thing to do with him in regard to his purity or his wealth whi[ch...] the many, his sentence shall be the same: he shall be sent [away.][9]

Both the hodayah, which will be considered below, and the set of regulations just quoted are about the same sort of problem. But the language each uses could not be more different. That is not a trivial matter. Each language offers its users a different symbolic structure, a different vocabulary of motives, a different type of society, a different sort of self. Consequently, the situation they serve to focus, the problem of disaffection, has a very different meaning in each of these available languages. In the Serek ha-Yaḥad the language is that of rule and breach, punishment and restoration. It is a language of utter impersonality. The characters are "the man who," "his neighbor," "the community," "they." There is no place here for the expression of emotion. Outrage, pain, doubt, disappointment, inner conflict—all such matters are simply unsayable in the language of rules and laws. One is inclined to think that they are unsayable because the central character in this language is not a person but an institution, the Yaḥad. That would not be quite correct, though it leads in the right direction. In other contexts one can speak as though a collective entity had personal qualities, even emotions. But the language of laws and penalties is a language in which one not only refrains from speaking of institutions as though they were persons but in which one speaks of persons as though they were components of

[9]Trans. Michael Knibb, *The Qumran Community* (Cambridge Commentaries on Writings of the Jewish and Christian World, 200 BC to AD 200; Cambridge: Cambridge University Press, 1987) 124.

an institutional system. The formalism of such language is not merely a matter of style. It also shapes the realities of which it speaks.

It is not just the affective dimension of existence that is obscured in the symbolic world of legal regulations. We are so accustomed to the language of legal authority that it is easy to overlook the constructive force of such language. The passage cited above lists a series of grave challenges to the authority of the community, an inventory of destabilizing behaviors. There is no reason to think that the legislation has a purely hypothetical character. And yet, an impression of instability and precariousness is not at all what one derives from that passage. Just the opposite is the case. But how is it that the text manages to speak of all these counter-institutional threats and yet leaves us persuaded of its authority and stability? In part, it is the way in which the parties to the conflict are presented. The transgressor is a single individual ("a person who does such-and-such"), whereas the punishing agent is the collectivity. The prospect of large-scale defection or challenges to authority, a situation that would put in question the very efficacy of law, is simply not contemplated. Transgression is always limited and punishable. This projection of relative power is also implied in the way in which defection is treated. The text does not deal with defection per se. It does not hold up for our inspection a case in which someone is beyond the power of the community. Instead it contemplates cases of expulsion of disaffected members (7:15-18, 24-25) and cases in which a defector seeks readmission (7:18-24). In the case of the one who has been a member for less than two years, it grants readmission on stringent terms. For the one who has been a member for more than ten years, it denies readmission. What the reader of the text sees is the power of the community in dealing with deviants and suppliants.

There are other ways, too, in which the authority of the community is constructed in the language of the rules. The world placed before the reader of these rules (and indeed of most legal texts) is an ahistorical, apolitical world in the sense that the conflicts, compromises, chances, and necessities that produced its particular fabric of rights and obligations are repressed. Its contingent character is completely obscured. All that appears are the assertions of norms, the catalogues of possible infractions, and the mechanisms for restoring equilibrium. In the case of the Serek ha-Yaḥad this quality of absoluteness even extends to the authoritative voice of the text. Traditionally, Israelite law drew authority from the identification of the speaking voice as that of God or a mediator such as Moses. But if one asks who authorizes the rules in the Serek ha-Yaḥad, there is no personal voice to which they may be attributed. Rather, their authority is projected precisely by the lack of any such voice. This is simply "the way things are," "how one does things." It is the authority of sheer obviousness, of utter matter-of-factness.

In sum, the regulations at the end of col. 7 of the Serek ha-Yaḥad give instructions for dealing with various expressions of serious disaffection from members of the community. But they do much more than that. The resources of the legal language itself, the limits its sets to what can be said, and the selection of examples all work together to create a text that persuades its reader to a belief in the authority, legitimacy, and effectiveness of the community. To the disgruntled it serves as a word of warning; to the one who doubts the stability of the community it speaks a word of confidence; and to the members who must from time to time take disciplinary measures, it coolly reassures them of the rightness and efficacy of their actions. Although we are not accustomed to thinking of such legal language as rhetorical, it is every bit as much a rhetorical act as the highly charged words of the Hodayot.

But how differently the Hodayot deals with the same sort of problems that 1QS 7 treats. The confessional "I"-style of the Hodayot organizes its rhetorical world around the experiences of a single ego. The rhetorical ground is not that of institutional but of personal relations. Disaffection is not a breach of obligations but a matter of betrayal. Correspondingly, it is not the dispassionate language of institutional procedure that one finds, but the language of the emotions. The immediate resolution provided by the regulations is missing here. Far more important than the possible action that could be taken against the transgressors is the process of giving a character to each of the parties. The betrayers are portrayed as monstrous villains. The one betrayed, far from being depicted as able to discipline or expel his opponents, is rather shown as one who suffers deeply from their attacks. His vulnerability is very much a part of the rhetorical strategy. The audience, too, is persuaded to a different stance. Rather than confident assurance, it is urged to solidarity.

The rhetorical strategy followed here can be better appreciated if we take a closer look at the prayer itself. Although the text does not have a strongly marked formal structure, there is a fairly regular alternation of topics. After an introduction blessing God for not abandoning the speaker (5:20-22 [P. 13:22-24]), the prayer may be outlined as follows:

A^1. Antagonism of the speaker's associates (5:22-25 [P. 13:24-27])

B^1. Divine assistance (5:25-26 [P. 13:27-28])

A^2. Antagonism of the speaker's associates; effect on the speaker (5:26-32 [P. 13:28-34])

B^2. Divine assistance (5:32-33 [P. 13:34-35])

A^3. Antagonism of the speaker's associates; effect on the speaker (5:33-6:3 [P. 13:35-14:6])

B^3. Divine assistance (6:3-19 [P. 14:6-22])

A^4. Defection of "those who had attached themselves to my witness"; effect on the speaker (6:19-24 [P. 14:22-27])

Carol A. Newsom

B^4. Divine assistance (6:24-? [P. 14:27-41 (?)]
A^5. Antagonism of speaker's associates (?); effect on speaker (7:1-5 [P. 15:1-8])

The most noticeable thing about the structure of the text is that it ends, not with a celebration of divine assistance (as would seem most fitting for a prayer of thanks) but with a description of the speaker's distress. This alone should alert one that something else is going on here besides simple thanks to God. But we need to follow the sequence of the prayer as it unfolds in order to assess its rhetorical strategies.

Although the introductory lines do not contain the pronoun "I," there is no doubt that the speaker is claiming for himself a traditional identity within a well-known moral language. He himself is to be seen as the "orphan" and "the poor one." By the second century BCE these were terms that not only drew on the ancient paternalistic ethos of the Near East but also on a specifically religious reinterpretation of those terms as labels of rectitude and piety.

Following this initial claim, the first movement of the text (A^1 and B^1) begins to sketch the conflict. Here, again, the speaker draws on traditional imagery from the psalms of complaint. He is "a cause of controversy and quarrels with my neighbors, and an object of jealousy and anger to those who enter into covenant with me," etc. In traditional psalmic language, such statements are not merely descriptive but function as implicit claims that the speaker's antagonists are the ones in the wrong. Only toward the end of the section is the specific, sectarian context of the antagonism indicated: "with the secret you have hidden in me they go about as slanderers to the children of destruction." Betrayal of esoteric knowledge to those outside the restricted group is hardly the type of misfortune addressed by the traditional psalms of complaint and thanksgiving. In actual fact, to whom such knowledge belonged and the morality of separating from a (possibly autocratic) leader or community may have been deeply ambiguous issues. The speaker here uses traditional language to colonize the new moral territory of sectarian ethics. Since the betrayers are unlikely to have been part of the audience that overhears this prayer of thanksgiving to God, the clarification is evidently intended for those who have not defected but whose loyalty needs to be reinforced. "Spin control," it would appear, has always been with us. The statement of divine assistance, though brief, is to the point. The speaker is vindicated, his opponents are judged, and their efforts are claimed to have been unavailing.

The text, however, does not appear to be as concerned with the topic of divine assistance as with the vivid characterization of the conflict, to which it quickly turns again (A2, 5:26-32 [P. 13:28-34]). Indeed, the statement of divine assistance in 5:33 (P. 13:35) does not really bring the prayer to a moment of rest but merely serves as a transition to a renewed description of the conflict and its effects on the speaker (A^3,

5:33-6:3 [P. 13.35-14.6]). The verbal quality of the conflict is aptly captured in the image of snakes with their darting tongues and poisonous venom, and again with the noisy songs of complaint to which the speaker is subjected by his opponents. Even more than the highly colored description of the faithless ones, the lengthy descriptions of the emotional state of the speaker form the central focus of this part of the prayer.

The adaptation of the personal language of the complaint psalm to the sectarian communal context is evident in the following section, which describes the divine assistance (B^3, 6:3-19 [P. 14:6-22]). Although the speaker's suffering has been described in wholly personal terms, the relief is God's provision of a community of repentance. The way in which the topic of the community is introduced is somewhat surprising. "[But you, O my God,] you opened my ears [to the correc]tion of those who reprove in righteousness." Although several lines are unfortunately broken, there are other references to the moral discipline of the life of the covenanted community. "I know that there is hope for those who repent of sin and for those who abandon transgression"; "you refine them in order to purify (them) from guilt"; "in your kindness you judge them with overflowing compassion and abundant forgiveness." Although cast in positive terms, the aspects of community life to which these expressions broadly refer had the potential for being occasions for disgruntlement and social friction. We know from the Serek ha-Yahad that members were encouraged to reprove one another concerning their faults and lapses. Indeed, the Serek ha-Yahad is aware of the potential for social friction and regulates the ways in which reproof was to be conducted (1QS 5:24-6:1). The conduct of members was regularly reviewed, and offenses against the community's understanding of Torah could result in a reduction of status. Though I would not care to go too far in specifying the situation to which this hodayah is a response, in general terms at least, the system of moral examination, mutual critique, and status hierarchy would have provided the environment in which "refractory murmurers" could be expected to have been a recurrent problem. By developing the theme of the community as the source of hope and reassurance to the suffering speaker, the prayer makes an appeal for the value of the practices of the community, even those that may not have been pleasant. But the appeal is bolstered by the further description of the benefits of membership in this elect group—universal acclaim, communion with the angels, a metaphorical account of the community as the world tree, and as a "spring of light" in which all the guilty will be burned up.

There is a recapitulation of the scenario of conflict and relief in A^4 and B^4 (6:19-36 [P. 14:22-41]). Again the fault is identified as defection ("they, who had attached themselves to my witness, have let themselves be persuaded by [...]," and as departure from "the way of ho[liness]"). The speaker's distress is presented under the image of a sailor caught in a raging storm, while the image of deliverance is that of a secure and fortified city. As before, the image culminates in a description of eschatological judgment, this time in a military idiom. Although the connection is not made explicitly in the text, Delcor is probably correct that the image of the fortified city is intended to suggest the covenanted community.[10] If so, it is curious that the community, which has in fact proved to be a place of instability, is described as sure and reliable. And the leader, who, on the evidence of this prayer, is a figure to be reckoned with, presents himself as deeply vulnerable, rescued from death and dissolution by the strength he receives from this community of God's truth. Indeed, the very image of the fortified city is one that refers to the leader's protection of the community in another text (7:6-25 [P. 15:9-28]). But perhaps this reversal is not so curious after all. Precisely in situations where the resolve of a group is in doubt, there may be an advantage in putting before them images of their proper role and crediting them with fulfilling their function, even if their performance has been a bit shaky.

It is now more explicable why the prayer ends as it does. The last lines of col. 6 (P. 14) and the first lines of col. 7 (P. 15) are unfortunately missing. Presumably they contained another description of faithless defection, for the last lines of the prayer are yet one more account of the speaker's suffering. Unlike the previous accounts, there is no following word of divine aid. We leave the speaker with his frame shaking, bowels heaving, and heart fluttering. Such an ending would be odd even in a psalm of complaint (see only Psalm 88), not to mention one that begins "Blessed are you, O Lord, for you have not abandoned the orphan." To conclude with the speaker's distress is to leave an empty space at the margin of the text. Four times the audience has been told that God has aided the speaker. In the last two cases the aid has been elaborately described as the faithful life of the community itself. By leaving what I have described as the empty space, the text forces the audience out of passivity and into commitment.

The two texts examined in this study offer the reader distinctive vocabularies of motive, images of the self, and experiences of community. Whether or not they originated from different types of social organization at different periods in the life of the sect, for much of the existence of the Qumran community, the Hodayot and the Serek ha-Yaḥad were both part of the discourse of Qumran sectarian life. That such different moral languages should exist side by side is not so surprising. Our own lives are intersected by a multiplicity of divergent discourses. In the case of the Qumran community the complementary resources of the impersonal language of institutional authority in the Serek ha-Yaḥad and the emotional language of personal relations in the Hodayot helped to negotiate some of the chronic problems of sectarian organization.

---

[10]M. Delcor, *Les Hymnes de Qumran (Hodayot)* (Paris: Letouzey et Ané, 1962) 180.

SOME OBSERVATIONS ON BLESSINGS OF GOD IN TEXTS FROM QUMRAN

Eileen Schuller
McMaster University

One of the classical forms of speech in the Hebrew Scriptures and one which became normative in the statutory prayer of the liturgy is the *berakah*, the "blessing" in which God's beneficient action is acknowledged and praised by the individual or the community. Both the actual form and pattern of the *berakah* as it appears within the Old Testament and the question of the meaning of blessing (especially when a human "blesses" God) have been the object of a number of detailed studies.[1] More recently, form-critical and historical methodologies have been adopted in studying the *berakot* in the Siddur.[2] Today it is generally acknowledged that there is an intrinsic link between the short spontaneous biblical expressions of adoration and joy (e.g., Gen 24:27, Ex 18:10, 1 Sam 25:32, 2 Sam 18:20, Ruth 4:4) and the liturgical *berakot* of statutory prayer, although the line of development between the two is complex and still not totally understood.[3]

The purpose of this paper is neither to retrace nor to offer new explanations of the biblical or the liturgical material per se, but rather to introduce into the discussion certain reflections on another corpus of *berakot*, those found in the nonbiblical manuscripts from Qumran. Much of this material has been accessible for some time now, but for the most part has been drawn only secondarily or peripherally into the

---

[1]The most recent study is C. W. Mitchell, *The Meaning of BRK "To Bless" in the Old Testament* (SBLDS 95; Atlanta: Scholars, 1987). Certain articles have been formative in shaping the discussion of blessings of God, specifically, J. P. Audet, "Esquisse historique du genre littéraire de la 'bénédiction' juive et de l'"Eucharistie' chrétienne," *RB* 65 (1958) 371-99; E. Bickerman, "Benediction et prière," *RB* 69 (1962) 524-32; W. S. Towner, "'Blessed be YHWH' and 'Blessed art Thou, YHWH': The Modulation of a Biblical Formula," *CBQ* 30 (1968) 386-99.

[2]J. Heinemann, *Prayer in the Talmud: Forms and Patterns* (Studia Judaica 9; Berlin: de Gruyter, 1977), particularly chap. 3, "The Patterns of the Liturgical *Berakah* and their Origins," 77-103. For a summary of earlier works, see R. S. Sarason, "On the Use of Method in the Modern Study of the Jewish Liturgy," in W. S. Green, ed., *Approaches to Ancient Judaism* (Missoula: Scholars, 1978) 97-172.

[3]This is evidenced in particular by the unusual combination of second and third person in the liturgical *berakot*.

discussion of the blessing formula;[4] other relevant material has become available only more recently.[5] In our overall effort to understand developments in the formulaic pattern and function of the *berakah*, it is surely significant that we now have the actual texts of over seventy blessings of God[6] in Hebrew from the Second Temple Period.[7]

The texts to be considered can be divided into four groups: (1) blessings in hymns and psalms; (2) blessings and curses formularies; (3) blessings in prayers from a liturgical ritual; (4) blessings in prayers within narrative. Although it is not possible to comment in detail on every example, we will look at the form and function of the blessings in major texts from each category.

1. *Blessings in Hymns and Psalms*

A study of the *Hodayot* (1QH) enables us to examine both the pattern and the function of the formula within a distinct body of material. There are six instances of the *baruk* formula: 10:14; 11:27, 29, 32; 16:8; frg. 4, 15; in addition, in 5:20 אודכה is deleted (by dots above and below) and ברוך אתה is written in above. The formula has been restored in a few other places: in 14:8, many commentators reconstruct, probably correctly, ברוך אתה, although others suggest אודכה;[8] frg. 15, 6 may be

---

[4]Most often the Qumran material has been treated in a footnote or an appendix by selecting (often randomly it seems) a small number of examples; for instance, Towner, "'Blessed be YHWH,'" 393, n. 15; J. Scharbert, "Die Geschichte der *baruk*-Formel" *BZ* 17 (1973) 20; Heinemann, *Prayer*, 86 (n. 13), 92, 121 (n. 38); for a more comprehensive survey of the Qumran material, see E. J. Wisenberg, "Gleanings of the Liturgical Term 'Melekh Ha^{c}olam,'" *JJS* 17 (1966) 61-63.

[5]In particular, there are many blessing in the texts published by M. Baillet, *Qumrân Grotte 4 III*, (DJD 7; Oxford: Claredon, 1982). According to the *Preliminary Concordance to the Hebrew and Aramaic Fragments from Qumran Caves II-X* (Jerusalem), there are about a dozen *berakot* in unpublished Cave 4 materials.

[6]Probably we should include here also the blessings of the "name" of God, e.g., 1QM 14:8 (= 4Q491 frgs. 8-10, 1:6), 1QM 18:6, 4Q511 frg. 63, 4:2, 11QBer frgs. 1-2, 3-4.

[7]The numerous *berakot* scattered throughout the Apocrypha and Pseudepigrapha are also a relevant and important body of material, but demand a separate study; they will be included only occasionally for comparative purposes.

[8]E. Puech ("Quelques aspects de la restauration du Rouleau des Hymnes (1QH)," *JJS* 39 [1988] 55) has recently argued that אודכה is required since the scribe would then have begun writing exactly in the middle of the line as is his usual style. Puech, however, now agrees (oral communication) that this rule of spacing is not absolute; cf. col. 3:19. In ten cases in 1QH the formula is אודכה אדוני (אלי) כי. There are two examples without כי (11:15, 14:23) but none with אודכה followed by a participle. The formula ברוך אתה plus a participle is attested in 1QS 11:15 and this is a strong argument for the reconstruction of ברוך אתה in 14:8.

134

Eileen Schuller

reconstructed to read ברוך] אתה אדוני אשׂ]ר;[9] and, more tentatively, ברוֹ]ך אתה has been suggested in 15:8.[10] In addition, 1QS concludes with a hymn (10:9-11:22) which is very similar to the "Hymns of the Community" in 1QH; 11:15 is a blessing ברוך אתה אלי הפותח לדעה לב עבדכה.

Given the difficulty of establishing where each unit begins and ends in 1QH, the discussion of how a blessing functions in a given psalm can often only be tentative. The *baruk* formula is clearly felt to be an appropriate way to begin a composition. It is unmistakably used in this way (after a *vacat*) in 10:14, in 14:8 (if this is the correct restoration) and in the corrected version of 5:20. Various scholars have proposed divisions so that one or more of 11:27, 29 and 32, 15:8 and 16:8 begin a new psalm, but these are all much more tentative.[11] In 1QS 11:15 too, the blessing seems to start a new stanza or section.[12] The impetus to begin a psalm with the *baruk* formula is not a direct imitation of a biblical prototype, since in the Psalter only Ps 144 begins in this way (ברוך יהוה צורי). The correction/substitution in 5:20 suggests that ברוך אתה was considered interchangeable with אודכה, which is attested as a biblical opening formula.[13] It can be observed that the group of *Hodayot* that have been designated "Hymns of the Teacher" uses only אודכה as an introductory formula

---

[9]If E. Puech is correct with this restoration ("Un hymne essénien en partie retrouvé et les Béatitudes," *RevQ* 13 (1988) 59-88), his reading of the rest of the line (5:15), ת]כופר רוח בשר אשׂ]ר, is problematic, since there is no precedent for an imperfect verb after אשׂר in a *baruk* formula. It is preferable to follow Sukenik's reading of the traces אשׂ]ר ה]כינתה.

[10]This is the reconstruction of H. Stegemann. See H.-W. Kuhn, *Enderwartung und gegenwärtiges Heil* (SUNT 4; Göttingen: Vandenhoeck & Ruprecht, 1966) 103-104, n. 6.

[11]Where three *baruk* expressions occur in such close proximity in col. 11, it is clear that not all can begin a new psalm. If 11:29 is an introductory blessing, as suggested by S. Holm-Nielsen (*Hodayot: Psalms from Qumran* [Denmark: Åarhus, 1960]), 11:27 would be an example of a blessing at the very end of a psalm. J. Licht (*The Thanksgiving Scroll* [Jerusalem: Bialik Institute, 1957] in Hebrew) proposes a triple blessing within a single psalm, with a new composition beginning only in the first part of col. 13.

[12]Theoretically, the blessing could be the conclusion of a section, as suggested by Sh. Talmon, "'The Manual of Benedictions' of the Sect of the Judaean Desert," *RevQ* 2 (1960) 477. However, the presence of a sign in the margin and two dots between הפארתו and ברוך indicate a scribal error at this point, probably the omission of a *vacat* before ברוך to indicate a new section.

[13]For the formula, see Isa 12:1, Ps 138:1; also 75:2. On the close relationship of *brk* and *ydh* as verbs of praise, see C. Westermann, *Praise and Lament in the Psalms* (Atlanta: John Knox, 1965, 1981), 25-30. Note the LXX translation of *ydh* in Isa 12:1 and 38:19 with εὐλογεῖν and the discussion of R. Ledogar, *Acknowledgement: Praise Verbs in the Early Greek Anaphora* (Rome: Pontifical Biblical Institute, 1968) 99-114.

135

(2:31, 4:5, 5:5, the original of 5:20,[14] 7:6, 8:4), while the "Hymns of the Community" have either אודכה (3:19, 11:3) or ברוך אתה (10:14, and probably 14:8) as the opening phrase.

A number of features of the actual form deserve comment. All of these *berakot* are cast in the second person ברוך אתה. There are only two biblical precedents, 1 Chr 29:10 and Ps 119:12.[15] The consistent use of the second person in the *Hodayot* is in marked contrast to the third-person form which is so regular in biblical texts and in many non-biblical compositions.[16] The second person transforms the *berakah* into a direct address to God (rather than a "proclamation" about God)[17] and allows it to blend easily into the rest of the psalm which is in the second person.

In contrast to the biblical blessings,[18] the tetragrammaton is never used in the *Hodayot*. This is, of course, part of a wider phenomenon, the non-use of the divine name in free compositions of the Qumran community.[19] All of the blessings have instead אדוני or אלי (1QS 10:15), except for 11:29 and frg. 4, 15, which move immediately to the ascription.

About half of the biblical blessings contain an ascription, that is, a descriptive phrase or epithet after the divine name and before the motive clause or doxological praise. In the bible, the most common phrase is "God of Israel" or a similar expression such as "God of our fathers" (Ezra 7:27) or "your God" (2 Sam 18:28). In contrast, in 1QH an ascription is used less frequently and is always אל plus an attribute of God: 10:14, [חסד] אל הרחמים; 11:29, אל הרחמים והחנינה; אל הרחמים; frg. 4, 15, אל הדעות; similar phraseology comes in the blessing in 1QM 14:8, אל החסדים.

---

[14]The introduction of ברוך אתה into a "Hymn of the Teacher" suggests that at least at one stage the scribe/community was not conscious of the distinction of two groups of hymns. It is difficult to establish on paleographic grounds whether the corrector is the second scribe of 1QH, or if this is the work of a third hand.

[15]Sometimes the MT in Neh 9:5b is emended to give a second person blessing; see the discussion of H. G. M. Williamson, *Ezra, Nehemiah* (Word Commentary; Waco: Word Books, 1985) 303-304.

[16]Cf., e.g., 1QM 14:4, 11QPsª 19:7-8, 26:13-14.

[17]For the distinction, see Towner, "'Blessed be YHWH,'" 392-93.

[18]The only biblical blessings without the tetragrammaton are Gen 14:20 and Dan 3:28, which are blessings by foreigners, although in other cases (e.g., 1 Kgs 5:21, 10:9) the biblical authors have not hesitated to put the name of God on the lips of pagans.

[19]See H. Stegemann, "Religionsgeschichtliche Erwägungen zu den Gottesbezeichnungen in den Qumrantexten," in M. Delcor, ed., *Qumrân: sa piété, sa théologie et son milieu* (BETL 46; Paris: Duculot, 1978) 139-217 and E. Schuller, *Non-Canonical Psalms from Qumran: A Pseudepigraphic Collection* (HSM 28; Atlanta: Scholars, 1986) 40-41.

Eileen Schuller

The "motive clause" is usually introduced by אשר (11:27, frg. 4, 15, frg. 15, 6) or כי (10:14, 11:32-33, 5:20). Both can be found in the Psalter,[20] but apart from the psalms אשר is normative for biblical blessings. The verb of the clause is in the second person perfect and this is a distinctive feature of the *Hodayot*; in biblical and rabbinic blessings the verb is third person.[21] Two blessings (11:29 and 16:8) are distinctive in that they do not have a clause describing the action of God in the past which has generated the blessing, but rather continue with general descriptive praise of God's qualities in nominal form. The absence of specific praise recalls in some ways the "doxologies" of the Psalter,[22] but the *Hodayot* blessings do not have the distinctive "forever and ever" language.

The blessing in 1QS 11:15 is to be noted specially; here the motive for praise is not a past divine deed, but God's present and on-going action expressed by a participle.[23] Given the extensive discussion about the origin and development of the participle in standard rabbinic blessings,[24] it is important to observe the number of cases where participles occur in blessings from the Second Temple period. A few examples, in fact, come from the Psalter itself (Pss 144:1, 135:21 and especially 72:18).[25] In addition to the occurrence in 1QS 11:15, we have already noted that 1QH 14:8 is probably to be restored as [ברוך אתה] אדוני הנותן. Other examples are to be found in the Daily Prayers (4Q503 frgs. 1-6, 3:7, frg. 16, 6:8) and Prayers for the Festivals (4Q509 frg. 4, 4, frg. 206, 1). The War Scroll has preserved fragments of two thanksgiving hymns, both probably of Maccabean origin, in which *baruk* is followed by a participle: 14:4, a blessing of God in the strict sense, ברוך אל ישראל השומר, and 14:8, a blessing of God's name, [ברוך] שמכה אל החסדים השומר (and in the parallel text in 4Q491 frg. 8-10, 1:6, ובר[וך] שמך אל ה[ח]סדים המ[פ]ליא). Finally, there are a few examples in 11QPs[a], all in psalms which are non-Qumranic in origin: the Plea for Deliverance (19:7-8) ברוך יהוה עושה צדקות מעטר חסידיו;

[20]For כי, see Pss 28:6, 31:22; for אשר Ps 66:20; for ש Ps 124:6.

[21]Heinemann (*Prayer*, 77-79) points out that the second person is not entirely unknown in rabbinic blessings and gives a few examples.

[22]Cf. Pss 41:14, 89:53, 106:48, 1 Chr 29:10. See the discussion of Heinemann, *Prayer*, 83 (n. 9) and 134-38.

[23]J. Murphy O'Connor ("La Genèse littéraire de la règle de la Communaute," *RB* 76 [1969] 544-46) has suggested that certain distinctive features of the hymn in 1QS (the expanded promise, the absence of a soteriological confession) indicate that this was "un hymne réservé a l'usage d'un group particulier ... eux qui allaient être admis comme membres au cours de la cérémonie." If so, the choice of a participle is particularly appropriate.

[24]Heinemann, *Prayer*, 85-93.

[25]It is surprising to find Heinemann so adamant that no blessings "with the main content clause in the form of an active participle" are to be found in the doxologies of the Psalter (*Prayer*, 89 n. 18); he does not explain how he reads a text like Ps 72:18.

137

the Hymn to the Creator (26:13-14), ברוך עושה ארץ בכוחו מכין תבל בחוכמתו,
and probably Ps 154 (18:18), ברוך] יהוה גואל עני.[26] The example of the Hymn of
the Creator, which is clearly related to Jer 10:12 = 51:15, is to be noted; it furnishes
strong support for Heinemann's suggestion that the *baruk* formula has been combined
with "various attributes of praise in the active participial form gleaned from the
Bible."[27]

In addition to the *Hodayot*, 4Q510-511, "Cantiques du Sage," provide a few
additional examples of blessings within Qumranic hymnic texts (4Q511 frg. 16, 4;
frgs. 52-59, 3:4 [largely restored], frg. 63, 4:2).[28] For the most part, the context is
very fragmentary, although in one instance (frg. 63, 4:2) a doxological-type blessing,
ברוך שמכה לעולמי עד אמן אמן, clearly forms the conclusion of a unit. As in the
Hodayot, these are in the second person form. The ascription in 4Q511 frgs. 52-59,
3:4 is to be noted: ברוך את[ה אלי מלך הכבו]ד, particularly when considered along
with the one example which we have of a blessing pronounced by the angels in the
heavenly liturgy (4Q403 frg. 1, 1:28) ברוך [ה]אד[ו]ן מל[ך ה]כול. These two texts
provide our earliest evidence for the mention of God's kingship in a benediction, a
feature which became an intrinsic component of the rabbinic *berakot*.[29]

2. Blessings and Curses

At Qumran there is a small but distinctive group of texts which deal with the
pronouncement of blessings and curses within the context of covenant. 1QS 1:16-
3:12 describes the ceremony of entrance into the community, including the rubric that
the priests and Levites "shall bless the God of salvation and all the deeds of his
faithfulness" (1:19), but no actual texts of the blessings of God are preserved.
4QBerakot (4Q286-90 and possibly 4Q291-93)[30] are copies of a liturgical collection

---

[26]Following the suggestion of J. Strugnell, "Notes on the Text and Transmission
of the Apocryphal Psalms 151, 154 (= Syr II) and 155 (= Syr III)," *HTR* 59 (1966) 275.
Contrast J. A. Sanders (*The Psalms Scroll of Qumrân Cave 11* [DJD 4; Oxford: Claredon
1965] 64), who restores [ברכו].

[27]Heinemann, *Prayer*, 92. Heinemann, however, wants to reconstruct a "pure"
pattern, ברוך אתה אדוני with a participle. The evidence of these text does not support
this understanding of the process of development since so many of these blessings are
in the third person.

[28]A few other traces may suggest additional blessings; e.g., 4Q511 frg. 169, 1,
ב.[רוך]. It is possible to restore another blessing in 4Q511 frg. 30, 2-3, ברוך] אתה אלי
חתמתה בעד כולם although the omission of אשר is unusual (but cf. 4Q504 frg. 3, 2:2).

[29]B. Ber. 12a, j. Ber. 9:12d. The inclusion of the phrase מלך העולם is usually
judged to be a second century CE reaction to Gnosticism, or a protest against Roman
emperor-worship; see Heinemann, *Prayer*, 94-97, and the extensive bibliography there.

[30]J. T. Milik, "Milkî-ṣedeq et Milkî-reša‘ dans les anciens écrits juifs et
chrétiens," *JJS* 28 (1972) 130-37.

of blessings and curses for use at the annual Renewal of Covenant, but unfortunately for our purposes the curse section is much better preserved than the blessings.

When this covenant material is taken up secondarily and incorporated into a battle ritual within the War Scroll, we do have the actual text of a blessing of God, 1QM 13:2, ברוך אל ישראל בכול מחשבת קודשו ומעשי אמתו.[31] The third-person proclamatory style seems more common in this type of material; note that two of the three-fold curses in 4Q286 frg. 10, 2:1-12 are third person, though the curse of the Angel of Destruction and the Spirit of Abbadon is a direct address in the second person. Similarly, the nominal construction with ב (rather than an אשר or כי clause) may be influenced by the curses (e.g., 4Q286 frg. 10, 2:2-7, 1QM 13:4, 1QS 2:5).

3. Liturgical Ritual Texts

Some years ago, it was suggested that the Qumran community must have provided some sort of a "Manual of Benedictions" for the various set times of prayer which were instituted to replace sacrifice as the core of their liturgical life.[32] Five collections of such prayers have recently been published, our only examples of liturgical prayers from the Second Temple period; the very fact that they were put into writing reflects a somewhat different perspective than that of the rabbis who warned that "those who write down prayers are like those who burn the Torah" (*b. Shab.* 115b). All of these prayers include blessings, although there is considerable variation in both the formal pattern and the placement of the *berakah*.

One of the lengthiest texts is 4Q503, a collection of blessings to be recited in the evening and morning of each day of the month. The dependence upon the lunar calendar and the absence of specific sectarian terminology suggest that these prayers reflect an early stage in the development of the community.[33] The pattern is relatively fixed, though with some flexibility. After a standardized dating formula followed by the rubric וברכו וענו ואמרו, the prayer begins with the set phrase ברוך אל ישראל, partially or completely preserved or restored in over twenty instances. There is evidence, however, of some variation, as in the prayers for the twenty-fifth day, ברוך אלוהי כול קודשים (frgs. 37-38, 12:13-14, 18-19), and occasionally the opening blessing may need to be reconstructed in the second person (frgs. 33-35-36, 11:1, 6-7).[34] This is followed either by אשר with a third-person verb as in the

---

[31]For a more detailed exegesis of col. 13, see J. L. Duhaime, "La rédaction de 1QM XIII et l'évolution du dualism à Qumrân," *RB* 84 (1977) especially 227-32.

[32]Sh. Talmon, "'The Manual of Benedictions,'" 476.

[33]J. M. Baumgarten, "4Q503 (Daily Prayers) and the Lunar Calendar," *RevQ* 12 (1987) 399-407.

[34]Note the singular appearance of ברו]ך אל א|שר in frgs. 33-35-36, 11:11, but the reconstruction here is far from certain. The extended ascription reconstructed by Baillet in frgs. 48-50, 7-8 אלו]ים ברוך אל יש]ראל אל כול צבאות is suspicious. The absence of a standard formula in Baillet's presentation of frgs. 1-6, 3:12-13 is further reason to

biblical pattern (frgs. 24-25, 7:4; frgs. 29-32, 8:2-3; frg. 76, 2) or, particularly where the motive clause refers to the cosmic order, with a participle (frgs.1-6, 3:6-7; frg. 16, 6:8).[35] A second *baruk* formula comes at the end of the prayer, reminiscent of the *ḥatima*/eulogy blessing in the statutory prayers. In this position, the form is either ברוך אל ישראל (e.g., frg. 65, 4) or ברוך שמכה אל ישראל (e.g., frg. 66, 2-3) or a second person ברו[ך אתה אל ישראל אשר העמדת] (frgs. 33-34, 10:20). In the latter example, the verb continues in the second person as in the *Hodayot*. All of these prayers end with a distinctive response-like formula שלום/שלום אל עליכה ישראל.

4Q504-506 is a collection of prayers for each day of the week.[36] The absence of strictly sectarian language and the early date of the manuscript might suggest a non-Qumranic origin. In contrast to 4Q503, there is no introductory *berakah*, but rather the prayer for each day (with the exception of the Sabbath, frgs. 1-2, 7:4) begins with the formula זכור אדוני (4Q504 frg. 5, 2:3, 8:1, and most probably frg. 4, 16).[37] All the prayers end with a *berakah* (followed by אמן אמן). The pattern is consistent: all are third person (אדוני [ברוך frg. 4, 14 and ל[אל הא ברוך frg. 3, 2:2), and followed by a perfect verb (frgs. 1-2, 7:2 הצילנו אשר; frg. 4, 14 הודי[ענו אשר; frg. 3 2:2, where Baillet already noted the unusual absence of אשר). The blessing in frg. 6, 20, ברוך אדוני, is to be noted, since it indicates that the *baruk* formula could also occur within the body of a prayer and not only in the closing benediction. Given that the prayers themselves are direct addresses to God in the second person, the blessing formula necessarily seems somewhat isolated and retains its biblical flavor as proclamatory praise "about" rather than "to" God.

Prayers for the festivals are preserved in 4Q507-509 and an overlapping copy of parts of the same text in 1Q34 and 34[bis]. These prayers are similar in form to the Daily Prayers in 4Q504 in that they begin with זכור אדוני.[38] Although the preserved portion of these prayers is often very fragmentary, they all seem to conclude

suspect that the fragments have been wrongly placed (see the discussion of Baumgarten, "4Q503 (Daily Prayers)," 401).

[35]Perhaps a participle could be reconstructed in frgs. 7-9, 4:6-7, and also in frg. 64, 8 rather than a nominal phrase as Baillet suggests.

[36]Following the interpretation of Baillet (DJD 7, 137) and E. Chazon, "Is *Divrei Ham-me'orot* a Sectarian Prayer?" in D. Dimant and U. Rappaport, eds., *The Dead Sea Scrolls: Forty Years of Research* (Jerusalem: Ben-Zvi, 1990). For a contrary view which sees this text as an early version of *Taḥanun* for Monday and Thursday, see M. T. Lehmann, "A Re-Interpretation of 4QDibrê Ham-Me'oroth," *RevQ* 17 (1964) 106-10; also M. Weinfeld, "Prayer and Liturgical Practice in Qumran," *The Dead Sea Scrolls: Forty Years of Research.*

[37]Although not preceded by a full *vacat* line (as in frgs. 1-2, 7:3, frg. 3, 2:4), frg. 4, 16 is almost certainly the beginning of a prayer for a new day. E. Chazon notes (oral communication) that in her reordering of the fragments, there is just enough room to restore the title of the prayer in the lacuna at the beginning of the line.

[38]4Q507 frg. 3, 3, 4Q508 frg. 2, 2 = 1Q34[bis] frg. 2+1, 6, 4Q509 frg. 131, 2:5.

with a *berakah* in the third person ברוך אדוני.[39] In the prayer for the New Year this is followed by a כי clause with a perfect verb, and elsewhere by a participle.[40] A distinctive feature is that the concluding blessing is itself preceded by a profession of praise and a long rubric-like introduction, e.g., for the Day of Atonement ואנו נודה לשמך לעולם ועד כי לזאות בראתנו וזה אשר נשיב לך ברוך.[41]

4Q502 contains a number of blessings, most only partially preserved; on the basis of certain phraseology, Baillet had entitled this "Rituel de Mariage" but more recently it has been suggested[42] that this is a ritual to honor an elderly couple joining the sect. In any case, the vocabulary here is much more clearly sectarian than in the prayers examined so far (cf. frg. 16 and 1QS 4:4-6). The most completely preserved blessing comes in frg. 24, 2, ברוך אל ישראל אשר עזר[ון]; other blessings, though only partially preserved, indicate that this was a set pattern (frg. 19, 6, frg. 30, 3, frg. 31, 1, frg. 96, 2, frg. 101, 3, frg. 104, 4, frg. 125, 4).[43] As in 4Q503, the blessing comes at the beginning; the texts are too fragmentary to establish whether the prayer also ended with a *berakah*.

Finally, 4Q512 is a combination of halakic regulations and blessings, presumably recited as part of a purification ritual. None of the blessings is preserved completely, but the second person formula, ברוך אתה אל ישראל, is surprisingly standard;[44] in frg. 41, 3, the scribe wrote ב[רוך אל ישר]אל, then added את above the line, which may suggest that the formula was not automatic. The motive clause is expressed by אשר and a second person verb (frg. 1-6, 12:8; also frg. 30, 7:8-9).

From the cumulative evidence of these five collections of prayers,[45] it is clear that the custom of beginning or ending a ritual prayer with a *berakah* (or, more rarely, using the blessing in both positions) was well established in the Second Temple Period. The pattern of the blessing is relatively, though not absolutely, fixed within each collection. The majority of these blessings are in the third person as in the

---

[39] 4Q507 frg. 2, 2, frg. 3, 1; 4Q509 frg. 3, 9 = 1Q34[bis] frg. 2+1, 4, 4Q509 frg. 4, 4.

[40] 4Q509 frg. 4, 4, possibly also frg. 206, 1.

[41] 1Q34[bis] frg. 3, 6-7 = 4Q508 frg. 1, 2-3; also 4Q509 frg. 3, 8-9.

[42] J. M. Baumgartnen, "4Q502, Marriage or Golden Age Ritual?" *JJS* 34 (1983) 125-35.

[43] Given the regularity of the third person, Baillet is probably correct in not reconstructing any second person blessings, even where this is theoretically possible (frgs. 7-10, 14, frg. 14, 4, frg. 32, 1); furthermore, frg. 14, 4 would be the only example from Qumran of ברוך אתה followed by a third-person verb, as in the classic rabbinic pattern.

[44] See, e.g., frg. 35, 4:6; frg. 30, 7:8, 21; frgs. 1-6, 12:1-2, 7-8; frg. 43, 2:2.

[45] 4Q513 may have also contained some blessings along with halakic material, but we only have the evidence of one occurrence of ברוך with no context (frg. 14, 2). Note also 4Q519 frg. 1, 4, ברוך, from "fragments non classés."

standard biblical pattern; the second person comes only in the Purification Ritual and occasionally in 4Q503. It can be observed that sectarian texts (those actually composed at Qumran) i.e., 1QH, 1QS, 4Q510-511, and 4Q512, all use the ברוך אתה form consistently, although a text like 4Q502 which seems to be of Qumran provenance has the third-person form throughout.

4. Blessings Within a Narrative

In the manuscripts from Qumran there are a few blessings which occur within a narrative context. In 1QapGen 20:12 Abraham begins his prayer בריך אנתה אל עליון מרי לכול עלמים. Although the earliest biblical spontaneous prose prayers never begin with a *berakah*, such an introduction is attested in many individual prayers from the post-exilic period.[46] The blessing in the second person allows an easy and spontaneous flow into the prayer itself in which God is addressed directly.

The beginning of a blessing is preserved in the Psalms of Joshua, 4Q379 frg. 22, 2:5 ברוך יהוה אלהי י[שראל, just before the famous curse of Joshua. In her initial publication of this fragment,[47] Newsom suggests that the previous lines probably narrated the destruction of Jericho and the victory celebration; she briefly relates the *baruk* phrase to the closing formula of some of the biblical psalms. While it is certainly possible that line five concludes a psalm begun in lines 1-4, it may be that what we have here is rather a short, spontaneous blessing of one and one-half to two lines. In addition to the dozen or so biblical examples, this type of brief affirmation of praise in a non-cultic setting continued to be popular in Second Temple narrative texts.[48] Given that the Psalms of Joshua are modeled so closely on biblical language and style, the author may have placed on the lips of Joshua a spontaneous blessing in praise of God who wrought the destruction of Jericho.

A number of texts recount a spontaneous blessing of God by an individual on the occasion of receiving a revelation.[49] The Aramaic of *1 Enoch* 22:14 is preserved in 4QEn[d] frg. 1, 11:2 להוה בריך דין קושפֿ]. In terms of form, it can be noted that the Aramaic confirms the third-person form of the blessing (as found in most Ethiopian manuscripts) in contrast to the second person in the Greek which was probably influenced by the common Septuagintal second person blessing pattern.[50]

---

[46]Cf., e.g., 1 Kgs 8:15, 8:56; 1 Chr 29:10; Tob 3:11, 8:5, 11:14; *1 Enoch* 84:2; *Jub.* 25.12; 1 Macc 4:30.

[47]Carol Newsom, "The 'Psalms of Joshua' from Qumran Cave 4," *JJS* 39 (1988) 68-69.

[48]Cf. 2 Macc 1:17, 15:34; *Par. Jer.* 5:8, 12; *Jos. and Asen.* 3:3; *Bib. Ant.* 27:13, 31:9; *Jub.* 8:17.

[49]Cf., e.g., *1 Enoch* 25:7, 27:5, 36:4 81:3, 90:40; Dan 2:19.

[50]For the pattern, cf. Tob 3:11, 8:5, 15; Pr Azar 3, 29. For the sake of completeness, it should be noted that J. T. Milik (*The Books of Enoch: Aramaic*

Eileen Schuller

Our study of blessing of God found in texts at Qumran has purposefully been mainly descriptive. Yet even this preliminary collation of materials leaves no doubt as to the frequency of the blessing formula in a wide variety of hymns and prayers of the Second Temple period, both those composed at Qumran and those from other sources. This material, particularly when combined with similar blessings in the Apocrypha and Pseudepigrapha, can afford us a glimpse into the diversity, perhaps even the experimentation with forms and patterns at a time prior to the rabbinic concern with standardization. Yet even at this stage all is not chaos, and more careful attention to form-critical details of the *berakah* can often be an invaluable guide in the restoration of fragmentary texts.

Fragments of Qumran Cave 4 [Oxford: Oxford University Press, 1976] 289-90) restores another blessing in 4QEnastr[b] frg. 23, 4, reading עלמא בר[י]ך אא or בר[י]ך מ[ן עלמא. The restoration is very uncertain both because the phrase is unusual and because the overlapping text in 4QEnastr[c] frg. 1, 2 does not have space for בריך.

4Q185 AND JEWISH WISDOM LITERATURE

Thomas H. Tobin, S.J.
Loyola University, Chicago

The purpose of this article is twofold. First, I want to explore the relationship of 4Q185 to other Jewish literature, including the texts found at Qumran. Second, based on this exploration, I shall suggest something about the possible dating and provenance of the text.

The remains of 4Q185 consist of three columns.[1] Each of the three columns originally consisted of fifteen lines. Of these three columns the first five or six lines of col. 1 are fragmentary; most of col. 3 is fragmentary, and it is only in frgs. 1-2, 3:8-11 that there is enough material to gain some sense of context; finally while col. 2 contains all fifteen lines, a small center section in almost all of the lines is missing.

The text is in the form of a wisdom instruction or admonition.[2] In this respect, 4Q185 is similar to sections from Proverbs 1-9 (especially 3:13-24; 4:1-9) and Ben Sira (especially 6:18-37; 14:20-15:10; 16:24-18:14). Those to whom the text is addressed are referred to in various ways: "sons of man" (frgs. 1-2, 1:9), "my people" (frgs. 1-2, 1:13), "you simple ones" (frgs. 1-2, 1:14), "my sons" (frgs. 1-2, 2:3). With the exception of "my people," the forms of address are common in Jewish wisdom literature.[3] There is no indication from the text of 4Q185 of who the speaker is. Based on the forms of address, the speaker was probably meant to be Solomon around whom wisdom traditions tended to cluster or a sage such as Ben

---

[1]4Q185 was originally published in J. M. Allegro (with the collaboration of A. A. Anderson), *Qumrân Cave 4: I (4Q158–4Q186)* (DJD 5; Oxford: Clarendon, 1968) 85-87, plates XXIX-XXX. Allegro's work has been extensively corrected and revised by J. Strugnell, "Notes en marge du volume V des 'Discoveries in the Judaean Desert of Jordan,'" *RevQ* 7 (1970) 269-73. Further revisions are to be found in H. Lichtenberger, "Eine weisheitliche Mahnrede in den Qumranfunden (4Q185)," in M. Delcor, ed., *Qumrân: Sa piété, sa théologie et son milieu* (BETL 46; Paris-Gembloux: Duculot, 1978) 151-62. English translations of 4Q185 are found in Allegro, Strugnell, and G. Vermes, *The Dead Sea Scrolls in English* (3d ed.; London: Penguin, 1987) 242-43.

[2]Strugnell, "Notes en marge," 269; Lichtenberger, "Eine weisheitliche Mahnrede," 151-52.

[3]"My people" does appear, however, as the opening address of Ps 78:1, a sapiential psalm.

Sira. There is nothing to suggest that the work is meant to be taken as the admonition of someone like Enoch or one of the patriarchs.

The point of the instruction or admonition is to exhort the hearers not to follow vanity but to seek God's wisdom and follow his will. In this way one can withstand the judgment of God's angels. While it is not completely clear whether the hearer is to seek God's wisdom or his law, frgs. 1-2, 1:14 ("draw wisdom from the mighty wisdom of God") suggests that God's wisdom is the immediate reference in the speaker's mind.[4]

In general, both the content and the language of 4Q185 are quite similar to Jewish wisdom literature such as Proverbs, Ben Sira, and the sapiential Psalms. The only element in 4Q185 not found in these Jewish wisdom texts is that of the angels serving as agents or instruments of judgment (frgs. 1-2, 1:8-9; 2:6). This will be of some help in situating 4Q185 within the history of Jewish wisdom literature and of Qumran literature.

One of the overall characteristics of 4Q185 is the extent to which it draws upon other biblical texts. 4Q185 is quite anthological in style; much of its imagery and language is drawn from the Psalms and other Jewish sapiential literature. The following are some of the more notable borrowings.

(1) The images which dominate frgs. 1-2, 1:9-13 are heavily influenced by a number of biblical texts. The most obvious of these texts is Isa 40:6-8. Both texts use metaphors of grass (חציר) and the fading beauty (חסד) of the flower (ציץ) to describe human life. In addition both texts speak of the breath (רוח) of God blowing (נשבה) on human beings and their consequent withering (יבש). While the parallels with Isa 40:6-8 are the most striking, very similar imagery is also found in Ps 90:5-6, Ps 92:5-9, and especially in Ps 103:15-17. As in frgs. 1-2, 1:13 (and possibly 11) the image of the fading flower is linked to that of the shadow in Job 14:1-2. A similar linking of these two images is also found in Ps 102:11 and Ps 144:3-4.

(2) 4Q185 frgs. 1-2, 1:14-15 ("Remember the wonderful works he did in Egypt and his miracles in [the land of Ham].") clearly draws on Ps 105:5 ("Remember the wonderful works that he has done, his signs, and the judgments he uttered.") and Ps 105:27 ("He [God] sent Moses his servant and Aaron whom he had chosen. They wrought his signs among them and miracles in the land of Ham.").

(3) Much of the imagery and language of 4Q185 frgs. 1-2, 1:13-2:15 is drawn from Jewish wisdom literature, especially from Proverbs.

(a) The forms of address:

    (i) "you simple ones" (פתאים) (frgs. 1-2, 1:14): Prov 1:22, 32; 8:5; 9:6; 14:18; 17:12 (see Pss 19:8; 116:6; 119:130).

    (ii) "(my) sons" (בני) (frgs. 1-2, 2:3): Prov 4:1; 5:7; 7:24; 8:32.

(b) Calls to listen (שמע) (frgs. 1-2, 1:13; 2:3): Prov 1:8; 4:1; 5:7; 7:24; 8:32.

---

[4]See Strugnell, "Notes en marge," 269, 273.

(c) Exhortations to seek wisdom:
  (i) "to search for" (חקר) (frgs. 1-2, 2:1): Prov 25:2; 28:11.
  (ii) "to seek" (בקש) (frgs. 1-2, 2:14): Prov 2:4; 11:27; 14:6; 15:14;
       17:11; 18:15; 28:5.
  (iii) "to cling to (החזיק) (frgs. 1-2, 2:14): Prov 3:18; 4:13.
(d) Words for "path" and "way."
  (i) "a way to life" (דרך לחיים) (frgs. 1-2, 2:1-2); Prov 6:23.
  (ii) "way" and "path" linked together (דרך נתיבה) (frgs. 1-2, 2:4):
       Prov 1:15; 7:25; 8:2; 12:28.
  (iii) "highway" (מסלה) (frgs. 1-2, 2:2): Prov 16:17.
(e) Promised rewards:
  (i) "length of days" (ארך ימים) (frgs. 1-2, 2:12): Prov 3:2, 16.
  (ii) "fatness of bone" (דשן עצם) (frgs. 1-2, 2:12): Prov 15:30.
  (iii) "gladness" (שמחה) (frgs. 1-2, 2:12): Prov 10:28; 14:10, 13; 21-25.

Obviously none of the above words or phrases is found exclusively in Proverbs, but the clustering of them in both Proverbs and 4Q185 indicates that the writer of 4Q185 drew heavily on the language and the imagery of Proverbs.

(4) The image of the "snare of the fowler" (פח יקוש) (frgs. 1-2, 2:5) is found in Ps 91:3 and in Hos 9:8.

(5) While col. 3 is very fragmentary, the image of God searching and trying human hearts (frgs. 1-2, 3:11-13) reflects Jer 11:20; 17:10, 20:12.

While the above list is not exhaustive, it should be sufficient to indicate that the author of 4Q185 drew heavily on the images and the language of various biblical texts, especially wisdom texts, in order to write his own admonition on wisdom.

The use of an anthological style of composition in 4Q185 is very similar to that used by Ben Sira. At the end of the 19th century, Solomon Schechter, in his edition of the Hebrew text of Ben Sira found in the Cairo Genizah, pointed out that Ben Sira "though not entirely devoid of original ideas, was, as is well known, a conscious imitator both as to form and as to matter, his chief model being the Book of Proverbs."[5] Schechter then went on to list over 350 phrases, idioms, typical expressions, and even whole verses which were used by the author of Ben Sira and which were drawn from various biblical texts.[6] While Schechter's list is at least exhaustive and probably excessive, the style of Ben Sira is clearly anthological.[7] Both the author of 4Q185 and Ben Sira were clearly making use of the same stylistic technique. While an argument from similar compositional techniques cannot be

[5]S. Schechter and C. Taylor, *The Wisdom of Ben Sira* (Cambridge: Cambridge University Press, 1899) 12.

[6]Ibid. 13-25.

[7]P. Skehan and A. Di Lella, *The Wisdom of Ben Sira* (AB 39; Garden City, NY: Doubleday, 1987) 40-45.

pressed too far since much of post-exilic Jewish literature tends to draw on older biblical texts, 4Q185 and Ben Sira are in this respect stylistically closer to each other than either of them is to Proverbs.

When one turns from the style of 4Q185 to the description of wisdom, 4Q185 is also similar to sections from Proverbs 1-9 and Ben Sira. While the text of 4Q185 is fragmentary, it is reasonably clear that wisdom in 4Q185 is personified as a woman who is to be honorably courted and who will reward the one who does so.

> Let the one who glories in her (wisdom) say,
> "Let him gain possession of her
>   for she is sufficient for him [...] her yield."
> Indeed with her is length of days and fatness of bone and
>   gladness of heart [...]
> and her youth is mercies for him, and salvation [...].
> Happy the man who acquires her
>   and does not play tricks with her
>   [and with a spirit] of deceit does not seek her
>   nor with flatteries cling to her. (frgs. 1-2, 2:11-14)

This type of personification of wisdom is quite similar to that found in Prov 3:13-18; 4:4-9; 7:4 and in Sir 6:23-31; 14:20-15:10. 4Q185, at least in what has been preserved, does not, however, contain any speeches of wisdom herself such as one finds in Prov 1:20-33; 8:1-36 and in Sir 4:11-19; 24:1-33. What has been preserved does, nevertheless, reflect a type of personification found in both Proverbs and Ben Sira.

Since 4Q185 was found among the documents of the community at Qumran, the question arises about the relationship of 4Q185 to the community at Qumran. Was the document written by someone in the community at Qumran, or was it written elsewhere but used by the group at Qumran? Several indications in the text suggest the latter alternative.

(1) The tetragrammaton is used in frgs. 1-2, 2:3. There is no clear example of the use of the tetragrammaton in any sectarian Qumran text which was not considered by them as "canonical." Even in the pesharim, where the copyist uses the tetragrammaton in quoting the biblical text, he does not use it in the actual interpretation of the biblical verse(s). All of the evidence that we have suggests that the Qumran community consistently avoided using the tetragrammaton in works of their own composition.[8]

---

[8]See H. Stegemann, "Religionsgeschlichtliche Erwägungen zu den Gottesbezeichnungen in den Qumrantexten," in M. Delcor, ed., *Qumrân: Sa piété, sa théologie et son milieu* (BETL 46; Paris-Gembloux: Duculot, 1978) 195-217. If the *Temple Scroll*

Thomas H. Tobin, S.J.

(2) When the term "wisdom" (חכמה) occurs in Qumran sectarian writings, it is not personified as it sometimes is in Proverbs, Ben Sira, and 4Q185. The term "wisdom" occurs a number of times in Qumran sectarian literature (e.g., 1QS 4:3, 18, 22, 24; 1QH 1:7, 14, 19; 3:15; 9:17; 10:2; CD 2:3). In Qumran sectarian texts, "wisdom" most often either refers to the providence with which God created and sustains the world (e.g., 1QH 1:7, 14-15, 19-20; 9:17; 10:2) or is connected with the mysteries revealed to the Qumran sectarians (e.g., 1QS 4:3, 18, 22). The closest that they came to a personification of wisdom is in the Damascus Document.

> God loves knowledge.
> Wisdom (חכמה) and understanding He has before Him,
> And prudence and knowledge serve Him.
> Patience and much forgiveness are with Him towards those
>   who turn from transgression. (CD 2:3-5)[9]

Yet even here it seems clear that a simple metaphor is being used that does not involve the personification of wisdom. The way in which wisdom is used in 4Q185, then, is quite unlike the way it is used in Qumran sectarian texts, has none of the sectarian overtones of 1QS, and is much closer to the way that it was used in Proverbs 109 and Ben Sira.

(3) The closest parallel to 4Q185 in any non-biblical text found at Qumran is in 4Q370 (An Admonition Based on the Flood).[10] There are clear literary affinities between 4Q185 frgs. 1-2, 1:13–2:3 and 4Q370 2:5-9. As Carol Newsom has pointed out, the literary affinities are such that there must be some literary relationship between 4Q185 and 4Q370 but that it may not be possible to determine clearly what that relationship was, that is, which text depended on the other.[11] She does conclude, however, that it is unlikely that 4Q370 was composed by the Qumran community. It has none of the distinctive theological themes or terminology found in clearly sectarian writings from Qumran. In addition 4Q370 also uses the tetragrammaton.[12] Because the Qumran text to which 4Q185 has the closest

---

(11QTemple) is a sectarian document, then it probably was considered "canonical," and the tetragrammaton could then be used.

[9]Translations from Qumran texts other than 4Q185 are from G. Vermes, *The Dead Sea Scrolls in English* (sometimes slightly altered).

[10]C. Newsom, "4Q370: An Admonition Based on the Flood," *RevQ* 13 (1988) 23-43.

[11]Ibid. 24, 39-42. She does point out, however, that the parallel section in 4Q370 is significantly shorter than the one in 4Q185 and that one usually assumes that the shorter and more succinct text is the older, i.e., that 4Q185 depends on 4Q370.

[12]Ibid. 23.

affinities was probably not composed at Qumran, this is an additional indication that 4Q185 too was not composed at Qumran.[13]

Although 4Q185 does not reflect the theological or terminological characteristics of the sectarian documents of Qumran, there are several elements in 4Q185 which move beyond what one finds in Proverbs or Ben Sira and which the Qumran sectarians would have found compatible with their own viewpoints.

(1) In frg. 1-2, 1:14 the word גבורה (might) seems to be used in the sense of "mighty wisdom." With the possible exception of Prov 8:14, that word is not used in biblical texts with that meaning. Yet as Strugnell has pointed out, the word is used fairly commonly in that sense at Qumran (see 1QS 4:3; 10:16; 1QH 12:13).[14] Its use in that sense in 4Q185 does not, however, give any indication of a meaning peculiar to Qumran sectarianism. While the use of גבורה in the sense of "mighty wisdom" goes beyond what one finds in biblical wisdom literature and is similar to what one finds in Qumran sectarian texts, its use does not carry along with it the ideological baggage that would suggest that 4Q185 was written at Qumran.

(2) A much more important element in 4Q185 is the role played by the angels in God's judgment of human beings. Although the text is somewhat broken, 4Q185 frgs. 1-2, 1:8-9 seems to read:

And who can stand before his angels (מלאכיו)?
For with a flaming fire [they] will judge [according] to his spirits.[15]

The same motif also seems to be present in frgs. 1-2, 2:6-7:

[and to be secure] before his angels (מלאכיו) for there is no darkness or gloom.

The use of the motif of God using his angels as instruments of judgment goes beyond what is found in Jewish wisdom literature such as Proverbs and Ben Sira.

In Qumran sectarian texts, of course, angels play an important role as instruments or agents of judgment. They appear most prominently in the War Scroll

---

[13]Lichtenberger ("Eine weisheitliche Mahnrede," 161), furthermore, suggests that the defective spelling in 4Q185 also points to its non-Qumran origin. See also E. Qimron, *The Hebrew of the Dead Sea Scrolls* (HSS 29; Atlanta: Scholars, 1986) 17-18.

[14]Strugnell, "Notes en marge," 270.

[15]Lichtenberger ("Eine weisheitliche Mahnrede," 153) prefers to fill in the lacuna at the beginning of frg. 1-2, 1:9 with a singular verb form (He [God] will judge...). Since the previous line is speaking about God's angels, it makes better sense to take "angels" as the subject of "judge" in 1-2, 1:9. "His spirits" in 1-2, 1:9 probably refers to God's spirits. There is no notion in what is preserved of 4Q185 of a sectarian doctrine of "two spirits."

Thomas H. Tobin, S.J.

(1QM). In the War Scroll they fight on the side of the Qumran community against the "sons of darkness" (see 1QM 1:15; 7:6; 10:11; 12:1, 4, 8; 13:11, 12, 14; 17:6). In a passage from the Damascus Document, the author speaks about "angels of destruction" (מלאכי חבל):

> But power, might, and great flaming wrath by the hand of all the angels of destruction towards those who depart from the way (דרך) and abhor the precept (חק). (CD 2:5-6)

These angels of destruction also appear in the Rule of the Community (1QS) in much the same role:

> The visitation of all who walk in it (i.e., ways of darkness) will be a multitude of blows at the hand of the angels of destruction (מלאכי חבל) to fell them forever in the furious wrath of God the Avenger, everlasting terror and continuous reproach, with the humiliation in darkening fires. (1QS 4:11-13)

While the parallels between 4Q185 and these quotations from some Qumran sectarian documents concerning the role played by angels in God's judgment of human beings is certainly clear, they do not lead to the conclusion that 4Q185 was a specifically sectarian document from the Qumran community. This is the case for two reasons. Firstly, an angelic role in divine judgment is not restricted to Qumran. It is also found, for example, in Dan 12:1-4 and, more extensively, in *1 Enoch* 1:9; 10:9-10; 20:1-4; 88:1-3; 90:20-27; 91:15-16; 97:2; 99:3; 100:4-5, 10; 102:3, neither of which is a Qumran sectarian document.[16] Second and more importantly, the avenging role of the angels in Qumran sectarian literature is against those who are not members of their own particular community and who do not accept their teachings or observe their practices, and it is exactly that sectarian bias that is missing from 4Q185. Although 4Q185 frgs. 1-2, 1:1-8 are very fragmentary, there is no indication that the document is talking about judgment on all those who do not have their very particular religious outlook. The answer to the rhetorical question about who can stand before his angels is that no one can (frgs. 1-2, 1:8). 4Q185 does not connect the angels' role in divine judgment with any sectarian viewpoint characteristic of Qumran. What it does indicate, however, is that the author of 4Q185 was in contact with and had accepted notions similar to those found in Jewish apocalyptic literature such as Daniel and sections of *1 Enoch*, especially 91–105.

---

[16] *1 Enoch* 1:9=4QEn[a] frg. 1, 1:15; 10:9-10=4QEn[c] frg. 1, 1:15; 88:1-3=4QEn[e] frg. 4 1:11-13. The relationship of 4Q185 frgs. 1-2, 1:8-9; 2:6 to the admonitory speeches in *1 Enoch* 91–105 deserves to be examined in more detail.

These considerations once again suggest that there is no cogent reason to maintain that 4Q185 was written in the Qumran community. There are elements in 4Q185, both conceptual and verbal, which were also used by the sectarian group at Qumran, emphasized and given their own peculiar interpretation. But it is precisely those emphases and peculiar interpretations which are missing in 4Q185.

If the above analysis is fairly accurate, then 4Q185 is firmly rooted in the tradition of Jewish wisdom literature presented by such works as Proverbs or Ben Sira. Its anthological style connects it more closely with Ben Sira than with Proverbs. In addition, the presence of an angelic role in God's judgment of human beings moves beyond the kind of Jewish wisdom viewpoints found in Ben Sira. It is, however, a role found in Jewish apocalyptic literature and in the sectarian texts of Qumran. This suggests that 4Q185 comes from a point in the development of Jewish wisdom literature when that literature comes to be influenced by a more apocalyptic outlook such as is found especially in *1 Enoch* 91-105.

4Q185, however, does not contain any elements which are characteristic of the Qumran community and does contain several which are not found in Qumran sectarian documents (i.e., the use of the tetragrammaton and the personification of wisdom). 4Q185, then, represents a viewpoint beyond that found in Ben Sira but prior to the sectarian viewpoints found at Qumran.

This leads to the suggestion that the composition of 4Q185 is probably best situated in the period prior to the formation of the Qumran sect and among those groups out of which the sect eventually emerged, that is, in the last part of the third century or the first part of the second century BCE. Given the strongly sectarian character of the Qumran community, it is unlikely that they would have introduced a text written by someone outside the community after the community had been formed. All those outside of the sect were enemies and belonged to the "lot of Belial."[17] Yet, if 4Q185 was composed within the groups out of which the Qumran sectarians emerged, its preservation and recopying at Qumran would have been quite understandable since its outlook would have been perceived as compatible with their own.

---

[17] Confirmation for this is found in the apparent fact that no non-sectarian document found at Qumran needs to be dated late in the history of the sect.

TWO NOTES ON THE ARAMAIC LEVI DOCUMENT

Jonas C. Greenfield and Michael E. Stone
The Hebrew University, Jerusalem

The Aramaic Levi Document (= *ALD*) is known both from manuscripts from the Cairo Geniza and from a number of fragments from Qumran Caves 1 and 4.[1] In addition, fragments of a Greek translation of the work are preserved in one of the Greek manuscripts of the *Testaments of the Twelve Patriarchs*. We would like here to devote some remarks to this interesting document, which casts a certain light on the situation of Judaism in the third pre-Christian century.[2]

The *Testaments of the Twelve Patriarchs* is a work which has raised a good deal of controversy in recent decades. Issues of its origin, context of composition, language and date have been warmly debated. The *Testaments of the Twelve Patriarchs* is composed of the death-bed addresses of the twelve sons of Jacob, including Levi. The *Testament of Levi* as it occurs in *Testaments of the Twelve Patriarchs* will be referred to hereafter as *TPL*. The oldest text of *TPL* is in Greek. In the Cairo Geniza at the end of the last century fragments of an Aramaic document were found dealing with Levi.[3] It was quickly realized that this Aramaic document shared certain expressions and phrases with *TPL* although it was equally clear that it was not the original from which the Greek text of *TPL* had been translated. It contained rather a lot of material that was not found at all in *TPL*; *TPL* seemed to summarize other parts of it, while yet further parts of *TPL* did not occur at all in the Geniza document. The suggestion was made quite quickly that this Geniza *ALD*

---

[1]See M. E. Stone and J. C. Greenfield, "Remarks on the Aramaic Testament of Levi," *RB* 86 (1979) 214-30, where the witnesses are discussed. A full bibliography of the publication of the texts is given there. A recent annotated translation may be found in M. E. Stone, and J. C. Greenfield, "The Aramaic Levi Document," in H. W. Hollander and M. de Jonge, *The Testaments of the Twelve Patriarchs: A Commentary* (Leiden: Brill, 1985) 457-69. The Aramaic text is quoted from R. H. Charles, *The Greek Versions of the Testaments of the Twelve Patriarchs* (Oxford: Oxford University Press, 1908) with emendations as proposed by Greenfield and Stone, "Aramaic Levi." The Greek text is quoted from M. de Jonge et al., *The Testaments of the Twelve Patriarchs* (PVTG 1, 2; Leiden: Brill, 1978).

[2]See M. E. Stone, "Enoch, Aramaic Levi and Sectarian Origins," *JSJ* 19 (1988) 159-70, on the dating of Aramaic Levi Document.

[3]The first publications of the Geniza fragments were by H. L. Pass and J. Arendzen, "Fragments of an Aramaic Text of the Testament of Levi," *JQR* 12 (1900) 651-56, and R. H. Charles and A. Cowley, "An Early Source of the Testaments of the Patriarchs," *JQR* 19 (1907) 566-83.

might have been one of the sources from which *TPL* drew, but this suggestion did not meet universal approval.

This complicated situation was made yet more complex by a further discovery. One manuscript of *TPL* contained rather long expansions, introduced at diverse places throughout the work. Certain of these expansions, and parts of others, were recognized as being Greek translations of the same document that had been found in the Geniza. Moreover, certain Greek expansions in this particular manuscript of *TPL* contained material which did not occur at all in the surviving Aramaic fragments from the Geniza, but which could properly be regarded as translated from lost parts of the *ALD*. The debate about the antiquity of the *ALD* was definitely and finally resolved by the Qumran finds.

1. The Prayer of Levi

In 1956 J. T. Milik published some fragments of *ALD* from a manuscript of Qumran Cave 4.[4] These Aramaic fragments from Qumran confirmed the antiquity of the textual material in Aramaic that had been recovered from the Geniza sixty years before. They presented a prayer, not found among the Aramaic Geniza fragments, but known in Greek translation from the expansion inserted in one manuscript of *TPL* 2:3.[5] We wish to examine here one or two problems associated with this prayer which we will call *Prayer of Levi*.

The Greek translation of *Prayer of Levi* is inserted in *TPL* 2:3. We quote the whole passage of *TPL*:

> 2:1 I, Levi, was conceived in Haran and born there, and after that I came with my father to Shechem.
>
> 2:2 And I was a young man of about twenty years of age, when, with Simeon, I avenged our sister Dinah on Hamor.
>
> 2:3. And when we were feeding the flocks in Abelmaul, the spirit of understanding of the Lord came upon me, and I saw all men corrupting their way and that unrighteousness has built for itself walls and lawlessness sat on towers.
>
> 2:4 And I felt grief for the race of the sons of men and I prayed to the Lord that I might be saved.
>
> 2:5 Then a sleep fell upon me and I beheld a high mountain (that was the mountain of the Shield in Abelmaul);
>
> 2:6 and behold, the heavens were opened and an angel of God said to me: Levi, enter![6]

---

[4]T. Milik, "Le Testament de Lévi en araméen," *RB* 62 (1955) 398-408.

[5]The Aramaic text actually contains some lines preceding and following the material preserved in Greek.

[6] Hollander and de Jonge, *Testaments of the Twelve Patriarchs*, 131-32.

Jonas C. Greenfield and Michael E. Stone

TPL introduces the fragment from *Prayer of Levi* following the phrase "and that unrighteousness has built for itself walls," in verse *TPL* 2:3 although the motive for its introduction was surely the latter part of *TPL* 2:4, "and I prayed to the Lord that I might be saved."

One question which we would like to pose is the following. Does the position at which the *Prayer of Levi* was introduced into the Greek text of *TPL* provide any indication of where it might have stood in the original *ALD*? The first part of the prayer as it can be reconstructed from 4QTLevi^a, col. 1 and the Greek text, reads as follows (the words in bold print survive in 4QTLevi^a):

4QTLevi^a col. 1
lines

4	
5	]**this**
6	]**I**

Greek and 4QTLevi^a

Greek		4QTLevi^a, col. 1
verses		*lines*
*1	Then **I** laundered my garments	6
	and having purified them with pure water,	
	I also [**washed**] my whole self in living water,	7
	and I made **all** my paths upright.	
*3	Then **I lifted up** my eyes and my countenance **to heaven,**	8
	and I opened my mouth and spoke.	
*4	And I stretched out **the fingers of my hands**	9
	and my hands [ ] for truth over against (towards) the holy ones,	
	And I prayed **and said**	10
*5	**O Lord, you** know all hearts,	
	And **you alone understand** all the thoughts of minds.	11
*6	And now my children are with me,	
	And grant me all the **paths of truth.**	12⁷

The first four lines of the text have been lost. The very fragmentary lines 5-6 have no parallel in *Prayer of Levi* as preserved by *TPL*. Presumably the fragmentary lines 6-7 correspond to parts of vv 1-2 of the Greek translation of the *Prayer of Levi*. From *Prayer of Levi* v 6, however, it appears that Levi is surrounded by his children

---

[7] This is a revised form of the authors' translation, published in Hollander and de Jonge, *Testaments*, 458-59.

as he relates events to them. This is reminiscent of an *Abschiedsrede* context, not coherent with the present setting of the prayer referred to in *TPL*.[8]

Following the prayer itself, in *ALD* some further aspects of the context are given, albeit by text which is sadly incomplete.

4QTLevi[a] col. 2, continued

lines
11 **Then I continued on[**
12 **to my father Jacob and ..[**
13 **from Abel Mayyin. Then[**
14 **I lay down and I remained[**
15   **Then I was shown visions[**
16 **In the vision of a vision and I saw the heaven[s**
17 **beneath me, high until it reached to the heaven[s**
18 **to me the gates of heaven, and an angel[**

Thus, according to *Prayer of Levi*, Levi concludes his prayer, goes to his father Jacob, and then goes elsewhere from Abel-Mayyin. At this new location he sees a vision of heaven, and a mountain below him reaching up to heaven. The gates of the heaven are opened. This order of events differs from that to be found in *TPL*. Moreover, *TPL* does not have the text of the prayer, simply saying ηὐξάμην κυρίῳ. ὅπως σωθῶ (2:4) which is, at best, a very limited summary of the material in *ALD*.

M. de Jonge considers, however, that there are definite points of contact between *ALD* col. 2:14-18 and *TPL*. He points to two phrases, *TPL* 2:5, τότε ἐπέπεσεν ἐπ' ἐμὲ ὕπνος and *TPL* 5:1, τὰς πύλας τοῦ οὐρανοῦ.

The whole of *TPL* 5:1 reads: "The angel opened to me the gates of heaven, and I saw the holy temple and the Most High upon a throne of glory." De Jonge points out that the words τὰς πύλας τοῦ οὐρανοῦ are "in any case awkward after the descriptions of several heavens in the previous chapters" of *TPL*.[9] This observation supports the view that *TPL* uses *ALD*. It does not necessarily prove that in *ALD* the *Prayer of Levi* occurred at the point at which it does in *TPL*, i.e., at 2:4, or that the vision, which follows the prayer directly in *ALD*, was in fact the same event as is referred to in *TPL* 5:1.

Some further observations are also in order in this connection. First, it seems likely that *ALD* vv 1-2 are not an integral part of the incident of the prayer related in vv 3ff. but are the end of a preceding event. Both v 1 and v 3 start with τότε and nothing in the text indicates a necessary continuity between them.

---

[8] The fact that the whole of *TPL* is a Testament, and that it opens with Levi summoning his children, does not obviate this difficulty.

[9] M. de Jonge, "Notes on Testament of Levi II-VII," M. S. H. G. Heerma van Voss, ed., *Travels in the World of the Old Testament: M. A. Beek Festschrift* (Assen: van Gorcum, 1974) 138.

Next, it can be questioned whether the present reference to a prayer in *TPL* 2:4 constitutes any sort of evidence for the original location of the prayer presently preserved in the Greek fragment of the *Prayer of Levi*. Did it occur in the original complete *ALD* (of which we have only excerpts and fragments) at a position corresponding to *TPL* 2:3? The chief argument supporting such a view is that adduced by Hollander and de Jonge, i.e., that *TPL* 4:2 reflects the prayer. That verse reads: εἰσήκουσεν οὖν ὁ ὕψιστος τῆς προσευχῆς σου, τοῦ διελεῖν σε ἀπὸ τῆς ἀδικίας, καὶ γενέσθαι αὐτῷ υἱὸν καὶ θεράποντα καὶ λειτουργὸν τοῦ προσώπου αὐτοῦ. "The Most High, therefore, has heard your prayer to separate you from unrighteousness and that you should become to him a son and a servant and a minister of his presence." This verse claims that God has granted three petitions which were made by Levi in his prayer: (a) "to separate you from unrighteousness"; (b) "that you should become to him a son"; (c) "and a servant and minister to his presence." Yet, if the prayer itself is examined, only element (a) is to be found. Thus we read:

Greek   4QTLevi[a], col. 1[10]
  v 7 **Make far** from me, O Lord, the unrighteous spirit,
        and **evil** thought **and fornication**,   line 13
        and **turn** pride **away** from me.

The second and third elements of the prayer to which *TPL* 4:2 refers do not seem to occur in the Aramaic and Greek text of *ALD*. While the third element, a reference to the Levitical and priestly functions of Levi, might be thought to be commonplace, the same can scarcely be said of the second element.

We venture to suggest, however, that in fact both the second and third element in *TPL* 4:2 actually do derive from *ALD*, but that they represent a misconstrual of its text. In cols. 2:10 of *ALD* we read: לבר עבדך מן קֺדֺמיך. The Greek text of *ALD* reads here (v 19): καὶ μὴ ἀποστήσῃς τὸν υἱὸν τοῦ παιδός σου ἀπὸ τοῦ προσώπου σου πάσας τὰς ἡμέρας τοῦ αἰῶνος. The words קֺדֺמיך in 4QTLevi = ἀπὸ τοῦ προσώπου of *ALD* and are reflected by the words "to his presence" of *TPL* 4:2. Equally, the word עבדך (rendered in the Greek translation of *ALD* as τοῦ παιδός σου, a common enough translation) stands behind the words a "servant and minister" of *TPL* 4:2. It remains only to suggest that the reworker of the *ALD* materials in *TPL* misread לבר as "for a son." He might have read this word as if there were a final *kap* on it, "for your son," or read the next word as if a *waw* preceded, "for a son and for..." It is not our claim, of course, that this understanding or interpretation of the Aramaic text is correct; to the contrary.[11] It

[10]The translation of *TPL* is that of Hollander and de Jonge. The translation of the Aramaic Levi Document is that of Greenfield and Stone. Words in Roman type occur only in the Greek text. Those in bold type occur also in the 4Q fragment.

[11]Compare *ALD* Greek v 15: "And turn not your countenance aside from the son of your servant Jacob."

serves, however, to clarify how the text of *ALD* might have been utilized by the redactor of the materials in *TPL*. This observation, of course, provides some further support for Hollander and de Jonge's view that the prayer found in *ALD* is that presumed by the words in *TPL* 4:2. It does not necessarily follow, however, that the order of events in the two documents is the same. The evidence to date is not in favor of *ALD* sharing the order of events in *TPL*. The arguments set forth above, concerning the events preceding the actual prayer, relating to the farewell address context assumed by the prayer, and pointing out the different sequence of events following it, show that the author of *TPL* has changed the original context and sequence of events of *ALD* rather radically.

2. Mebaqqer

In *ALD* there is a section which deals with the the wood that may be burnt upon the altar.[12] Before putting the parts of the slaughtered animal upon the altar one is ordered to examine the wood carefully. The text (9:11; col. c, lines 9-10) reads in Aramaic: ובקר אינון לקדמין מן תולשא "and beforehand examine them for worms." The Greek translation of this in the Athos manuscript reads ἐπισκοπῶν αὐτὰ πρῶτον ἀπὸ παντὸς μολυσμοῦ.[13] This portion of the text has not been recovered from Qumran, but there can be no doubt that the Geniza text is very close to that which would have been found at Qumran.[14] As can be seen from comparing the two texts, the Aramaic *bqr* is translated by a form of the verb ἐπισκοπεῖν. This fits in very well with the practice of the LXX to translate *bqr* and the nominal forms of this root (as well as many occurrences of פקד) by forms of ἐπισκοπεῖν. Since the meaning of *baqqer* in the passage from *ALD* quoted above partakes of a very particular and basic nuance, this occurrence has not been used in the discussion of the *mebaqqer*, the "overseer" or "supervisor" in the Cairo Damascus Covenant (= CD) or in the Rule of the Community (= 1QS), to which we will now turn our attention.

The occurrence of *baqqer* in *ALD* and its translation by ἐπισκοπεῖν, as well as the use of *baqqer* in another text that has not been discussed from this point of view, is the occasion for a brief review of the use of *mebaqqer* in the CD and 1QS.

It is difficult to assess who first associated the ἐπίσκοπος of the early church with the *mebaqqer* of the *Damascus Covenant*, but in the late twenties this equation was proposed by Jeremias.[15] It was discussed and debated by various scholars and was accepted by the *TWNT*.[16] With the discovery and publication of the Rule (1QS)

---

[12]Aramaic text in Charles, *Testaments*, 248.

[13]Greek text in de Jonge, *Testaments*, 46.

[14]As comparison of the two texts shows when both are extant.

[15]J. Jeremias, *Jerusalem zur Zeit Jesu* (Leipzig: Pfeiffer, 1929) 2B.132 ff. See also W. Nauck, "Probleme des frühchristlichen Amtstverstndnisses (I Ptr 5,2f.)," *ZNW* 48 (1957) 200-20.

[16]*TWNT* 2, 604-17, esp. 614-15; *TDNT* 2, 608-22, esp. 618-19.

Jonas C. Greenfield and Michael E. Stone

in which the *mebaqqer* also has an important role, the equation *mebaqqer* = ἐπίσκοπος has received general acceptance. The *mebaqqer* also bears the title פקד בראש הרבים (official in charge of the "Many"). In his function as outlined in the Rule, it is clear that he inducts new members into the group (1QS 6:14) and is in charge of the possessions of the "Many" (מבקר על מלאכת הרבים [1QS 6:20]).[17] These functions are more explicit in the Damascus Covenant where the *mebaqqer* has an important role as an instructor, a leader and an adjudicator (CD 13:7-10). He also inducts new members and and keeps the lists of those admitted into the "Many." The CD, which is a later document, and is set in a broader social context than that of 1QS, speaks also of a מבקר לכל המחנת (overseer of all the camps [CD 14:8-10]) who also functions as an adjudicator of disputes. The *mebaqqer* in CD receives part of the wages earned by members of the "Many" and is in charge of the disbursement of funds for "charitable purposes" (CD 14:12-16). These include support for the aged and orphans (CD 14:12-16).

Of the two terms *paqid* and *mebaqqer*, it is clear that *paqid*, which is less frequently used, is, as has been recognized, a term taken from the biblical repertoire, while *mebaqqer*, as used in these texts, is essentially a new term. In Biblical Hebrew *baqqer* has two closely related usages: "to examine closely" and " to pay attention to." The first usage seems to be limited to examining animals for ritual or other purposes (Lev 13:36; 27:33),[18] and the second usage for a shepherd looking after his flock (Ezek 34: 11f.).[19] The use of *baqqer* for "examining" the wood used for sacrifices quoted above from *ALD* is an extension of the first usage[20] while *baqqer* for "visiting the sick" usual in Mishnaic Hebrew is an extension of the second usage.

A use of *baqqer* that has also not been noted in the discussion of *mebaqqer* is found in the *Genesis Apocryphon* (22.29). God appeared to Abraham in a vision and

---

[17]This is in agreement with those scholars who. are of the opinion that the *paqid* and the *mebaqqer* are one and the same person, e.g., P. Wernberg-Møller, *The Manual of Discipline* (Leiden: Brill, 1957) 107; J. Licht, *The Rule Scroll* (Jerusalem: Mosad Bialik, 1965) 115-16 (in Hebrew). Licht's discussion of the role of the *mebaqqer* and of the community, although brief, is very useful and has been followed here. M. Weinfeld has also dealt with the *mebaqqer*, cf. *The Organizational Pattern and the Penal Code of the Qumran Sect* (Fribourg: Fribourg University/Göttingen: Vandenhoeck & Ruprecht, 1986) 19ff., 48, 76-7.

[18]Many scholars take *lebaqqer* in 2 Kgs 16:15 to refer to examining the entrails of sacrificial animals for omens.

[19]The *mebaqqer* is also supposed to be a shepherd to his flock (13,9).

[20]In Mishnaic Hebrew this use of *baqqer* is limited on the whole to the examination of an animal for imperfections; see J. Levy, *Wörterbuch über die Talmudim und Midrashim* (4 vols.; Berlin: Harz, 1924; reprinted, Darmstadt: Wissenschaftliche Buchgesellschaft, 1963) 1.255; E. Ben Yehuda, *Thesaurus totius hebraitatis et veteris et recentioris* (8 vols.; New York and London: Yoseloff, 1959) 1.600a.

reminded him that it was ten years since he had left Haran, and that he was now much better off than previously and orders him as follows:

וכען בקר ומני כול די איתי לך

"and now examine closely and count all that you possess."[21]

Abraham would then see that his wealth had indeed increased greatly. The use of the two verbs (*baqqer* and *manni*) rather than one is typical of Aramaic, and this stylistic device is frequent in the *Genesis Apocryphon*. The use of these two verbs together for examining and keeping count of wealth fits well with the role of the *mebaqqer* as being על מלאכת הרבים, "in charge of the possessions of the 'Many.'"

In the discussion of ἐπίτροπος it has been noted by various writers that this title was also used in the Hellenistic religious guilds.[22] But it is not a clearly defined designation and the role varied from place to place as the inscriptional evidence shows, "the ἐπίσκοποι like the ἐπιμεληταί are simply officers who exercise supervision and control."[23] The *mebaqqer*, as noted above, had clearly defined functions according to 1QS and the CD.

It is of interest that in the Babatha archive from Nahal Hever the title ἐπίτροπος is used in two documents of a woman in charge of the monetary affairs of orphans.[24] After the death of Judah son of Eleazar Khthousion, his possessions were taken over by his second wife Babatha claiming that these devolved to her in place of unpaid obligations. Judah's brother Jesus (Yeshua), who probably was also recently deceased, had left orphan sons, and their guardians instituted proceedings to recover properties which they claimed legally belonged to their wards. In the first case (text no. 20) they sued Shelamzion, Judah's daughter by his first wife, claiming that property that she had received from her father belonged to the orphans. They conceded that the property rightfully belonged to Shelamzion. In the second case (text no. 25) Babatha is called before the court since she is accused of seizing property that rightfully belongs to the orphans. There were two guardians. The first Jesus (YeshuTa) son of Besa bears the expected title ἐπίτροπος while the other Julia Crispina is called an ἐπίσκοπος. She is in all likelihood to be identified with a Julia Crispina who is known from a contemporary document from Egypt, and as a Roman citizen could appear before the court.[25] In P. Yadin 20 (130 CE) they both

---

[21]A late usage in Mishnaic Hebrew has *baqqer* with the nuance "to examine accounts;" see the lexica cited in the previous note.

[22]*TDNT* 2.612-14; see the discussion of *mebaqqer* by Weinfeld, *Organizational Pattern*, 20.

[23]*TDNT* 2.613.

[24]See Naphtali Lewis, ed., *The Documents from the Bar Kokhba Period in the Cave of Letters, Greek Papyri* (Jerusalem: Israel Exploration Society, 1989) no. 20, lines 25, 43 and no. 25, line 3.

[25]See the note to no. 25, line 2 (*Cave of Letters*, 111).

summoned Shelamzion to appear before the court, but in P. Yadin 25 (131 CE) Julia Crispina alone summoned Babatha to appear before the court. The editor notes "that the technical distinction between the two terms ἐπίσκοπος and ἐπίτροπος escapes us" and thinks that it may be a technical matter and that ἐπίσκοπος was used because a woman could not be an ἐπίτροπος.[26] There may have been a rationale for the use of the term ἐπίσκοπος reflecting a Near Eastern usage in which ἐπίσκοπος is used for those who supervise monetary affairs and it may possibly reflect the role of the *mebaqqer*. This then takes us back to the use of *baqqer umanni* in the *Genesis Apocryphon* with Abraham instructed to make an accounting of his possessions.[27]

The use of the title ἐπίσκοπος in the New Testament has been frequently discussed. However, in the light of the material adduced above it may be worthwhile to return to the subject briefly. As used in Acts 20:28 the ἐπίσκοπος is a faithful shepherd, and, as has been noticed by various scholars, this fits the usage of *mebaqqer* in CD 13:9. However nothing of his function can be gathered from that passage. In two other passages—1 Tim 3:1 and Titus 1:7—the moral qualities needed in an ἐπίσκοπος are described; the difference between the two descriptions is that in the first the ability to manage the household is mentioned (v 4) and in the second it is the ability to teach (v 9). The *mebaqqer*, one may assume, surely had the necessary moral qualities and in addition he was supposed to teach and to manage the monetary affairs of the "Many." Perhaps in the light of the use of *baqqer* in the text from the *Genesis Apocryphon* quoted above, we may assume that managing the household means that the ἐπίσκοπος had the important function of taking charge not only of the spiritual needs of his flock but also of their financial affairs.

This is an interesting example of how the study of the use of a particular root in an overlooked text may help to cast light on a variety of passages from the same period. The interrelations of the Hebrew, Aramaic and Greek usages help elucidate one another.

---

[26]Prof. R. Katzoff has suggested, orally, that Julia Crispina was a freed-woman who simply served as a caretaker for the orphans. This is surely possible, but could she then appear before a Roman court as sole guardian?

[27]Note the use of *baqqer* in late Mishnaic Hebrew. See n. 20 above.

THE GENDER OF Ιαηλ IN THE JEWISH INSCRIPTION FROM APHRODISIAS*

Bernadette J. Brooten
Harvard Divinity School

The primary purpose of this paper is to ascertain whether Ιαηλ in line 9 of the principal Jewish inscription from ancient Aphrodisias in Asia Minor is a feminine or a masculine name. I argue that no convincing evidence has been adduced to read it as a male name and that the female biblical figure of Jael was well known among both Greek- and Aramaic-speaking Jews of the Roman period and probably inspired this use of the name. While arguing the case of this specific name, I propose the methodological principle that Septuagintal manuscript variants of personal names are not a reliable source for Jewish onomastics, i.e., that such variants help us to understand scribal transliteration policies, but not actual naming practices among Greek-speaking Jews. A certain overlap between the biblical names occurring in the inscription and the biblical figures mentioned in a synagogal prayer preserved in the *Apostolic Constitutions* raises the question whether there is a more general correlation between Jewish naming practices and synagogue liturgy, i.e., the cycle of readings and synagogal prayers. Further research on this point is required.

The Inscription

Joyce Reynolds and Robert Tannenbaum have provided an invaluable service to the scholarly world with their publication of the principal Jewish inscription from Aphrodisias in Asia Minor.[1] The cooperation between an epigraphist and a historian

---

* Thanks are due to those who have assisted me in various ways with this project: Denise Buell, Ruth Clements, Sara Hazel, John Lanci, and Laurel Schneider. My deepest gratitude goes to John Strugnell, my teacher and mentor, from whom I have learned the philological and historical methods employed in this piece. May he learn through this volume how important he has been to a generation of scholars.

[1] Joyce Reynolds and Robert Tannenbaum, *Jews and God-Fearers at Aphrodisias: Greek Inscriptions with Commentary* (Cambridge Philological Society, Supp. 12; Cambridge: The Cambridge Philological Society, 1987). The principal question to date that has engaged scholars studying this inscription has been that of the God-Fearers. In line 34 of face *b* of the inscription, the phrase "and those who are God-Fearers (or pious)" (Καὶ ὅσοι θεοσεβῖς) occurs after a break and is followed by a list of Greek and Latin names (pp. 6f.). See esp. Robert S. MacLennan and A. Thomas Kraabel, "The God-Fearers—A Literary and Theological Invention," *BAR* 12:5 (1986) 46-53, 64;

of Judaism has multiplied the advantages for the reader and is a model for future work. The inscription in question is in Greek on a marble block inscribed on two faces, *a* and *b* (faces *a* and *c* 45-43 cm [w] x 280 cm [h]; face *b* 46-42.5 cm [w]).[2] Faces *a* and *b* are from different hands, with face *b* displaying the greater stone-cutting skills.[3] The editors conclude that both faces are of the third century. Because the inscription contains no explicit date, their dating is based on palaeography (face *a* contains both angular and lunate *epsilon* and *sigma*, lunate *omega*, *alpha* with both a straight and a dropped bar and *omicron* frequently written small; ligatures and many abbreviations occur;[4] face *b* contains letters more consistent in form: lunate *epsilon*, *sigma* and *omega*, but *alpha* with both the straight and the dropped bar; many abbreviations also occur here, but they are often unmarked,[5] and on the names occurring in the lists). *Aurelius/a* names and their derivatives do not occur, which may point to a date before the Antonine Constitution of 212, which granted wide-scale citizenship and left its mark on nomenclature through wide-spread adoption of the emperor's *nomen*, Aurelius. While lists of this length might not have included an *Aurelius/a* even just after 212, the absence is striking.[6] The occurrence of *Antoninos* in line 20 of face *a* may provide a *terminus post quem* during the reign of Antoninus Pius (138-161).[7] The editors consider a later date (fifth/sixth century) for face *a* on the basis of the varying forms and sizes of the letters, the poor alignment, the improper calculation of space and the many abbreviations and lack of uniformity in them.[8] Pointing to parallels to these features, however, they stick to a date for face *a* only slightly later than for face *b*, i.e., they date both to the third century.[9]

Reynolds and Tannenbaum have transcribed face *a* of the inscription as follows:

Col.   (i)   Θεὸς βοηθός, πατέλλᾳ ? δο[.1 *or* 2.]
                 Οἱ ὑποτεταγμέ-
                 νοι τῆς δεκαν(ίας)
                 τῶν φιλομαθῶ[ν]

Robert F. Tannenbaum, "Jews and God-Fearers in the Holy City of Aphrodite," *BAR* 12:5 (1986) 54-57; Louis H. Feldman, "The Omnipresence of the God-Fearers," *BAR* 12:5 (1986) 58-64, 66-69.

[2]Reynolds and Tannenbaum, *Jews*, 3.

[3]Reynolds and Tannenbaum, *Jews*, 20.

[4]Reynolds and Tannenbaum, *Jews*, 3.

[5]Reynolds and Tannenbaum, *Jews*, 4.

[6]Reynolds and Tannenbaum, *Jews*, 20.

[7]Reynolds and Tannenbaum, *Jews*, 21.

[8]Reynolds and Tannenbaum, *Jews*, 20.

[9]Reynolds and Tannenbaum, *Jews*, 21f. G(len) W. Bowersock, in an earlier unpublished paper, had dated face *b* to the early third century and face *a* to not much earlier than the fifth century ("The Jews of Aphrodisias," April 6, 1981, pp. 11, 14).

```
        5      τῶν κὲ παντευλογ(—ων)
               εἰς ἀπενθησίαν
               τῷ πλήθι ἔκτισα[ν]
               ἐξ ἰδίων μνῆμα
Σ α -          Ἰαηλ προστάτης
μ ο υ  10      ν. σὺν υἱῷ Ἰωσούᾳ ἀρχ(οντι?)
η λ           Θεόδοτος Παλατῖν(ος?) σὺν
π ρ ε σ        ν. υἱῷ Ἱλαριανῷ vac.
β ε υ -        Σαμουηλ ἀρχιδ(έκανος?) προσήλ(υτος)
τ ῆ ς          Ἰωσῆς. Ἰεσσέου vacat
Π ε ρ -15      Βενιαμιν ψαλμο(λόγος?)
γ ε -          Ἰούδας εὔκολος vacat
ο ύ ς          Ἰωσῆς προσήλυ(τος)
               Σαββάτιος Ἀμαχίου
               Ἐμμόνιος θεοσεβ(ής) υ. υ.
        20     Ἀντωνῖνος θεοσεβ(ής)
               Σαμουηλ Πολιτιανοῦ
               Εἰωσηφ Εὐσεβίου προσή(λυτος)
               κα[ὶ] Εἰούδας Θεοδώρ(ου)
               καὶ Ἀντιπές Ἑρμή(ου?)
        25     καὶ Σαβάθιος νεκτάρις
               [?κα]ὶ Σαμο[υ]ηλ πρεσ-

               βευτὴς ἱερεύς[10]
```

Reynolds and Tannenbaum give a tentative translation of lines 1-8:

God our help. {Givers to / Give to / Gift to / Building for} the soup kitchen.[11] Below (are) listed the (members) of the decany of the {students / disciples / sages} of the law, also known as those who {fervently / continually} praise God, (who) erected, for the relief of suffering in the community,[12] at their personal expense, (this) memorial

---

[10]Reynolds and Tannenbaum, *Jews*, 5. For face *b*, which is another list of names, see Reynolds and Tannenbaum, *Jews*, 6f.

[11]Reynolds and Tannenbaum suggest as an alternative in line 1: "God help the {givers to / gift to / building for} the soup-kitchen."

[12]For lines 6-8 Reynolds and Tannenbaum give as an alternative: "for the alleviation of grief in the community ... (this public) tomb." Reynolds and Tannenbaum are to be congratulated for their care in presenting and explaining several alternative translations.

(building).[13]

Following the commentary of Reynolds and Tannenbaum, I offer the following tentative translation of lines 9-27:

(Margin:)

Samouel,	Iael, {president / patron},
envoy(?), 10	with (her) son Iosouas, archon (?);
from	Theodotos, former court employee (?), with
Perge	(his) son Hilarianos;
	Samouel, head of the decany (?), proselyte;
	Ioses, son of Iesseos;
15	Beniamin, psalm-singer (?);
	good-tempered Ioudas;
	Ioses, proselyte;
	Sabbatios, son of Amachios;
	{pious Emmonios / Emmonios, God-Fearer};
20	{pious Antoninos / Antoninos, God-Fearer};
	Samouel, son of Politianos;
	Eioseph, proselyte, son of Eusebios;
	and Eioudas, son of Theodoros;
	and Antipeos, son of {Hermes / Hermeas};
25	and sweet Sabathios;
	and (?) Samouel, en-
	voy (?), priest[14]

Iael occurs first in this list of names. Only Iael, in line 9, and Theodotos, in line 11, have their sons' names listed. The titles of Jewish leadership (president or patron, archon [?], head of the decany [?], and envoy [?]) occur clustered at the beginning. Lines 26f. were erased; Reynolds and Tannenbaum suggest that Samouel's name may have been moved up from lines 26f. to the margin of lines 9-17 because of his status as a leader or because he was not a regular member of the community, i.e., either he was moved up to accord him greater honor or he was moved to the margin because he

[13]Reynolds and Tannenbaum, *Jews*, 41.

[14]While I have left the names in their Greek form, a number are, or may be biblical. The following may be equivalencies: Iael = Jael; Samouel = Samuel; Iosouas = Joshua; Ioses = hypocoristic form of Joseph; Iesseos = Isaiah; Beniamin = Benjamin; Ioudas/Eioudas = Judah; Eioseph = Joseph; Hermeas = Jeremiah (possible, given that the rough breathing was no longer pronounced and that the *eta* was pronounced as an *iota*; otherwise this name could be a theophoric name from Hermes).

166

was on the margin of the community.[15] These two facts, namely the clustering of leadership titles at the beginning and the listing of only two persons' sons, and these at the beginning, make it probable that the names are not in random order. Being listed at the beginning may have been a special honor.

Ιαηλ as a Name and 2 Esdras 10:26, 43[16]

Reynolds and Tannenbaum note:

> Jael may be a woman's name: the title is no obstacle to its being so here, since women are often given titles of high synagogue or community office in the diaspora; but it is more probably a man's...[17]

They refer to several examples of women having titles of leadership in the ancient synagogue and to my own work on these and other titles.[18]   They suggest that in light of the Septuagintal usage of Ιαηλ for a man in 2 Esdras 10:26, 43, Ιαηλ should be read as masculine in this inscription. They also recognize that the Septuagint has Ιαηλ as a feminine name in Judges, but argue that, since "the lists here are otherwise demonstrably and consistently masculine ... the feminine should be rejected in favor of the masculine here."[19]   This is not a convincing argument against the femininity of Iael. Throughout Western history, women accorded special honor have often been in the minority. Whether προστάτης[20] means "president" or "patron,"[21] Iael could

[15]Reynolds and Tannenbaum, *Jews*, 10, 30, 41f.

[16]See B(ruce) M. Metzger's "Table of Titles Given to Books Associated with Ezra (and Nehemiah) in Selected Versions" for help in sorting out the confusing nomenclature, in James H. Charlesworth, ed., *The Old Testament Pseudepigrapha* (2 vols.; Garden City: Doubleday, 1983-85) 1.516. In the LXX 2 Esdras is the translation of the Hebrew books of Ezra (= 2 Esdras 1-10) and Nehemiah (= 2 Esdras 11-23).

[17]Reynolds and Tannenbaum, *Jews*, 41.

[18]*Women Leaders in the Ancient Synagogue: Inscriptional Evidence and Background Issues* (Brown Judaic Studies 36; Chico: Scholars, 1982). The work focuses on nineteen Greek and Latin inscriptions from the Roman and early Byzantine periods in which women bear the titles "head of the synagogue," "leader," "elder," "mother of the synagogue" and "priestess." See also Ross S. Kraemer, "A New Inscription from Malta and the Question of Women Elders in the Diaspora Jewish Communities," *HTR* 78 (1985) 431-38. Kraemer presents an excellent discussion of an inscription from Malta, in which a woman named Eulogia bears the title πρεσβυτήρα (sic); Kraemer critically reviews the evidence for the seven other Jewish inscriptions in which women bear similar titles.

[19]Reynolds and Tannenbaum, *Jews*, 101.

[20]This form of the title could apply either to a man or a woman, since women sometimes bear the form of a title that would otherwise apply to a man, e.g., Rufina, a Jewess, ἀρχισυνάγωγος (*CII* 741 = *Inscriptiones Graecae ad res romanas pertinentes* IV

well have been a feminine minority of one. Women with leadership positions have been rare in Western religious and civic history. The question is, how many women does an inscription honoring leaders and respected community members have to contain before there can have been one?[22] The same would apply if Iael were a patron. Women have less often had sufficient economic power to be able to make major donations or serve as patrons, but individual wealthy women certainly served such functions in the ancient world.[23]

As to the philological argument based on the LXX, a closer look at 2 Esdras and at Judges is required. 2 Esdras 10:26, 43 is a translation of Ezra 10:26, 43. These verses are part of a list of male returning exiles who had married foreign women and were now repudiating them. Therefore, all the names in the list are by definition masculine. A number of theophoric names appear in Ezra 10. Those which end in אֵל- include: יְחִיאֵל (10:2, 21, 26) and יְעִיאֵל (10:43; see also 8:13).[24] The Septuagintal manuscript tradition as a whole includes many variants among transliterated Semitic names, and the names of 2 Esdras 10 are no exception. The level of chaos may even be a little higher here than usual; see, e.g., the note by

1452); Phoebe, διάκονος (Rom 16:1).

[21]For discussion of the meaning of προστάτης here, see Bernadette J. Brooten, "Iael προστάτης in the Jewish Inscription from Aphrodisias," in Birger Pearson, et al., eds., *The Future of Early Christianity: Festschrift for Helmut Koester* (Minneapolis: Augsburg-Fortress, forthcoming).

[22]Will future historians assume, since British Prime Minister Margaret Thatcher has to date, with but one exception, The Baroness Young, Lord Privy Seal and Leader of the House of Lords (1983), presided over all-male cabinets, that Thatcher herself was not a woman? See *Whitaker's Almanack* (London: Whitaker and Sons, 1980 [p. 314], 1981 [p. 310], 1982 [p. 310], 1983 [p. 309f.], 1984 [p. 309], 1985 [p. 309], 1987 [p. 308], 1988 [p. 238]); John Paxton, ed., *The Statesman's Yearbook* (New York: St. Martin's, 1981-82 [1981, pp. 1299f.], 1987-88 [1987, p. 1296]).
Female leaders in the company of all-male groups occur in antiquity as well; e.g., Nikippe, [προ]ερανίστρια of a cultic club of Sarapis worshipers, is named first in a list of men, the first three of whom are also office-holders (Athens, 215-214 BCE: Ladislaus Vidman, ed., *Sylloge inscriptionum religionis Isiacae et Sarapiacae* [Religionsgeschichtliche Versuche und Vorarbeiten 28; Berlin: de Gruyter, 1969] 4-6, no. 2).

[23]For an epigraphic collection of women as donors in synagogues of the Roman and early Byzantine periods, see Brooten, *Women Leaders*, 157-65. On women's philanthropic activity in Asia Minor, see esp. Riet Van Bremen, "Women and Wealth," in Averil Cameron and Amélie Kuhrt, eds., *Images of Women in Antiquity* (Detroit: Wayne State University Press, 1983) 223-42.

[24]For other theophoric names in אֵל-, see Ezra 10:15, 22, 30, 34, 41, 43. Shmuel Safrai drew my attention to the number of אֵל- names in this chapter. Note that these differ from the יָעֵל of Judges, which has ע, rather than א in its root. The Greek cannot distinguish between the two.

Rahlfs at 10:30: "multa nomina propria in mss. falso distincta sunt."[25] At 10:26 some manuscripts have Ιαηλ (BdhpEthiopic[26]) for יְחִיאֵל. At 10:43, some have Ιαηλ (BNShEthiopic) for יְעִיאֵל. The manuscripts are not even internally consistent; they may transliterate the same Hebrew name differently within the space of a few verses. Thus, while BdhpEthiopic have Ιαηλ for יְחִיאֵל at 10:26, BScdhjp* have Ιεηλ for יְחִיאֵל at 10:2, and BSdhm have Ιεηλ for יְחִיאֵל at 10:21. A (= Alexandrinus, mid fifth century) has Ιεειηλ for יְחִיאֵל at 10:2, Ιειηλ at 10:21, and Αιειηλ at 10:26, while for יְעִיאֵל at 10:43 it has Ιεειηλ and at 8:13 it seems to have Ειηλ. B (= Vaticanus, mid fourth century) has two different transliterations of יְחִיאֵל: Ιεηλ at 10:2, 21 and Ιαηλ at 10:26. B also has two different transliterations of יְעִיאֵל: Ιαηλ at 10:43 and Ευεια at 8:13. Note that Ιαηλ in B is the transliteration of both יְחִיאֵל (10:26) and יְעִיאֵל (10:43). Looking just at the two verses upon which Reynolds and Tannenbaum base their case, one finds the following variants: 10:26, יְחִיאֵל: Ιαηλ (BdhpEthiopic), Ιαειηλ (S), Ιειηλ (be₂), Αιειηλ (A), Ιαιηλ (N and the others); 10:43, יְעִיאֵל: Ιαηλ (BNShEthiopic), Ιεειηλ (A), Ιεηλ (d; the η was added by a corrector), Ειηλ (b), Ιειηλ (the others). In sum, the individual manuscripts often transliterate the same name in different ways and different names in the same way, and this within the space of a few verses. The manuscript tradition as a whole is chaotic in the transliteration of these and other Semitic names.

A general methodological principle follows from this. The forms Ιαηλ, Ιειηλ, Αιειηλ or Ευεια as male names in 2 Esdras do not constitute documentation that male, Greek-speaking Jews ever bore these names. Finding a particular form of a name in the LXX is qualitatively different from finding an inscription or a papyrus document in which a Jewish man or woman bears a particular name. Inscriptions and documentary papyri constitute evidence that at least one historical person bore a particular name. In contrast, the LXX constitutes evidence as to what *Vorlage* translators and scribes may have had, as to how they functioned in their work, and occasionally as to how they pronounced Hebrew and Greek.

In the case of names, one can never say never. There may be a boy named Sue or a man named Maria. Take the latter example. Was not Rainer Maria Rilke a man? Yes, but surely this usage is a matter of modern Catholic Marian piety, rather than of ancient Jewish onomastics. But consider 2 Esdras 10:42. There BSh have Μαρια as a transliteration of אֲמַרְיָה. The weight of Vaticanus and Sinaiticus (= S, fourth

---

[25]Alfred Rahlfs, ed., *Septuaginta* (2 vols. in 1; Stuttgart: Deutsche Bibelstiftung, 1935) 1.922.

[26]For this and the following readings, see Alan England Brooke and Norman McLean, eds., *The Old Testament in Greek* (3 vols.; Cambridge: Cambridge University Press, 1906-40) vol. 2/4, *I Esdras, Ezra-Nehemia* (A. E. Brooke, N. McLean, and Henry St. John Thackeray, eds.,1935) 620, 624, 626-28.

century) led Brooke, McLean and Thackeray to print Μαρια (Μαριά) in their text.[27] Does this constitute evidence that ancient Greek-speaking Jews used Maria as a male name? This kind of evidence is not comparable to inscriptions or documentary papyri. In contrast, Greek Jewish inscriptions in which Μαρια occurs are evidence for actual historical usage (e.g., *CII* 137, daughter of (P)rokopios; 374, wife of Saloutios; 701 = *Inscriptiones Graecae* IX/2. 988*c*, wife of Leontiskos; 1535, daughter of Phamsothis—probably Jewish[28]). Thus, Reynolds and Tannenbaum have not paid sufficient attention to the nature of the LXX as evidence for onomastic studies.

Jael in the Book of Judges and in Post-Biblical Jewish Literature
    The name יָעֵל occurs six times in Judges (4:17, 18, 21, 22; 5:6, 24). Since Judges is counted among the Prophets, those attending synagogue services could have heard the story of Jael slaying Sisera as part of the Haftara, thus making the name well-known among Jewish families.[29] Judg 5:24 reads: "Most blessed of women be Jael, the wife of Heber the Kenite, of tent-dwelling women most blessed" (RSV). The Targum Jonathan has: "May Jael the wife of Heber the Shalmaite be blessed with the blessing of good women; may she be blessed like one of the women who serve in the

[27]*The Old Testament in Greek*, 2/4.628.

[28]On documentary evidence for the name Maria, see G. H. R. Horsley, *New Documents Illustrating Early Christianity* (vols. 1- ; North Ryde: Macquarie University, 1981-) 4 (1987) 229f.

[29]Ben Zion Wacholder lists Judg 5:14 (מני אפרים) as the Haftara for Num 7:48 (נשיא לבני אפרים [אפרים] ביום השביעי) in the ancient Palestinian three-year cycle, giving the early medieval payyetan Yannai (ca. late 6th/early 7th century) as a source for Num 7:48, but no source for Judg 5:14 (Jacob Mann, *The Bible as Read and Preached in the Old Synagogue* [2 vols.; Cincinnati: Hebrew Union College, 1940-1966; reprint ed., New York: Ktav, 1971] vol. 1, *The Palestinian Triennial Cycle: Genesis and Exodus*, Prolegomenon by Ben Zion Wacholder, lx-lxi). The reason for assuming that Judg 5:14ff. was read together with the Torah portion Num 7:48ff. in an early Palestinian three-year cycle (rather than the Babylonian one-year cycle) may be the "Ephraim" in both texts. Yannai composed a liturgical poem on Num 7:48ff., with the last word of each line being "Ephraim," but I see no direct reference to Judg 5:14ff. in that poem (Menahem Zulay, *Piyyute Yannai: Liturgical Poems of Yannai* [Palestine: Schocken, 1938] 187f.). In another poem (listed as dubious by Zulay) Yannai quotes part of Judg 5:5, but we cannot be certain whether this quotation means that Judg 5:5, or the Jael story, which begins in Judg 5:6, was part of the Haftara (Zulay, *Piyyute Yannai*, 367). Judg 5:5 is not quoted at the end of the third stanza, which, according to Wacholder, is the usual position for the first verse of the Haftara (Mann, *The Bible*, Prolegomenon, xl). In general, Yannai is significant for reconstructing a triennial Palestinian cycle because his liturgical poems are woven around the first verse of the weekly Torah portion, the second verse of the seder, and the first verse of the Haftara (Mann, *The Bible*, Prolegomenon, xl).
    Judg 4:4-5:31 is the Haftara to the Torah portion בשלח (Exod 13:17-17:16) in the cycle of readings in use in contemporary Orthodox synagogues.

houses of study."[30]

In the Septuagintal manuscripts of Judges, Ιαηλ is the best attested form of the name at Judg 4:17, 18, 21, 22; 5:6, 24 and is printed by both Brooke/McLean and Rahlfs. Variants do exist, however: Ιααηλ, Ηαηλ, Ιηλ, Ισραηλ (sic), Αηλ.[31] While the Ιαηλ of the Aphrodisias inscription does coincide with the best attested Greek form of the Hebrew name יָעֵל in the manuscripts of the LXX, I am not basing my argument on this fact. The LXX displays such great variety in the forms of proper names that it is an inadequate base for an exact identification of Greek names occurring in inscriptions.

Josephus recounts the story of Jael (Ιαλη, *Ant.* 5.5.4 § 207f.).[32] Pseudo-Philo recounts her story at some length. In all, Pseudo-Philo mentions Jael (*Iahel* in an indeclinable form in the Latin) sixteen times by name.[33] The Hebrew fragments of Pseudo-Philo's *Liber Antiquitatum Biblicarum* as preserved in the *Chronicles of Jerahmeel* (fourteenth century MS) also contain the account of Jael (יעל).[34] Rabbinic

[30]Daniel J. Harrington and Anthony J. Saldarini, tr., *Targum Jonathan of the Former Prophets: Introduction, Translation and Notes* (Wilmington: Glazier, 1987) 69. See Alexander Sperber, ed., *The Bible in Aramaic* (4 vols.; Leiden: Brill, 1959-73) vol. 2, *The Former Prophets According to Targum Jonathan* (1959) 57. Harrington has observed that the *Targum Jonathan* on Judges 5 has "a more explicit theological framework" and is more adapted to the conditions of the targumist's time than the rest of *Targum Jonathan of the Former Prophets*, which is generally a close rendering of the Hebrew text. He notes that adding "the houses of study," "modernizes the biblical text and puts it in a rabbinic context" ("The Prophecy of Deborah: Interpretive Homiletics in Targum Jonathan of Judges 5," *CBQ* 48 [1986] 437, n. 64; see also 433, 439-42). Harrington argues that it is impossible to date *Targum Jonathan* of Judges 5 precisely, but that, "It probably existed prior to and independent from *Targum Jonathan* as a whole" (ibid., 441).

[31]A. E. Brooke and N. McLean, eds., *The Old Testament in Greek*, vol. 1/4, *Joshua, Judges and Ruth* (1917) 800-802, 807; Rahlfs, *Septuaginta*, 1.421-23, 426.

[32]Benedikt Niese, ed., *Flavii Iosephi Opera* (7 vols.; Berlin: Weidmann, 1887, 1885-95) 1.333. Adolf Schlatter comments that Josephus may have read יָעֵל rather than יָעֵל (*Die hebräischen Namen bei Josephus* [Beiträge zur Förderung christlicher Theologie 17:3; Gütersloh: Bertelsmann, 1913] 63). Abraham Schalit also suggests that Josephus may have read יָעֵל or יָעֵלָה (Karl Heinrich Rengstorf, ed., *A Complete Concordance to Flavius Josephus* [4 vols.; Leiden: Brill, 1973-83] Supplement 1, *Namenwörterbuch zu Flavius Josephus*, ed. Abraham Schalit [1968 (1969)] 56).

[33]*Liber Antiquitatum Biblicarum* 31f.; Daniel J. Harrington et al., eds., and French tr., *Pseudo-Philon: Les antiquités bibliques* (2 vols.; SC 229-30; Paris: Cerf, 1976) 1.238-43, 250f. D(aniel) J. Harrington, tr., in *OTP*, 2.344-46.

[34]*Chronicles of Jerahmeel* 58.4f. (parallels *Liber Antiquitatum Biblicarum* 31.3-7, 8); Daniel J. Harrington, ed. and tr., *The Hebrew Fragments of Pseudo-Philo's* Liber Antiquitatum Biblicarum *Preserved in the* Chronicles of Jerahmeel (SBLTT 3; Missoula: Scholars, 1974) 58f.

sources refer to Jael both by name[35] and indirectly.[36] The discussion focuses in part on the assumption of some that Sisera had sexual intercourse with Jael.[37] *Ruth Rabbah* 1.1 contains the suggestion of R. Huna that "the judges" of Judg 2:17 refers to Deborah, Barak and Jael.[38]

Jews in the late Roman period may also have invoked the name of Jael in synagogue services. The Christian *Apostolic Constitutions* contain prayers which several scholars have identified as Hellenistic Jewish prayers taken over with only slight Christian interpolations.[39] The reasons for this identification are similarities to known synagogue prayers and the striking absence of peculiarly Christian content. Where references to Christ occur, they are usually in discreet units only loosely connected to the surrounding material. *Apost. Const.* 7.37.1-5 is such a prayer. The only explicitly Christian material is a brief christological formula at 7.37.1 which bears great resemblance to Rom 1:3 and another reference to Christ at the end. The prayer is an invocation to God to receive the prayers of God's people, even as God has "received the gifts of the righteous in their generations" (7.37.1). There follows a list of well-known biblical figures: Abel, Noah, Abraham, Isaac, etc. The list is roughly in chronological order. For this reason it is surprising to find "Barak and Deborah, in the days of Sisera" at 7.37.2 and "Jael (Ιαηλ) in praises" at the very end of the list (7.37.4). Samuel, which occurs five times in the Aphrodisias inscription (Σαμουηλ, *a*, lines 9-11 left margin, 13, 21, 26; *b*, line 30), appears in the prayer (Σαμουηλ, 7.37.2), as does Manasseh (inscription: Μανασης, *b*, line 5; *Apost. Const.* 7.37.3: Μανασση). There may be two further cases of overlap: Joshua (inscription: Ιωσουας, *a*, line 10; *Apost. Const.* 7.37.2: Ιησου, the [son of] Naue in Galgal) and Jonah (inscription: Ιουν (?), *b*, line 43; *Apost. Const.* 7.37.4: Ιωνα), but the

[35]Cf., e.g., *b. Nazir* 23b; *b. Hor.* 10b; *b. Sanh.* 105b; *b. Meg.* 15a; *Gen. Rab.* 48.15; *Exod. Rab.* 4.2; *Lev. Rab.* 23.9f.; *Num. Rab.* 10.2; *Ruth Rab.* 1.1.

[36]Cf., e.g., *Sipre Deut.* 35; *Mek.*, Pisḥa 17.130-34 (ed. Lauterbach); *b. Yebam.* 103a; *b. Nid.* 55b; *b. Menaḥ.* 36b; *b. Sanh.* 105a-b; *Exod. Rab.* 15.22.

[37]Cf., e.g., *b. Yebam.* 103a; *b. Nazir* 23b; *b. Hor.* 10b; *b. Sanh.* 105a-b; *Lev. Rab.* 23.10.

[38]This may be the R. Huna who was a second-generation Babylonian Amora (died 297) and was himself a judge (*b. Sanh.* 7b). See also *Eccl. Rab.* 2.8, 1, which contains a reference to male and female judges.

[39]See D(avid) A. Fiensy's introduction to "Hellenistic Synagogal Prayers," in *OTP*, 2.671-76. See also Erwin R. Goodenough, *By Light, Light: The Mystic Gospel of Hellenistic Judaism* (New Haven, 1935; reprinted, Amsterdam: Philo, 1969) 306-58; K. Kohler, "The Origin and Composition of the Eighteen Benedictions with a Translation of the Corresponding Essene Prayers in the Apostolic Constitutions," *HUCA* 1 (1924) 387-425; W. Bousset, "Eine jüdische Gebetssammlung im siebenten Buch der apostolischen Konstitutionen," *Nachrichten von der Königlichen Gesellschaft der Wissenschaften zu Göttingen. Philol.-hist. Kl. 1915*, 3 (Berlin: Weidmann, 1916) 435-89.

Bernadette Brooten

spelling divergences make these uncertain.[40]
David A. Fiensy dates these prayers to between 150 and 300 CE, thus roughly
contemporaneous with the Aphrodisias inscription. The provenance is uncertain, but
since the *Apostolic Constitutions* are generally thought to have been compiled in
Syria, the prayers were probably in liturgical use there.[41]   The significance for
Jewish onomastics of this and of the other prayers containing lists of biblical names
is that worshipers presumably repeated these names on a regular basis, which made the
names more familiar. While the actual biblical narratives of Jael, Samuel, Manasseh
and the others may have been read or referred to in the sermon infrequently, a prayer
recalled their names to memory on a regular basis. Perhaps the overlap between the
Greek prayer with biblical names and the Greek inscription with biblical names is not
accidental.
    The cumulative significance of the references to the biblical Jael in Josephus,
Pseudo-Philo, rabbinic literature and the prayer in *Apost. Const.* 7.37.1-5 is that they
make clear that post-biblical Jews discussed and disputed the biblical accounts of Jael.
This held true within rabbinic circles and among Greek-speaking diaspora
communities.
    Thus it becomes evident that the Jael of Judges is a well-known biblical figure,
mentioned by name six times in Judges and referred to in post-biblical Jewish
literature as well, while the Jehiel of Ezra 10:26 and the Jeiel of Ezra 10:43 are
obscure figures in whatever form or language.[42] The male biblical names of the
Aphrodisias inscription tend to be of illustrious figures: Samuel, Benjamin, Judah,
Joseph, possibly Isaiah and Jeremiah. The female Jael of Judges is by far the best
known Jael of the bible and of post-biblical Judaism. Reynolds and Tannenbaum have
not given sufficient explanation why the obscure should take precedence over that
which is near at hand.

[40]Franziskus X. Funk, ed., *Didascalia et Constitutiones Apostolorum* (Paderborn:
Schoeningh, 1905) 436-38.   D. R. Darnell, tr., "Hellenistic Synagogal Prayers," in
OTP, 2.684f.; David Fiensy includes text and translation of this prayer in his *Prayers
Alleged to Be Jewish: An Examination of the* Constitutiones Apostolorum (Brown
Judaic Studies 65; Chico: Scholars, 1985) 80-83.

[41]Introduction to "Hellenistic Synagogal Prayers," in *OTP*, 2.673; idem, *Prayers*,
215-28.

[42]Aaron Hyman (*Sefer Torah ha-ketuvah veha-mesurah* [2d ed., rev. and enl. by
Arthur Hyman; 3 vols.; 1938-39; Tel-Aviv: Dvir, 1979] 3.237) gives no references to
Ezra 10:26 or 10:43 in all of the rabbinic literature he has surveyed.   Nor does the
companion volume to this work, compiled by Arthur Hyman, give references to these
verses (*Sefer ha-Hashlamot* [Jerusalem: "Peri ha-Aretz"] 194).

TIBERIUS JULIUS ALEXANDER AND THE CRISIS IN ALEXANDRIA ACCORDING TO JOSEPHUS

Robert A. Kraft
University of Pennsylvania

The context of this examination of Josephus' information about Tiberius Julius Alexander is set by my article on "Philo and the Sabbath Crisis" (Koester Festschrift) and by the independent (and prior) treatment by Daniel Schwartz of "the governor of *De Somniis* 2.123-32."[1] Philo speaks with strong feelings and in some detail about a crisis caused in "Egypt" in the recent past by "one of the rulers" who attempted to bully the observant Jews into forsaking their sabbath customs, for some unexplained reason. Philo sees this as the first step towards pulling Jews completely away from their "ancestral customs." Philo describes the episode in the context of a fairly unsympathetic treatment of the dreams of Joseph the patriarch (*On Dreams* 2.110-154) and the entire Joseph symbolism here could be read as referring to a Roman ruler of Jewish origin. Since the most obvious and best known Jewish Roman ruler in Egypt around the time of Philo was Philo's nephew, Tiberius Julius Alexander (= TJA), it seemed logical to examine the surviving reports about TJA to see whether he might qualify as the antagonist in Philo's tale. Schwartz argues that Philo may be referring to the early 40's, when TJA held one of his first Roman assignments, as "epistrategos" of the Thebaid.[2] Josephus does not mention that appointment, but he does narrate in some detail an episode that deserves close attention from a considerably later period, to which we shall turn below.

The results of this probe are not conclusive. The descriptions by Philo of the "sabbath crisis" and by Josephus of the Alexandrian riots around the time that TJA became Roman governor of Alexandria and Egypt (66-70) can be made to complement each other without too much difficulty. But there is not enough detail

[1] Daniel R. Schwartz, "Philonic Anonyms of the Roman and Nazi Periods: Two Suggestions," *The Studia Philonica Annual* 1 (1989) 63-73. I did not see the article by Schwartz until my essay on "Philo and the Sabbath Crisis: Alexandrian Jewish Politics and the Dating of Philo's Works" had been submitted to the Helmut Koester Festschrift (Birger Pearson, et al., eds., *The Future of Early Christianity* (Minneapolis: Augsburg-Fortress, forthcoming), but I am pleased at the ways in which our independent insights and hypotheses supplement each other.

[2] See E. G. Turner, "Tiberius Iulius Alexander," *Journal of Roman Studies* 44 (1954) 54-64 (esp. 58). We know of this appointment not from ancient historical records, but from an inscription on the temple at Dendera (OGI 663).

and corresponding overlap in the two accounts to be sure that they depict the same events. If Philo is referring to the activities of his nephew as governor of Alexandria/Egypt, however, this would necessitate a radical revision of the chronology of Philo's later life and his literary career. It seems to me that the evidence is sufficiently suggestive to encourage such a reevaluation, even if all the details of the following discussion are not considered persuasive.

Tiberius Julius Alexander in the Antiquities

As has sometimes been noted, Josephus' attitude to TJA seems somewhat more positive in the *War* than in the *Antiquities*.[3] Actually, Josephus mentions TJA only once in the *Antiquities*, the famous passage in which TJA is described as not maintaining the ancestral customs (Josephus does not say that TJA "apostasized," despite the frequent claims to that effect!). The complete context is as follows (*Ant.* 20.5.2 § 100-03), in an intentionally wooden/mechanical rendering:

> Now there came as successor to Fadus, Tiberius Alexander, son of the Alexander who was also alabarch in Alexandria, who both in family heritage and in wealth surpassed those there with him. He also differed in his piety to God from his son Alexander, for that one did not remain steadfast in the ancestral customs. [101] At this time also the great famine in Judea came about, when also Queen Helena, having purchased with much money grain from Egypt distributed it to the needy, as I related previously. [102] Along with these events, the sons of Judah the Galilean, who caused the people to revolt against the Romans when Cyrenius was taking a census of Judea, as I made clear in the previous accounts, were brought to trial—Jacob and Simon—whom Alexander ordered to be crucified. [103] Herod King of Chalcis, having removed from the high priesthood Joseph son of Camei, gave the succession of office to Ananias son of Nedebaius. And to Tiberius Alexander, Cumanus became successor.

Tiberius Julius Alexander in the War, *Part One*

This account of events in Judea around the years 46-48 is somewhat fuller than the parallel passage (published more than a decade earlier) in the *War*. It also depicts TJA in a light not even hinted at in the *War* references. Indeed, Josephus makes it a point to say in *War* 2.11.6 § 220 that neither TJA nor his immediate predecessor Cuspius Fadus made any changes to the traditional Jewish patterns when they

---

[3]So, for example, Shaye J. D. Cohen, *Josephus in Galilee and Rome: His* Vita *and Development as a Historian* (Leiden: Brill, 1979) 150; Turner, "Tiberius Iulius Alexander," 63.

governed Judea without significant incident.[4] TJA is not contrasted with his father (or with anyone else) with regard to "piety," nor is there any mention of the execution of Jewish insurgents. The entire passage runs as follows, speaking about the death of Agrippa I in 44 CE:

> Now [Agrippa] left three daughters born of Cypros—Bernike and Mariamme and Drusilla—and a son from the same mother—Agrippa. Since he was entirely a child, when Claudius again made the kingdoms a province he sent Cuspius Fadus as a governor, then Tiberius Alexander, who [plural], since neither did anything that disturbed the local customs, kept the nation in peace. [221-222 tells of the death of Herod of Chalcis, his survivors, and his relation to the larger family of Herod the Great.] [223=12.1] Now after Herod, who ruled over Chalcis, died, Claudius inserted into the kingdom of his uncle, Agrippa son of Agrippa. But of the other province Cumanus received the governorship from Alexander, and under him began disturbances and again there occurred destruction of Judeans/Jews.

A few paragraphs later (2.12.4 § 235), Josephus mentions an undifferentiated "Alexander" as a leader, along with Eleazar son of Deinaeus, of retaliatory actions of Jews against Samaritans during the governorship of Cumanus. This Alexander does not appear in the parallel passage from *Antiquities* (20.6.1 § 120), and it would seem difficult to identify him with TJA since the actions described here are immediately countered by Cumanus and his troops. Still, in the aftermath of the situation, Cumanus is recalled to Rome and the Jews are vindicated in their complaints against the Samaritans, so it is not completely impossible that somehow TJA was involved in the situation and his political career furthered (or at least not hindered) thereby. But the ancient sources do not give us enough information to pursue this possibility with any confidence.

We next encounter TJA, in Josephus' account of the Jewish *War*, when TJA becomes governor of Egypt under Nero (66 CE). The context is the trouble in Jerusalem under the Roman governor Florus who provokes an escalation of Jewish unrest when he takes money from the temple treasury (2.14.6 § 293-308). Josephus notes that (2.15.1 § 309):

> At this very time King Agrippa happened to have gone to Alexandria so that he might get together with Alexander who had been entrusted with Egypt by Nero and who had been sent to manage (it).

---

[4] In *Ant.* 20.1.1-2 § 1-14 and 20.5.1 § 97-99, the rule of Fadus is depicted as encountering various problems with Jewish unrest.

Josephus does nothing else with TJA at this point in the narrative. The picture returns to Jerusalem, where Agrippa's sister Bernike attempts unsuccessfully to pacify matters. Finally, Agrippa himself returns from Alexandria in 2.16.1b § 335, with no further mention of TJA. Agrippa gives a lengthy speech that emphasizes the futility of resisting Roman might (2.16.4-5 § 345-404), but is ultimately unsuccessful as civil war and open rebellion against Rome break out in Jerusalem and throughout the Syro-Palestinian area (2.17.1-18.6 § 405-86). Josephus does not hesitate to give examples of how the hope of saving one's life could lead to partial or complete abandonment of one's prior position, both by Romans (the Roman commander Metilius agrees "to Judaize to the extent of circumcision" in 2.454) and by Jews (e.g., Simon son of Saul at Scythopolis in 2.469-76, who first fights with the Scythopolis Jews against his marauding countrymen, then, at the treachery of the non Jewish Scythopolitans, "corrects" his misguided actions by slaughtering his family and committing suicide). The question of taking up arms on the sabbath is an explicit issue (see 2.392-93 [Agrippa's pleas], 2.456 [the deceitful victory of the Jerusalem rebels], 2.457 [the massacre of Jews at Caesarea]), as is the matter of Jews accepting in the temple precincts the reverential acts and gifts of "outsiders" (2.414) and of Jews making offerings in the temple for the Roman rulers (2.410).

Tiberius Julius Alexander in the War: *the Alexandrian Crisis*
It is against this background that TJA reappears in Josephus' narrative, as follows (2.18.7 § 487)—again an intentionally wooden/mechanical representation of the Greek is provided:

> Now in Alexandria there was continuous antagonism against the Jewish community by the indigenous people, ever since having received support from the Jews against the Egyptians Alexander gave them the privilege of alliance [or, a gift for assistance] to dwell in the city having an equal portion with the Greeks. [488] The honor was continued for them even by the successors (of Alexander) who also partitioned for them their own place so that more purely it might provide a better mode of living than by mixing with foreigners, and they permitted them to be called "Macedonians." And when the Romans acquired Egypt neither the first Caesar nor any of his successors supported reducing the honors of the Jews bestowed by Alexander... [489] But there were collisions of them unceasingly with the Greeks, and although the rulers punished many day by day from both sides the antagonism was fanned instead. [490] And then, since also elsewhere there was disorder, theirs was loosed all the more. And indeed, when the Alexandrians were gathered concerning an embassy they were about to send to Nero there streamed together into the amphitheater along with the Greeks

many of the Jews. [491] Now when the adversaries caught sight of them, immediately they cried out saying "enemies" and "spies." Then rushing forward they laid hands on them. And the rest were scattered since they fled, but when they captured three men they dragged them off to burn them alive. [492] Now the whole Jewish community arose in defence and at first threw stones at the Greeks, but then grabbing lanterns they ran to the amphitheater threatening to burn in it the attendees to a man. And they quickly would have done this except he—Tiberius Alexander the governor of the city—repelled their angers. [493] Now he did not, indeed, by using weapons begin to enlighten them but by secretly sending the notables to them he exhorted (them) to cease and not to provoke the Roman army upon themselves. But scoffing at the exhortation the insurgents ridiculed Tiberius. [494] And he, understanding that without a major calamity those rebelling would not cease, let loose on them the city-based two divisions of Romans and with them 2,000 soldiers from Libya by chance in transit to the destruction of the Jews. And he permitted (them) not only to destroy but also to ravage their possessions and to burn down their houses. [495] Now they by rushing eagerly into the so-called "D" district (for the Jewish community was concentrated there) fulfilled their orders, but not without shedding their own blood. For the Jews by closing ranks and placing the better of their armed persons to the front resisted as long as possible, but once having collapsed they were killed without further ado. [496] And manifold ruin was theirs; some were seized in the field, some were forced together into the houses. And the Romans set those afire after plundering their contents, and neither mercy for infants nor respect for old age came to their minds but through every age bracket they advanced slaughtering, [497] so that the whole district was flooded with blood and five myriads of dead were heaped up; and not even the remnant would be left if they had not turned to supplication. But having compassion on them Alexander ordered the Romans to move off. [498] They, then, by custom being obedient stopped the killing on command, but the populace of Alexandrians because of excessive hatred were hard to restrain and with difficulty were dragged off of the corpses. [499] Such was the calamity that took place at Alexandria. But Cestius decided no longer to keep quiet since on all fronts the Jews were being involved in war. [500] And taking from Antioch the twelfth...

The story strikes me as extremely peculiar in various respects. The main villains seem to be the anti-Jewish "indigenous people" or "foreigners" at first, who conspire with and then give way to the antagonistic "Greeks" at some point, who in turn seem to be equivalent to the "populace of Alexandrians" near the end. What characterizes them, regardless of what they are called, is enmity towards the "Jewish community" of Alexandria, which seems to be treated as a unit once the hostilities erupt. At the outset, however, only some Jews attend the meeting of the "Alexandrians," along with some "Greeks," and the opponents take issue with this Jewish presence. Based on Josephus' claim that Jews of Alexandria had special priviliges and equal rights with the "Greeks," it is not clear whether there was anything illegal or suspicious about Jews attending an assembly of Alexandrians! Nor is it stated why an embassy to Nero was contemplated, or whether Jewish issues were under discussion in that context. Indeed, the "privileges" emphasized by Josephus at the beginning of the narrative have to do with status in Alexandria, and make no mention of peculiarly Jewish practices or perspectives. Even when TJA tries to solve the (unexplained) problem by sending a delegation of "notables" to mediate with the "insurgents," we are not told what was discussed. We are left completely in the dark with regard to any specific issues other than hatred of Jews by the general (non-Jewish) populace.

The secondary villain of the story seems to be the Roman troops, which include not only those from the local Alexandrian garrison but also a contingent from Libya that apparently is enroute to Palestine to help quell the disorders there. At one point, the troops are mentioned almost as though they had independent authority to act in such situations (the Jewish insurgents are warned not to provoke the wrath of the army on themselves!), although it soon becomes clear that they answer to TJA's orders—he turns them loose, allows them to kill and plunder, and later in pity he commands them to withdraw. Thus TJA is described as being in control, at least of the troops, of acting wisely in attempting to find a peaceful solution, and of showing compassion and thus saving some of the Jews who were being slaughtered by the tens of thousands. He does not seem to be seen as a villain in the whole episode! Apparently, from Josephus' point of view in the *War*, TJA did what needed to be done to control the situation in Alexandria while the rebellion in Palestine grew rapidly out of hand.

Later References to Tiberius Julius Alexander in the War

There are several subsequent references to TJA in the *War*:

In 4.10.6 § 616-18 is found the story of how Vespasian quickly sought support from TJA, while the latter was still governor of Alexandria and Egypt, in order to consolidate power in the east when Vespasian's soldiers forced the imperial office upon him—TJA enthusiastically complies, and Vespasian's rule henceforth is officially dated from that event.

In 5.1.6b § 45-46, TJA is praised for his good will and insight as well as for his experience and maturity in military matters as Titus appoints him leader of the reconstituted army once the principate of Vespasian had been secured.

180

Robert A. Kraft

In 5.5.3b § 205 is a brief mention of TJA that serves to identify his father Alexander who had plated the gates of the temple with silver and gold (this is the only mention of TJA's family in the *War!*).

In 5.12.2 § 510 TJA is entrusted with the second watch, after Titus, around the besieged city of Jerusalem.

In 6.4.3 § 237-42 Titus confers with TJA—who is again pictured as being in charge of all the forces in some sense—and with the four generals of specific armies and with the procruator of Judea about whether to destroy the temple; Titus decides not to do so, and gains support from TJA and two others.

Clearly, the Josephus of the *War* presents TJA as an important and positive figure, one of the better examples of Roman officialdom. Interestingly, in the *War* Josephus never dwells on the "Jewishness" of TJA or his family, although if one knows, one can see it shining through (e.g., TJA sends secret messengers to the Jews in Alexandria, and takes pity on them; his father plates the temple gates in precious metals! TJA opposes burning the temple, in agreement with Titus and two others). Still, if the reader of the *War* did not know that TJA was of Jewish descent, that fact would not be particularly obvious from the narratives themselves. And almost nothing is learned of TJA's family from his various appearances in the *War*.

It is in the *Antiquities* that the larger family is given a role in Jewish history, with TJA's rich and genealogically well-connected father Alexander (described as "alabarch" in *Ant.* 18.259, 20.100, and in 19.276 also as an "old friend" of the emperor Claudius, for whose mother Antonia he had served as trustee!) as moneylender to Cypros and thus to her husband the Jewish king Agrippa (*Ant.* 18.159-60); with TJA's uncle Philo heading the Alexandrian Jewish delegation to Gaius (*Ant.* 18.259-60); with TJA's brother Marcus Julius Alexander as husband to princess Bernike, daughter of Agrippa (*Ant.* 19.277); and with TJA himself as not maintaining the ancestral laws, in contrast to his father's piety towards God.

Conclusions and Suggestions

The reason for such contrasting treatments by Josephus is not immediately apparent. Perhaps TJA was still alive and in power when Josephus published the surviving Greek edition of the *War* around the year 80.[5] There is some reason to believe that TJA was located in Rome after the close of the Jewish Palestinian

---

[5]On the date of Josephus' *War*, see Cohen, *Josephus*, 84-90. Cohen himself concludes that "in BJ 1-6 we have a relatively coherent uniform work finished as a whole before 81" (p. 90), which was one stage in a series of revised editions. Thus Vespasian may have seen parts of the work in progress, but probably not the whole work as we have it.

181

rebellion in the early 70's.[6] Perhaps Josephus knew, or suspected, that TJA would not appreciate a published discussion of his Jewish background and connections, for whatever reasons. In any event, both Vespasian and Titus are mentioned as recipients of copies of at least sections of the *War* in Greek (*Life* 358-63), and they certainly qualify as having been powerful supporters of TJA—good reason in itself for Josephus to deal with TJA carefully and sympathetically! That Josephus moved in the circles of "notable Jews" (see, e.g., *War* 7.447-50) who would be likely to know much more about TJA than is indicated in the *War* is certain, if his autobiography can be trusted on this matter (correspondence with Agrippa II is reported in *Life* 364), although it could be argued that much of the detailed family information was digested by him only after the *War* had been published. In any event, the passage of more than a decade between the appearance of the *War* in Greek and the publication of the *Antiquties* the may have encouraged Josephus to speak with more freedom, although still very briefly and mostly respectfully, about these matters associated with TJA.

Is it possible to make a strong connection between Philo's account of "the sabbath crisis" (*On Dreams* 2.123-32) and Josephus' story of the Alexandrian confrontation under TJA around the year 66? The general situation as described can be made to have some common elements; a (presumably Jewish) Roman ruler of Egypt[7] tries to deal with a serious crisis involving the Jewish community. In Philo, he resorts directly to threats; in Josephus, TJA sends respected Jewish mediators secretly to try to persuade the rebels to submit, with at least an implied threat (don't provoke the army!). Philo does not report the outcome. His point is the deity-usurping arrogance of the ruler—a perspective to be compared to Josephus' words about how the insurgents ridiculed ("blasphemed"!) TJA. But how could Philo fail to mention the catastrophic results, if indeed the slaughter permitted by TJA and described by Josephus was in view? It could be answered that the wonder is that Philo came this close to describing any specific events from his own times in his exegetical treatise, not that he failed to describe more! He gives such little explicit attention to contemporary situations in these writings. It was not his aim to discuss the fate of the Jewish community in this context and we cannot demand that he do so, although we can marvel that he did not.

[6] See Turner, "Tiberius Iulius Alexander," 61-64, on TJA as prefect of the praetorian guard in Rome.

[7] Philo's language seems to me to be stronger than Schwartz allows in his attempt to identify the ruler with TJA as a minor Roman official hundreds of miles from Alexandria. Philo's wording requires not only "rulership" of some sort, but also "the leadership and protection of Egypt" (a stock phrase in Philo for people in authority). While this might be stretched to refer to a young "epistrategos" in the Thebaid, that does not strike me as the most likely possibility.

Robert A. Kraft

The ruler in Philo's story is advocating abandonment of sabbath observance, as a step (thinks Philo) towards changing external Jewish habits in general; it is not clear what the specific issues are behind Josephus' story. Elsewhere, Josephus does report on attempts to force the cultically observant Jews to give up keeping sabbath—a Roman ruler in Asia Minor two centuries earlier tried this but was officially rebuffed (*Ant.* 14.10.21 § 245), and not long after the TJA episode, Josephus reports, the son of a Jewish leader in Syrian Antioch incites the anti-Jewish Antiochians against the Jews and tries to prove his opposition to Jewish customs by (among other things) forcing the Jews not to rest on sabbath (*J.W.* 7.3.3 § 46-53; Josephus claims that this policy spread briefly to other cities as well!).

As was noted above, sabbath plays another role in Josephus' story of the background of the *War*—in Agrippa's lengthy conciliatory speech to the incipient insurgents in *J.W.* 2.16.4 § 345-404, he paints them this paradox: to oppose Rome effectively, you will have to fight on sabbath, but if you do that, how can you hope for the divine assistance you will need (2.390-394)?! Sure enough, sabbath fighting soon proved necessary (see *J.W.* 2.17.10b § 456, with Josephus' strong disapproval; note the contrasting result in 2.18.1a § 457, "on the same day"!; see also 2.19.2 § 517). Josephus' own attitude is probably accurately reflected in 2.21.8 § 634, where he as a general avoids taking military action on sabbath. If TJA had advocated abandonment of sabbath observance, Josephus could hardly have mentioned it with sympathy—with the possible exception of permitting Jews to resist attacks on sabbath (see *Ant.* 12.6.2 § 274-77; 14.4.2 § 63; 18.9.2 § 319-24).

What, then, can we make of Philo's ruler's attack on sabbath keeping? Was he urging the Jews to defend themselves even on the sabbath? That would explain the language about an imminent threat to life and goods, but it somehow doesn't feel like this was the issue in Philo's mind. Was he attempting to break down the distinctions between Jews and other Roman subjects by removing any special Jewish privileges that were resented by others (not having to go to court on sabbath, for example, which Josephus notes as a privilege granted observant Jews [*Ant.* 16.6.2 § 163])—and thus quell the riots? There are many hints in Josephus and other ancient sources that significant and influential groups of non-cultic Jews existed in antiquity, of whom TJA might be a selfconscious representative.[8] Or perhaps he

[8]The presumably official language of some of the edicts cited by Josephus in *Ant.* 14 already seems to point in this direction, as I suggested many years ago ("Judaism on the World Scene," in S. Benko and J. J. O'Rourke, eds., *The Catacombs and the Colosseum* [Valley Forge, PA: Judson, 1971] 85) note, for example, *Ant.* 14.10.23 § 258, "Jewish men and women who are so inclined may keep the sabbaths and fulfil the sacred rites in accord with Jewish law" (which suggests that not all Jews were so inclined); 14.10.16 § 234 (see 14.10.13 § 228; 14.10.18 § 237; 14.10.19 § 240), "those Jews who are Roman citizens, who seem to me to have and to observe Jewish rites in Ephesus" (which could mean that some Jews did not seem to so observe).

183

was trying to enlist Jewish soldiers to help deal with the current crises, and needed to overcome the appeal for exemption on the basis of observance of sabbath and other Jewish laws (see *Ant.* 14.10.12. § 226-27) to do so? We cannot know. Why were the Alexandrians under TJA planning to send an embassy to Nero? Why was Jewish presence at the meeting viewed as "spying"? Josephus does not say. But perhaps it is to some extent on the basis of TJA's actions in the Alexandrian riots that Josephus, in the *Antiquities*, describes him as not abiding by the ancestral customs.

Although the attempt to equate Philo's "sabbath crisis" with the Alexandrian confrontation under TJA may fall short of being persuasive, it is an attempt worth considering. That it probably requires Philo to be in his 70's (or even 80's) when the event happened is not sufficient reason to disqualify such a possibility. Other related considerations are how much time might have elapsed between the event and the writing of *On Dreams*, and how many other Philonic writings were produced after *On Dreams*. Did Philo live through part or all of the catastrophic events in Palestine in 66-73? If so, why did he make no mention of them in his later writings? Did he ever reconcile in his own mind the role of his nephew, TJA, in those events? I suspect that perhaps he did, based on his treatment of the memorials to his "Joseph" (see *Migr.* 16-24).

III. New Testament and Christian Origins

DANIEL 7 AND THE HISTORICAL JESUS

Adela Yarbro Collins
University of Notre Dame

Interest in the historical Jesus has revived in the 1980s. A national research seminar has been at work reconstructing the teaching of Jesus. A section of the national meeting of the Society of Biblical Literature has been devoted to the subject. A major factor in this resurgence of interest has been the recognition that it is virtually impossible to come to an understanding of Christian origins without having a theory on the teaching and life of Jesus. In particular, it is difficult to discuss early christologies without being clear about what kind of a basis they have in the life of Jesus. One such early christology is the portrayal of Jesus as Son of Man.

A recent and influential theory has been put forward to explain the origin of this christology. The proposal is that it originated in Jesus' use of an Aramaic idiom. I would like to suggest that this theory is inadequate and to reopen the question of the role played by Daniel 7 in Christian origins.

The work of Geza Vermes

A major stimulus to the discussion of the Son of Man sayings was the publication in 1967 of Geza Vermes' thesis that the Son of Man sayings originated in Jesus' use of a Semitic idiom, namely, בַּר נָשׁ ("a son of man") or בַּר נָשָׁא ("the son of man") in a generic or indefinite sense, or, especially, as a circumlocution for "I."[1] Vermes held it to be significant that the phrase "son of man" in the New Testament occurs frequently in the gospels, once in Acts, and twice in Revelation. He thought it odd that, if the phrase were a Christological formula, it never occurred in Paul or the other epistles. Further, like others, he was struck by the fact that the phrase occurred almost exclusively on the lips of Jesus. He reminded his readers that the phrase is not idiomatic in Greek. The Greek phrase that occurs in the gospels and Acts, ὁ υἱὸς τοῦ ἀνθρώπου, would normally mean "the son of the man" or "the man's son." Since there is a Semitic idiom related to the Greek phrase and since he assumed that Jesus spoke Aramaic, Vermes turned to Aramaic texts to illuminate the origin of the phrase in the New Testament. The Semitic idiom appears in the

---

[1]Geza Vermes, "The Use of בַּר נָשׁ/בַּר נָשָׁא in Jewish Aramaic," Appendix E in Matthew Black, *An Aramaic Approach to the Gospels and Acts* (3d ed.; Oxford: Clarendon, 1967) 310-30; see also idem, *Jesus the Jew: A Historian's Reading of the Gospels* (Philadelphia: Fortress, 1973) 160-91.

Aramaic text of Dan 7:13. It is quite clear that the idiom was used in virtually all periods in a generic sense to mean "a man" or "the man" (as such, the human being in general). It is also generally accepted that the idiom was used widely in an indefinite sense to mean "one" or "someone." In fact, Vermes does not use either of these firmly established uses to explain the origin and meaning of any saying in the New Testament. Rather, the crucial underpinning of his thesis is the hypothesis that there existed in Aramaic literature what he calls a circumlocutional use of the idiom. In other words, an Aramaic speaker would use the phrase "son of man" to refer to himself, when a direct statement about himself would have seemed immodest or brought discomfort to the speaker. For example, Vermes takes the saying of Mark 2:10 as probably an actual saying of Jesus. This saying occurs in the narrative about the healing of the paralytic and reads, "But that you may know that the son of man has authority on earth to forgive sins . . ." It is followed then by the remark, "I say to you, rise, take up your pallet and go home." According to Vermes, the phrase "son of man" was used by Jesus, because the direct claim, "I have the authority to forgive sins on earth" would have sounded immodest.[2] The Son of Man sayings that contain the prediction of Jesus' suffering, death, and resurrection are said originally to have predicted only Jesus' imminent martyrdom. In these cases, the Aramaic idiom was used to avoid direct reference by the speaker to his own violent death.[3] Finally, Vermes argues that the apocalyptic Son of Man sayings were created by the apocalyptically minded Galilean followers of Jesus, who gave an eschatological interpretation of Jesus' neutral manner of speech by connecting it with Dan 7:13.[4]

Vermes' critics and followers
Vermes' thesis has been criticized by Joseph Fitzmyer because the Aramaic evidence cited to support the circumlocutional form of the idiom is later than the first century CE.[5] There is another objection, and in my view it is fatal. In all the examples cited in which the speaker uses the phrase "son of man" in Aramaic to refer to himself, the reference is to himself as a human being, as a member of humankind. In no case is the reference to the speaker as distinct from other men or as having

---

[2]Vermes, *Jesus the Jew*, 180.
[3]Ibid., 181-82.
[4]Ibid., 186.
[5]The work of Joseph A. Fitzmyer on this topic has been cited and summarized by John Donahue, "Recent Studies on the Origin of 'Son of Man' in the Gospels," in *A Wise and Discerning Heart: Studies Presented to Joseph A. Fitzmyer, S.J. in Celebration of His Sixty-Fifth Birthday, CBQ* 48 (1986) 486-90.

special authority or a special role.[6] For example, one of the texts cited by Vermes is the following story:

> If a son of man is despised by his mother, but honoured by another of his father's wives, where should he go? Yohanan replied: He should go where he is honoured. Thereupon Kahana left. Then Rabbi Yohanan was told: Kahana has gone to Babylon. He exclaimed: What! Has he gone without asking leave? They said to him: The story he told you was his request for leave.[7]

It should be clear that, in this story, "son of man" is used in an indefinite sense, meaning a man, any man. The saying is applied to the speaker, but only as a particular example of a general rule.

This text, and it is typical of Vermes' data, does not help us understand the Son of Man sayings as we have them in the gospels. For example, in Mark 2:10, such a reference by Jesus to himself would merely mean that a man, any man, has the authority to forgive sins on earth. In the context the saying surely means that Jesus has this power by virtue of his special nature or role. Even Matthew, who comments that the crowds glorified God, who had given such authority to men (human beings), probably implies the extension of Jesus' authority to his disciples, not to some general ability any person might exercise.[8]

Although Vermes' thesis regarding a circumlocutional use of the phrase "son of man" in Aramaic has been severely criticized, it has continued to be used in a modified form, even by some of his critics.[9] For example, Maurice Casey claims that the idiom in question has two levels of meaning. The first is a general statement. The second level is that at which the speaker says something about himself. Casey assumes that the saying about the son of man having authority to forgive sins in Mark 2:10 was spoken originally by Jesus in Aramaic. He takes it as a general statement used by Jesus deliberately to say something about himself. So far so good, but then Casey claims that the general statement was that healers could forgive sins. Thus the "general statement" is not general at all, but alleged to apply

---

[6]For a fuller discussion of this point, see Adela Yarbro Collins, "The Origin of the Designation of Jesus as 'Son of Man,'" *HTR* 80 (1987) 397-98.

[7]Vermes, *Jesus the Jew*, 164 (in his translation of the text, Vermes left *bar nash* untranslated. I have translated it, but otherwise quote from his version.

[8]Matt 9:8; cf. 16:18-19 and 18:18.

[9]See also Yarbro Collins, "The Origin of the Designation of Jesus as 'Son of Man,'" 397; Donahue, "Recent Studies on the Origin of 'Son of Man' in the Gospels," 489.

to a particular group.[10] The Aramaic evidence outside the New Testament does not support such a restricted use of the idiom.

Barnabas Lindars, like Casey, rejects the circumlocutional theory. He also rejects Casey's solution. But his own is equally vulnerable. He proposes that there was a use of the idiom in which "son of man" referred to a class of persons with whom the speaker identifies himself. This use he thinks is the key to the Synoptic sayings. The phrase "son of man" in this usage should be translated "a man in my position." Unfortunately, Lindars can give only one example of this usage, one of the texts cited by Vermes. Further, his interpretation of that text is not compelling. It can perfectly well and more simply be understood in the usual generic sense, that, in the situation envisaged, includes the speaker.[11] Similarly to Casey, Lindars takes the saying about the Son of Man forgiving sins in Mark 2:10 as a generic use of the idiom. But he denies that the reference is to any man.[12]

A further problem with this whole approach to the Son of Man sayings in the gospels is that it fails to explain why, if Jesus used a perfectly understandable Aramaic idiom, it was translated into Greek in such an unidiomatic way. If Jesus used the phrase generically, it could have been translated simply as "a man" in Greek and the context would have shown that Jesus was including himself in the reference. The unidiomatic translation into Greek can be explained by the hypothesis that Jesus used the phrase "son of man," not as a simple idiom, but with a particular meaning that needed to be preserved in Greek. I suggest that this particular meaning was an allusion to the wording of Dan 7:13. The phrase in that text was used idiomatically, in a generic sense: I saw (one) like a man. In the teaching of Jesus, the phrase became definite because of the allusion to "the" or "that (son of) man," namely, the one in Dan 7:13. The phrase was translated unidiomatically in Greek to make the allusion to that text clear.[13]

---

[10]Maurice Casey, *Son of Man: The Interpretation and Influence of Daniel 7* (London: SPCK, 1979) 228-29.

[11]Barnabas Lindars, *Jesus Son of Man* (London: SPCK, 1983) 22-24.

[12]Ibid., 44-45. Carsten Colpe occasionally makes a similar argument ("ὁ υἱὸς τοῦ ἀνθρώπου," *TDNT* 8 [1972] 430-31).

[13]See the discussion in Yarbro Collins, "The Origin of the Designation of Jesus as 'Son of Man,'" 404-405; on this point I agree with C. F. D. Moule (*The Origin of Christology* [Cambridge: Cambridge University Press, 1977] 13-17). I disagree with his conclusion that the referent of the one like a son of man in Daniel 7 is "the devout Jews who, in the days of Antiochus Epiphanes' persecution, had remained resolutely loyal" (ibid., 13). I agree with those who conclude that the referent of the phrase in Daniel is an angelic being (Yarbro Collins, "Daniel 7 and Jesus," forthcoming in the *Journal of Theology*, published by United Theological Seminary in Dayton, Ohio). I also disagree with Moule's conclusion that Jesus understood the human figure in Daniel 7 as a collective symbol, representing himself and his disciples as "the saints" (*The Origin of Christology*, 14). I think it more likely that he

Adela Yarbro Collins

The historical Jesus

It is unlikely that an actual saying of Jesus stands behind each of the so-called "present Son of Man sayings," referred to by Vermes, Casey and Lindars. The question arises then, how these sayings arose. First of all, the theory that the disciples of Jesus identified him with the man-like figure of Daniel 7, in light of the resurrection appearances, makes a good deal of sense, even more so if Jesus had referred to that figure in his life-time. After the death and vindication of Jesus, the two figures were easily collapsed into one, just as the "pre-existent" Son of Man of the Similitudes of Enoch was identified with the translated Enoch.[14]

My thesis then is that Jesus used the phrase "son of man" exegetically and not as a title. In other words, there was no Son of Man concept or title detachable from Daniel 7 in Jesus' life-time. The Similitudes of Enoch, and possibly 4 Ezra 13 as well, start with the text of Daniel 7, not with a universally recognized title. By concluding that Jesus used the phrase exegetically, I do not mean that he was a professional scribe or engaged in a sophisticated pesher-type method of interpretation. I am suggesting that his use of the phrase was allusive to a particular text and that the use he made of the phrase in his teaching constituted an interpretation of that text.

The hypothesis that Jesus used the phrase exegetically and not as a title, but in close relationship with himself and his mission, fits with the fact that the phrase, even when used in a quasi-titular way, is almost always on the lips of Jesus. When it is placed on the lips of the crowd in John 12, they are quoting Jesus (v 34). When it is placed on the lips of Stephen, it is in a scene modeled on the trial and execution of Jesus and Stephen's words are modeled on Jesus' words (Acts 7:56).

Some may wonder why I do not go a step further and conclude that, not only did Jesus speak of the son of man in Daniel 7, but also identified himself with that figure. In the Similitudes of Enoch, "that son of man" in Daniel 7 is identified with the Messiah.[15] Since the latest historical allusions in the work are to the Parthian invasion of Palestine in 40 BCE and to Herod's treatment in the springs of Callirrhoe, the usual methods of dating point to a date around the turn of the era. If the

---

understood that figure as a high angel or heavenly being and that he did not identify himself with that being (Yarbro Collins, "The Origin of the Designation of Jesus as 'Son of Man,'" 404–407; "Daniel 7 and Jesus").

[14]See further Yarbro Collins, "The Origin of the Designation of Jesus as 'Son of Man,'" 405-406.

[15]The parallelism between "that Son of Man" and the Messiah in chaps. 48 and 52 suggest that the two are identical. The Chosen One is characterized in chap. 49 in terms of the messianic prophecy of Isa 11:3; it is clear from many passages that the Chosen One and the Son of Man are the same figure (cf. chaps. 45 and 55 with 69:24-29).

messianic interpretation of the man-like figure was already current, may we not conclude that Jesus considered himself to be the messiah and thus also the Son of Man?

The first issue to address is whether Jesus considered himself to be the messiah. Many scholars have moved from a concern for the messianic consciousness of Jesus to the inference of a christology implicit in his life and message. One reason for this shift is that many attempts to articulate the consciousness of Jesus have involved psychologizing and have issued in portraits of Jesus that look very much like the scholars who have painted them, or at least that reflect their ideals. Another reason is a matter of contemporary taste. Many scholars feel that, if the claims about his own nature attributed to Jesus in the gospels were to be taken as historical, the resulting historical Jesus would be a man suffering from delusions of grandeur.[16] But even the attempt to discern an implicit christology yields significant results.

Most scholars agree that it is historically sound to conclude that Jesus was baptized by John the Baptist. This conclusion implies that Jesus accepted him as an agent of God (prophet) and accepted his message about "the wrath to come." At the same time, it is also historically likely that Jesus' eschatological ideas and lifestyle were different from John's. The themes of fulfillment and the presence of the Kingdom of God are characteristic of the teaching of Jesus in the tradition, themes that are lacking in the tradition about John. Further, the striking contrast between John, who "came neither eating nor drinking" and Jesus, who came eating and drinking to the extent that he was called "a glutton and a drunkard," is likely to be historically accurate, even if the saying itself was not spoken by Jesus (Matt 11:18-19/Luke 7:33-34). This contrast is best explained if John considered himself a prophet pointing to the imminent intervention of God, whereas Jesus considered himself a different kind of divine agent, perhaps a messianic figure. The main point I want to make is that the difference between their teachings and life-styles suggests that they saw themselves in different places on the eschatological time-line. Jesus' public life, after his baptism, implies a time of a greater degree of fulfillment than that of John. But we simply have no hard evidence for Jesus' precise self-understanding or for his preference with regard to a title or term designating his role.[17]

The second, related issue is whether Jesus could have identified himself with the man-like figure of Dan 7:13. Although it is clear that this figure was interpreted messianically before and after the life of Jesus, it is important to note that in the earlier of the two texts that attest this development, namely the Similitudes, the Messiah as Son of Man is a heavenly being. There is some tension in the vision of

---

[16]Norman Perrin, *A Modern Pilgrimage in New Testament Christology* (Philadelphia: Fortress, 1974) 49-50.

[17]So also E. P. Sanders, *Jesus and Judaism* (Philadelphia: Fortress, 1985) 308.

4 Ezra 13 between the portrayal of the mythic "man" and the interpretation of the vision, that emphasizes the human, earthly qualities of the messiah. It may be that the vision is an older mythic source that the author of 4 Ezra treats as an allegory of historical events.[18] The emphasis on the heavenly character of the man-like figure in Daniel itself, the extensive role of angelic beings at Qumran, and the heavenly character of the Son of Man/Messiah in the Similitudes make it somewhat more probable that Jesus, as a restoration- eschatological or apocalyptic leader, would have understood the son of man as a heavenly figure and not identified himself with that figure.

Since Jesus' use of the phrase "son of man" was exegetical, his disciples would have been encouraged to engage in further exegetical reflection. Thus, although Jesus probably did not interpret Dan 7:13 in relation to a human messiah, his disciples probably did so after his vindication. If "Son of Man" then came to mean "Messiah," the simple designation "Messiah" (Christ) would have been sufficient whenever the context of Daniel 7 was not in view. This would explain why the term "Son of Man" does not occur in Paul and the other epistles. Further, it may be that the language, perspective and current Jewish interpretation of Daniel were considered too oriented to Israel for use in the universal Gentile mission. In addition, the political and national connotations of Daniel may have been unappealing to many Greek-speaking Christians of the Diaspora, even to some Jewish Christians like Paul.[19]

Conclusion

I have attempted to show that the case for the origin of the Son of Man sayings in Jesus' use of an Aramaic idiom to refer to himself is extremely weak. Not only is this theory poorly supported by the Aramaic evidence outside the New Testament, it does not help us understand the history of the tradition. A more illuminating hypothesis is that Jesus used the phrase "son of man" to allude to the human figure of Dan 7:13 whom he interpreted as a heavenly being who would have an eschatological role in the near future. After Jesus died and was vindicated in the eyes of his followers, they reinterpreted Dan 7:13 in such a way as to identify him with the "son of man" mentioned there and interpreted this phrase messianically. The messianic interpretation allowed the use of the term as a quasi-title or even name, parallel to "Christ." The epithet was not used by Paul and many other Christians of the Diaspora probably because of the political implications it carried, due to its connection with Daniel 7.

---

[18]See Michael Stone, "The Concept of the Messiah in IV Ezra," in J. Neusner, ed., *Religions in Antiquity: Essays in Memory of E. R. Goodenough* (Leiden: Brill, 1968) 308-10.

[19]Note the striking departure from the synoptic apocalyptic discourse in the reference to "the *Lord* coming on the clouds of heaven" in Didache 16:8.

THE MIXED RECEPTION OF THE GOSPEL: INTERPRETING THE PARABLES IN MATT 13:1-52

Daniel J. Harrington, S.J.
Weston School of Theology

Matt 13:1-52 features seven (or eight) parables. Taking over some material from Mark 4:1-34, Matthew has enlarged and supplemented his source, making it into the third major discourse of Jesus. As the third of Jesus' five discourses and placed in the middle of the Gospel, the "day of parables" assumes pivotal significance. With this discourse the audience for Jesus' teaching shifts from the crowds and disciples to the disciples alone.

The major theme in Matthew's presentation of Jesus' parables in Matt 13:1-52 is the mystery of Jewish acceptance and rejection of Jesus' message of the kingdom. Thus Matthew was confronting what was a reality both during Jesus' public ministry and within his own experience toward the end of the first century CE. These parables helped Matthew to illumine what was a painful reality for Jewish Christians: not all Jews accepted the Christian claims about Jesus.

The situation facing Matthew and his community was similar to that treated by Paul in Romans 9--11.[1] There Paul sought to solve the problem of Jewish rejection and Gentile acceptance of the gospel by the image of the olive tree. The remnant (Jewish Christians such as Paul) constituted the principle of continuity. Gentile Christians had been grafted onto the olive tree, while non-Christian Jews had been cut off from it. That this mystery was in accord with God's will is "proved" by many quotations from Scripture.

Matthew's problem was the same as Paul's—the mystery of varied reactions to the gospel and how to deal with them. It is unlikely that Matthew was entering directly into conversation with Paul on the matter. At any rate, he shows no knowledge of Paul's adventurous solution to the mystery: "A hardening has come upon part of Israel, until the full number of the Gentiles come in, and so all Israel will be saved" (Rom 11:25-26).[2] Although Matthew does exploit the "hardening" motif (see 13:10-17), he has no interest in a fixed

---

[1]V. Mora, *Le Refus d'Israël: Matthieu 27,25* (LD 124; Paris: Cerf, 1986).

[2]D. J. Harrington, "Israel's Salvation according to Paul," *Bible Today* 26 (1988) 304-308.

number of Gentiles or the final (eschatological) salvation of "all Israel." He writes some thirty years after Paul and in a different place. The problem of the mixed reception of the gospel remained a real one. Matthew's solution is more limited than Paul's was. It focuses on the present and the past, not the future.

In this reading of Matthew 13, the parables concern relations between Jewish Christians (and their Gentile associates) and other Jews, between those who accept Jesus' "word of the kingdom" and those who do not. This is not the usual approach to the text today. In light of redaction-critical study of Matthew 13, it has become common to view the parables as confronting the "mixed" character of the Christians within the Matthean community, that is, the "bad" Christians and their actions.[3] Another common line of interpretation takes the parables as concerned with the Church over against Israel.[4] My approach is different. The Matthean community sees itself as part of Israel, indeed the "best" part. It must explain to itself and to anyone else who may be interested why some Jews accept the gospel and some do not.

Thus the problem facing Matthew was an inner-Jewish one, not unlike the problem that Jesus encountered in his preaching. The difference, of course, arose from the cross and resurrection, from the claims made by Christians and the scandal that they constituted for other Jews.

This approach to the parables in Matthew 13 is suggested first of all by the literary context. The theme of Israel's acceptance and rejection of Jesus and his message runs through chapters 11--15. The "day of parables" is bracketed by Jesus' definition of his true family (12:46-50) and the rejection of Jesus by people in his hometown (13:53-58). The parables in Matt 21:28--22:14 and 24:36--25:46, which flank the infamous woes against the scribes and Pharisees in chapter 23, carry on the same theme of the mixed reception of the gospel within Israel. This reading of the parables also allows a smoother movement from the Jesus-level of Matthew's story to Matthew's own time. Jesus and Matthew address the same problem, whereas the "inside the church" and the "church versus Israel" approaches involve a radical revision of the problem at issue.

The "within Israel" approach adopted in this paper is also recommended by the circumstances in which Matthew wrote his Gospel. I read Matthew's Gospel as one of several Jewish responses to the destruction of the Jerusalem temple in 70 CE. The Matthean community somewhere in Syria or Palestine still existed

---

[3] J. R. Donahue, *The Gospel in Parable: Metaphor, Narrative, and Theology in the Synoptic Gospels* (Philadelphia: Fortress, 1988) 66-70.

[4] J. D. Kingsbury, *The Parables of Jesus in Matthew 13: A Study in Redaction-Criticism* (Richmond, VA: John Knox, 1969) 130-37.

Daniel J. Harrington, S.J.

within the framework of Judaism but in tension with other Jewish groups—
especially the early rabbinic movement apparently in control of "their
synagogues" (Matt 4:23; 9:35; 10:17; 12:9; 13:54), which are synagogues of the
hypocrites (6:2, 5; 23:6, 34). The stakes were high (the survival of Judaism),
the transition from a Temple- and land-centered Judaism to some other kind was
at a very early stage (late first century CE), and tensions were severe (as Matthew
23 and other texts show). Matthew's theological problem should be viewed as
an attempt to show how the Jewish tradition is best preserved in a Jewish-
Christian context. An obvious problem for Matthew and his community was
the mixed reception of the gospel within Israel. Why did some Jews not accept
the gospel? How should Jewish Christians (and their Gentile associates) react to
such Jews?

The Parable of the Sower and Its Interpretation
     The first part of Matthew's "day of parables" (13:1-23) follows Mark 4:1-20
closely. The general structure is the same: the setting (Matt 13:1-3a; Mark 4:1-
2), the parable of the sower (Matt 13:3b-9; Mark 4:3-9), the reason for speaking
in parables (Matt 13:10-17; Mark 4:10-12), and the interpretation of the parable
(Matt 13:18-23; Mark 4:13-20). Whereas Matthew basically reproduced the
Markan parable and its interpretation, he expanded the setting somewhat and
added greatly to the part about the reason for speaking in parables. This
overview indicates that what especially concerned Matthew was Jesus' reason for
speaking in parables and the contrasting reactions to his parables.
     The scene (Matt 13:1-3a) is taken over from Mark and embellished to
connect the narrative with what now precedes it. Since Jesus in Matt 12:46-50
was in a house, he must now go forth from the house. The picturesque scene of
Jesus seated in a boat off the shore and the crowd standing on the shore is taken
over from Mark. Matthew's reader would be expected to envision some point
along the western shore of the Sea of Galilee. The scene provides an appropriate
setting for the final parable of the series—the dragnet (Matt 13:47-50).
     The so-called parable of the sower (13:3b-9) really focuses on the seeds and
their respective yields. The sower merely initiates the action. If we assume that
this parable goes back to Jesus (as most interpreters do), it would have been
especially appropriate for an audience made up largely of Galilean farmers. Even
non-farmers in an agricultural society would have had some familiarity with
seeds and harvests. There is every reason to assume that Matthew's readers knew
something about such matters and could easily relate to them.
     That the parable of the sower concerns something beyond agriculture,
however, is suggested by two texts in 4 Ezra, a Palestinian-Jewish writing
composed around 100 CE that reflects on the theological implications of the
destruction of Jerusalem and its temple in 70 CE. In this work roughly

contemporary with Matthew's Gospel, the seed/harvest imagery is prominent: "For just as the farmer sows many seeds upon the ground and plants a multitude of seedlings, and yet not all that have been sown will come up in due season and not all that were planted will take root; so all those who have been sown in the world will not be saved" (4 Ezra 8:41). In 4 Ezra 9:31 the seed is equated with the Law ("I sow my Law in you"), and a distinction is made between the eternal character of the seed (the Law) and the perishable character of those who receive the Law but sin (9:32-37). In the Christian context the seed is Jesus' "word of the kingdom" (Matt 13:19). But there is a common concern in the Jewish apocalyptic and early Christian traditions for explaining why not all the plantlings reach an abundant harvest and why only some will do so.

Matthew's most extensive rewriting and adaptation appears in the section about the reason for Jesus' speaking in parables (Matt 13:10-17). He has simplified and clarified the setting, added a saying (13:12) from Mark 4:25, given the full Septuagint text of Isa 6:9-10, and included a Q saying found also in Luke 10:23-24. The effect of all these editorial modifications and additions is to heighten the contrast between those who have received Jesus' word of the kingdom and those who have not.

The theological presupposition of Matt 13:10-17 (and Mark 4:10-12) is the "hardening" motif found in Isa 6:9-10. [5] The allusion to this text in Mark 4:12 is taken over in Matt 13:13, and then the full text is provided in Matt 13:14-15. The biblical context is God's commissioning of Isaiah the prophet. At the end of Isaiah's vision of God's majesty, the prophet is sent forth with the paradoxical mission of increasing the obduracy of those to whom he proclaims God's will. The prophet is to continue until the destruction and exile occur and only a "stump" or remnant remains (see Isa 6:13). The text would have been an effective tool for early Christians in their efforts at relating Jesus to major biblical figures (here Isaiah) and to explain why not all Jews accept the message of Jesus. It also appears in Acts 28:26-27 and John 12:40, and is alluded to in Romans 9--11. Without explaining precisely why the message of Isaiah and of Jesus is rejected, the quotation describes the phenomenon of "hardening" on the people's part and presents it as in accord with Scripture and therefore God's will.

The reasons for the people's hardening are spelled out in the "allegorical" interpretation (Matt 13:18-23) taken over from Mark 4:13-20. The vocabulary is more typical of the Epistles than of the Gospels. The situations described in it probably reflect the failures of some early Christians. It is often taken as a kind

---

[5] J. Gnilka, *Die Verstockung Israels: Isaias 6,9-10 in der Theologie der Synoptiker* (SANT 3; Munich: Kösel, 1961).

of examination of conscience or sermon outline based on the parable of the sower. Even the most persistent champion of the authentic words of Jesus attributed this text to the early church. Joachim Jeremias confessed: "I have long held out against the conclusion that this interpretation must be ascribed to the primitive church; but on linguistic grounds alone it is unavoidable." [6]

Even though the content and vocabulary of the interpretation suggest an origin within the early church, such an origin does not necessarily determine Matthew's use of the text. Matthew's major interest was to explain why some Jews refused Jesus' "word of the kingdom." He used the interpretation as a list of reasons why his fellow Jews did not accept and act upon Jesus' preaching: the evil one's activity (13:19), personal shallowness (13:20-21), and worldly concerns and desire for wealth (13:22). He contrasted them with the ideal disciple who "hears the word and understands" (13:23). Whereas the original interpretation may well have circulated to explain problems within the Christian community, Matthew set it back into the ministry of the earthly Jesus and used it to illumine the mysterious situation in which some Jews accepted and some Jews rejected Jesus' preaching.

Other Parables

The rest of Matthew's "day of parables" combines material from Mark, Matthew's special tradition (M), and Matthew himself: the parable of the wheat and weeds (13:24-30), the parable of the mustard seed (13:31-32), the parable of the leaven (13:33), the reason for Jesus' use of parables (13:34-35), an explanation of the parable of the wheat and the weeds (13:36-43), the parables of the hidden treasure (13:44) and the pearl (13:45-46), the parable of the dragnet (13:47-50), and the parable of the householder (13:51-52). Matthew used Mark for 13:31-32, 34-35. He probably composed the two explanations (13:36-43, 49-50) by himself. The remainder (13:24-30, 33, 44-48) is most likely attributable to the special tradition found only in Matthew (M).

The parable of the wheat and weeds (13:24-30) follows well on the parable of the sower. The setting is agricultural, and the subject is the mixed reception accorded to Jesus' message. The problem is the fact that some Jews accept and others reject the gospel.[7] The issue before the Matthean Christians is: how do we react to this reality? The parable, which surely has allegorical features (though not as many as Matt 13:36-43 supplies), counsels patience and tolerance

---

[6] J. Jeremias, *The Parables of Jesus* (rev. ed.; New York: Scribner's, 1963) 77.

[7] For another "within the church" approach see G. Barth, "Auseinandersetzungen um die Kirchenzucht im Umkreis des Matthäusevangeliums," *ZNW* 69 (1978) 158-77.

in the present. The assumption behind this counsel is the confidence that at the final judgment there will be a separation between the just and the unjust along with appropriate rewards and punishments.

The same dynamic underlies the parable of the dragnet (13:47-48). Though not the elaborate story that Matt 13:24-30 is, the problem is the same: how to deal with the mixed response accorded to the gospel. And the solution is also the same: patience and tolerance until the final judgment, when God will set matters straight.

The parables, which are so close as to constitute a pair, reflect an approach common in Jewish apocalyptic writings. A good example is the "instruction on the two spirits" in the Qumran *Manual of Discipline* (1QS cols. 3--4), which divides humankind into two segments: the "sons of light" who follow the Prince of Light and do the deeds of light, and the "sons of darkness" who follow the Angel of Darkness and do the deeds of darkness. These two groups walk in their two ways until the final end. But God "has set an end for the existence of perversity; and at the time of the visitation he will destroy it forever. Then truth shall arise in the world forever" (4:18-19). The same point is made in 1QS 4:25: "For God has allotted these spirits in equal parts until the final end, the time of renewal."[8]

The two parables and the Qumran text deal with what their writers reckoned as misguided and even morally wrong behavior. The particular problem facing both is how the "insiders" are to react. Their solution is to leave judgment to God in the end-time. For the present the proper response is patience and tolerance born from the conviction that in the end God will make all things right.

The other four parables (13:31-32, 33, 44, 45-46) come in pairs. The mustard seed and the leaven (13:31-33) stress the contrast between the small beginnings of the kingdom and the great result. The hidden treasure and the pearl (13:44-46) emphasize the extraordinary value of the kingdom and the single-minded response that it should elicit. In all four parables the kingdom is a present, though inchoate, reality. The great result that can be expected in the future and the extraordinary value that the kingdom possesses in the present make its rejection all the more puzzling and implausible.

If it is correct to attribute the explanations of the two parables (13:36-43, 49-50) to Matthew himself, then it seems that his special interest was the future judgment. Nevertheless, he was sufficiently concerned with the theme of patient

---

[8]Translations of 1QS are from A. Dupont-Sommer, *The Essene Writings from Qumran* (Cleveland/New York: World, 1962) 78-79.

tolerance that he included the two parables (13:24-30, 47-48). The quotation of Ps 78(77):2 added to the saying about Jesus' use of the parables in teaching the crowds (13:35) asserts that this style of teaching—and its resultant incomprehension—was in accord with God's will.

Conclusion

How did Matthew intend his first readers to understand the parables of the kingdom in chap. 13? The literary and historical context as well as the content indicate that for Matthew and his community these parables concerned the mixed reception of the gospel. Some Jews and even some Gentiles accepted it, and some did not. Matthew used the parables to highlight the mystery involved in receiving or rejecting the word of the kingdom (13:19) offered in Jesus' preaching. He also advised his fellow Christians about how to deal with Jews who rejected the gospel: patient tolerance in the present, and leaving the future judgment to God.

Matthew and his community remained within the framework of Judaism. Indeed, they were convinced that faith in Jesus led to the fullest kind of Judaism. They did not yet view themselves as practicing a separate religion as the "church versus Israel" approach suggests. Neither was their focus of attention the problems within the community caused by "bad" Christians. Their major concern was to understand why some Jews rejected the gospel and how those who accepted it should look upon those who did not.

JOHN 10 AND THE FEAST OF THE DEDICATION

James C. VanderKam
North Carolina State University

After he presents the section about Jesus as the good shepherd (John 10:1-21), the author of the fourth gospel introduces a new episode at 10:22-23 by noting that "it was the feast of the Dedication at Jerusalem; it was winter, and Jesus was walking in the temple, in the portico of Solomon."[1] On this occasion "the Jews" surround Jesus and ask him for a definitive statement at long last: "If you are the Christ, tell us plainly" (v 24c). Jesus' answer is, in effect, "yes," but as he replies he points to the unbelief of the audience: his works, which are done in his Father's name, should answer their query, but they do not believe because they do not belong to his sheep (vv 25-26). This segment of the scene (vv 24-30)—his initial response which recalls the good shepherd language at the beginning of the chapter (see the addition in some MSS at v 26: καθὼς εἶπον ὑμῖν) and thus unites the two pericopes—concludes with Jesus' forthright declaration: "I and the Father are one" (ἐγὼ καὶ ὁ πατῆρ ἕν ἐσμεν [v 30]).

His astounding answer makes "the Jews" wish to stone him. When Jesus asks which of his works have elicited their reaction, they reply: "It is not for a good work that we stone you but for blasphemy; because you, being a man, make yourself God" (ὅτι σὺ ἄνθρωπος ὢν ποιεῖς σεαυτὸν θεόν [v 33]). Jesus, who acknowledges tacitly that he has in fact claimed divinity for himself, then cites scriptural support for calling human beings "gods" (Ps 82:6). He argues that if the psalm (which he labels "your law" [v 34]) could properly designate those who received the divine word as "gods," how could his interrogators question his claim, when he was the one "whom the Father consecrated and sent into the world" (v 36)? His second exchange with the audience proves no more successful than the first. This time they want to arrest him (v 39).

John 10:22-39 is one of a series of scenes in which the evangelist connects the actions and words of Jesus with a festival—a familiar feature that distinguishes John from the Synoptic Gospels. In fact, that part of the fourth gospel which scholars have grown accustomed to calling the Book of Signs (chaps. 2-12) is, in large sections, organized around references to sabbaths, passovers, and other holidays.

---

[1] All biblical citations are from the *RSV*.

These feasts evidently were very important elements in the way in which the writer chose to present Jesus to his audiences. Though there are several mentions of a passover at earlier points in the Book of Signs (2:13, 23; cf. 2:45), it is especially in chaps. 5-10 that holidays play the most prominent roles. R. Brown refers to these chapters under the title "Jesus and the Principal Feasts of the Jews."[2]

In this intriguing section of the gospel—that is, chaps. 5-10—the writer first relates how Jesus performed a healing miracle on the sabbath (5:1-15); following this account, one reads discourses in which the significance of his action on the day of rest is elaborated (16-47). It is worth noting that in this opening segment of chaps. 5-10 Jesus' opponents not only fault him for violating the sabbath but also because he "called God his own Father, making himself equal with God" (ἴσον ἑαυτὸν ποιῶν τῷ θεῷ [5:18])—a charge that will be repeated at the close of the section (10:33). The following chapter centers about Jesus' feeding of the 5,000 at the time of passover and the meaning that the writer attaches to the event. Jesus' speech at this time involves the assertion that he is the heavenly manna (v 31) and the bread of life (35). A number of scholars have demonstrated that the themes which are developed in the discourse draw upon traditional associations of passover and the lectionary readings which synagogue audiences probably heard around the time of the festival.[3]

The next, more extended section finds its setting at the festival of tabernacles (at least chaps. 7-8, and perhaps 9 as well). Here, too, Jesus' major statements stand in direct relationship with the holiday, but in this instance his words build upon the ceremonies which took place in the temple. On the last day of the festival he called himself the source to whom the thirsty should come and drink (7:37-38) and the light of the world (8:12). As all commentators note, these two claims reflect or were occasioned by the prominence of water and light in the spectacular celebration of the

---

[2] R. Brown, *The Gospel According to John i-xii* (AB 29; Garden City, NY: Doubleday, 1966) 200-204. These chapters form what he classifies as the third part of the Book of Signs; 4:46-54 serve as an introduction to it.

[3] See Brown, *John*, 255-56, 262, 265, 272-74, 277-80; and C. H. Dodd, *The Interpretation of the Fourth Gospel* (Cambridge: Cambridge University Press, 1968) 333-45, for surveys of passages and views. Cf. also P. Borgen, *Bread From Heaven: An Exegetical Study of the Concept of Manna in the Gospel of John and the Writings of Philo* (SNT 10; Leiden: Brill, 1965; 2d ed. with revisions, 1981); *Philo, John and Paul: New Perspectives on Judaism and Early Christianity* (Brown Judaic Studies 131; Atlanta: Scholars, 1987) esp. Part II, chaps. 6 and 7; and A. Guilding, *The Fourth Gospel and Jewish Worship: A Study of the Relation of St. John's Gospel to the Ancient Jewish Lectionary System* (Oxford: Clarendon, 1960) 58-68.

autumn festival.[4] The light imagery continues into chap. 9 in which Jesus heals the man born blind. Dodd has chosen to classify this chapter as part of a new section in the Book of Signs ("Judgment by Light"),[5] but one can at least say that it is not entirely divorced from the symbolism of the chapters that precede it. The final holiday in this series is the Feast of the Dedication which is mentioned in 10:22. The Johannine Hanukkah and its relations with its context in John 10 are the subjects of the present essay. The pages that follow offer, first, a survey of the suggestions that have been made about the relations between the winter festival and John 10:22-39 and, second, a proposal regarding an additional point of contact between chap. 10 and the historical associations of Hanukkah.

Most commentators on John 10:22-39 are satisfied with noting simply that the festival commemorated the rededication of the temple and altar by Judas Maccabeus in 165 or 164, after they had been profaned for some years by the pagan worship and practices which Antiochus IV Epiphanes had imposed upon his Jewish subjects. It is also regularly observed that since the eight-day festival began on Chislev 25 it was a winter holiday, as the evangelist mentions in v 22. Some expositors go on to explain that it was appropriate that Jesus be walking in Solomon's portico at this time of year. As Brown writes, this is a "... detail of local color that is very acccurate. At this winter season, when the cold winds sweep in from the east across the great desert, we find Jesus in the east portico of the Temple, the only one of the porticoes whose closed side would protect it from the east wind..."[6]

It would not be surprising if the reference to Solomon would have evoked more than a literal reaction in the reader. The great king was, of course, the first temple-builder in Israel's history, and he was also the first to dedicate one. As is well known, the verb that is used for his dedicating the temple in 1 Kgs 8:63; 2 Chr 7:5, 9 (וַיַּחְנְכוּ) is the one to which the noun *hanukkah* is related. Moreover, Josephus implies that the portico of Solomon was a structure from the first temple that had

---

[4]For references, see Str-B 2.490-93, 521-22, 774-812; Guilding, *The Fourth Gospel*, 92-120; Brown, *John*, 326-29, 343-44; and Dodd, *The Interpretation*, 348-51.

[5]*The Interpretation*, 354-61. See also Brown, *John*, 376; and Guilding (*The Fourth Gospel*, 121-26), who thinks that for this chapter "... the sequence of lectionary readings seems to indicate a date at the end of Tishri or, more likely, at the beginning of the eighth month, Cheshvan" (121).

[6]Brown, *John*, 405. J. Giblet ("Et il y eut la dédicace ... Jean 10, 22-39," *Bible et vie chrétienne* 66 [1965] 18) thinks that more is involved: "Nous savons par les souvenirs conservés dans les Actes des Apôtres que les chrétiens se sont réunis souvent dans cette partie extérieure du Temple [Acts 3:11] et on peut penser que le rapprochement n'est pas fortuit. Car la controverse qui va suivre, fut aussi celle que, bien souvent sans doute, les premiers disciples du Christ eurent à soutenir en ces mêmes lieux."

somehow escaped destruction and had become part of the second sanctuary. In *J.W.* 5.5.1 (§ 185) he relates that Solomon, "having walled up the eastern side, a single portico was reared on this made ground" (cf. also *Ant.* 15.11.3 [§ 401]).[7] In *Ant.* 20.9.7 (§ 221) he again attributes this great portico to Solomon. The place in which Jesus was walking may, then, have been more widely believed to be the only part of the temple that had endured from the beginning of the structure to the present—the lone physical connection between the two temples of Israel's long history. In this remarkable portico, with its historic symbolism and supposed continuity, there now walks the new son of David who, for John, would replace it by building the temple of his body (2:19-22).

Scholars have spotted in the ensuing narrative and discussions a few additional details that may have some connection with the festival of Hanukkah. First, the fact that the audience's initial question concerns Jesus' messianic status has occasionally been seen as a reflection of the nationalistic associations of the holiday—associations which might have included the expectation of a new deliverer. As B. F. Westcott put it: "The special mention of the time appears to be made in order to connect the subject of the Lord's teaching with hopes associated with the last national deliverance. The Hymn which is at present used in Jewish Synagogues at the Festival records the successive deliverances of Israel, and contains a prayer for yet another."[8] There seem not to be, however, any indications in the sources that there were, in the first century, special associations between Hanukkah and hopes for national deliverance led by a messiah.

One final detail in the text has been isolated as possibly being conditioned by Hanukkah. Jesus refers to himself as the one whom the Father *consecrated* (v 36). The verb which he uses ($\dot{\eta}\gamma\iota\alpha\sigma\epsilon\nu$) is also employed in Num 7:1, which is the first verse in the Torah passage for Hanukkah.[9] If this parallel is admitted, then the several occurrences of the verb חנך (vv 1 [twice], 10, 84, 88; in these last three verses both the construct form of the noun *hanukkah* (חֲנֻכַּת) and the niphal infinitive

---

[7]Translation of H. St. J. Thackeray, *Josephus III: The Jewish War, Books IV–VII* (LCL; Cambridge: Harvard University Press, 1928). See also Brown, *John,* 402; and E. Lohse, *"Solomon," TDNT* (1971) 464.

[8]B. F. Westcott, *The Gospel According to John* (2 vols.; London: John Murray, 1908) 2.64. E. Nodet ("La dédicace, les Maccabées et le messie," *RB* 93 [1986] 321–75) discusses the changing perceptions of the festival and argues that it originally had messianic associations (as attested by John 10:22-39) but other views developed, with the result that Hanukkah fell in importance—a process that reached its culmination with the failure of the messianic revolt of Bar Kokhba.

[9]Brown, *John,* 404, 411.

James C. VanderKam

of רשמ appear) in the same chapter of Leviticus should also be noted in connection with the question about Jesus' messianic status.

Beyond general connections of these sorts, exegetes have found little else in John 10:22-39 that might be explained as having been occasioned by the festival of Hanukkah. This is fairly surprising when one recalls the importance for the gospel text of the holidays which are named in the the preceding chapters. But a glance at the standard commentaries indicates that their authors consider the reference to the holiday as of little consequence. No less an authority than C. K. Barrett maintains that its purpose was merely "... that of indicating the lapse of a short interval; it does not seem possible to detect any symbolical correspondence between the conduct of the feast and the ensuing discussion..." [10] R. Schnackenburg states the matter thus:

> All in all, the mention of this feast does not carry the same weight as is the case with the other feasts, and it is rather to be thought of, in effect, as being an incidental remark. It remains open to question whether the subject of pastoral discourses was selected in view of this feast, on which occasion corresponding O.T. passages occurred in the three-yearly cycle of synagogue readings.[11]

Schnackenburg's reference to the synagogal lections for Hanukkah brings to mind A. Guilding's intriguing contribution to the understanding of the festal sections in the Gospel of John. She has argued that the lectionary passages of the triennial cycle that were read at the times of the great festivals have played a fundamental role in John's development of themes around his frequent references to holidays. As she formulates her thesis:

> It is suggested, then, that the Fourth Gospel appears to be a Christian commentary on the Old Testament lectionary readings as they were arranged for the synagogue in a three-year cycle. The order of the Gospel follows the cycle of the Jewish lectionary year, which was so arranged that a suitable portion of scripture was read at each of the feasts, and the evangelist's many allusions to Jewish festivals are not

---

[10]C. K. Barrett, *The Gospel According to John: An Introduction with Commentary and Notes on the Greek Text* (2d ed.; Philadelphia: Westminster, 1978) 379. For similar assessments, see L. Morris, *The New Testament and the Jewish Lectionaries* (London: Tyndale, 1964) 66; and Giblet, "Et il y eut la dédicace," 24-25.

[11]R. Schnackenburg,*The Gospel According to John* (3 vols.; New York: Seabury, 1968, 1980, 1982) 2.305.

merely casual references but are fundamental to the structure of the Gospel.[12]

Basic to her case are her two related claims that, first, there was "... a regular system of lectionary readings already in use by the first century,"[13] and that, second, it appears "... probable that by the first century CE the triennial cycle was in use."[14] Once she has established these points to her satisfaction, she proceeds to reconstruct from later sources the likely form of the lections—both Torah and haphtarah—for each sabbath of the three years and also for the various holiday seasons.[15] It must be objected, however, that her conclusions go considerably beyond what the texts which she cites allow. A more widely held view today is that one cannot draw definitive conclusions from the much later data about a fixed lectionary system in the first century. The issue is not, of course, whether selections from the Torah and prophets were read on sabbaths in the synagogues; that is obvious, with the New Testament itself providing the clearest and earliest examples (Luke 4:16-30; Acts 13:15). The question is rather: were there, for each sabbath, *stipulated* passages from the law and prophets as there were at later times. As B. Z. Wacholder writes:

> Unfortunately, it is impossible to reconstruct the respective readings of the Torah and Prophets for the Sabbaths when Jesus and Paul appeared in the synagogues of Nazareth and Antioch. Adolph Buchler's article ... claiming to do so has misled some scholars into believing that our present knowledge permits us to reconstruct the cycles for the Scriptural selections during the pre-70 period, thus making it possible to fix seasons for events recorded in the Gospels. Except for the Festival readings, and even here much doubt remains, there is no evidence of a cycle of Scriptural readings linked with the calendar. The so-called 'Triennial Cycle' ... is probably of a later date, and was not tied to a particular season of the year.[16]

---

[12]*The Fourth Gospel*, 3.

[13]Ibid., 8.

[14]Ibid., 10. In fact, she claims more: "... the origin of the triennial cycle can be traced back to approximately 400 BC, so that by the first century the lectionary readings of this cycle were no novelty but already old—established and fixed" (24).

[15]Ibid., 10-23; see also 24-44.

[16]B. Z. Wacholder, "Prolegomenon: A History of the Sabbatical Readings of Scripture for the 'Triennial Cycle'" in J. Mann, *The Bible as Read and Preached in the Old Synagogue*, vol. 1: *The Palestinian Triennial Cycle* (reprinted New York: KTAV, 1971) xvi-xvii (Wacholder's Prolegomenon was republished in his *Essays on Jewish*

James C. VanderKam

Yet, even if one agrees with Wacholder (and others) and thus rejects Guilding's claims about the existence in the first century of a fixed triennial system, it is still possible that she is correct in seeing a close connection between the Johannine references to festivals and certain biblical passages which later became fixed lections for these holidays. The true test of her case comes in how well it explains the passages in question; and here it must be admitted that she has produced some fascinating insights, particularly for the passover and tabernacles sections which were treated above.

Guilding has also subjected the tenth chapter of John to a lectionary analysis and has found ample connections with passages which, according to later notices in Jewish literature, were read around the time of Hanukkah. She treats the whole of the chapter—both the Good Shepherd section (vv 1-21), which precedes the reference to the holiday, and the discussion that is explicitly dated to the time of the Dedication (vv 22-39). The Mishnah and Babylonian Talmud identify the Torah and haphtarah readings for Hanukkah itself. According to *m. Meg.* 3.6, "At the [Feast of the] Dedication [they read the section] 'The Princes'" (= Num 7:1-89).[17] The comment on this passage in the Babylonian Talmud adds: "On Hanukkah we read the section of the Princes and for *haftarah* [on Sabbath] that of the lights in Zechariah. Should there fall two sabbaths in Hanukkah, on the first we read [for *haftarah*] the passage of the lights in Zechariah and on the second that of the lights of Solomon."[18] The two "lights" passages in the prophets are Zechariah 4 and 1 Kings 7:40-50.

The sabbath that precedes Hanukkah is also important for Guilding's argument. On her reconstruction, the first-year Torah passage for this sabbath would be Gen 46:28-47:31, in which one finds shepherding language (see 46:33; 47:3 where Jacob and his sons identify themselves to the pharaoh as shepherds). Ezek 37:16ff., the haphtarah for the preceding seder (Gen 44:18ff.), may, she thinks, once have been associated with the reading of Gen 46:28ff. Also, Ezekiel 34 was the haphtarah for

Chronology and Chronography [New York: KTAV, 1976] 137-211). The essay of Buchler to which he refers is "The Triennial Cycle," *JQR* 5 (1893) 420-68; 6 (1894) 1-73. A verdict similar to Wacholder's was reached by E. Schürer, *The History of the Jewish People in the Age of Jesus Christ (175 B.C.-A.D. 135)* (rev. and ed. by G. Vermes, F. Millar, and M. Black; 3 vols.; Edinburgh: Clark, 1973-1987) 2.450-51; and S. Safrai, "The Synagogue" in S. Safrai and M. Stern, eds., *The Jewish People in the First Century* (CRINT 1, 2; Assen: van Gorcum; Philadelphia: Fortress, 1976) 927-30. For a detailed expose of weaknesses in Guilding's book, see Morris, *The New Testament and the Jewish Lectionaries.*

[17]Translation of H. Danby, *The Mishnah* (Oxford: Oxford University Press, 1933) 205.

[18]Translation of M. Simon in *The Babylonian Talmud, part 2: Seder Mo'ed* (4 vols.; I. Epstein, ed.; London: Soncino, 1938) 4.190.

the second year. Both of these passages from Ezekiel use pastoral imagery not only for God but also for the davidic shepherd whom God will appoint (37:22, 24 [note the reference to the sanctuary to be set in their midst in vv 26-28]; 34:23-24 [according to 34:27 God will break the bars of the yoke of those who oppress his people]). Thus, the biblical lections which would be heard just before Hanukkah make Jesus' discourse about himself as the good shepherd (placed immediately before the reference to Hanukkah) and also the discussion about Jesus as messiah in 10:27-30 most timely.[19]

Guilding also thinks that the subject of blasphemy in 10:33 can be explained from the lectionary cycle. In the second year of the triennial readings, Lev 24:1-25:13 (or to 25:34) would be the Torah portion. It comes just after chap. 23 which deals with the festivals, the last of which is Tabernacles—the final holiday mentioned in John before chap. 10. Moreover, chap. 24 begins with a treatment of the permanent light in the tabernacle—a theme that would have been most pertinent during the Dedication with the prominence of lights in its celebration. Then, in Lev 24:10-16 there is a description of blasphemy and the punishment for it. Note v 16: "He who blasphemes the name of the Lord shall be put to death; all the congregation shall stone him; the sojourner as well as the native, when he blasphemes the Name, shall be put to death." Blasphemy and stoning are, of course, two other important subjects in John 10.[20]

Thus one may say with confidence that, though the evidence has not allowed her to establish the existence of a fixed triennial lectionary system in the first century, Guilding has uncovered some noteworthy connections that associate the scriptural portions that—at least in later sources—are attested as having been read at the season of Hanukkah and the themes that dominate John 10: shepherding; the davidic shepherd/ messiah; and blasphemy/stoning. Her work rather effectively refutes the claims of those who find little more than surface contacts between Hanukkah and the concerns of John 10. Yet, though she has advanced a considerable distance beyond her predecessors, she has not exhausted the fund of Hanukkah associations in this passage. In particular, she has not dealt with the importance of Jesus' claim *at this precise occasion and in this very location* to being one with God. Guilding suggests, in discussing the major themes of Hanukkah, that there may be something here but she contents herself only with these general comments:

---

[19]Guilding, *The Fourth Gospel,* 129-32.

[20]Ibid., 131. It is difficult to see the point of Morris' (*The New Testament and the Jewish Lectionaries,* 48) brief critique of Guilding's conclusions about the lections and Hanukkah. She finds echoes of both the sabbath and special lections for the holiday in John 10; why should this be considered "unusual" in connection with her overall argument?

Thus in New Testament times Hanukkah would doubtless be associated in Jewish and Christian minds with two contrasting sets of ideas: the blasphemy of false worship, the Man of Sin, and the Temple defiled: the true worship of a regathered Israel (an idea found already in 2 Maccabees 2.18), the return of the Shekinah, and the Temple restored.[21]

The notions of "the blasphemy of false worship" and "the Man of Sin" deserve further exploration.

In dealing with the possible relations between the festival and the passage in John's gospel, it is important to remember that there could be different kinds of relationships. There are the obvious connections (time of the year, etc.) that most commentators note, and there are the more profound interconnections of scriptural lections as Guilding has shown. But one might also ask whether the historical associations of the events that inspired the first Hanukkah might be on the minds of Jesus and his audience or on that of the author. The festival did indeed commemorate the rededication of the altar and temple to the worship of Israel's God, but it is difficult to believe that Jewish people would not be thinking about the defiled conditions of the temple and cult from which the Maccabean forces had to cleanse and reconsecrate them. In this connection it should be recalled that Antiochus IV not only banned the practice of Judaism and the temple cult but that he also imposed new forms of worship which included veneration of himself as a god in Jerusalem's temple. Jesus' strong assertions that he and the Father are one (10:30), that he was the Son of God (10:36), and that the Father was in him as he was in the Father (10:38) were uttered at a time when the blasphemous pretensions of Antiochus IV to be a god would have been particularly fresh in the minds of Jewish people. The vigorous reactions of the Jewish audience to Jesus' claims are especially understandable against this historical backdrop. A study of the texts which treat Antiochus' divinity reveal some interesting points of similarity with the argument between Jesus and "the Jews" in John 10:22-39 and with the words that immediately precede this section.

For Antiochus' claims to divinity there is the testimony of history and archeology, while for his imposition of the cult of himself in Jerusalem there is the evidence of 1-2 Maccabees. The extant coins that were minted during Antiochus IV's reign prove that he, like a number of other hellenistic monarchs, advertised himself as a god. Although the older theory that Antiochus identified himself with Zeus

---

[21]Ibid., 129.

should now be abandoned,[22] he does appear to have been the first of the great hellenistic kings to "... introduce divine epithets such as 'God Manifest' and 'God Manifest, the Victorious' on his coins."[23] The Greek wording for these titles is: βασιλέως 'Αντιόχου θεοῦ ἐπιφανοῦς and βασιλέως 'Αντιόχου θεοῦ ἐπιφανοῦς νικεφόρου. One also finds the shorter inscription βασιλέως 'Αντιόχου θεοῦ on some of his coins.[24] Thus, it is a fact that he used the word θεός for himself, though it is apparent that not all were convinced by Antiochus' use of the cult of the sovereign. As Polybius reports, after describing some of the king's more unusual capers: "In consequence all respectable men were entirely puzzled about him, some looking upon him as a plain simple man and others as a madman (μαινόμενον)."[25] It is to Polybius that we owe the quip that he was not ἐπιφανής, but ἐπιμανής.[26]

The Jewish texts which deal with the fateful years of Antiochus' reign and his relations with the Judean populace echo the themes of his supposed divinity and anti-godly arrogance and hold them up for judgment or ridicule. The earliest references are found in Daniel 7, 8, and 11. In the former two chapters, the seer watches visions in which Antiochus is represented as a little horn. According to chap. 7, this little horn (vv 8, 20), who makes war with the saints of the Most High (21), will "speak words against the Most High and shall wear out the saints of the Most High..." (25). Chap. 8, too, presents the arrogance and pride of the little horn as it opposes God himself: "It grew right up to the armies of heaven and flung armies and stars to the ground, and trampled them underfoot. It even challenged the power of that army's Prince; it abolished the perpetual sacrifice and overthrew the foundation of his sanctuary..." (8:10-11). The "army's Prince" is God himself, as is "the Prince of princes" (8:25) whom the little horn challenges.[27] A more explicit account of Antiochus' divine pretensions emerges in Dan 11:36-37: "And the king shall do according to his will; he shall exalt himself and magnify himself above every god, and shall speak astonishing things against the God of gods.... He shall give no heed to the gods of his fathers, or to the one beloved by women; he shall not give heed to

[22]So O. Mørkholm, *Antiochus IV of Syria* (Classica et mediaevalia, dissertationes 8; Copenhagen: Gyldendalske, 1966) 130-31.

[23]Ibid., 132.

[24]Ibid., 113, 132, n. 56.

[25]Translation of W. R. Paton, *Polybius, The Histories*, vol. 5 (LCL; London: Heinemann, 1926) 483 (= Book 26.1, 7).

[26]*The Histories* 26.1a.

[27]J. A. Montgomery, *A Critical and Exegetical Commentary on the Book of Daniel* (ICC; Edinburgh: Clark, 1927) 335 (where he detects echoes of Isaiah 14) and 351.

any other god, for he shall magnify himself above all." While some details of this passage remain obscure, Antiochus' divine pretensions are not.

1-2 Maccabees confirm the impression gained from Daniel in different ways. First, if one observes the sequence of events in the two books, it becomes apparent that the first sacrifice was offered on the pagan altar in the temple on Chislev 25 (which became the first day of Hanukkah) because that was the date on which Antiochus' birthday was celebrated with sacrifices in temples where the ruler cult was practiced (see especially 1 Macc 1:59 with 2 Macc 6:7).[28] In other words, Antiochus, a man whom the author of 2 Maccabees calls a "blasphemer" (9:28), was revered as a god in the Jerusalem temple during the years when the king's decrees were in effect.

The most interesting passage in connection with Antiochus' divinity figures in his dramatic deathbed speech in 2 Maccabees 9. It is obviously not necessary to think that 2 Maccabees provides a historically reliable account of the king's last words; the anguished speech is blatantly fictitious. The important point is that this fanciful report became part of the Jewish literary heritage about King Antiochus. 2 Maccabees relates that, as the king nears his end amid the unspeakable torments of his body and the unbearable stench of his rotting flesh, he experiences a belated flash of insight and exclaims: "It is right to be subject to God, and no mortal should think that he is equal to God" (δίκαιον ὑποτάσσεσθαι τῷ θεῷ καὶ μὴ θνητὸν ὄντα ἰσόθεα φρονεῖν [9:12]).[29] The reported words of Antiochus resemble in an ironic way the response of Jesus' interrogators to his claim to being one with God: "... you, being a man, make yourself God" (σὺ ἄνθρωπος ὢν ποιεῖς σεαυτὸν θεόν).

It seems to be no accident that John dated Jesus' assertion of his divinity to the festival of Hanukkah when the blasphemies of Antiochus IV, the self-proclaimed god manifest, were remembered. Jesus' unbelieving audience who do not belong to his sheep see in the divine Son only another blasphemer who, like the Seleucid king, claimed to be god. Perhaps it is also no coincidence that just two verses before the notice about Hanukkah one reads: "Many of them said, 'He has a demon, and he is mad... ' " (10:20: the word is μαίνεται). Is this charge meant to remind one of Antiochus whom some considered a madman (μαινόμενος)?

In sum, it is evident that the reference to the Dedication in John 10:22 is not merely a note of little importance meant only to indicate the passage of time. It is,

---

[28]See J. VanderKam, "2 Maccabees 6,7A and Calendrical Change in Jerusalem," *JSJ* 12 (1981) 52-74.

[29]The Greek text is cited from A. Rahlfs, ed., *Septuaginta id est Vetus Testamentum graece iuxta LXX interpretes* (2 vols.; Stuttgart: Wurttembergische Bibelanstalt, 1935).

rather, another in the series of Johannine festivals whose associations deeply influenced the context in which the evangelist placed them.[30]

[30]My colleague Professor William Adler has suggested the possibility that in the Jewish demand to have Jesus reveal himself "plainly" (10:24 [παρρησία]) readers might see some parallel with the Jewish rejection of Antiochus' claim to be god "made manifest."

CURSE AND COMPETITION
IN THE ANCIENT CIRCUS

John G. Gager
Princeton University

1. *Preliminary Observations*

The study of ancient curse tablets (*katadesmoi* or *defixiones*) is currently undergoing a modest revival and threatens to become a respectable, perhaps even an indispensable component in the study of ancient Mediterranean culture. First exploited systematically in 1897 by Richard Wünsch[1] and greatly expanded in 1904 by Auguste Audollent,[2] curse tablets languished in relative obscurity[3] until the recent work of David R. Jordan[4] and Christopher Faraone.[5] More recently still,

---

[1]R. Wünsch, *Defixionum Tabellae* (= IG III.3 Appendix); contains 220 items from Greece, most of which have long since disappeared and many of whose readings seem uncertain, with extensive indices. Wünsch became known among classicists and archaeologists of his time as *the* great expert on *defixiones*. His publications are numerous, among them *Antike Fluchtafeln* (Bonn: Marcus und Weber, 1912), an annotated selection of six tablets.

[2]A. Audollent, *Defixionum Tabellae* (Paris: Fontemoing, 1904), a classic work which vastly expanded the range of available texts, includes 301 separate items and 137 pages of indices (unfortunately, excluding the items published by Wünsch in 1897). It covers the entire Mediterranean region, Greek as well as Latin, though it pays no attention to Semitic or Egyptian materials.

[3]There has been intermittent interest: M. Jeanneret, "La langue des tablettes d'exécration latines," *Revue de philologie* 40 (1916) 229-58 and 41 (1917) 5-99; M. Besnier, "Récents travaux sur les *Defixionum Tabellae*: 1904-1914," *Revue de philologie* 44 (1920) 5-30; Eugen Kagarow, *Griechische Fluchtafeln* (Leipzig: Ministry of Public Instruction, 1929); several synthetic works by K. Preisendanz, including "Die griechischen und lateinischen Zaubertafeln," *Archiv für Papyrusforschung* 9 (1930) and 11 (1933), and "Fluchtafel (Defixio)," *RAC* (1972) 1-24; H. Solin's survey of Latin *defixiones* published between 1914 and 1968, *Eine neue Fluchtafel aus Ostia* (Helsinki: Societas Scientiarum Fennica, Commentationes Humanarum Litterarum, 42, nr. 3, 1968) 23-31; and D. Wortmann, "Neue magische Texts," *Bonner Jahrbücher* 168 (1968) 56-111.

[4]Jordan is the Wünsch of current scholarship. His publications are too numerous to mention. The most significant of them include "A Survey of Greek Defixiones Not Included in the Special Corpora," *GRBS* 26 (1985) 151-197 and "Defixiones from a Well near the Southwest Corner of the Athenian Agora," *Hesperia* 54 (1985) 198-255.

R. O. S. Tomlin has published a remarkable set of 130 Latin *defixiones* from the shrine of Sulis Minerva at Bath (England),[6] while an equally important collection from Uley (England) still awaits full publication. One quantitative datum illustrates a basis for our renaissance—in 1977, a modest total of ten curse tablets had been discovered in England; today this figure is close to 300. A few general observations may bring the topic into sharper focus:

A. All *defixiones* share a common goal: to constrain the actions and motivations of individuals through formulaic appeals to deities, spirits and *daimones*. They are private acts by private persons directed at other persons but are not, despite common assumptions, always designed to harm or kill. The figurines or dolls, frequently found with "love" spells and often pierced by nails or needles, are clearly not meant to harm the "victim" but instead to constrain or bind that person according to the wishes (and fantasies) of the client. Thus a better name for *defixiones* might well be binding-spells rather than curse tablets.

B. The total number of known *defixiones* exceeds 1,500, with many still unpublished.

C. In addition to the tablets themselves, *defixiones* are attested by numerous literary sources ranging from Plato to Christian saints' lives. Beyond this, several professional handbooks of ancient *magoi* have survived, preserving recipes for the preparation and sale of curse tablets, e.g., the large collections in the Greek magical papyri,[7] the Jewish material in *Sepher ha-Razim*,[8] and a Syriac collection known as *The Book of Protection*.[9]

D. The geo-cultural zone of their usage reaches from Britain to Mesopotamia, from southern Russia to Egypt and North Africa.

E. The earliest *defixiones* date from the sixth century BCE (Greek Sicily), while the latest reach into the sixth century CE; i.e., they cover more than a millennium of ancient history.

[5]Faraone is the author of several important articles on curse tablets and also the coeditor, with D. Obbink, of a forthcoming volume, *Magika Hiera* (Oxford University Press). This volume will include an important essay by Faraone, tentatively entitled "The Agonistic Context of Early Greek Binding Spells."

[6]Tomlin's work appears as chap. 4 ("The Curse Tablets") in B. Cunliffe, ed., *The Temple of Sulis Minerva*, vol. 2: *The Finds from the Sacred Spring* (Oxford: Oxford Committee for Archaeology, 1988) 59-277.

[7]Now available in Hans Dieter Betz, et al., eds., *The Greek Magical Papyri, including the Demotic Spells* (Chicago: University of Chicago Press, 1986).

[8]Originally edited from fragments by Mordecai Margalioth in 1966 and prepared in English by Michael Morgan, *Sepher Ha-Razim: The Book of Mysteries* (SBLTT 25; Chico: Scholars, 1983).

[9]Edited and translated in 1912 by Hermann Gollancz as *The Book of Protection, being a Collection of Charms* (London: Henry Frowde, 1912).

John G. Gager

F. Tablets appear in numerous languages, e.g., Greek, Demotic, Hebrew, Aramaic, Latin, Coptic.

G. Similar or identical names, formulas, invocations and the like appear without regard to location, language, or chronology, that is, this material travelled widely in the hands of professional practitioners who shared a common pool of mostly written recipes. In many places, multiple examples made according to the same master copy have survived.

H. By and large the material used for curses are thin metal strips, usually of lead or lead alloys, although gold, silver, copper, and iron are called for in various recipes. In addition, curse formulas also appear on wood, ostraka, potsherds, papyrus, and ceramic bowls.

I. *Defixiones* were customarily commissioned from a local professional who inscribed them using fixed formulas taken from books. Once prepared, the tablet was generally rolled up, pierced with a nail, and deposited in a burial site, a well or a spring, or at the site of its desired effects, e.g., the home of a "loved" one or the starting gates of the hippodrome.

J. The invocations address a wide range of deities (many, though not all, chthonic), spirits of dead persons and *daimones*, always by their proper names and epithets and often through their proper signs or *charaktêres* (see below). In many cases, though not until the Roman period, these names appear as *voces mysticae*, i.e., brief or lengthy strings of letters and "words" not recognizable from any ancient language. These *voces* are not to be taken as "gibberish" but rather, in line with a universal tendency, as the secret and powerful names and epithets known only to the professional *magos* who prepares the tablet.[10]

K. Most *defixiones* are poignantly particular: the occasion of the enmity is usually spelled out; the client's name sometimes appears; the designated target of the spell is always identified, usually by name, sometimes by profession, neighborhood, family and friends, and frequently by the name of his/her mother.

L. The use of *defixiones* extended to all levels of society and to all cultures; it was not an exclusively "popular" phenomenon. The tablets from classical Greece name philosophers (Socrates, Aristotle), orators (Demosthenes, Lycurgus), and famous politicians (Cassander, Demetrius of Phalerum), as well as cooks, potters, metalworkers, pub-owners, courtesans, and prostitutes.

M. *Defixiones* constituted a regular feature, largely ignored by modern historians, of precisely definable arenas of ancient culture: sex and love; political and personal disputes; appeals for justice and revenge, notably in connection with stolen

---

[10]See the discussions of such "words" in S. J. Tambiah, "The Magical Power of Words," *Man* 3 (1968) 175-208 and P. C. Miller, "In Praise of Nonsense," in A. H. Armstrong, ed., *Classical Mediterranean Spirituality* (New York: Crossroad, 1986) 481–505.

217

property but also with the protection of burial sites; lawsuits and public trials; and the category discussed and illustrated here, athletic and other forms of public competition.

What follows is a brief excursion into the murky realm of ancient *defixiones*. We will first look at some of the broader issues surrounding their widespread use in various forms of public competition, e.g., theater and hippodrome, and then turn to a single tablet, commissioned for use against rival charioteers in the hippodrome of Apamea (Syria) sometime in the fifth or sixth century CE.

2. Forms and Functions of Defixiones

In the major cities of the Mediterranean, much of life unfolded in public settings: theaters, amphitheaters, hippodromes, odeums, stadiums and circuses.[11] While large installations like stadiums and circuses tended to be limited to cult centers (Greece) and large cities (Rome), theaters and odeums were much more common.[12] Depending on the size of the building, crowds could vary considerably: several hundred in small theaters; several thousand in larger theaters (e.g., Pompeii); perhaps 50,000 in the Roman Colosseum and the stadium of Herodes Atticus at Athens; as many as 250,000 (almost one-quarter of the city's population) for chariot races in the Circus Maximus at Rome.

In Greece, from classical to Roman times, games were celebrated not so much in the cities as at major cult sites (Olympia, Delphi, Isthmia/Corinth, Nemea, Epidaurus), although the later Panatheneian games did take place in Athens. Such games were great festivals for all Greeks (*panegyreis*) and occurred once every two or four years; in short, they were relatively infrequent events and heavy with political, national, and religious trappings.[13] Originally created for wealthy aristocrat-citizens who competed as amateurs, the games became increasingly professionalized so that by the second century BCE the competitors were all professionals; the theatrical

---

[11]On Greek and Roman public performance generally see E. N. Gardiner, *Athletics of the Ancient World* (Chicago: Ares, 1955); J. P. V. D. Balsdon, *Life and Leisure in Ancient Rome* (New York: McGraw-Hill, 1969) esp. 244-339; H. A. Harris, *Sport in Greece and Rome* (Ithaca: Cornell University Press, 1972); H. W. Parke, *Festivals of the Athenians* (Ithaca: Cornell University Press, 1977); W. Sweet, *Sport and Recreation in Ancient Greece: A Sourcebook with Translations* (New York: Oxford University Press, 1987); D. Sansone, *Greek Athletics and the Genesis of Sport* (Berkeley: University of California Press, 1988).

[12]For a brief review of the various types of structures used for games, racing, and theater see Harris, *Sport*, 161-72; Balsdon, *Leisure*, 252-61; and J. H. Humphrey, *Roman Circuses: Arenas for Chariot Racing* (Berkeley: University of California Press, 1986) 1-24.

[13]The religious origins and setting of the Greek games is stressed by M. Nilsson, *Greek Folk Religion* (New York: Harper & Brothers, 1961) 97-101.

events were probably professional from the beginning. A list of prizes from Athens in the fifth century BCE reveals the games' comprehensive character: rhapsodes reciting Homer; singers accompanied by harp or flute; instrumentalists on harp or flute; athletes in various events for men and boys;[14] equestrian events, including four- and two-horse chariot racing; various team competitions; and a regatta for ships. Complementing this cycle of biennial and quadrennial competitions was the annual dramatic festival of Dionysus at Athens when dramatists competed for the right to stage their plays,[15] as well as other occasions throughout the year where poetry was publicly recited and songs chanted. All these occasions involved competitions of one kind or another, usually among choruses of singers, dancers and reciters and their leaders. As we shall see, the competitive nature of these occasions—where both employment and status were on the line—regularly prompted the use of curse tablets in order to hinder one's opponents and to enhance one's own chances of success. No less a figure than Augustine of Hippo, Christian bishop and former professor of rhetoric, illustrates the long history of ties between such competitions and the use of curse spells. In his *Confessions* 4.2, written some 800 years after the earliest Greek tablets, he relates that "once, when I had decided to enter a competition for reciting theatrical verse, a sorcerer (*haruspex*) sent to inquire of me how much I would pay him to guarantee a victory."

In the period which concerns us here, i.e., the second century CE onward when most of the athletic curse tablets occur, Roman hegemony throughout the Mediterranean meant that Greek games were adopted by Romans but also that distinctively Roman games, especially chariot racing and gladiatorial contests, could be found everywhere, West and East. Unlike their Athenian counterparts, Romans enjoyed a calendar literally bursting with various forms of competition: festivals (*feriae*), games (*ludi*) and shows (*munera*) of every kind and combination.[16] In the period which produced the surviving *defixiones*, the earlier religious character of festival days had largely been assimilated to the pattern of games (various theatrical performances and chariot racing) so that by the year 300 CE there were 177 days of games, including sixty-six days of racing in the circus. Finally, we must take account of lavish and lusty shows and of gladiatorial contests involving both men and wild animals, which occurred on a non-regular basis several times a year, sometimes as part of the games and sometimes separately.

---

[14]Harris (*Sport*, 40f.) argues that before the Christian era, women had competed in separate games at Olympia; from the first century CE onward, women's athletic events, including wrestling, took place alongside men's at the same games.

[15]See A. Pickard-Cambridge, *The Dramatic Festivals of Athens* (Oxford: Clarendon, 1968) 40-42 and 74-83 for a discussion of the competitive aspects of dramatic festivals at Athens and other Greek cities.

[16]See Balsdon, *Leisure*, 244-52, 267-70.

What Greek and Roman performances shared was a keen sense of competition, copious rewards and enormous popularity. The number of actual competitors may have been limited, but the tally of those interested in the events was enormous and encompassed the full spectrum of the social order, from emperor to slave. For winning performers the tangible rewards were fame and fortune, while for the spectator-participant there was suspense over the outcome, exaltation at the competition and, depending on the outcome, gloating in victory or despair in defeat.

All in all, the stakes were high. For all involved, much depended on the outcome, and, as at all times, competitors and fans sought advantages wherever they could find them.[17] Among these advantages was the use of *defixiones*, here understood quite literally as an effort to bind one's competitors—their tongues, limbs, minds, etc.—through spells addressed to gods, spirits and *daimones*. There can be no doubt that such tablets played a regular and persistent role in the life of the circus. The number of surviving examples is considerable; their find-spots stretch right across the Roman world; and literary testimonies of various kinds support the picture sketched by the tablets themselves.[18]

The earliest surviving tablets stem from Greek cities in Attica and Sicily from the 5th to the 3rd centuries BCE. These focus on theatrical rather than athletic competition. Thereafter no further examples survive until a Latin *defixio* of the second century CE and two Greek tablets directed against actors a century later.[19]

As for athletics, all of the many *defixiones* are relatively late and concern a variety of events; five from Athens in the third century CE are directed against professional wrestlers in matches against named opponents.[20] One from

---

[17]In his essay, "The Agonistic Context," Faraone (20f.) suggests that curses were used in order to even up contests where the opponent seemed to have an unfair advantage. The wide usage of curse tablets indicates that while "evening up the odds" may have been an occasional motive, perhaps even a rationalization, their real goal was precisely to create an unfair advantage, to "fix" the outcome. At the same time, it must be recalled that those who resorted to the use of *defixiones* did so in the full knowledge that their opponents were up to the same tricks.

[18]Faraone ("The Agonistic Context," 20) observes that the first literary instance of a curse in athletic competition occurs in Pindar (fifth century BCE), in his first *Olympian Ode* (lines 76-78) where Pelops, the son of Tantalus, competes with Oenomaos for the hand of his daughter, Hippodameia. In preparation for this all-or-nothing battle with spears and chariots, Pelops prays for help to Poseidon: "Block the bronze spear, and grant me the swifter chariot ... and surround me with power..."

[19]Jordan ("Survey," 167) notes the discovery, from the area of the gymnasium at Corinth, of a lead scroll which invokes "holy and powerful nymphs" against "a retired (?) mimic actress."

[20]The tandem of curses and wrestlers shows up again in later Christian saints' lives. In one (*Life of Saint George of Choziba*), a professional wrestler is released from spells cast on him by his opponents only by becoming a monk himself. In the

John G. Gager

Oxyrhynchus in Egypt a century later names a runner.[21] Gladiators are named in a series of tablets from Carthage in the second and third centuries CE. But by far the greatest number of tablets concerns chariot racing in the Roman world.[22] Numerous examples have survived, all from three areas, Rome itself, North Africa and Syria. Here again, however, it would be a mistake to doubt that curse tablets were deployed wherever racing took place. Indeed, excavations at Antioch (Syria) and Lepcis Magna (North Africa) have recovered tablets from spots around the circuses and hippodromes where they were originally deposited in accordance with prescribed procedures.[23]

It would be difficult to overestimate the cultural significance of chariot racing in the Greco-Roman world. The earliest literary account appears in Homer (*Iliad* 23.262ff.), as part of the funeral games in honor of Patroclus, where it was the first event. More than a millennium and a half later, Byzantine civilization could still be described, in the words of Norman Baynes, as honoring two heroes: the Christian holy man and the triumphant charioteer.[24] Certainly, Roman authors, even when they professed dislike for this facet of life, recognized and described it well. Tacitus, late in the first century CE, speaks disparagingly of "the peculiar vices found in our city, which seem to be conceived already in the mother's womb—a partiality for the stage and a passion for gladiators and horse-racing."[25] Some 300 years later, Ammianus Marcellinus mockingly depicts race fans who argue that the state itself will fall unless their favored team is first from the starting gates and negotiates the turn in proper fashion. For such folk, he writes, "their temple, their dwelling, their assembly and the height of all their hopes is the Circus Maximus."[26] For winners,

other (*Life of Saint Theodore of Sykeon*), a wrestler unable to compete because of pain in his body is released from a demon introduced by a curse tablet. For a discussion of both texts, see H. J. Magoulias, "The Lives of Byzantine Saints as Sources of Data for the History of Magic in the Sixth and Seventh Centuries: Sorcery, Relics and Icons," *Byzantion* 37 (1967) 245f.

[21] Jordan ("Agora" 214) notes the discovery of a *defixio* from Isthmia against a runner. In addition, one of the tablets from the find in the Athenian Agora, directed against a certain Alkidamos, probably concerns a foot-race ("Agora," 221f.)

[22] On chariot racing see especially Alan Cameron, *Porphyrius: The Charioteer* (Oxford: Clarendon, 1973) and *Circus Factions: Blues and Greens at Rome and Byzantium* (Oxford: Clarendon, 1976).

[23] See now the discussion in D. Jordan, "New Defixiones from Carthage," in J. H. Humphrey, ed., *The Circus and a Byzantine Cemetary at Carthage*, vol. 1 (Ann Arbor: University of Michigan Press, 1973) 117-20.

[24] Baynes, *The Byzantine Empire* (London: Oxford University Press, 1925) 33.

[25] Tacitus, *Dialogue on Oratory*, 29.

[26] Ammianus Marcellinus' account of racing and its popularity in Rome (37.4.28-31) appears in his catalogue of the vices of the Roman people (38.4). His history of the later Roman empire, of which only the portions covering the years 353-378 have survived, was written in Rome sometime after 378 CE.

the gain was enormous fortunes; Juvenal utters the familiar complaint that the Red driver, Lacerta, earned one hundred times the fee of a lawyer.[27] Betting was omnipresent and riots not infrequent. Emperors regularly proclaimed loyalty to favorite drivers or factions, while the powerful factions themselves (Reds, Whites, Blues, Greens) organized the financial, technical and professional side of the sport and spread eventually to every major city of the empire.[28] In the sixth century, the historian Procopius writes that "in every city the population has been divided for a long time into the Blue and Green factions."[29] Vivid accounts of races survive in a youthful poem of Sidonius, later a Christian bishop in Gaul in the 470's, and in the epic poem entitled *Dionysiaca* by Nonnus, a writer of the fifth or sixth century CE. Such accounts make it easy to understand the remarkable persistence of chariot racing into the Christian empire despite the resistance of figures like John of Ephesus (sixth century CE) who responded to the Patriarch of Antioch's plan to build a hippodrome by labelling it "the church of Satan."[30] Indeed, it is the Christian writer Cassidorus, also in sixth century CE, who provides an elaborate interpretation of the circus and its races as an astrological and astronomical symbol of the entire universe: the twenty-four races each day are the twenty-four hours; the seven laps of each race are the days of the week; the twelve portals at the entrance are the signs of the zodiac; the turning posts are the tropics and so on.[31]

For these reasons and more, curse tablets and binding spells played a potent and abiding role in the world of chariot racing.[32] Whether commissioned and deposited by supporters[33] or by the drivers themselves,[34] they were a regular feature of

[27]*Satires* 7.114; see the discussion in Cameron, *Porphyry*, 244.

[28]In their discussion of a lead tablet discovered in the circus at Lepcis Magna, J. H. Humphrey, F. B. Sear and M. Vickers propose the attractive idea that the use of Greek in the *defixiones* from the Latin West may indicate that most of the professional charioteers came from the Greek-speaking East; see *Libya Antiqua* 9-10 (1972-73) 97.

[29]*Persian War* 1.24.

[30]On Christian attitudes to racing see Magoulias, "Lives" 242-45, and Harris, *Sport*, 227-37. Tertullian's *On the Games/Spectacles* (written ca. 200 CE) illustrates the sharply antagonistic attitude, while Cassiodorus' history of chariot racing, written in the early sixth century CE by a Roman aristocrat who served as secretary to Theodoric and later founded a monastery in Italy, indicates just how central an institution the circus remained in Christian Rome.

[31]Spelled out in Cassiodorus, *Variae* 51, and discussed by Cameron, *Factions*, 230f.

[32]Brief discussions of *defixiones* and chariot racing in Harris, *Sport*, 234-37; Balsdon, *Leisure*, 318f.; Cameron, *Porphyry*, 173, n. 3 and 245, and *Factions*, 56, 61f., 194, 200 and 345 note. Once again, Christian texts provide further evidence regarding the use of curse tablets in racing; see Cameron, *Porphyry*, 245, and *Factions*, 345 note.

[33]So Cameron, *Porphyry*, 245.

John G. Gager

competition, each faction and charioteer seeking advantage not just by tricks and skills on the course—described in precise detail not only by Sidonius and Nonnus but spelled out in several of the tablets (see below)—but by hampering the performance of man and beast through *defixiones*. The targets of these spells include both horses and drivers—often impossible to separate, usually named, commonly identified by the color of their faction and regularly listed under specific races on a given day.

Finally, there is good reason to assume that everyone believed the tablets to be effective, even those who disapproved. In his vast encyclopedia (*Natural History* 28.19), Pliny the Elder offers cogent observations on how curses worked and concludes that, in any case, "There is no one who is not afraid of being constrained by curse tablets." How else to understand a practice attested over such a stretch of time and geography? Certainly the legal evidence points in this direction. For, in the fourth century CE, a highpoint in the construction of Roman circuses,[35] Roman emperors began to issue decrees specifically aimed at the notorious connection between charioteers and the use of spells and curses.[36] A remarkable passage in Cassiodorus' edition of imperial documents issued during his years as secretary to Theodoric illustrates several facets of this connection:

> *King Theodoric to Faustus, Praetorian Prefect (of Rome):*
> Since constancy in actors is not a very common virtue, therefore with all the more pleasure do we record the faithful allegiance of Thomas the Charioteer, who came here long ago from the East, and who, having become a champion charioteer, has chosen to attach himself to the seat of our Empire; we therefore decide that he shall be rewarded by a monthly allowance. He embraced what was then a losing side in the chariot races and carried it to victory—victory which he won so often that envious rivals declared that he conquered by means of witchcraft. For they were driven to attribute his victories to magic when they could not account for them by the strength of his horses.[37]

---

[34]So in Humphrey, Sear and Vickers, *Libya Antiqua*, 97.

[35]See Humphrey, *Roman Circuses*, chap. 11.

[36]See the *Theodosian Code* 9.16.11, an imperial decree issued in 389 and renewed subsequently by later emperors. The decree requires anyone with knowledge of persons practicing magic to expose them publicly. It goes on to forbid charioteers to contravene the edict by carrying out the punishment by themselves! In line with this, the historian Ammianus Marcellinus, writing in the 370's, records three instances in which charioteers were punished for involvement with illegal spells (26.3.3; 28.1.27; 29.3.5); see the discussions in Harris, *Sport*, 234f. and Cameron, *Porphyry*, 245.

[37]The translation is adapted from Thomas Hodgkin's condensed translation of Cassiodorus' edition, known commonly as *Variae Epistolae* (3.51) and written in the

"The circus was indeed," in Alan Cameron's words, "a microcosm of the Roman state."[38] But it does not require a mystical turn of mind to perceive this, nor is the symbolism of the circus limited to the visible realm of social and political power unmistakably displayed in the boxes for the emperor, senators and so on "down" to slaves and children in the upper galleries. The inconspicuous lead tablet, inscribed, folded and buried in the dust beneath the starting gates, symbolized the invisible world of Rome—a world of gods, spirits and *daimones* on the one side, of aspirations, tensions and implicit power on the other—in short, a world where emperors, senators and bishops were not in command.[39]

3. A Defixio

The following tablet was discovered at Apamea, an important Greek city in Syria, on the Orontes River, along with a second smaller tablet among miscellaneous debris.[40] Both are of lead and were originally rolled up. The larger tablet, treated here, measures 11.8 by 5.2 cm. The smaller has a hole in the center, probably made by a nail. Both date to the late fifth or early sixth centuries CE. The figures invoked in the spells are especially interesting. The text appeals to the *charaktêres*, known from numerous other tablets and texts. At the end of the text, two unusual names appear: *topos*, a designation of the highest god in other texts; and Sablan/Zablan, an uncommon name with angelic and astrological associations in Jewish texts of the same period. The setting of the spell is chariot racing in the hippodrome of Apamea and in particular, intense rivalry between the major teams or factions, the Blues and the Greens, known from a passage from Procopius (*Wars* 2.11.31-35). On a "visit" to Apamea, the Persian general Chosroes issued orders for a special set of races in the city's hippodrome. Knowing that the Roman emperor Justinian favored the Blues, Chosroes decided to support the Greens. When the Blues took an early lead, Chosroes commanded his agents to slow down the Blue team in order to guarantee a Green victory. The targets of this spell are named: Porphyras, Hapsicrates and Eugenius, all blues. The client is not named but presumably represented or supported the Greens. Above the first line of text, which invokes the *charaktêres*, appear several lines of signs, or, more precisely, the *charaktêres* themselves. These

years 507-511 CE; see T. Hodgkin, *The Letters of Cassiodorus* (London: Frowde, 1886) 226.

[38] *Factions*, 231.

[39] On charioteers and curses, see the excellent essay of Peter Brown, "Sorcery, Demons, and the Rise of Christianity," in Mary Douglas, ed., *Witchcraft Accusations and Confessions* (London: Tavistock, 1970) 25f.

[40] W. van Rengen, "Deux défixions contre les bleus à Apamée (VIe siècle apr. J.-C.)," *Apamée de Syrie* (Brussels: Centre Belge de Recherches Archéologiques à Apamée de Syrie, 1984) 213-34; SEG 34 (1984) no. 1437; Jordan, "Survey," 192f.

signs are identical on the two tablets and similar to representations of the *charaktêres* elsewhere. The editor of this tablet is the first to transcribe these signs carefully (Appendix II) and to analyze them seriously. The text itself is virtually complete (Appendix I). What follows below is a full English translation, with accompanying notes.

> Most holy Lord *Charaktêres*,[41] tie up, bind the feet, the hands, the nerves, the eyes, the knees, the courage, the leaps, the whip,[42] the victory and the crowning of Porphyras[43] and Harpsicates, who are in the middle-left, as well as his co-drivers of the Blue-colors in the stable of Eugenius.[44] From this very hour, from today, may they not eat or drink or sleep;[45] instead, from the (starting) gates may they see spirits (of those) who have died prematurely, spirits (of those) who have died violently,[46] and the fire of Hephaestus;[47] ... in the hippodrome at the

[41]We must suppose a close connection between the signs on the first two lines of the tablet, above the text, and the verbal invocation of the *charaktêres* here. These signs embodied the higher powers invoked to carry out the spell. What exactly these powers were thought to be is not clear, although the magical papyri make it clear that all superior beings possessed their own characters or signs as empowered signatures. The presence of exactly thirty-six signs on the two tablets from Apamea leads van Rengen to argue that the connection or association here may be with the thirty-six decans or divisions of the heavens common in Egyptian astrology. Elsewhere, the *charaktêres* are associated with the protective powers and functions of angels and archangels. From these associations follows the use of *charaktêres* on amulets designed to ward off spells and hostile powers. In this tablet, there may well be a tie between archangels and decans, with the former understood as in charge of the latter.

[42]The text reads *taura*, a word otherwise unattested. The editor suggests a miswriting for *tauria/taureia* = "whip."

[43]Porphyras no doubt stands for Porphyrius, a common name for horses and jockeys. The most famous jockey of this name was a professional who enjoyed phenomenal success in the mid sixth century and received numerous public honors; cf. Cameron, *Porphyrius*.

[44]The Eugenius named here in connection with the *stablon* (a Latin word taken into Greek) is no doubt the *factionarius* or professional manager, later the leading jockey, of a team; on the term *factionarius* and its development, see Cameron, *Circus Factions*, 5-13.

[45]In this case, the client's wish is that the spell begin immediately, not just at the time of the race. Thus the horses are marked for trouble not just during the race but for unfavorable conditions in advance.

[46]The spirits of those who had died prematurely or by violent means were thought to be particularly terrifying and thus were regularly invoked as agents in spells of all kinds.

moment when they are about to compete[48] may they not squeeze over, may they not collide, may they not extend, may they not force (us) out, may they not overtake, may they not break off (in a new direction) for the entire day when they are about to race. May they be broken, may they be dragged (on the ground), may they be destroyed; under Topos[49] and under Zablas.[50] Now, now, quickly, quickly!

[47]Hephaestus, the classical Greek god of fire and the foundry. More appropriately here, he is also known as the first Greek "magician," though his name appears in just one other surviving magical text (PGM XII, lines 177f.). The point is clear: the horses are to see the fire of Hephaestus as they leave the starting gates and thus be frightened into a bad race. In general on Hephaestus, see M. Delcourt, *Héphaistos ou la légende du magicien* (Paris: Les Belles Lettres, 1957).

[48]The following series of verbs is not merely repetitive but lists the various techniques or tricks used by charioteers to gain an advantage over their competitors. There is a close parallel in Audollent, *Defixionum*, no. 187 (Rome): "... may they not get a good start, may they not pass..."

[49]The phrase *kata topo(n)* and the following phrase *kata Zablan* are unusual and a bit puzzling. The sense seems to be that the figures are here invoked as the divine agents through whose authority (*kata*) the *charaktêres* are to carry out the spell. *Topos* ("the place") as a divine name occurs commonly in Jewish texts, translating Hebrew *makom* which is commonly used to designate the deity (e.g., Philo, *Dreams* 1.63). The same term appears in Valentianian Gnostic texts where it designates the demiurge or creator-god (cf. Clement of Alexandria, *Excerpts of Theodotus* 34, 37-39). And in the *Corpus Hermeticum* 2.12 (from Egypt and dating to the same period as the curse tablets), *topos* is described as "that in which everything moves ... the incorporeal ... a mind which contains its own self entirely, free from any form of bodily nature, unerring, above emotion, intangible, immutable in itself, containing all things and redeeming all things ... from which the good, the truth and fountainhead of what is spiritual emanate like rays..." Thus, while *topos* appears in no other binding spell, it certainly falls within the range of powerful spiritual beings which could be useful in circumstances like these.

[50]The only other known occurrence of Zablas/Sablas is in a Coptic amulet from around 600 CE (Kropp, *Ausgewählte Koptische Zaubertexte* [Brussels: Fondation Egyptologique, 1931] vol. 1, text F, line 37). It appears in a list of the seven angels who assisted god in the creation of Adam; the theme of angelic cooperation in the act of creation is a common one in Jewish and Christian texts of this period. This helps to understand the connection between *topos*, taken as referring to the Biblical god, and Zablas, an angel. What about their connection to the *charaktêres*, depicted in the first two lines above the text and invoked in the first line of the text? As van Rengen observes, angels and archangels were thought to control and command not only spirits and demons generally, but the thirty-six decans specifically, i.e., the thirty-six equally divided portions, also known as world rulers, of the heavenly sphere or zodiac according to Egyptian astrological tradition. Thus the thirty-six *charaktêres* of the first two lines of our text almost certainly represent the thirty-six astrological decans; see the convincing argument of van Rengen, pp. 216-19. Furthermore, in a widely circulated Jewish document known as *The Testament of Solomon*, the thirty-six decans

John G. Gager

Appendix I:

κύριοι ἁγιώτατοι χαρακτῆρες δῆτε καταδήσα-
τε τούς πόδα τὰς χῖρας τὰ νερα τοὺς ὀφθαλ-
μοὺς τὰ γόνατα τὰ θράση τὰ ἅλματα τὴν ταύραν τὴν νίκην
4   τὴν στεφάνωσιν Πορφυρᾶν κὲ ʼΑψικράτην μεσαρίστερον κὲ
τοὺς σὺν α-
ὑτ[οι]ῷ συνελαύνοντας χρόας καλαείνων στάβλου Εὐγενίου ἐκ τῆς
ἄρτι ὥρας ἐκ τῆς σήμερον ἡμέρας μὴ φάγωσιν μὴ πίωσιν μὴ κοι-
μηθῶσιν ἀλλὰ βλεπέτωσαν [ἀ]πὸ θυρῶν δέμ[ο]νας ἀώρο[υ]ς
8   δέμονας βιέους ʻΗφέστου πῦρ απ[....]ὲν τῷ ἱ[ππ]οδρόμῳ ὅτε
μέλουσιν ἀγωνίζασθε μὴ χιάσωσιν μὴ παρα-
βύσωσιν μὴ ταθῶσι μὴ ἐκβάλω[σ]ιν μὴ παρέλθωσιν μὴ πε-
ρικλάσωσιν δι ʼ ὅλης τῆς ἡμέρας ὅτε μέλοσιν ἀγωνίζασθε
12   κλασθῶσιν συρῶσιν ἀφανισθῶσιν κατὰ τόπο κὲ κατὰ Ζαβ-
λαν ἤδη ἤδη ταχὺ ταχύ

are summoned to appear before Solomon, where they announce their names, their powers and the particular angel to whom they are subjugated: "I am the first decan of the zodiac and I am called Ruax. I cause the head of men to suffer pain and I cause their temples to throb. But if I even hear, 'Michael, imprison Ruax,' I retreat immediately" (18.5). Unfortunately, none of the thirty-six decans summoned before Solomon specialized in chariot racing and none is named Zablas. But it is quite evident that there was great variability in the names and functions of spirits from one text to another. In short, there is a close connection in our tablet between the *charactêres* on the one hand, who are summoned to carry out the spell, and, on the other hand, *topos* and Zablan under whose power and authority they stand.

Appendix II:

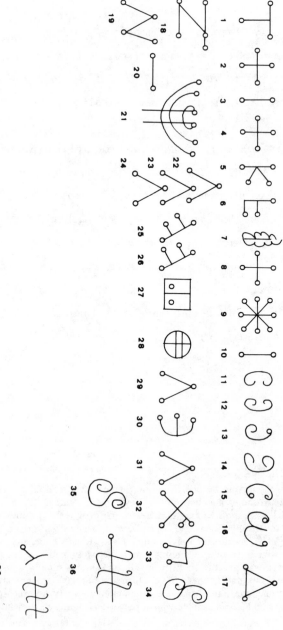

THE ANTI-JUDAIC POLEMIC OF EPHREM SYRUS' HYMNS ON THE NATIVITY

Katheen E. McVey
Princeton Theological Seminary

Christian polemic against Judaism both within the New Testament and in the Patristic literature has received a good deal of attention in recent scholarship.[1] The Syriac Christian writers have commanded a share of this attention. Kazan supplemented his publication of Isaac of Antioch's "Homily against the Jews" with a survey of the relevant Syriac Christian writings from the fourth to the twelfth centuries.[2] Several subsequent studies have expanded on the views of individual writers[3] or have broadened the general discussion to include second- and third-century materials.[4] The two great Syriac writers of the fourth century, Aphrahat and Ephrem, address several themes common to the Greco-Roman anti-Judaic literature,

---

[1] A helpful survey of the literature from 1948-82 is provided by J. Gager, *The Origins of Christian Anti-Semitism: Attitudes toward Judaism in Pagan and Christian Antiquity* (Oxford: Oxford University Press, 1983) 13-34; to this we must add R. Wilken, *John Chrysostom and the Jews: Rhetoric and Reality in the Late 4th Century* (The Transformation of the Classical Heritage 4; Berkeley: University of California, 1983) and other recent works cited by L. T. Johnson, "The New Testament's anti-Jewish slander and the conventions of ancient polemic," *JBL* 108 (1989) 419-41.

[2] S. Kazan, "Isaac of Antioch's Homily against the Jews," *OrChr* 45 (1961) 30-53; 46 (1962) 87-98; 47 (1963) 89-97; 49 (1965) 57-78; a survey of previous secondary literature stands at the beginning of Kazan's general study, *OrChr* 46 (1962) 87-88.

[3] On Aphrahat: J. Neusner, *Aphrahat and Judaism* (SPB 19; Leiden: Brill, 1971) but for more recent bibliography and overview of this literature, cf. M.-J. Pierre, *Aphraate le Sage Persan: Les Exposés* (Tome I; SC 349; Paris: Cerf, 1988) esp. 19-20, 112-31. On Aphrahat and Ephrem: R. Murray, *Symbols of Church and Kingdom: A Study in Early Syriac Tradition* (Cambridge: Cambridge University Press, 1975) esp. 41-68. For bibliography and some discussion on Ephrem, cf. K. E. McVey, *Ephrem the Syrian: Hymns* (Classics of Western Spirituality; New York: Paulist, 1989) 3-59, esp. 11-12. On Jacob of Serug: M. Albert, *Jacques de Saroug, Homélies contre les juifs* (PO 38.1; Turnhout: Brepols, 1976). On Sergius the Stylite: A. M. Hayman, *The disputation of Sergius the Stylite against a Jew* (CSCO 338-39, Scr. Syr. 152-53; Louvain: Secrétariat du CSCO, 1973).

[4] P. Hayman, "The Image of the Jew in the Syriac Anti-Jewish Polemical Literature," in J. Neusner and E. S. Frerichs, eds., *"To See Ourselves as Others See Us": Christians, Jews, "Others" in Late Antiquity* (Chico: Scholars, 1985) 423-41; H. J. W. Drijvers, "Jews and Christians at Edessa," *JJS* 36 (1985) 88-102.

such as criticism of circumcision, the sabbath and food laws, on the basis of typological exegesis of Hebrew Scripture. Other motifs are uniquely emphasized by the two Syriac writers: the replacement of the Jewish people by the "peoples," arguments based on the interpretation of historical events, and a defense of celibacy as a vocational choice.[5] Ephrem Syrus' formative role for the style and content of the subsequent Syriac anti-Judaic polemic is clear.[6] Ephrem's animosity has been contrasted with the civility of his older contemporary, Aphrahat,[7] or with other early Syriac sources such as the *Odes of Solomon*, the Bardaisanite *Book of the Laws of the Countries*, the "Letter of Mara bar Serapion," the *Acts of Judas Thomas*, the *Didascalia*, and earlier strata of the *Doctrina Addai*.[8]

Various explanations have been brought to bear on the attitudes of Aphrahat and Ephrem. Since Mesopotamia was an arena of political and military conflict between the Roman and Persian Empires in the second half of the fourth century, adherence to Judaism or to Christianity had divergent political implications. The Jewish communities in both empires, while a minority, were not subject to severe legal restrictions or persecution.[9] On the other hand, when Christianity became the favored religion of the Roman Empire, Christians became politically suspect in Sassanid Persia, especially after Constantine's ill-advised letter of 337; from 344 until 379 they were subject to sporadic but intermittently severe persecution.[10] The fact that Sassanian persecution of Christians coincides with Christian polemics against Judaism led Gavin to suppose that Persian Christians, having originated mainly as converts from Judaism and having maintained close intellectual and social ties with Judaism, must have been tempted to embrace Judaism as a reasonable

---

[5]Although Kazan ("Homily," *OrChr* 46 (1962) 90-91; *OrChr* 49 (1965) 70-78) refers to the "tradition of Ephraem Syrus," he makes it clear that Aphrahat shares much of its content, although not Ephrem's tone; Neusner, *Aphrahat*, esp. 131-44, 196-244; Murray, *Symbols*, esp. 67; McVey, *Ephrem*, 23.

[6]Kazan, "Homily," esp. *OrChr* 49 (1965) 70-78; Albert, *Jacques*, esp. 20-21; Hayman, *Sergius*, 50*-51*; more importantly, Hayman, "Image," esp. 423-34.

[7]On Ephrem's animosity, cf. Kazan, "Homily," *OrChr* 46 (1962) 96 and *OrChr* 47 (1963) 92. On Aphrahat's civility, cf. Neusner, *Aphrahat*, 5, 244. Contrasting the two, cf. Murray, *Symbols*, 19, 41, 65-68; and Hayman, "Image," 424, 426-27.

[8]Brief consideration of all in Hayman, "Image," 424-26, 433; more extensive treatment only of the *Doctrina Addai* in Drijvers, "Jews."

[9]E. Mary Smallwood, *The Jews under Roman Rule: From Pompey to Diocletian* (SJLA 20; Leiden: Brill, 1976); A. H. M. Jones, *The Later Roman Empire 284-602: A Social, Economic and Administrative Survey* (Norman: University of Oklahoma, 1964) esp. 92-93, 116, 944-50 et passim; J. Neusner, *A History of the Jews in Babylonia* (SPB 14; 4 vols.; Leiden: Brill, 1969) esp. 4.35-36.

[10]S. Brock, "Christians in the Sasanian Empire: A Case of Divided Loyalties," *Studies in Church History* 18 (1982) 1-19.

compromise between apostasy and martyrdom.[11] Parisot and Kazan assumed that such pressures were felt by Persian Christians not simply out of their own theological tendencies combined with the differing circumstances of the Christian and Jewish communities under Shapur II, but because of Jewish proselytism.[12] Although he has not directly addressed the question of Jewish proselytism among Mesopotamian Christians, Neusner has suggested that there was a much broader competition in the previous centuries between rabbis and Christians for the allegiance of the "Jews of the oriental diaspora" with the former enjoying greater success in "Nisibis and central Babylonia" and the latter in "Edessa and Adiabene."[13] He argues that the competition continued in some form in the fourth century, perhaps now including gentile Christians in the number of potential converts to rabbinic Judaism.[14]

The changed tone of Christian writings about Judaism in the later fourth century is attested not only by Ephrem but also by the *acta martyrum* and the later version of the *Doctrina Addai*.[15] Whereas Hayman sees the difference as rooted essentially in Ephrem's intolerant personality, rhetorical gifts and subsequent influence,[16] others have stressed the possible contribution of some environmental factors. Murray surmised that Ephrem was emboldened by the security of his location "within the Roman Empire, where the Jews are already a persecuted nation."[17] Drijvers has argued that the movement of the "Palutians" toward consistent orthodoxy and against "heresy" in Edessa led naturally to Ephrem's anti-Judaic stance.[18] On the other hand, several scholars have seen especially in Ephrem's third *Sermon on Faith* and in his

---

[11]F. Gavin, "Aphraates and the Jews," *Journal of the Society of Oriental Research* 7 (1923) 95-166, esp. 125-26; reiterated by J. G. Snaith, "Aphrahat and the Jews," in J. A. Emerton and S. E. Reif, eds., *Interpreting the Hebrew Bible: Essays in honor of E. I. J. Rosenthal* (Cambridge: Cambridge University Press, 1982) 237 and 250; and Hayman, "Image," 426.

[12]I. Parisot, *Aphraatis Sapientis Persae: Demonstrationes* (Patrologia Syriaca 1 and 2; Paris: Firmin-Didot, 1894 and 1907) esp. 1.xxv-xxviii; Kazan, "Homily," *OrChr* 46 (1962) 90-95.

[13]Neusner, *Aphrahat*, 2

[14]Neusner, *Aphrahat*, 124-27, 144-47, 168-69. On the other hand, Pierre (*Aphraate*, esp. 129-31) has remarked that Aphrahat provides no clear internal evidence that his concern is with Christians who convert or return to Judaism rather than with judaizing Christians and other rigoristic sects without any relation to the Persian persecution.

[15]Drijvers, "Jews," 99; Hayman, "Image," 433-34.

[16]Hayman, "Image," 423, 428-34.

[17]Murray, *Symbols*, 67; but this picture of persecuted Jewry is problematic (cf. n. 9 above).

[18]Drijvers, "Jews," 96-98.

Kathleen E. McVey

Hymns on the unleavened bread evidence of a judaizing movement among his Christian contemporaries.[19] The impact of the Emperor Julian's brief reign, especially his attempt to rebuild the Temple in Jerusalem has been noted.[20] Although the Sassanian persecution had begun at least by the time Aphrahat wrote his twenty-first *Demonstration*, where he attests and attempts to refute a Jewish polemical use of this historical circumstance, his last extant writing was only a year later, whereas the persecution continued until Shapur's death in 379 CE.[21] Neusner has rightly questioned Wiessner's too easy assumption of Jewish collusion in the persecution, but the question of Christian defection to Judaism and the related question of Jewish proselytism in the period between 344 and 379 also needs to be addressed.[22] As yet no one has pressed the question whether the difference in tone as we pass from Aphrahat to Ephrem has to do with Jewish proselytism among Christians in the face of full-scale Sassanian persecution. This is the question I propose to raise here by a consideration of a source heretofore unexplored in studies of Ephrem's anti-Judaic polemic, his *Hymns on the Nativity*.

The core of the collection of twenty-eight *Hymns on the Nativity* published by Beck is a smaller collection (*Hymns 5-20*) on a single melody; these were evidently composed by Ephrem as a unit for a particular purpose.[23] One obvious use for this collection of sixteen hymns—as for the larger collection—was for the liturgy of Christmas-Epiphany, celebrated in Ephrem's time as a single feast on the sixth of January.[24] Recognition of this liturgical function does not, of course, exhaust the possible intentions of its composer. Examination of the style and content of the hymns shows that one of their central concerns, if not their principal theological intent, is the presentation of a theology of the incarnation in the face of Jewish criticism of this and related Christian beliefs.

[19]E. Beck, *Ephraems Reden über den Glauben* (Rome: Herder, 1953) 73, 118-20; Kazan, "Homily," *OrChr* 46 (1962) esp. 96-98; OrChr 47 (1963) 89-90; Drijvers, "Jews," 98-100; Hayman, "Image," 432-33.

[20]Kazan, "Homily," *OrChr* 46 (1962) 96; Drijvers, "Jews," 98-99; McVey, *Ephrem*, 19-23, 34-39, 221-257.

[21]For the dating of Aphrahat's work, cf. Pierre, *Aphraate*, 42.

[22]Neusner, *History* 4.26, n. 2; cf. G. Wiessner, *Zur Märtyrerüberlieferung aus der Christenverfolgung Schapurs II* (Abhandlungen der Akademie der Wissenschaften in Göttingen. Philologisch-Historische Klasse. 3. Folge, 67; Göttingen: Vandenhoeck & Ruprecht, 1967); further, cf. J. Neusner, "Babylonian Jewry and Shapur II's persecution of Christianity from 339 to 379," *HUCA* 43 (1972) 77-102.

[23]E. Beck, ed., *Des heiligen Ephraem des Syrers Hymnen De Nativitate (Epiphania)* (hereafter *HNat.*) (CSCO 186-87, Scr. Syr. 822-83; 2 vols. in 1; Louvain: Brill, 1959); on the core of the collection, cf. ibid., CSCO 187, v. For English translation and comments, cf. McVey, *Ephrem*, esp. 29-34, 105-72.

[24]*HNat.* 5.13-14; for discussion, cf. Beck, *HNat.*, CSCO 186, v-vi.

In the *Hymns on the Nativity* Ephrem meditates on the feast in three ways: liturgically, exegetically and dogmatically. If Christmas-Epiphany is understood as the celebration of the manifestation of Christ to the world, the applicability of each of these themes is transparent. His liturgical motif is the interpretation of the feast of birth of Christ as the "victory of the unconquered sun" over the darkness.[25] His exegetical subject is the infancy narratives of Matthew and Luke, possibly viewed through the lens of the *Diatessaron*.[26] His dogmatic theme is the wondrous paradox of the incarnation.[27] As he enlarges on his exegetical and dogmatic materials, Ephrem enters upon a defense of the virginal conception in the face of "slanderers." The "slanderers" have questioned not only Mary's virginal conception but also the resurrection of Jesus and the chastity of Christian women devoted to celibacy.[28] He attributes all three "slanders" to the Jewish people.[29]

On the one hand Ephrem responds positively to these challenges by constructing a tripartite typological argument. For the first part of the argument he has selected from Hebrew Scripture a series of women who had been barren but conceived by divine grace. He argues that Mary is like Sarah, Rachel and Anna in that they all became mothers through divine intervention and for the sake of the history of salvation. Yet Mary is superior since "without vows and without prayer in her virginity she conceived and brought forth the Lord of all of the sons of her counterparts ... pure and just men, priests and kings."[30] The second group of types consists of prominent Hebrew women whose sexual behavior was questionable: Tamar, Ruth and Rahab.[31] He argues that their bold behavior was justified by the purposes of God, which they mysteriously discerned. Mary, he implies, appears to be like them, yet she is quite different in her chaste conception of Jesus: "I who am slandered have conceived and given birth to the True Judge Who will vindicate me. For if Tamar was acquitted by Judah, how much more will I be acquitted by You!"[32] In Ephrem's third use of feminine typology in these hymns, Mary is anticipated by

---

[25]*HNat*. 5, esp. 13-15.

[26]*HNat*. 5.4, 12, 16-18; 6.7-21; 7.1-8; 8.6; 11.7-8; 15.2-9; 16.8; 17.2-3; 18.1-3.

[27]*HNat*. 5.5-6, 19-24; 6.9-11, 14; 8.1-4, 17; 9.1-2; 11.1-8; 12.1; 13.6-24; 18.4-36; 19.12-17.

[28]Slander against Mary's virginal conception: *HNat*. 6.3; 12.4, 10; 14.12, 14; 15.7. Against the resurrection of Jesus: *HNat*. 10.5, 12. Against both together: *HNat*. 10.9. Against chaste Christian women: *HNat*. 12.5, 9; associated with slander against Mary: *HNat* 12.6-11.

[29]*HNat*. 10.10; 14.11-15.

[30]*HNat*. 8.16.

[31]*HNat*. 9.7-16.

[32]*HNat*. 15.8, cf. *HNat*. 16.12, 14.

inanimate sacred symbols of the Jewish cult. He implies that Mary fulfills the type of the *Shekhinah*; she is like the dwelling place of God, the Ark of the covenant, and the tablets of the Law of Moses.[33] The consecrated virgin, moreover, is "the Holy of holies," and Christ is the High Priest.[34]

On a theological level, Ephrem relates the notion of Mary's virginal conception to the incomprehensibility and omnipotence of God, again using a *qal wa homer* type of argument: "Our Lord, no one knows how to address Your mother. [If] one calls her "virgin," her child stands up, and "married"—no one knew her [sexually]. But if Your mother is incomprehensible, who is capable of [comprehending] You?"[35] His essential approach to the incarnation is to state the paradox baldly and to assert a notion of *kenosis*, thereby indicating an awareness of the inherent difficulty in maintaining that the creator of the universe became a human being, without compromising his affirmation that it is true. Since Ephrem places many of the hymns in the mouths of biblical *dramatis personae* and especially of Mary, he is able to use the dramatic form to assert these apparent contradictions without further explanation. So Mary sings, "Who has granted to the barren one to conceive and give birth to the One [Who is also] many, to the small [Who is also] great, Who is fully present in me yet fully present in the universe."[36] Or a choir sings about Mary:

> The womb of Your mother overthrew the orders;
> The Establisher of all entered a Rich One;
> He emerged poor. He entered her a Lofty One;
> He emerged humble. He entered her a Radiant One,
> and He put on a despised hue and emerged.
>
> He entered, a mighty warrior, and put on fear
> inside her womb. He entered, Nourisher of all
> and He acquired hunger. He entered, the One who
> gives drink to all, and He acquired thirst.
> Stripped and laid bare,
> He emerged from [her womb], the One who clothes
> all.[37]

---

[33]*HNat.* 16.16-17.
[34]*HNat.* 17.5
[35]*HNat.* 11.1.
[36]*HNat.* 5.19.
[37]*HNat.* 11.7-8; cf. *HNat* 11.5-6; 16.2 and 18.5.

His other approach to the problem of incarnation is a simple assertion of Jesus' dual parenthood. Again, he gives no explanation of the manner in which it is possible but simply states that God is the Father of Jesus while Mary is his mother. A choir of women addresses the following words to the Divine Infant:

How humble You are! How powerful You are!
O Infant, Your judgment is powerful;
Your love is sweet. Who is able
to stand against You? Your Father is in heaven,
and Your mother on earth. Who is able to speak
about You?

If anyone seeks Your hidden nature
behold it is in heaven in the great womb
of Divinity. And if anyone seeks
Your revealed body, behold it rests and looks out
From the small womb of Mary![38]

Another aspect of Ephrem's exegetical concern with issues of integrity and social status is his portrayal of Joseph's inner dilemma: "Who has given me the Son of the Most High to be a son to me? I was jealous of Your mother and wanted to divorce her. I did not know that in her womb was a great treasure that would suddenly enrich my poverty."[39] In the following verse he gives attention not only to Joseph's worries about his wife's fidelity, but also to his lowly status as a carpenter. Despite his Davidic descent, he admits, "instead of a king I am a carpenter."[40] In his poetic response Ephrem turns even the humble profession of Jesus and Joseph into an asset by means of a typological interpretation. Carpenters arriving with farmers and laborers in the vineyard address Joseph: "Blessed is your offspring, the Chief of carpenters by Whom was drawn even the Ark. By Him was constructed the temporal Tabernacle."[41]

On the other hand, Ephrem also responds to these challenges to his belief in Mary's virginal conception and its importance with a graphic and bitter anti-Judaic polemic, centering on Jewish women, female personifications and sexual mores. The Jewish people as a whole are represented by the figure of the daughter of Sion. Startled by the acclamation of Christ "the Watcher" who awakens all, "she killed the

[38]*HNat.* 13.6-7; cf. *HNat.* 8.2; 9.2, 11.1-4, 14.2.
[39]*HNat.* 5.17.
[40]*HNat.* 5.18.
[41]*HNat.* 8.10; cf. 8.11-12.

Watcher."[42] When he rises up from the grave, Christ awakens the Gentiles instead, who are properly grateful. Not only is Mary favorably contrasted with Tamar "who reeked of the smell of her father-in-law" and yet "was acquitted,"[43] but all Israel is personified as a whore and contrasted to Zipporah, Moses' wife, who maintained chastity "altogether she was the daughter of [pagan] priests."[44] Recalling the daughter of Saul, who criticized David for his dance and called him dissolute, he warns that because she "vomited forth evil, her womb was deprived of childbearing." Clearly addressing his Jewish contemporaries, he continues, "Daughter of Sion, hold your tongue about the Son of David Who surpasses you in glory. Be not like the daughter of Saul whose family history is complete."[45] He even considers the Deuteronomic legislation concerning proofs of the virginity of brides and tests of accusations of adultery to argue that slanderous accusations in these matters are to be expected, particularly from "the unclean people."[46]

In responding to questions about the reliability of the earliest witnesses to the resurrection, Ephrem links the theme of Mary's virginity to the resurrection by a theologically and symbolically related defense of the truth of the "empty tomb." The sealed womb of Mary and the stone sealing the tomb of Christ are both proof of Christ's divinity in the face of "the slanderers" who say that Christ was conceived by "human seed" and that the resurrection was "human robbery."[47] Daniel sealed in the lions' den and Lazarus sealed in his tomb are taken as types predicting both the Virgin Birth and the Resurrection.[48] Ephrem argues further that just as some went in search of Elijah after his ascent, thus demonstrating their doubts, how much more it is to be expected that "the impure" will doubt the resurrection of Jesus.[49] Elijah, Elisha and Moses are presented as examples of the power granted to the practitioners of chastity.[50]

Ephrem presents additional typological arguments for the authority of Jesus: as the descendent of Melchizedek, David and Abraham, he has inherited the priesthood, kingship and the right to constitute the people of God.[51] Most striking and original, however, is his extensive typology rooted in the image of the shepherd and the lamb.

[42]*HNat.* 6.23-24.
[43]*HNat.* 16.14 and 15.8
[44]*HNat.* 14.19.
[45]*HNat.* 14.9-10.
[46]*HNat.* 14.11-15.
[47]*HNat.* 10.9.
[48]*HNat.* 10.4.
[49]*HNat.* 10.11-12.
[50]*HNat.* 14.16-18.
[51]*HNat.* 9.3.

Beginning with the worship offered by the shepherds of Luke's infancy narrative, he portrays Moses, shepherding his unruly flock in the desert, Noah, pacifying the animals on the Ark, and David as shepherds whom Jesus has superceded. By killing the "wolf that killed Adam, the innocent lamb who grazed and bleated in paradise," Jesus has restored the lost youth of Adam and Eve and of all people, especially those who live in chastity.[52] Christ, the second Adam, is also the Paschal Lamb—a common enough designation by the fourth century, but here with new ramifications: he is the "Paschal Lamb who ... offered the Passover for all ... [and who invites the] lamb of the flock to give thanks that our Lord did not kill him as Moses [did]."[53] The starting point for this imagery is once again the Lucan infancy narrative, but Ephrem elaborates from it an argument for the superiority of Jesus to Moses based on his putative compassion for the sacrificial animals. So a lamb brought by the shepherds at Bethlehem bleats to thank "the Lamb that came to free the sheep and oxen from sacrifices."[54] As Ephrem was perhaps aware, the Scripture reading for the feast of Hanukkah describes the dedication offerings of each of the twelve tribes, including dozens of sacrificial animals.[55] Finally, Ephrem's complex of imagery is completed with Sampson and Samuel, on the one hand, and Isaac, on the other, as types of Jesus to show that he is both powerful and gentle, and that his meekness is superior to the *lex talionis* of Moses.[56]

It is clear, then, that this group of hymns contains a forceful, coherent and often bitter anti-Judaic polemic centering on the New Testament accounts of the conception and birth of Jesus, his social status and the authenticity of the resurrection. In addition to these exegetical and historical themes, in relation to which Ephrem states clearly that he has been provoked to respond by "slanderers" among his Jewish contemporaries, he elaborates poetically on the doctrines of incarnation and mariology. If in reality he was engaged in a polemic with his Jewish contemporaries, we might hope to find traces of it in Jewish sources. Although it is well known that we are far less informed about Jewish arguments against Christianity in antiquity than about the corresponding Christian polemics, the difficulty is not entirely bereft of a solution. Berger has suggested that Jewish arguments as presented in Christian dialogues may be critically assessed through comparison with medieval Jewish polemical materials as well as through a

---

[52]*HNat.* 7.5-11.
[53]*HNat.* 18.18-19.
[54]*HNat.* 7.4.
[55]Num 7.1-89; cf. Meg. 3.6; H. Danby, *The Mishnah* (Oxford: Oxford University Press, 1933) 205, n. 19.
[56]*HNat.* 13 throughout, but esp. 13.3-5, 15-17; further on Isaac, cf. *HNat.* 18.30; 20.5.

Kathleen E. McVey

consideration of their "inherent plausibility."[57] This approach enables us to press the discussion of Ephrem's putative opponents a little farther. The *Toledoth Yeshu*,[58] a popular medieval Jewish folk polemic against Christianity has earlier roots and also contains materials which mirror Ephrem's arguments to some extent. The exegetical polemics that Ephrem addresses here—doubts about the virginal conception, Joseph's confusion, Jesus' lowly status as "son of a carpenter," and the suggestion that the empty tomb was a hoax—are addressed in several other early Christian writings, always attributed to Jewish critics of Christianity: in Matthew's gospel,[59] in Ephrem's *Commentary on the Diatessaron*,[60] in Origen's *Contra Celsum* and a few other patristic writers.[61] They probably correspond to a series of scattered pejorative references in the Talmud to Jesus ben Panthera and Jesus ben Stada.[62] Eventually these putative allusions to Jesus and his movement were brought together, not in the form of a dialog or debate, but rather as a pamphlet aimed at a popular audience, the *Toledoth Yeshu*, the "Book of the Generations of Jesus." Views on the date of composition of this counter-gospel have varied widely—from the first to the tenth century CE; the place of composition is likewise unknown.[63] The question is complicated by the existence of at least five major recensions and by the lack of a complete critical edition.[64] Krauss argued for the

---

[57]D. Berger, *The Jewish-Christian Debate in the High Middle Ages: a critical edition of the Nizzahon Vetus with an introduction, translation and commentary* (Philadelphia: Jewish Publication Society, 1979) 7-8.

[58]For bibliography and discussion of the literature, cf. G. Schlichting, *Ein jüdisches Leben Jesu: Die verschollene Toledot-Jeschu-Fassung Tam u-muᶜad: Einleitung, Text, Übersetzung, Kommentar, Motivsynopse, Bibliographie* (WUNT 24; Tübingen: Mohr [Siebeck], 1982).

[59]Matt 1:18-25 (cf. Luke 1:26-38); Mark 6:3, Matt 13:55 and 28:11-15. For discussion of these issues with regard to the infancy narratives of both Matthew and Luke, and for bibliography, see R. Brown, *The Birth of the Messiah* (New York: Doubleday, 1977) 534-46.

[60]E.g., on Joseph's view of Mary, cf. L. Leloir, *Ephrem de Nisibe, Commentaire de l'Evangile Concordant ou Diatessaron* (SC 121; Paris: Cerf, 1966) 65-70; on *HNat.* 10.20-10, cf. ibid., 385-86.

[61]Origen, *Con. Cels.* 1.28-32; 2.26, 61-73; for other patristic references, cf. H. Chadwick, *Origen, Contra Celsum* (Cambridge: Cambridge University Press, 1965) 31, n. 3.

[62]Cf. Johann Maier, *Jesus von Nazareth in der Talmudische überlieferung* (Erträge der Forschung 82; Darmstadt: Wissenschaftliche Buchgesellschaft, 1978).

[63]Schlichting, *Ein jüdisches Leben*, 2.

[64]For delineation of the five basic recensions of the *Toledoth*, cf. E. Bischoff, "Klassificirung der Texte," in S. Krauss, *Das Leben Jesu nach jüdischen Quellen* (Berlin: Calvary, 1902) 27-37. Schlichting's text is of Bischoff's fourth type (Schlichting, *Ein jüdisches Leben*, 8).

Kathleen E. McVey

existence of an early version, antedating any of the surviving complete accounts and lacking the allusions to Nestorius, Simon Stylites and the papacy which would otherwise necessitate a date later than the fourth century. On the basis of Aramaic fragments of the Toledoth discovered in the Cairo Geniza, Krauss argued that this "Ur-Toldot" was an Aramaic composition strongly influenced by Syriac syntax and dating to the late fourth century. On a linguistic basis the most probable place of origin for this version would then be Mesopotamia.[65] The confusion of Barsauma with Nestorius in the story of "Nestorius" indicate the existence of a Babylonian recension by the late sixth or early seventh century.[66]

The Jewish community of Persian Mesopotamia was well-established, prosperous and politically secure, relatively speaking, in the fourth century.[67] In contrast to Syriac-speaking Christianity, rabbinic Judaism also shared with the Zoroastrianism of Sassanid Persia a high estimation of marriage and saw the family unit as an essential component of the social structure. Although direct evidence of the economic condition of the Mesopotamian Christians is lacking, Ephrem's many allusions to the poor and his frequent use of imagery drawn from manual labor suggest that the Christians may have been less well-to-do.[68] Whether or not they were economically disadvantaged, the Christians were certainly in a more vulnerable political position on the Persian side of the shifting border in the fourth century. Why should a Mesopotamian Jewish community that enjoyed a superior position in so many respects bother to polemicize against the Christians?[69] Neusner has suggested that the majority of Jews in Mesopotamia had to be persuaded to interpret their Judaism in the manner of the rabbis.[70] As in Roman Palestine of Jesus' day, the majority of Jews still had little concern for rabbinic prescriptions. While Christian antinomian proselytization would scarcely be a threat to the social, economic and political position of Jews in the Persian Empire, it could have been a threat to rabbinic proselytization within the Jewish community. If Neusner's assessment of the relations between the rabbis and the general Jewish population is correct, then it is reasonable to suggest that the rabbis of fourth-century Mesopotamia would have had good reason to promote popular forms of polemic

[65]S. Krauss, "Neuere Ansichten über "Toldoth Jeschu," *MGWJ* 76 (1932) 586-603, 77 (1933) 44-61, esp. 46-58; but Heller demurs ("Über das Alter der jüdischen Judas-Sage und das Toldot Jeschu," *MGWJ* 77 (1933) 198-210, esp. 206-210).

[66]S. Gero, "The Nestorious Legend in the *Toledoth Yeshu*," *OrChr* 59 (1975) 108-20.

[67]Neusner, *History of the Jews*, esp. 4.35-56.

[68]Cf. e.g., *HNat.* 8.7-12, 20.

[69]This implausibility constitutes Heller's central reason for rejecting Krauss' "Ur-Toldot," cf. n. 65, above.

[70]Neusner, *History of the Jews* 4.125-26, 279, 360, 386 et passim.

among Jews not yet committed to a rabbinic interpretation of their faith, as well as among Christians wavering due to the Sassanian persecution, and even pagan Semites.[71] Both the tone and the content of Ephrem's *Nativity Hymns* support this hypothesis.

[71]On the last group, cf. M. Simon's suggestion in *Verus Israel: Etude sur les rélations entre chrétiens et juifs dans l'Empire Romain (135-425)* (Paris: Boccard, 1948) 351-55.

THE ORIGINAL LANGUAGE OF THE ACTS OF THOMAS*

Harold W. Attridge
University of Notre Dame

Since the original publication of the Syriac text of the Acts of Thomas there has been considerable debate about the work's original language of composition. Scholars, including W. Wright, the editor of the London (British Museum) MS through which the Syriac was first made known, initially presumed that the Greek was primary.[1] Subsequently, many have argued that the extant Greek was translated from Syriac, which would then presumably be the original language. This tradition began with Th. Nöldeke in 1883.[2] A series of articles by F. C. Burkitt laid the foundation for most subsequent discussion.[3] Occasional contributions subsequently added new evidence.[4] When Bornkamm wrote his introduction to the *Acts of Thomas* in the second edition of Hennecke-Schneemelcher, he simply noted (428): "As is today scarcely disputed, the ATh were originally composed in Syriac." Bornkamm, like most other scholars who have treated the work, still gave priority to the form of the text found in the Greek witnesses.

---

*A version of this paper was presented at the Consultation on New Testament Apocrypha at the 1989 Annual Meeting of the Society of Biblical Literature. I am happy to offer it here as a small token of thanks to Prof. John Strugnell, with whom I first explored Syriac Christian literature and much else pertinent to Christian origins.

[1]Wright (*Apocryphal Acts* [2 vols. in 1; London-Edinburgh: Williams and Norgate, 1871] 1.xiv) was followed by M. Bonnet (in R. A. Lipsius and M. Bonnet, *Acta Apostolorum Apocrypha* (2 vols., vol. 2 in two parts; Leipzig: Teubner, 1903; reprinted, Hildesheim/New York: Olms, 1972) 2.2.xx).

[2]Th. Nöldeke in R. A. Lipsius, *Die apokryphen Apostelgeschichten* (Braunschweig: Schwetschke, 1883) 2.2,423; F. C. Burkitt, E. Preuschen, "Thomasakten," in E. Hennecke, *Handbuch zu den neutestamentlichen Apokryphen* (Tübingen: Mohr [Siebeck], 1904) 563; G. Bornkamm, "The Acts of Thomas," in E. Hennecke and W. Schneemelcher, *New Testament Apocrypha* (Philadelphia: Westminster, 1965) 2.428, and A. J. F. Klijn, *The Acts of Thomas: Introduction-Text-Commentary* (NovTSup 5; Leiden: Brill, 1962) 5-7. The position is accepted by E. Plumacher, "Apokryphe Apostelakten," *PWSup* 15 (1978) 34.

[3]"The Original Language of the Acts of Judas Thomas," *JTS* 1 (1900) 280-90; idem, "The Name Habban in the Acts of Thomas," *JTS* 2 (1901) 429; idem, "Another Indication of the Syriac Origin of the Acts of Thomas," *JTS* 3 (1902) 94-95.

[4]See P. Devos, "Actes de Thomas et Actes de Paul," in *AnBoll.* 69 (1951) 119-30, esp. 123.

It remains possible that the work, or some parts of it, was originally composed in Greek, translated into Syriac and then back into Greek, although evidence for such a development would be difficult to find.[5] It is also possible that sources, perhaps underlying the episodic miracle stories in the first half of the work, were originally composed in Greek. Yet for the ATh as a whole the general current consensus, represented in such treatments as Klijn's commentary or the introduction by Drijvers in the new Hennecke-Schneemelcher,[6] is that the original language was Syriac. A few scholars remain unconvinced. Some, such as J. Ysebaert, rather casually affirm the priority of the Greek.[7] Others, such as Michael Lafargue, argue for it on the basis of literary characteristics (particularly word plays) in the Greek text.[8] In the 1988 consultation on the apocryphal acts in the context of the annual meeting of the Society of Biblical Literature, Dennis MacDonald suggested that the Greek of Thomas, generally agreed to be one of the later of the acts once attributed to Leucius Charinus, shows evidence of direct dependence on other Greek acts. In light of this residual doubt about the original language, it might be profitable to review some of the evidence.

Semitisms

That the ATh were composed in a Semitic milieu is clear. The Greek version displays numerous Syriac idioms, such as "cultivation of the stomach" for gluttony (chap. 28; 144,3-4)[9]; "Lord of the debt" for creditor (chap. 29; 145,19); or "husband of your maidenhood" (chap. 114; 225,5) for "husband of your youth." There are also a few Semitic syntactical features, such as the resumptive used with the relative converter (Syriac ܕ), e.g., "I have neither son nor daughter from you that I might take consolation in them" (chap. 100; 212,13-14); predicates marked with the preposition εἰς (= Syriac ܠ), as in "May this eucharist be life," etc. (chap. 158; 269,4-5); third-person resumptive pronouns in direct address (chap. 133; 240,8 and frequently). Such

---

[5]M. R. James (*The Apocryphal New Testament* [Oxford: Oxford University Press, 1945] 364) detected in the smoother Greek recension of the martyrdom an independent witness to the original Greek text.

[6]H. J. Drijvers, "Thomasakten," in W. Schneemelcher, *Neutestamentlische Apokryphen in deutscher Übersetzung* (2 vols., 5th ed.; Tübingen: Mohr [Siebeck], 1987-89) 2.289-367, esp. 290.

[7]J. Ysebaert, *Greek Baptismal Terminology: Its Origins and Early Development* (Nijmegen: Dekker & Van de Vegt, 1962) 4.

[8]Michael Lafargue, *Language and Gnosis* (HDR 18; Philadelphia: Fortress, 1985) 9. He later notes word plays in Greek, such as that in chap. 3 between "price" (τίμημα) and "value, honor" (τιμή). The sentence in which this particular play appears is absent from the Syriac and is probably an addition in the Greek. The Greek translation obviously involved some embellishment.

[9]References are to page and line of the Greek critical text by Lipsius-Bonnet.

H. W. Attridge

features are not, however, decisive for the original language and could be explained by the character of Greek used in a Semitic environment.

Inner-Greek Corruptions

Judgment about the original language involves assessment of the significance of variants between the Syriac and the Greek. These fall into several categories. First are cases where the Syriac preserves what would appear to be a better reading, but where the corruption could be due to an inner-Greek error. These cases are not absolutely decisive for deciding the question of the original language.

For example, in chap. 28 (144,11) the Greek article ἡ is corrupt for the negative conjuntion μή, which the context requires. In chap. 63 (179,18) the Greek reads "he says" (φησιν), while the Syriac reads the plural "they say" (= Greek φασιν), as the context requires.

In chap. 66 (183,6) the Greek reads, "while looking at their shepherds" (ἀπιδόντες τοὺς ποιμένας). The Syriac reads, "while their shepherd was away" (= Greek ἀπιόντος τοῦ ποιμένος). The Syriac fits better the biblical allusion, and the misreading of the participle would have been easy in Greek.

In chap. 75 (190,13) the Greek reads: "Have you returned, you who blot out our craft." The Syriac reads: "Have you returned, who blots out our traces." The more consistent imagery of the latter reading was destroyed by a mechanical confusion in the Greek between τέχνην and τὰ ἴχνη.

In chap. 78 (193,16) the Greek reads: "Why wonder about the physical healings that are performed" (ἐνεργεῖται). The Syriac reads: "Why do you wonder about his physical healings that are (eventually) dissolved." The contrastive language of the Syriac fits the context well. As Bonnet suggested, there was probably a corruption in the Greek verb from καταργεῖται.

In chap. 107 (219,11) the nonsensical πρόσδεξαί με may be corrupt for an optative, προσδεξαίμην, which would appropriately translate the Syriac imperfect. For a similar optative, cf. chap. 115 (226,8).

Omissions

Of similar value are several cases where the Greek displays a shorter text than the Syriac and the variants are due to obvious omissions in Greek.

In chap. 55 (171,19) the first of a series of chiasms is explicitly labelled in Syriac but not in Greek.

In chap. 57 (173,18-19) the Greek reads: "Some (*scil.* of those punished in one chamber of hell) are completely consumed and they are given to other punishments." The Syriac avoids the contradictory assertion and reads, "some completely consumed and others given over to other punishments."

In chap. 64 (181,5-6) the Greek reports the encounter of two women and their attendants with demons: "Afterwards I too saw them (i.e., the demons) coming toward

243

us and we fled from them, as the boys who were with us struck us and threw me against my daughter." The Syriac reads: "After her I too saw them coming toward us and the lads who accompanied us fled them. They struck me and my daughter and they threw us down." In the Greek the verb describing the flight of the attendants has been omitted, making the attendants, not the demons, the assailants.

In chap. 135 (241,9) the Greek labels Charisios (in Syriac, Carish or Curesh, the equivalent of Cyrus) as the husband of Tertia. Tertia, of course, is the wife of King Misdaios (in Syriac Mizdai, as in the divine name Ahura Mazda). Usually in the Syriac, and commonly in the Greek, Carish is identified as "the kinsman of Mizdai." The omission of the middle two words in the phrase τοῦ συγγενοῦς τοῦ ἀνδρός is an easy parablepsis.

Later in chap. 135 (242,8-9), there is a balanced series of comments. The Greek reads: "You are wealthy with an abundance of servants." The Syriac adds, "but you have not set your own soul free from slavery." The antithetical style of the passage requires what the Syriac preserves.

In all such cases of inner-Greek error it is theoretically possible that the Syriac was translated from an uncorrupted Greek MS. These cases at least provide disjunctive errors indicating that the extant Greek is not the source of the Syriac. Their large number enhances the probability that the Greek was translated from the Syriac.

Awkward Greek and Misunderstood Syriac

An appeal to an inner-Greek and post-translation corruption is less likely in cases where an odd or corrupt Greek text is explicable on the basis of a misreading of the Syriac. An obvious example is the phrase in chap. 21 (134,7-8), "if you do not come with punishment against the head of that sorceror."[10] The awkward expression renders a simple Syriac idiom for "to punish" (literally, "put on the head"; ܟܨ ܝ ܣܡ). This phrase and related terms have repeatedly caused translators difficulty.[11] In chap. 76 (191,1) the Greek reads "he will give you punishment on your head." Here the Syriac does not use the common expression for punishment but simply says "you will receive blame." The last word ܟܫ ܝ has been confused with the word for head, ܟܫ ܝ in the expression for punishment.[12]

---

[10]The reading is that of the longer recension. The shorter, more elegant, recension has (134,16), "drive out that sorceror with a dread punishment."

[11]The phrase is used various times with slightly different translations. Cf. also 66 (184,10), 100 (213,8), 101 (214,12). The phenomenon was already noted by Burkitt, "The Original Language," 283.

[12]The case was noted by Burkitt, "The Original Language," 284.

In chap. 40 the Syriac reads: "I have been sent that I might give you rest and that thereby the faith of these people might be built,[13] and that this other faculty might be added to me, which today, because I was to serve you, I acquired." The Greek (158,5-8) reads, quite literally: "I have been sent to you for you to have rest by sitting on me and (that) I might gain faith and that this portion might be bestowed on me, which I am now about to acquire through the service that I have performed for you." There are two problems in the Greek. Since the term "portion" (ܡܢܬܐ; μέρις) must refer to the faculty of speech,[14] the Greek future (νῦν μέλλω κτᾶσθαι) is corrupt. The ass is not going to get what he already has. The tenses in the final clause of the passage have apparently been reversed from the Syriac (ܡܢ ܕܝܠܝ ܐܫܡܫ ܕܡܫܡܫܘ). There is also a corruption in the reference to those who are to acquire faith. The Syriac indicates that the crowds are in view. The variant may, of course, be an inner-Greek corruption (λαβώσιν to λάβω).

In chap. 63 (179,14-15) there is an awkward parataxis involving a curious use of Greek tenses: "I too stood in the road watching to see when she would come (πότε ἔλθῃ) and I would see (θεάσομαι) her[15] with my daughter." This is a woodenly literal reproduction of the idiomatic Syriac: "I too stood in the road watching to see when she would come, so that I would see her (ܐܚܙܝܗ) and greet my daughter with her."

In chap. 66 (182,15) the Greek reads: "Remain in this faith, preaching the good news of Jesus." The admonition is possible, but odd. The Syriac reads instead "Remain in this faith and hope in Jesus." An inner-Syriac variant or mistaken translation explains the difference. The pael of the verb ܣܒܪ means to hope or trust, which is more suitable in the context; the ethpael means to proclaim or preach. A similar error appears in chap. 139 (245,28).

In chap. 81 (196,14) the Greek awkwardly uses two verbal expressions: "I am not separated from you, nor I call upon you in disbelief." The Syriac is simpler: "I do not doubt you." The Syriac word for doubt (ܡܬܦܠܓ) etymologically means "separate, divide." The Greek gives two renditions of the same Syriac verb, one of which commits an etymological fallacy.

---

[13]For ܬܬܒܢܐ of the London MS, the basis of the editio princeps, Wright conjectures ܬܬܒܢܐ "be built," a reading confirmed in the other major witness to the Syriac, a Berlin MS, edited by P. Bedjan, *Acta Martyrum et Sanctorum* (3 vols.; Paris/Leipzig: Harrassowitz, 1892; reprinted, Hildesheim: Olms, 1968) 3.1-175, esp. p. 44. The edition uses the text of London MS as its base. Variants from the Berlin MS are indicated in the apparatus, or sometimes adopted as the text. On the problems of the edition see Klijn, *The Acts*, 1, n. 4.

[14]The Berlin MS (Bedjan, p. 44) in fact reads ܡܠܬܐ, "speech."

[15]One MS (U) adds "and greet" (ἀσπάσομαι) which is closer to the Syriac.

In chap. 85, part of a lengthy sermon inculcating certain virtues, there are major differences of organization and emphasis among the Greek witnesses and between them and the Syriac. There are, however, some common details. Much of the Greek of the longer recension, represented particularly in MS U,[16] is extremely awkward. Some of that awkwardness can be explained by the Syriac. At 200,33-201,2 (in U) comes the elliptical phrase: "(Be pleasing to God) in peacefulness, in stretching out the hand to the poor," etc. The image of stretching out the hand is a good Syriac idiom for liberality or generosity (ܐܝܕܐ ܡܫܛܚ ܐܝܟ). The Greek expresses this notion not with an abstract noun or an infinitive, but with a participle (τῷ διὰ χειρὸς ὀρέγοντι τοῖς πένησιν), apparently misconstruing the Syriac form.

In chap. 88 (203,18) there is an awkward Greek sentence. Part of the problem lies in the ever troublesome Syriac expression for punishment (ܒܝܫܬܐ ܡܣܡ), here the object of a preposition "with." The Greek has a infinitive construction (ὑπόδικον εἶναι), the syntactical position of which is unclear. Apparently the governing preposition in the Syriac (ܠܗܘܢ) has acquired in translation a prepositional object (αὐτῶν). The following conjunction (ܐܝܟܢܐ), which introduces a clause explaining the basis for punishment, is rendered with a prepositional phrase (ἐν ᾧ) designed to function in a similar way. The effect in the Greek, however, is obscure and awkward.

In chap. 115 (225,22) the Greek has Carish ask Mygdonia an apparently ironic question. "Who would bear this 'good' behavior of yours?" Carish follows this with a despairing comment, "What is left for me?" He then awkwardly refers to the beauties of Mygdonia: "Your fragrance is in my nostrils and your bright face is set in my eyes." The Syriac is more straightforward: "Or can I endure your lovely beauties that are always before me?" The following remark details the beauties that Carish cannot now stand to see: "Your sweet fragrance is in my nostrils and your lovely face is set before my eyes."

In chap. 116 (227,7) the Greek reads: "You are wealth and honor to me"; the Syriac: "I have wealth and honor." The following phrase, "and everyone knows that no one is my equal," common to both versions, indicates which comment is closer to the original. Carish clearly boasts of his own status, which Mygdonia has given up for Christ. The variant was probably caused by misreading the "there is" (ܐܝܬ) for "you (are)" (ܐܢܬ). That the Syriac version retains the form of the dialogue closer to the original at this point is confirmed by the sequel (chap. 117) in the Greek.[17] There Mygdonia responds to her husband's speech by contrasting the supreme worldy wealth and status that he has claimed to possess with the heavenly status of the apostle whom Mygdonia now loves.

[16]Romanus Vallicellanus B 35, from the twelfth century. This is the only witness to the complete text of the Acts, including the Hymn of the Pearl.

[17]I owe this observation to Prof. David Cartlidge, in discussion of this paper in the SBL consultation on the Apocryphal Acts.

In chap. 117 (227,17-18) Mygdonia prays to the Lord in the Greek that she might forget (ἐπιλαθέσθαι σε) her husband. In the Syriac she prays to God to "blot out" his deeds ("Don't remind me of your former activities with me, which I pray to the Lord to blot out for me."). The Greek has apparently misread the Syriac verb "to blot out" (ܪܚܩ) as "to forget" (ܪܚܩ).[18]

In chap. 130 (238,21) the Greek expression is awkward: "If you obey me, I know what I must do." The Syriac involves an idiomatic ellipse: "If you obey me, (fine), if not, I know what I must do." A Greek translator has apparently ignored or misconstrued the adversative ܐܢ ܘܐܢ[19] or perhaps misread it as "I" (ܐܢܐ).

In chap. 136 (243,5) there is reference in Greek to the "number of the servants" of Jesus. The Syriac reads, "number of the sheep." There is a simple confusion possible in Syriac between "his servants" (ܥܒ̈ܕܘܗܝ) and "his sheep" (ܥܢܗ). Hence the difference between the versions is clearly due to an error caused by an inner-Syriac phenomenon. Whether the current Syriac is closer to the original is not clear.

The relation of the two recensions of the martyrdom to the Syriac requires separate comment. That the recension represented in P[20] and related MSS (FLQSZ)[21] is not simply a reworking of the Greek of U is clear. It has several parallels with the Syriac not found in U (e.g., in the final prayer of Thomas, the phrases "and my toil found fruitless" at 253,13; "and let not tares be found in it, for your land does not accept his tares and they cannot fall into the storage bins of your husbandman" at 253,17-18; "I have planted your vine in the earth" at 253,19; "to the wedding feast I have been invited and I have put on white clothes" at 254,16-17; "May the powers not perceive me and the rulers not think of me. May the tax gatherers not see me nor the collectors harm me" at 257,10-12; and, in the narrative of the martyrdom, "For we are unable to guard him. For if your good fortune had not guarded the prisoners, they all would have escaped" at 274,15-17). Hence, this recension is often closer to the Syriac in content, though not in order, while it has a substantially smoother and less Semitizing style than the recension of U and its kin (AOKRV).

---

[18]See Paul Devos, "Actes de Thomas et Actes de Paul," in AnBoll. 69 (1951) 126-27, for this and other observations on the passage. The Berlin MS (Bedjan, p. 123) reads "forgive" (ܥܒܕܘܗܝ).

[19]This is the reading of the London MS. The Berlin MS (Bedjan, p. 138) has a fuller, but equivalent, expression ܘܐܢ ܠܐ.

[20]Parisiacus graecus 881, from the tenth century. This is the other major Greek witness to the ATh, containing all of the text apart from the Hymn of the Pearl.

[21]In these witnesses (PFSLZ) the prayer, found in the longer (U) Greek recension and the Syriac at chaps. 144-148, appears as the final prayer of Thomas. The Greek of this version of the martyrdom, for which MS Q is also a witness, is considerably smoother than that of the other witnesses to this portion of the work (AOKRUV).

That the P recension is a witness to an original Greek has been maintained,[22] but here too there is evidence of the Syriac original. One example will suffice. Three forms of Thomas' remark in chap. 167 may be compared. U (281,2-4) reads: "Give to those who carry out the command of Misdaios the King what is due them so that, free of them, I might go off and pray. When Vizan persuaded the soldiers, Judas turned to prayer, which ran..." P (281,14-16) reads: "Give to the servants of Misdaios that of which they are worthy so that they might let me go off and pray. Vizan persuaded the soldiers that they should let him go to pray. The blessed apostle Thomas went to pray..." The Syriac of the London MS reads: "Grant (ܒ ܗ) to the attendants that the will of their King Mizdai will be done. I shall go and pray. Vizan spoke to the servants and they let Judas go and Judas went and prayed and said..." It is difficult to see how the Syriac might be derived from either of the Greek versions, but easy to see how it accounts for the differences between them. The Syriac verb grant or give (ܒ ܗ) is misunderstood.[23] It takes as its object the whole clause which follows. Thomas asks Vizan to assure the soldiers that they will be able to do their duty. The P recension assumes that he is asking Vizan to give the troops a bribe. The disparaging reference to "their" king in the Syriac (ܢܘܗܠܝܕ) is construed as the object of the verb. In U that becomes the participle τὸ ὀφειλομενον; in P the relative οὖ εἰσιν ἄξιοι. U makes the sentence work by ignoring the verb "will be done" (ܟܢܗܝ); P by ignoring the noun "will" (ܗܢܝܒܨ).

Corrupt Syriac

The most decisive evidence of the direction of dependence are cases where an inner-Syriac *corruption* explains the state of the Greek. There are few clear cases of this which can be adduced. One is found in chap. 32. There the serpent claims (149,9) to be the one who "bound" (καταδήσας) the angels with lust for women. This reading follows that of the Berlin MS, "I bound" (ܟܪܡܐ). The London MS more sensibly reads "corrupted" them (ܟܪܡܚܕ), which could easily have been deformed into the reading found in the Berlin MS.[24]

In chap. 59, as the crowds offer thanks for Thomas' healing ministry, they describe themselves in Greek (177,1) as "healthy and rejoicing," a reading shared with the Syriac

---

[22]For James' position, see n. 5 above. Klijn (*The Acts*, 6-7) discusses this as well as further passages from the martyrdom with possible evidence of a Syriac source.

[23]Problems with the verb may have led to the form of the text in the Berlin M S (Bedjan, p. 171), which reads more concisely: "Allow (ܟܣܢܩ) the servants to fulfill the command of Mizdai. First I shall go and pray. And Vizan gave a command and they let him pray, and he prayed thus..."

[24]See Bedjan, p. 33. This example was first noted by Burkitt ("The Original Language," 284). See also Klijn, *The Acts*, 226.

H. W. Attridge

Berlin MS.[25] The Syriac of the London MS (Wright) has them "healthy and having sight." The difference in Syriac between "rejoicing" (ᴗᴗᴗ) and "seeing" (ᴗᴗᴗ) is slight. The variant is clearly due to an inner-Syriac corruption. The more likely collocation is the reading of the London MS, where the crowds refer to the healings that they have experienced, which provide the motive for their request to join God's flock. The Greek was apparently translated from a corrupt Syriac text like that of the Berlin MS.

In chap. 72 (187,22) the Greek reads "Jesus, who is blasphemed through knowledge of you (διὰ τὴν σὴν ἐπίγνωσιν) in this country." The expression is extremely awkward, and one MS (V) corrects to "through ignorance (ἄγνοιαν)."[26] The Greek is a literal rendition of the text represented in the London MS (ᴗᴗᴗ ᴗᴗᴗ). The Berlin MS reads more coherently: "Jesus, whose knowledge is rejected in this country" (ᴗᴗᴗ ᴗᴗ ᴗᴗᴗ).

In chap. 74 (189,16) the sentence may be translated: "But your activities are greater than the punishment which is reserved for you." The syntax, however, is extremely awkward. The predicate adjective is neuter (μείζονα) while the subject (αἱ ὑμέτεραι πράξεις) is feminine. The comparative is expressed with an unusual preposition (ἀπό). The awkwardness may be an attempt to render the difficult Syriac of a text like that of the London MS: "However great your bodies (ᴗᴗᴗ) may be, they are too small for your punishments." The odd preposition in Greek clearly reflects the Syriac where comparative is expressed with the normal preposition ᴗᴗ. The curious reference to "bodies" in the Syriac was apparently corrected, either in Syriac or in the process of translation, to "deeds" (ᴗᴗᴗ). The resulting Greek and the Syriac of the London MS remain obscure. Bedjan[27] suggests a simple inner-Syriac corruption of ᴗᴗᴗ to ᴗᴗᴗ. That would explain the whole sorry chain of readings. The original reading would be: "However great your torments, they are too small for your punishments" (i.e., they are less than you deserve).

Another corruption is found in the accounts of the martyrdom of Thomas. In chap. 146, frequently corrupt in the Greek of U, there is a reference to the prudent servant familiar from Gospel parables. The Greek (255,4-5) refers to the "bright prudence" (λαμπρᾷ σπουδῇ) of the man. This conforms to the Syriac, but the epithet is hardly apt. The text is probably corrupt, a scribe having read an original "prudent" (ᴗᴗᴗ) as "bright" (ᴗᴗᴗ).[28]

[25]See Bedjan, p. 64.
[26]Klijn (*The Acts*, 259) suggesting that the Greek may be original, apparently translates this Greek MS, although he does not note the fact.
[27]See Bedjan, p. 79.
[28]The Berlin and London MSS do not differ here.

249

Form-critical observations

Although perhaps not decisive, evidence confirming the priority of the Syriac can be found in the formulas used to introduce certain prayers (chaps. 94, 107). In each case the Syriac consistently preserves what is apparently the most traditional introduction using a form of the verb ܟܝ, a form found in biblical models and in the Qumran "Hodayoth." The Greek translates the introductory form using several terms (ὁμολογῆσαι and εὐχαριστεῖν) found in the LXX and the New Testament.[29]

Conclusion

Despite the fact that the Acts of Thomas and its famous hymns have been intensively studied for more than a century, much remains to be learned about the development of the text, the relationships among its various witnesses and and their relations with the history of religion in late antiquity. It is, however, clear that the range of witnesses now available to us ultimately depends on a Syriac original.

---

[29]For a detailed discussion of these formulas, see James M. Robinson, "Die Hodajot-Formel in Gebet und Hymnus des Frühchristentums," *Apophoreta: Festschrift für Ernst Haenchen zu seinem siebzigsten Geburtstag* (Berlin: Töpelmann, 1964) 194-235, esp. 199-201. Prof. Robinson himself suggested that the form-critical analysis might have implications for the discussion of the original language.

TWO ENOCHIC MANUSCRIPTS: UNSTUDIED EVIDENCE FOR EGYPTIAN CHRISTIANITY*

George W. E. Nickelsburg
The University of Iowa

We scholars of the Pseudepigrapha tend to use our manuscript resources almost exclusively for text-critical purposes. How can we arrive at the earliest form of the text, whether this be the text of the original or of a primary or secondary translation. Relatively seldom do we focus on codicological and contextual issues. Was a particular exemplar of the text copied into a manuscript that contained other texts? If so, can we discern a rationale for the collection? Such questions are significant, even if we have rarely asked them. Texts are, of course, created within communities and should be interpreted within that context. However, they are also *preserved* in communities, and it may be fruitful to ask why they were preserved, how they might have been understood and used, and what they might tell us about the people who preserved them.[1] In this essay, I shall raise these questions about the two major Greek manuscripts of *1 Enoch* and sketch some possible answers.

The various components of the collection of early Jewish apocalyptic texts known as *1 Enoch* were composed in Aramaic and then translated into Greek and from Greek into ancient Ethiopic. It is in this language alone that the whole corpus has been preserved, as an integral part of the Christian Bible. Of the original Aramaic text the Qumran materials have preserved fragments of eleven MSS that include various parts of the corpus and at least nine MSS that include fragments of the

---

*Scholarly credits rarely do justice to what we learn informally from teachers and friends. It was with John Strugnell that I first studied the Chester Beatty papyrus of *1 Enoch*, in 1965 while working on my dissertation, and in 1973 while preparing an extensive text-critical article, "Enoch 97-104: A study of the Greek and Ethiopic texts," *Armenian and Biblical Studies* (Jerusalem: St. James Press, 1976) 90-156. Subsequently, my study of early Judaism in general and *1 Enoch* in particular has been immensely helped, supported, and stimulated by our many conversations.

[1] A concern about this issue has been repeatedly expressed by Robert A. Kraft, formally first in an address on "The Christianity of the Pseudepigraphia" at the General Meeting of the SNTS at Durham, NC, in August, 1976. See also briefly in his article, "Reassessing the 'Recensional Problem' in Testament of Abraham," G. W. E. Nickelsburg, Jr., ed., *Studies on the Testament of Abraham* (SCS 6; Missoula: Scholars 1976) 135-37.

Book of Giants.[2] A significant part of the Greek translation of *1 Enoch* 1-36 has survived in the ninth-century chronography of George Syncellus.[3] More important, two codices have preserved, respectively, most of the Book of the Watchers (chaps. 1-36) and a substantial part of the end of the collection (chaps. 97-107). These two MSS are the subject of the present discussion.

1. *The Codex Panopolitanus*

This fifth- or sixth-century parchment codex, discovered a century ago in a grave at Akhmim (ancient Panopolis) in Upper Egypt, contains the only substantial pieces of the Greek versions of three ancient texts.[4] Bound between two boards, it contains thirty-three leaves, or sixty-six pages. An initial page contains only a Coptic cross. Pages 2-10 contain the *Gospel of Peter*.[5] The selection both begins and ends in mid-sentence and is thus probably a copy of a defective MS. It recounts a large part of the story of Jesus' trial, death, and resurrection. A blank leaf (pp. 11-12) is then followed in pp. 13-19 by an extract from the *Apocalypse of Peter*, bound upside down with a blank page at end. This fragment contains approximately one third of the text form of the *Apocalypse* preserved in Ethiopic, albeit in a different order.[6]

---

[2]For details, see J. T. Milik, *The Books of Enoch: Aramaic Fragments of Qumrân Cave 4* (Oxford: Clarendon, 1976) 4-7.

[3]For a critical edition of Syncellus, see Alden A. Mosshammer, ed., *Georgii Syncelli Ecloga Chronographica* (Leipzig: Teubner, 1984).

[4]For the *editio princeps* of the codex, see U. Bouriant, "Fragments grecs du Livre d'Enoch," *Mémoires publiés par les membres de la mission archéologique française au Caire* 9:1 (Paris: Leroux, 1892) 91-147. For the plates, corrections of the *editio princeps* of Enan, and the *editio princeps* of the *Gospel of Peter* and the *Apocalypse of Peter*, see A. Lods, "L'évangile & L'apocalypse de Pierre: Le texte grec du livre d'Énoch," *Mémoires publiés par les membres de la mission archéologique francaise au Caire* 9:3 (Paris: Leroux, 1893) 217-35 (with pp. 232-35 wrongly numbered as 32-335) + plates 1-34. For a description of the codex, see Bouriant, "Fragments," 93-94. For a fifth- to sixth-century date (rather than the eighth- to twelfth-century suggested by Bouriant ("Fragments," 83), see Milik (*Books*, 70), who cites Grenfell and Hunt, and see Eric G. Turner, *The Typology of the Early Codex* (Philadelphia: University of Pennsylvania, 1977) 185.

[5]For the most recent bibliography on the *Gospel of Peter*, see John Dominic Crossan, *The Cross that Spoke* (San Francisco: Harper & Row, 1988) 414-25.

[6]On the *Apocalypse of Peter*, see the discussion and translation by Christian Maurer and Hugo Duensing, "Apocalypse of Peter," Edgar Hennecke and Wilhelm Schneemelcher, *New Testament Apocrypha* (R. McL. Wilson, ed. and trans.; 2 vols.; Philadelphia: Westminster, 1964) 2.663-83. See also Martha Himmelfarb, *Tours of Hell: An Apocalyptic Form in Jewish and Christian Literature* (Philadelphia: University of Pennsylvania, 1983) 8-11 and passim, and Dennis Buchholz, *Your Eyes Will be Opened: A Study of the Greek (Ethiopic) Apocalypse of Peter* (SBLDS 97; Atlanta: Scholars, 1988).

George W. E. Nickeslburg

The fragment is mainly an account of Peter's tour of paradise and the places of punishment. The final forty-six pages of the codex contain almost all of the Enochic Book of the Watchers. The first two and a half pages include a short fragment: *1 Enoch* 19:3-21:9, beginning and ending in mid-sentence. Then, with no break in the text, the MS continues with *1 Enoch* 1:1-32:6, with a scribal change in mid-sentence at 14:22, at the top of page 50. Milik suggests that these Enochic pages, copied from two different MSS (the one ending at 21:9), had already been in circulation before they were gathered into the present codex.[7]

The Codex Panopolitanus is, then, a collection of extracts from three separate texts, two of them Christian and the third Jewish in origin. Two points of commonality are immediately evident: (1) The first two texts have a Petrine ascription; (2) The *Apocalypse of Peter* and the Book of the Watchers share, in part, a common form and subject matter; they are accounts of journeys to the world of the dead. We may press this similarity further. The *Apocalypse of Peter* is an example of a Christian apocalyptic genre which grew out of a Jewish revelatory journey tradition whose earliest known form is in the Book of the Watchers.[8]

A related point of similarity ties the *Gospel of Peter* (41-42) to both the *Apocalypse of Peter* and to the Book of the Watchers, viz., the reference to Jesus' descent into the realm of the dead. As is well known, the Enochic connection is more obviously present in 1 Pet 3:18-20, which mentions Jesus' mission to "the spirits in prison," who had disobeyed God in the days of Noah.[9]

The association between Petrine and Enochic traditions is much more widespread, however. Probably dependent on Jude, 2 Pet 2:4-5 alludes to the tradition about the rebellion of the Watchers and its context in the days of Noah.[10] The *Pseudo-Clementine Homilies* 8:11-15, in a sermon attributed to Peter, recounts the descent and sin of the Watchers with many close parallels to *1 Enoch* 8. Two other parallels with the Enochic traditions appear in canonical Petrine traditions. Peter's commissioning at Caesarea Philippi (Matt 16:16-19) is reminiscent of Enoch's commissioning near Mt. Hermon (*1 Enoch* 12-16).[11] Peter's dream vision about unclean animals symbolizes God's view that Gentiles are not unclean (Acts

---

[7]Milik, *Books*, 71. At the end of the codex is a single leaf extract from the Acts of St. Julian, stuck to the back board, see Bouriant, "Fragments," 146; Lods, "L'evangile," [2]33-35.

[8]See Himmelfarb, *Tours.*

[9]See W. J. Dalton, *Christ's Proclamation to the Spirits* (AnBib 23; Rome: Pontifical Biblical Institute, 1965).

[10]See Birger A. Pearson, "A Reminiscence of Classical Myth at II Peter 2.4," *GRBS* 10 (1969) 71-80.

[11]George W. E. Nickelsburg, "Enoch, Levi, and Peter: Recipients of Revelation in Upper Galilee," *JBL* 100 (1981) 575-600.

10). Enoch's second dream vision (*1 Enoch* 85-90) uses unclean animals to symbolize Israel's gentile oppressors and concludes with the obliteration of the distinction between Israel and the nations (90:37-38).[12]

In the light of these widespread parallels between Enochic and Petrine traditions, it is not surprising to find a single codex in which two Petrine texts have been supplemented by an extant manuscript of the Enochic text. This little book appears to have derived from a provenance in which the Petrine traditions continued to coexist with Jewish traditions that were, in part, their source.[13]

What might have been the rationale for the choice of texts bound in the Codex Panopolitanus? The *Gospel of Peter* refers to the dead to whom Christ preached between his death and resurrection, and it features a sensational narrative about Jesus' resurrection (35-42). The other texts deal with the realm of the dead, the judgment, and the hope of the righteous. Such concerns were eminently appropriate in a book laid in a Christian grave, and it would appear that the codex was compiled for this purpose.[14] Two relevant extracts from Petrine texts, perhaps copied for the purpose, were supplemented with a part from extant Enochic text and laid in the grave, following the old Egyptian custom of burying a copy of the Book of the Dead.[15] Such a burial deposit is not surprising. Evidence for the Jewish and/or Christian use of motifs in the Book of the Dead can be found in the long recension of the *Testament of Abraham* and in a fifth-century CE Coptic MS about Enoch.[16]

[12]On the Animal Vision, see idem, *Jewish Literature Between the Bible and the Mishnah* (Philadelphia: Fortress, 1981) 90-94.

[13]We cannot discuss here the evidence for Petrine traditions in Egypt. However, it is noteworthy that the two other extant fragments of the *Gospel of Peter* are from scraps of papyrus found at Oxyrhynchus. For a summary and bibliography, see Crossan, *Cross*, 6-9.

[14]Ernst Schürer (*Geschichte des jüdischen Volkes im Zeitalter Jesu Christ* [3 vols.; Hildesheim: Olms, 1970 reprint of 1909 ed.] 3.269, n. 42) notes a similarity in the theme of the three texts (eternal life) and suggests that "the scribe" chose the three fragments for inclusion in a burial gift. Milik (*Books*, 71) criticizes the theory that the whole book was hurriedly copied for this purpose.

A mathematical papyrus of eleven pages was also found in the same grave; J. Baillet, "Papyrus mathematique d'Akhmim," *Mémoires publiés par les membres de la mission archéologique francaise au Caire* 9:1 (Paris: LeRoux, 1982) 1-87 + plates I-VIII. Does this indicate an interest on the part of the buried person that would have been compatible with a study of the Astronomical Book of Enoch (*1 Enoch* 72-82)?

[15]See Thomas George Allen, ed., *The Book of the Dead* (Chicago: Oriental Institute, 1974).

[16]On the *Testament of Abraham* and the Book of the Dead, see Francis Schmidt, *Le Testament d'Abraham: introduction, édition de la recension courte, traduction et notes* (2 vols.; Diss. Strasbourg, 1971) 1.71-78; and George W. E. Nickelsburg, Jr., "Eschatology in the Testament of Abraham: A Study of the Judgment Scene in the Two Recensions," in Nickelsburg, *Studies*, 32-35. On the Coptic Enoch text, see Birger A.

George W. E. Nickeslburg

2. *Chester Beatty Biblical Papyrus XII*

This papyrus from the large Chester Beatty collection, dated by Kenyon to the fourth century CE, contains approximately two thirds of the Greek text of the last chapters of *1 Enoch* and all but the last few lines of the Homily on the Passion of Melito of Sardis.[17] Three other fragments contain a few partial lines of an "Ezekiel Apocryphon."[18]

The remains of this codex originally formed a quire of seven folded sheets, or fourteen leaves, some of which still contain the original page enumeration.[19] The first eleven and a half pages, which begin with page 15, contain a large part of the Epistle of Enoch plus the story of Noah's birth (*1 Enoch* 97:6-104:12; 106-107). The last sixteen and a half pages preserve Melito's treatise from a superscription almost to its final twelve-line doxology. Kenyon believes that the quire of fourteen leaves was "preceded by a quire of 8 leaves (one blank leaf and seven containing the numbered pages 1-14); or they may have been the central portion of a quire of 28 leaves, seven preceding and seven following the fourteen preserved leaves."[20]

In either case, comparative calculations of the Ethiopic text of *1 Enoch* 92–107 suggest that the Greek text of *1 Enoch* 92:1-97:6 would have filled approximately four of the first fourteen pages; the redactional chapter 91 would have taken another page. The remaining nine or ten pages would not have provided nearly enough space for the long Animal vision (chaps. 85–90). We may presume that the Epistle, with or without chap. 91, was preceded by another short text. Whether the Ezekiel text occupied this space or was placed after Melito's text, we shall discuss below.

It seems to have occurred to no one to ask whether there was a rationale for including *1 Enoch*, Melito, and the Ezekiel text in one codex. The three texts lack anything like the obvious similarities among the three components of the Codex Panopolitanus. Closer inspection indicates, however, that there are some significant

Pearson, "The Pierpont Morgan Fragments of a Coptic Enoch Apocryphon," in Nickelsburg, *Studies*, 227-83.

[17]The *editio princeps* of the Enoch text and of Melito and the Ezekiel text were both published by Campbell Bonner, *The Last Chapters of Enoch in Greek* (SD 8; London: Chatto and Windus, 1937); and *The Homily on the Passion by Melito Bishop of Sardis and Some Fragments of the Apocryphal Ezekiel* (SD 12; London: Christophers, 1940). The plates of the whole papyrus except Ezekiel were published with an introduction by Frederic C. Kenyon, *The Chester Beatty Biblical Papyri: Descriptions and Texts of Twelve Manuscripts on Papyrus of the Greek Bible: Fasciculus VII, Enoch and Melito* (London: Emery Walker, 1941).

[18]For the text and photos of the Ezekiel text, together with a brief discussion, see Bonner, *Homily*, 183-90 and plate 2.

[19]Kenyon, *Papyri*, 5-7.

[20]Ibid. 6.

parallels between the Enochic and Melitonic texts which may explain their presence in one codex.

Since Chester Beatty codex XII is a Christian document, one may ask how a Christian scribe or reader would have understood *1 Enoch* 92-107. To begin with, the Epistle would probably not have been understood as a Jewish product, but as a writing by the ancient seer, addressed especially to "the latter generations who will observe truth and peace" (92:1).[21] This audience would be, by definition, the Christian community for whom the codex was written. Enoch's books had been written to be revealed to them as latter-day life-giving wisdom (104:12-13).[22] Thus, Christian readers would identify themselves as the righteous and pious whom Enoch was admonishing to stand fast in the hope of the coming judgment.[23] The precise identity of the sinners, who are said to be guilty of oppression and of false religious teaching that perverted the ancient covenant (see esp. 98:9-99:2),[24] cannot be ascertained, since the codex's provenance in Egypt is unknown.[25] One group could have been rich and powerful pagans.[26] The false teachers could have been either Christian heretics or Egyptian Jews—a matter to which we shall return. The story of Noah's wondrous birth would also have had a special meaning for Christian readers. The generic parallels between the infancy stories in the gospels and this story and especially the account of Melchizedek's birth in *2 Enoch* are readily evident.[27] In a

[21]On the epistolary character of *1 Enoch* 92-105, see Milik, *Books,* 47 and 51.

[22]On the Epistle as eschatological wisdom, see George W. E. Nickelsburg, "The Epistle of Enoch and the Qumran Literature," *JJS* 33 (1982) 1-2 (= *Essays in honour of Yigael Yadin*) 334-43.

[23]See George W. E. Nickelsburg, "The Apocalyptic Message of 1 Enoch 92–105," *CBQ* 39 (1977) 309-28.

[24]On the specifically religious sins condemned in *1 Enoch* 92-105, see Nickelsburg, "Epistle," 334-39.

[25]Frederic G. Kenyon (*The Chester Beatty Biblical Papyri: Descriptions and Texts of Twelve Manuscripts on Papyrus of the Greek Bible: Fasciculus I, General Introduction* [London: Emery Walker, 1933], 5) states that the papyri come from Egypt. "Their place of origin is unknown ... however, it is plain that they must have been discovered among the ruins of some early Christian church or monastery; and there is reason to believe that they come from the neighborhood of the Fayum."

[26]Oppression by the rich is severely criticized throughout the Epistle; see George W. E. Nickelsburg, "Riches, the Rich, and God's Judgment in 1 Enoch 92-105 and the Gospel According to Luke," *NTS* 25 (1979) 324-32. For a criticism of idolatry, which easily leads to an identification of the sinners with pagans, see 99:6-9.

[27]On the story of Noah's birth and its parallels in the Qumran Genesis Apocryphon and in *2 Enoch,* see George W. E. Nickelsburg, "The Bible Rewritten and Expanded," in Michael E. Stone, ed., *Jewish Writings of the Second Temple Period* (CRINT 2:2; Assen van Gorcum; Philadelphia: Fortress, 1984) 93-94. On the

setting where typological exegesis flourished (see the discussion of Melito below), the story of Noah's miraculous birth, and its character as a portent of coming salvation, would easily have been read as a prototype for the miraculous birth of Jesus, whose name symbolized the salvation he was bringing (Matt 1:21; cf. *1 Enoch* 106:18; 107:3).

Thus, fourth-century Christians could have read the Enochic text as an epistle encouraging them as they waited for judgment and salvation and reminding them by ancient analogy that the eschatological Savior had already been born.

The relevance that Melito's homily would have had for a Christian scribe and his audience is much more evident; the text was composed by a Christian for Christians and deals explicitly with matters relevant to Christians.[28] Of special importance in the present context are its similarities to the Enochic epistle and the possibilities for a common interpretation. According to Melito, salvation had been given to the Jews at the time of the Exodus and had been sealed in the first paschal ritual. The death of Jesus, the true paschal lamb, was the latter day fulfillment of the ancient ritual. This typology is not dissimilar to the Noah typology suggested above; the one relates to Jesus' birth, the other to his death. In Melito's view the Jews were the agents of the crucifixion, and because they rejected their savior, they were condemned before God.[29] Over against Israel stood the gentiles, "the families of men" (766) called into the church, the true Israel, for whom the paschal lamb died. This contrast between apostate Israel and God's true people parallels our suggested Christian interpretation of Enoch's epistle, and, indeed, the Epistle refers to the salvation of "all the sons of the whole earth."[30] Thus, taken together, Enoch's Epistle and Melito's Homily allow a common reading in which Jews and gentile Christians play a prominent role negatively and positively with respect to judgment and salvation.

Finally, we may look for a rationale for the inclusion of the Ezekiel text. In spite of its fragmentary condition, a few details are clear. Fragment 1 recto contains part of a prayer of penitence, which probably addressed God as "Father" and appealed for the mercy that had been shown to Abraham, Isaac, and Jacob.[31] Fragment 1 verso is, in part, a paraphrase of Ezekiel 34. God promises to shepherd God's people

---

relationship of *1 Enoch* 106-107 to the NT infancy narratives, see the articles by Otto Betz and Joseph Fitzmyer cited in ibid., p. 94, n. 19.

[28] For a critical edition of Melito, see Stuart George Hall, ed., *Melito of Sardis: On Pascha and Fragments* (Oxford: Clarendon, 1979).

[29] On the anti-Jewish tendency in the homily, see already Bonner, *Homily*, 57-58, and especially A. T. Kraabel, "Melito the Bishop and the Synagogue at Sardis: Text and Context," in D. G. Mitten, et al., eds., *Studies Presented to George M. A. Hanfmann* (Cambridge: Harvard University Press, 1971) 77–85.

[30] For the notion of the salvation of "all the sons of the earth," see *1 Enoch* 105:1-2 and cf. 100:6; 101:1; and see Nickelsburg, "Epistle," 343-45.

[31] For the text, see Bonner, *Homily*, 185.

and give them rest on the holy mountain.[32] Here, too, one encounters the motifs of sin and judgment, but especially reference to repentance, salvation, and the consummation of the covenantal relationship.

One cannot be certain about the precise interpretation of this text in the context of the other two, because we have only a fragment of text and because it is uncertain whether the text stood at the beginning or the end of the codex. Depending on the original sequential order of the sides (recto-verso, as Bonner suggests, or verso-recto) and the structure of the codex (one or two quires), it could have stood before Enoch's Epistle or after Melito's homily.[33] These two possibilities for placement suggest different scenarios for interpretation.

The imagery of Ezekiel 34 is constitutive of the allegorical symbolism in the Animal Vision of Enoch, chaps. 85-90, which are separated from the Epistle in the Ethiopic tradition only by the redactional chap. 91. In that vision, Israel is depicted as the disobedient flock, left in the hands of negligent shepherds, beleaguered by the gentile beasts, but finally saved. If the Ezekiel text stood at the beginning of the codex, it would have occupied in the codex the same place as the vision which was partly inspired by it occupies in *1 Enoch*.[34] This order of the three texts in the codex would have suggested the following interpretation. God promised that Israel would return from exile and live on the holy mountain in a new covenantal relationship with God (Ezekiel). Israel, however, has continued to sin. Therefore, God has rejected the nation and accepted the church as the holy people. The promises made through Ezekiel have failed because of Israel's renewed disobedience—their perversion of the ancient covenant (Enoch) and their rejection of the Christ (Melito).

If the Ezekiel text followed Melito's homily, which is perhaps more likely (see n. 33), the sheep-shepherd language of Ezekiel would have been immediately preceded by a document that was dominated by the imagery of the paschal lamb. This sequence of the three texts suggests an interpretation very different from the previous one. According to both Enoch's Epistle and Melito's homily, Israel stands under God's judgment. However, if the people repent, in effect speaking the prayer partly preserved on fragment 1 recto, they will see the fulfillment of Ezekiel's prophecy and will return to the holy mountain. If we accept this scenario, we could revise somewhat our first suggestion for the codex's audience. It could have been written

---

[32]Ibid., 186. For another text from Qumran that paraphrases Ezekiel 37, interpreting it in an eschatological vein, see John Strugnell and Devorah Dimant, "4QSecond Ezekiel," *RevQ* 13 (1988) 49-52 (= *Mémorial Jean Carmignac*) 45-58.

[33]On the placement of the Ezekiel text in the codex, see Bonner, *Homily*, 183.

[34]In the Ethiopic corpus, the Animal Vision (chaps. 85-90) stands immediately before chap. 91. For its place in the fragments of the Aramaic scrolls, see Milik, *Books*, 4-7. In the texts of the Greek version, there is only the possible implicit evidence cited here.

not only for Christians, but also for Jews who were considering Christianity. Taken as a whole, it would be an appeal to them to turn from their unbelief and to identify with the eschatological community of the righteous and pious.[35]

3. Some Broader Implications

The Christian preservation and transmission of Enochic texts in Egypt needs to be studied further. Knowledge of *1 Enoch* in Egyptian Jewry is probably indicated by two texts. The so-called Slavonic Enoch (*2 Enoch*), which is very closely related to the whole of *1 Enoch*, reflects Egyptian influence and is often thought to have been composed in Egypt.[36] The Wisdom of Solomon indicates numerous important parallels to *1 Enoch*.[37] In addition to the two Christian codices discussed above, we have fragments of a fourth-century Greek papyrus from Oxyrhynchus, which appears to have contained (material from) both the Astronomical Book (chaps. 72-82) and the Animal Vision (chaps. 85-90).[38] The Book of the Watchers was also known by the fifth-century Alexandrian monks, Panodorus and Annianus, whose chronicles were used by the ninth-century Byzantine chronographer, George Syncellus.[39] One leaf of a sixth- to seventh-century MS contains part of a Coptic version of the Apocalypse of Weeks (*1 Enoch* 93:1–10 – 91:11–17).[40] A fifth-century Coptic MS of nine leaves

---

[35]See my discussion of the Epistle of Enoch, "Epistle," 343-45. There may be an analogy to this codex as thus interpreted. Birger A. Pearson has called my attention to the Mississippi Coptic Codex I (the Crosby Codex) a papyrus collection of texts written ca. 300 CE, which also contains Melito's Homily (in part), as well as 2 Macc 5:27-7:41, 1 Peter, the Book of Jonah, and an unidentified fragment. It has been suggested that this was a paschal lectionary, Allen Cabaniss, "The University of Mississippi Coptic Papyrus Manuscript: A Paschal Lectionary?" *NTS* 8 (1961-62) 70-72. One may also note, as in the Chester Beatty Papyrus XII, that Melito's homily is collected with two texts that emphasize repentance (2 Macc 5-7 and Jonah) and one that mentions it prominently (1 Pet 1:22–2:10).

[36]On the parallels between *1 Enoch* and *2 Enoch*, see Nickelsburg, *Jewish Literature*, 185-88. On Egypt as a likely place of origin, see the citations in ibid., p. 192, n. 87.

[37]On the probable Egyptian provenance of Wisdom, see ibid., 184. For the parallels between *1 Enoch* and Wisdom, see C. Larcher, *Etudes sur le livre de la Sagesse* (EBib; Paris: Gabalda, 1969) 106-12; and George W. E. Nickelsburg, *Resurrection, Immortality, and Eternal Life in Intertestamental Judaism* (HTS 16; Cambridge: Harvard University Press, 1972) 128–29.

[38]J. T. Milik, "Fragments grecs du livre d'Henoch (P. Oxy. XVII 2069)," *Chronique d'Egypte* 46 (1971) 321–43.

[39]For a detailed discussion of the chronographers, see William Adler, *Time Immemorial: Archaic History and its Sources in Christian Chronography from Julius Africanus to George Syncellus* (Washington, D.C.: Dumbarton Oaks, 1989).

[40]Sergio Donadoni, "Un Frammento della Versione Copta del 'Libro di Enoch,'" *AcOr* 25 (1960) 197–202.

preserves a Christian Enochic tradition related in some way to the *Testament of Abraham*.[41] Knowledge of Enochic traditions is also evident in the Epistle of Barnabas, Clement of Alexandria, and Origen,[42] as well as in the third-century *Pistis Sophia*.[43]

In this study, I have proposed a possible rationale for each of two collections of evidently disparate texts. Such questions should be posed to other non-traditional collections of ancient texts. Such study of these codices may yield precious evidence for the beliefs and practices of the communities that preserved and transmitted the texts. The study of Egyptian Christianity should take into consideration not only the "orthodox" and "heretical" Christian writings that originated in Egypt, but also the texts preserved in codices found in Egypt. Intense work of this sort has proceeded on the basis of the Nag Hammadi finds. Manuscripts like those discussed in this essay should also be taken into consideration. They are a small, but significant part of the broader historical picture of early Egyptian Christianity.

---

[41]See the edition and commentary by Pearson, "Pierpont Morgan Fragments." In n. 4, Pearson refers to fragments of what seems to be yet another Coptic Enoch text.

[42]See H. J. Lawlor, "Early Citations from the Book of Enoch," *The Journal of Philology* 25 (1897) 201-204.

[43]Ibid., 204, and Pearson, "Pierpont Morgan Fragments," 228, n. 4.

JULIAN'S ATTEMPT TO REBUILD THE TEMPLE:
AN INVENTORY OF ANCIENT AND MEDIEVAL SOURCES[*]

David Levenson
Florida State University

Over fifty sources from the fourth to the fourteenth century record the Emperor Julian's abortive attempt to rebuild the Jerusalem Temple in 363 CE. No Jewish texts mention the incident before the sixteenth century.[1] The one surviving pagan source, Ammianus Marcellinus, devotes only a brief report to the project, abandoned, he writes, when fires breaking out around the foundations made work impossible.

Christians, however, had good reason to narrate the episode fully and often. The first accounts come from within a year of the event and already reflect considerable embellishment. They report that sudden winds, storms, and earthquakes preceded the fire, which shot out suddenly from mysteriously opened gates. The sign of the cross, it was claimed, appeared in heaven and on the clothes of those present in Jerusalem, leading to mass conversions of unbelievers. What better proof could there be of the futility of pagan plans to undermine the church, the permanence of the divine

---

[*]The source-critical analysis upon which this report is based was originally part of a dissertation supervised by John Strugnell ("A Source and Tradition Critical Study of the Stories of the Emperor Julian's Attempt to Rebuild the Jerusalem Temple" [Harvard, 1980]). It was a continual source of amazement to find Prof. Strugnell as at home in the Byzantine and Oriental sources of late antiquity as in the Jewish and Christian texts of the Hellenistic and early Roman periods. Perhaps only those who have studied closely with him will ever fully appreciate the gentle humility and spirit of generosity with which he carries and tries to transmit his enormous learning. I would also like to thank Prof. Glen Bowersock for help on this project inspired by his seminar on Julian. In addition to summarizing the source-critical analysis of my thesis, I have included here a number of additional sources. Full discussion of the evidence, as well as analysis of the development of the tradition, will be found in my *Julian and the Jerusalem Temple: The Sources and the Tradition* (SJLA; Leiden: Brill, forthcoming).

[1]For ingenious, but unconvincing, attempts to find reflections of the incident in Rabbinic literature, see W. Bacher, "Statements of a Contemporary of the Emperor Julian on the Rebuilding of the Temple," *JQR* 10 (1898) 168-72; S. Liebermann, "The Martyrs of Caesarea," *AIPHO* 7 (1939-44) 412-16; E. Urbach, "Cyrus and his decrees in the eyes of the Sages," [Heb.] *Molad* 19 (1961) 372-74. The best candidate for a Rabbinic reflection on Julian's project is the story (set in the early second century!) in *Gen. Rab.* 64.10 about the emperor who decided to rebuild the Temple but changed his mind after Samaritan informers claimed the Jews would no longer pay taxes.

judgment pronounced against Jews and Judaism in 70 CE, and the truth of Jesus' prophecy that the Temple would never be rebuilt? Aside from its apologetic value for Christians, which has continued into the twentieth century,[2] the event has held a certain fascination for historians with a variety of interests. In addition to being the subject of a number of specialized studies,[3] it is duly narrated in every biography of Julian[4] and in virtually all the major histories of the Jews,[5] the early church[6] and the later Roman Empire.[7]

[2]J. C. Wagenseil, *Tela ignea Satanae* (Altdorf: Schönnerstaedt, 1681) 226-32; W. Warburton, *Julian; or a Discourse concerning the Earthquake and Fiery Eruption which defeated the Emperor's Attempt to rebuild the Temple at Jerusalem* (London: Knapton, 1750); J. H. Newman, *Two Essays on Biblical and Ecclesiastical Miracles* (3d. ed.; London: Pickering, 1873) 334-47; P. Allard, "Un précurseur du sionisme: Julien l'Apostat et les juifs," *Le Correspondant* (Aug. 10, 1901) 530-54 (implying that the modern enterprise would meet the same end as its ancient counterpart).

[3]J. M. Campbell, "Julian and Jerusalem, A.D. 363," *The Scottish Review* 35 (1900) 291-306; M. Adler, "The Emperor Julian and the Jews," *JQR* 5 (1893) 591-651; R. Konecki, "The Emperor Julian the Apostate's Attempt to Rebuild the Jewish Temple in Jerusalem," [Polish] *Przeglad Teologiczny* 2 (1921) 40-59; 3 (1922) 72-96. J. Vogt, *Kaiser Julian und das Judentum* (Leipzig: Hinrichs, 1939); Y. Levi, "The Emperor Julian and the Rebuilding of the Temple" [Heb.], *Zion* 6 [1941] 1-32, reprinted in *ᶜOlamot Nifgashim* [Eng. title: *Studies in Jewish Hellenism*] (Jerusalem, 1969) 221-54 (ET [without the important appendix on the authenticity of Julian's letter "To the Jewish Community"] in Lee Levine, ed., *The Jerusalem Cathedra* (3 vols.; Detroit: Wayne State University Press, 1981-83) 3.70-96.

[4]E.g., P. Allard, *Julien l'Apostat* (3d. ed.; 3 vols.; Paris: Lecoffre, 1910) 3.130-48; J. Geffcken, *Kaiser Julianus* (Leipzig: Dietrich, 1914) 110, 165; J. Bidez, *La vie de l'empereur Julien* (Paris: Les Belles lettres, 1930) 305-09; R. Browning, *The Emperor Julian* (Berkeley: University of California Press, 1976) 176; G. W. Bowersock, *Julian the Apostate* (Cambridge: Harvard University Press, 1978) 89-90, 120-22; P. Athanassiadi-Fowden, *Julian and Hellenism* (Oxford: Oxford University Press, 1981) 164.

[5]E.g., H. Graetz, *Geschichte der Juden* (4th. ed.; Leipzig: Leiner, 1908) 4.338-46, 457-59; J. Juster, *Les juifs dans l'empire romain* (2 vols.; Paris: Geuthner, 1914) 1.247-48; S. Baron, *A Social and Religious History of the Jews* (18 vols.; New York: Columbia Univeristy Press, 1952) 2.159-61, 392; J. Neusner, *A History of the Jews in Babylonia* (SPB 14; 4 vols.; Leiden: Brill, 1969) 4.29-34; M. Avi-Yonah, *The Jews of Palestine: Political History from the Bar Kokhba War to the Arab Conquest* (New York: Schocken, 1976; 1st Heb. ed., Jerusalem, 1946) 185-207; P. Schäfer, *Geschichte der Juden in der Antike* (Stuttgart: Katholisches Bibelwerk, 1983) 197-200.

[6]E.g., Sébastien Le Nain de Tillemont, *Mémoires pour servir à l'histoire ecclésiastique des six premiers siècles* (10 vols. in 5; Brussels: Fricx, 1732) 7.409-15; H. Lietzmann, *A History of the Early Church* (4 vols.; rev. ET; London: Lutterworth, 1953) 3.281-82; W. H. C. Frend, *The Rise of Christianity* (Philadelphia: Fortress, 1983) 606.

David Levenson

The past fifteen years have witnessed a renewed interest in the incident, as classicists have focussed more of their efforts on late antiquity and historians of ancient religion have made Jewish–Christian relations a major field of study.[8] Furthermore, the discovery of a manuscript purporting to be Cyril of Jerusalem's eyewitness account of the event has provided a new piece of evidence to be evaluated.

Despite their valuable contributions to understanding an incident which stands at the intersection of the struggle among Jews, Christians and pagans in late antiquity, no earlier study provides a complete list of the ancient and medieval accounts of the event nor attempts to trace the complex interrelationship among these sources. Some of the most influential studies not only fail to take into account all available sources, but offer inaccurate information about those they do consider and often treat demonstrably secondary elaborations as reliable early evidence.[9] To provide a firmer basis for both further historical and literary work on the tradition, I have tried to assemble here a complete inventory of the ancient and medieval references to the event, from the fourth to the mid fourteenth century.[10] Also included are the

[7]E.g., E. Gibbon, *The History of the Decline and Fall of the Roman Empire* (J. B. Bury, ed.; 7 vols.; London: Methuen, 1909-12) 2.478-85; E. Stein, *Histoire du Bas-Empire* (2 vols. in 3; Paris: Desclée, 1959) 1.164, 503; A. Piganiol, *L'empire chrétien* (2d. ed.; A. Chastognol, ed.; Paris: Presses universitaires de France, 1972) 155.

[8]C. Aziza, "Julien et le Judaïsme," in R. Braun and J. Richer, eds., *L'empereur Julien: De l'histoire à la légend (331-1715)* (Paris: Les Belles lettres, 1978) 141-58; F. Blanchetière, "Julien, Philhellène, Philosémite, Antichrétien: L'affaire du Temple de Jerusalem (363)," *JJS* 31 (1980) 61-81; J. Seaver, "Julian the Apostate and the Attempted Rebuilding of the Temple of Jerusalem," *Res Publica Litterarum* 1 (1978) 273-84; C. R. Phillips, "Julian's Rebuilding of the Temple: A Sociological Study of Religious Competition," SBLASP 1979, 2.167-172. See also the extensive treatment of the episode in F. Thélamon, *Paiens et chrétiens au IVe siécle: L'apport de "Histoire ecclésiastique" de Rufin d'Aquilée* (Paris: Etudes Augustiniennes, 1981) 294-309; R. L. Wilken, *John Chrysostom and the Jews: Rhetoric and Reality in the Late 4th Century* (Berkeley: University of California Press, 1983) 128-64, and M. Stern, *Greek and Latin Authors on Jews and Judaism* (2 vols.; Jerusalem: Magnes, 1980) 2.502-72 (on Julian) 601-603, 607-609 (on Ammianus).

[9]Adler's pioneering article is particularly bad in these respects. There are also a number of inaccuracies in the details in Avi-Yonah's generally insightful treatment of the incident, which occupies a central place in his history of the Jews in Palestine. In addition to containing several factual errors, his engaging narrative often consists of a harmonization of details added to increase the drama in accounts whose sources are extant. This is typical of the tendency of historians to rely primarily on the fifth-century Orthodox histories of Socrates, Sozomen, and Theodoret, even in cases, such as the Temple rebuilding story, when they rely entirely on sources to which we still have access.

[10]I am least confident that I have collected all of the medieval Latin accounts. I would be grateful for any further references.

263

sixteenth-century Jewish accounts because they have so often been cited (almost always with some inaccuracies) in the modern scholarly discussion.

Where they can be determined with virtual certainty, I have listed the sources of each account in brackets. Where there is some doubt, I have provided a brief discussion of the most likely possibilities. In addition, I have appended a note on the date of the event and the relationship between the fire in Jerusalem and the Palestinian earthquakes of May, 363, issues clarified, I believe, by a better understanding of the complicated interrelationship of the sources.

Fourth Century
1. Julian:
   a. *Ep*. 204, "To the Community of the Jews" (362/3 CE)[11]
   b. *Ep*. 134, "To the Jews" (363 CE)[12]
   c. *Ep*. 89b, "To a Priest" (363 CE)[13]

Julian nowhere discusses the events in Jerusalem.[14] He does, however, refer to his intention to rebuild the Temple in three places: *Ep*. 204, which ends with a promise to rebuild and repopulate Jerusalem; *Ep*. 134, of which only one sentence is preserved by John the Lydian, who says that while on campaign against the Persians (i.e., after March 5, 363) Julian wrote to the Jews, "I am rebuilding with all zeal the Temple of the Most High God"; *Ep*. 89b, a fragment of a letter to a pagan priest, in which Julian refers to the fact that the Temple has been destroyed three times and not yet rebuilt, something, he writes, "I intended after so many years."

[11] J. Bidez and F. Cumont, eds., *Imperatoris Caesaris Flavii Claudii Iuliani epistulae, leges, poemata, fragmenta varia* (Paris: Les Belles lettres, 1922) 280-82 (386d-398a). The authenticity of the letter has often been questioned. See Vogt, *Kaiser Julian*, 64-68, for the most extensive arguments against authenticity. Levi (*Emperor Julian*, 248-54), M. Hack ("Is Julian's Proclamation a Forgery?" [Heb.] *Yavneh* 2 [1940] 118-39; "Notes to the Article 'The Emperor Julian and the Rebuilding of the Temple'" [Heb.] *Zion* 6 [1940-41] 158-59), and W. den Boer ("Two Letters from the Corpus Iulianum," *VC* 16 [1962] 186-97) present decisive arguments in favor of Julianic authorship.

[12] Bidez-Cumont, 193 (apud Johannes Lydus, *De mensibus* 4.53).

[13] Bidez-Cumont, 128 (295cd).

[14] Adler concludes from the silence of Julian, Jerome, and others that the project was never begun and that Gregory was the *fons et origo* of the story. He fails to provide an account of how the features in the other sources might derive from Gregory, underestimates the considerably different and most likely reliable report of Ammianus, and ignores the important early evidence of Ephrem.

David Levenson

2. Ephrem of Nisibis, *Hymni contra Julianum* 1.16-40; 2.7; 4.18-26 (363/4 CE)[15](
3. Gregory of Nazianzus, *Or.* 5.3-7 (*Contra Julianum*) (363/4 CE)[16]
4. John Chrysostom:
   a. *De sancto Babyla* 22 (late 370's CE)[17]
   b. *Adversus Judaeos* 5.11; 6.2 (387 CE)[18]
   c. *Quod Christus sit Deus* 16 (386/7 CE)[19]
   d. *De laudibus sancti Pauli* 4.6 (386-398 CE)[20]
   e. *Exp. in Ps. 110* (386-398 CE)[21]
   f. *Hom. in Mt.* 4 (ca. 390 CE)[22]
   g. *Hom. in Acta Apost.* 41.3 (400/1 CE)[23]
5. Ambrose, *Ep.* 40.12 (388 CE)[24]
6. Ammianus Marcellinus, *Res Gestae* 23.2.3 (391/2 CE)[25]

Although it is impossible to determine with any degree of certainty the sources for the fourth-century accounts, two forms of the tradition are clearly discernable.

Ephrem and Gregory stand close to one another with their reports of storm, earthquake and fire from opened gates. This connection is not surprising since these two polemicists, writing soon after Julian's death, share a number of other

[15] E. Beck, ed., *Des heiligen Ephraem des Hymnen De Paradiso und Contra Julianum* (CSCO 174-75, Scr. Syr. 78-79; 2 vols. in 1; Louvain: Secrétariat du CSCO, 1957) 1.74-75, 77, 89-90.

[16] J. Bernardi, ed.,*Grégoire de Nazianze, Discours 4-5* (SC 309; Paris: Cerf, 1983) 298-306.

[17] PG 50.567-68; M. A. Schatkin, "Critical Edition of, and Introduction to St. John Chrysostom's *De Sancto Babyla, Contra Iulianum et Gentiles*" (Diss., Fordham University, 1967) 97-98. For discussion of authenticity, see Schatkin, "The Authenticity of St. John Chrysostom's *De Sancto Babyla, Contra Iulianum et Gentiles*," *Kyriakon* 1 (1970) 474-89.

[18] PG 48.900-901, 905.

[19] PG 48.835; N. G. McKendrick, "*Quod Christus sit Deus* of St. John Chrysostom" (Diss., Fordham University, 1966) 127-28.

[20] A. Piédagnel, ed., *Panégyriques de S. Paul* (SC 300; Paris: Cerf, 1982) 190-92.

[21] PG 55.285

[22] F. Field, ed., *Homiliae in Matthaeum* (Cambridge: Cambridge University Press, 1839) 1.40.

[23] PG 60.291.

[24] PL 16.1152-53.

[25] W. Seyfarth, ed., *Ammiani Marcellini Rerum gestarum libri qui supersunt* (Leipzig: Teubner, 1978) 1.294-95.

traditions.[26] The similarities are usually explained by a common knowledge of a widespread oral tradition about the emperor elaborated in Christian circles.

The accounts in Chrysostom and Ammianus, which mention only fire shooting out from the foundations, are closely related and share little with those in Gregory and Ephrem. Both Chrysostom and Ammianus are almost certainly dependent on Antiochene traditions. The failure to rebuild the Jerusalem Temple is only one of a number of events in Antioch that they both report, often using similar language, and whose significance was debated by Antiochene pagans and Christians.[27] Ammianus' account of the events in Jerusalem might well derive directly or indirectly from Alypius, his fellow Antiochene, whom Julian placed in charge of the project.[28]

[26]See J. Geffcken, "Kaiser Julianus und die Streitschriften seiner Gegner," *Neue Jahrbücher für das klassische Altertum* 21 (1908) 174-78, and S. Griffith, "Ephrem the Syrian's Hymns 'Against Julian': Meditations on History and Imperial Power," *VC* 41 (1987) 238-68 (passim).

[27]In all his reports, apart from those in *Adv. Jud.* and *Quod Christus sit Deus*, Chrysostom associates the fire in Jerusalem preventing the rebuilding the Temple with between three and seven other signs that occurred in Antioch indicating divine opposition to Julian's reign. Ammianus and often Libanius and Julian provide interpretations circulating among non-Christian Antiochenes, including (1) the purification of Daphne (cf. Amm. 23.1.5), (2) the burning of the Temple of Apollo (cf. Amm. 22.13.2-3; Julian, *Misopogon* 361B; Libanius, *Or.* 17.30), (3) the death of Julian's uncle (cf. Amm. 23.1.5), (4) the death of Felix (cf. Amm. 23.1.5), (5) the desiccation of the springs (cf. Amm. 23.13.4 and 14.1; Julian, *Misopogon* 369A), (6) the famine (cf. Amm. 22.14.1; *Misopogon* 386C-370C), (7) Julian's death (cf. Amm. 25.3.6; Zosimus 3.29; Lib. *Orations* 1.133, 17.32, 18.274-75, 24.6).

[28]Ammianus' closeness to Alypius or those near him might be indicated by his particularly full and sympathetic treatment of Alypius' unfair trial and exile for sorcery (Amm. 29.1.44). For Alypius as Ammianus' source for the events in Jerusalem, see G. Sabbah, *La Methode d'Ammien Marcellin* (Paris: 1978) 220-21.

It is likely that Ammianus' account is close to that of the *Universal History* of Eunapius of Sardis. That Eunapius and Ammianus had a significant amount of Julianic material in common is clear from the parallel traditions in Ammianus and in Zosimus' *New History*, which according to Photius was an epitome of Eunapius' work. Although Zosimus does not have the Temple rebuilding story, striking similarities between the accounts of Ammianus and Philostorgius, and, most significantly, the close relationship between Ammianus' story and that in the eleventh-century *Epitome of Histories* by John Zonaras point to the probability that the Greek Christian historians used Eunapius rather than Ammianus. (For Ammianus and Philostorgius, see L. Jeep, *Quellenuntersuchungen zu den griechischen Kirchenhistorikern* [*Jahrb. f. Klass. Philologie*, Supp. Bd., 14; Leipzig: Teubner, 1884] 56-64. For parallels between Ammianus and Zonaras, see E. Patzig, "Über einige Quellen des Zonaras," *BZ* 6 [1897] 324-29. For Philostorgius' use of Eunapius, see Jeep, 57-60, and J. Bidez and F. Winkelmann, *Philostorgius Kirchengeschichte* [GCS 21; 3d ed.; Leipzig: Hinrichs, 1981], cxxxviii-cxxxix.) M. DiMaio ("Zonaras' Account of the Neo-Flavian Emperors: A Commentary" [Diss., University of Missouri, 1977] 397) follows Patzig's

David Levenson

Like Chrysostom and Ammianus, Ambrose mentions only the fire, making it likely he knew a form of the tradition similar to theirs. His notice, however, is too brief to be certain about this, and, in any case, he reports other traditions about the Julianic period not shared by either Ammianus or Chrysostom.[29]

Fifth Century Historians
7. Rufinus of Aquileia *H.E.* 10.38-40 (ca. 403 CE)[30]
Most features of Rufinus' account can be explained as a conflation of elements from Gregory (some of whose orations he translated into Latin), Chrysostom, and Ammianus. Rufinus' report of the dialogue between Julian and the Jews was almost certainly invented by Chrysostom. He adds only three items: a reference to Cyril of Jerusalem's claim, based on Jesus' and Daniel's prophecies that the Temple would never be rebuilt, an account of porticoes which collapsed killing many Jews, and the notice that the fire started in an underground room beneath the Temple foundations.[31]

suggestion that Zonaras had access to Ammianus through the lost history of John of Antioch. For the Temple rebuilding story, he suggests Zonaras used Theophanes. It is unlikely, however, that Zonaras would have eliminated from his account all the distinctive Christian and miraculous elements in Theophanes (or Philostorgius) from his account and left only those features which happened also to be found in Ammianus. For a summary of the debate on the relationship between Ammianus' and Eunapius' histories, see J. Matthews, *The Roman Empire of Ammianus* (Baltimore: Johns Hopkins University Press, 1989) 164-75.

[29]Cf. *Ep.* 40.15, 17, 18, 21.

[30]T. Mommsen, ed., *Eusebius Werke. Die Kirchengeschichte* (GCS 9/2; Leipzig: Hinrichs, 1908) 997-98.

[31]Some have suggested Rufinus did little more than translate the lost Greek *Ecclesiastical History* of Gelasius of Caesarea, the nephew of Cyril of Jerusalem. A Greek version of at least part of Rufinus' history circulated in the Byzantine world and was associated with the name Gelasius. Whether it was a translation of Rufinus or its source remains unclear. (For reviews of the ancient and medieval evidence and surveys of modern scholarship on the issue, see F. Winkelmann, *Untersuchungen zur Kirchengeschichte des Gelasios von Kaisareia* [Sitzungberichte der deutschen Akademie der Wissenschaft zu Berlin. Klasse für Sprache, Literatur und Kunst 1965, Nr. 3; Berlin: Akademie, 1966], and J. Schamp, "Gélase ou Rufin: Un fait nouveau. Sur des fragments oubliés de Gélase de Césarée (*CPG*, N° 3521)," *Byzantion* 57 [1987] 360-90.) Since the terminal point for Gelasius' history is uncertain and Rufinus' account of the Julianic period shares a number of verbal parallels with Latin sources, including Ammianus (cf. Ruf. 10.8 and Ambrose, *De obitu Theodosii* 43-47; Ruf. 10.37 and Amm. 25.3.6), it seems best to conclude that Rufinus, who spent twenty years on the Mt. of Olives, either supplemented the earlier accounts with Jerusalem oral traditions about Cyril's prophecy, the collapsed portico, and the underground room, or that he invented these features based on a reading of Cyril's *Catech.* 15.15 and his knowledge of the site of the Temple Mount.

267

8. Jerome, *In Dan.* 11.34 (407 CE)[32]

9. Orosius, *Historia adversus Paganos* 7.30 (418 CE)[33]

Neither Jerome nor Orosius mentions the attempt to rebuild the Temple, although both contain related traditions. Jerome reports that Julian "affected a love for the Jews, promising to sacrifice in their temple." Orosius says that Julian built an amphitheatre in Jerusalem in which he planned to sacrifice the Christians upon his return from Persia. Jerome's source might well be Julian's letter to the Jewish community (*Ep.* 204).[34] The source of Orosius' distorted reflection of the Temple rebuilding incident is impossible to determine.[35]

10. Philostorgius, *H.E.* 7.9 and 7.14 (425-433 CE)

    a. Photius, 7.9; 7.14[36]   b. *Artemii Passio* 58; 68[37]

In his magisterial edition, Bidez reconstructed Philostorgius' account of the attempted rebuilding from Photius' ninth-century epitome and the eighth-century *Artemii Passio*, which cites Philostorgius for background to the martyrdom.[38]

---

[32] F. Glorie, ed., *Commentariorum in Danielem Libri III (IV)* 11.34 (CChrL 75A; Turnhout: Brepols, 1964) 923-24.

[33] C. Zangemeister, ed., *Pauli Orosii Historiarum adversus paganos libri vii* (CSEL 5; Vienna: Gerold, 1882) 510.

[34] Cf. Blanchètiere, "Julien," 62.

[35] Possibly he heard the story on his visit to Jerusalem where he attended the council of 415.

[36] J. Bidez and F. Winkelmann, 95-96, 99-100.

[37] Bidez-Winkelmann (above); B. Kotter, *Die Schriften des Johannes von Damaskos* vol.5 (PTS 29; Berlin: de Gruyter, 1988) 225-26; 242.

[38] Based on several manuscripts, Bidez assigned the *Artemii Passio* work to an otherwise unknown ninth-century John of Rhodes, but recent scholarship attributes it to the eighth-century Palestinian monk, John of Damascus. For a full discussion of authorship and date, see Kotter, *Die Schriften*, 185-87.

Bidez included the Temple rebuilding story in his reconstruction of an anonymous Arian historian whose work he believed was one of Philostorgius' main sources. Basing himself on earlier studies, Bidez argued that fragments of the lost Arian history have been preserved in Jerome's *Chronicon* and in various Byzantine and Oriental chronicles, the most important of which are the Chronicon Paschale and Theophanes. (Bidez-Winkelmann, *Philostorgius*, cli-clxiii; the texts Bidez believed could be used to reconstruct the text are printed in an appendix [202-41]). Accordingly, he argued that Theophanes' *Chronographia*, the Syriac *Chronicon miscellaneum*, the Arabic *Universal History* of Agapius of Memjib and the *Chronicle* of Michael the Syrian preserve the Arian historian's account of the attempt to rebuild the Temple. Michael, however, depends ultimately on Theophanes (see below). The others are just as likely to have derived their information ultimately from Philostorgius (whose work is also only partially preserved) as from a lost source. Furthermore, the fact that the story is not found in either the *Chronicon Paschale* or in Jerome's *Chronicon* and that the *Chron. misc.* only mentions earthquakes in Palestine and does not include the Temple

David Levenson

Philostorgius' sources were probably Rufinus, Chrysostom, Eunapius (or Ammianus, and possibly Gregory. A doublet reveals the conflation of at least two sources: there are two accounts of the fire, one deriving from Rufinus and the other from either Chrysostom or Eunapius (or Ammianus). The accounts of Palestinian earthquakes and the uniquely Philostorgian story of the discovery of a copy of the gospel of John underneath the foundations of the Temple may be derived from Jerusalem traditions Philostorgius might have learned on his trip to Palestine (7.3).

    11. Socrates, *H.E.* 3.20 (early 440's CE)[39] [Rufinus][40]
    12. Sozomen, *H.E.* 5.22 (ca. 443 CE)[41] [Julian, *Ep.* 204, Greg., Chrys., Ruf., Philost., Soc.][42]
    13. Theodoret, *H.E.* 3.20 (ca.450 CE)[43] [Ruf., Philost., Greg.][44]

Fifth and Sixth Century Syriac Popular Literature
    14. *Martyrium Simeon bar Sabba ᶜe* 13; *Narratio Simeon bar Sabba ᶜe* 13-15 (fifth cent. CE)[45]
    The *Martyrium* presents a shorter and the *Narratio* a longer recension of the story of the saint's martyrdom under Shapur II. Wiessener concluded that both depend on a common source rather than being directly related.[46] The reference to the attempt to

rebuilding story all make it unlikely that it was found in the common source of these documents and Theophanes.

[39] R. Hussey, ed., *Socratis Scholastici Historia Ecclesiastica* (3 vols.; Oxford, 1853) 1.437-40.

[40] For Socrates' use of Rufinus, see the programmatic statement in *H.E.* 2.1 and F. Geppert, *Die Quellen des Kirchenhistorikers Socrates Scholasticus* (Leipzig: Dieterich, Weicher, 1898).

[41] J. Bidez and G. C. Hansen, eds., *Sozomenus, Kirchengeschichte* (GCS 50; Berlin: Akademie, 1960) 229-32.

[42] For the sources, see the *apparatus fontium* in the Bidez-Hansen edition.

[43] L. Parmentier and F. Scheidweiler, eds., *Theodoret Kirchengeschichte* (GCS 44; 2d. ed.; Berlin: Akademie, 1954) 198-200.

[44] For Theodoret's use of Rufinus, see A. Güldenpenning, *Die Kirchengeschichte des Theodoret von Kyrrhos: Eine Untersuchungen ihren Quellen* (Halle: Niemeyer, 1889) 26-39 (28-30 discuss the Temple rebuilding story). L. Parmentier (*Theodoret Kirchengeschichte* [GCS 44; Leipzig: Hinrichs, 1911] lxxxix) points to the common elements in the stories of Theodoret and Philostorgius, but argues they both depend on the anonymous Arian historian (for the problem with that view, see above, n. 38). Neither Güldenpenning nor Parmentier seemed to recognize that Theodoret, like Sozomen, regularly conflated several sources for his description of individual incidents.

[45] M. Kmosko, ed., *S. Simeon bar Sabb ᶜe* (*Patrologia Syriaca* 1/2; Paris: Firmin-Didot 1907) 739, 807-811.

[46] G. Wiessner, *Zur Märtyerüberlieferung aus der Christenverfolgung Schapurs II* (Abhandlungen der Akademie der Wissenschaften in Göttingen. Philologisch-Historische Klasse. 3. Folge, 67; Göttingen: Vandenhoeck & Ruprecht, 1967).

rebuild the Temple is too brief to establish a clear link to any other source, although it shares some elements with Theodoret's account, whose history, as well as that of Socrates, was frequently cited in Syriac literature. The notice of a "deceiver" announcing Julian's plan to the Jews of Mahoza and Bet Aramaye and exhorting them to return to Jerusalem and their subsequent destruction by Shapur's army might well depend on Syriac Christian traditions such as those found in the *Julian Romance*.

15. *The Syriac Julian Romance,* pp. 108-16, 132-38 (early sixth cent. CE)[47]

The lengthy narratives of Julian's negotiations with Jewish leaders, in which they are persuaded to eat non-kosher food and commit idolatry, and their subsequent attempt to betray Edessa and punishment by expulsion probably reflect popular Christian traditions emerging from Jewish-Christian conflict in the region. The novelist begins to tell of the events in Jerusalem, but stops short, claiming that another writer has already described them "as they actually took place." The beginning of the story bears some resemblance to Socrates' account, although direct dependence is far from demonstrable.

16. A Letter attributed to Cyril of Jerusalem on the Rebuilding of the Temple (fifth or sixth cent. CE).[48]

Sebastian Brock's discovery and publication of this fascinating document, which presents itself as the Bishop of Jerusalem's eyewitness account of the miraculous events confirming Jesus' prophecy, has received surprisingly little scholarly attention. Brock argued that the work was a forgery dating from the early fifth century, but that the date (Iyyar 19) is trustworthy. Only Philip Wainwright, so far as I know, has defended the document's authenticity, although he admits that the last section, listing cities destroyed by the earthquake and reporting Julian's death, are later additions.[49] Most likely the letter is a late fifth- or early sixth-century

---

[47]J. G. E. Hoffmann, ed., *Iulianos der Abtrünnige, Syrische Erzaehlungen* (Leiden: Brill, 1880).

[48]S. P. Brock, "A Letter Attributed to Cyril of Jerusalem on the Rebuilding of the Temple," *BSOAS* 40/2 (1977) 267-86. The complete letter is found only in a modern manuscript, dated 1899. A late sixth-century manuscript contains the first half.

[49]P. Wainwright, "The Authenticity of the Recently discovered letter attributed to Cyril of Jerusalem," *VC* 40 (1986) 286-93.

A forger's hand is betrayed by a number of elements in addition to Brock's general observation that, although the letter was supposedly sent to all the churches of the world, no one seems to know of it. It is highly unlikely, for instance, that Cyril would have said that the city of Jerusalem (rather than the Jews or the Temple site) was punished. (In *Catech.* 10.11 and 15.15, Cyril writes that Matt 24:2 refers to the "Temple of the Jews," not the city of Jerusalem as the letter states). Several times the author speaks of Jerusalem as if it were a foreign city (e.g., "the foundations of Jerusalem" [3]; "the Mt. of Olives, which is east of Jerusalem" [6]; "the statue of Hadrian which stood in Jerusalem;" [9] ["Herod" in the MS is a corruption introduced by a scribe influenced by the apocryphal correspondence between Herod and Pilate

document belonging to the same provenance as the *Julian Romance*, which also includes a number of fictitious letters. Perhaps the letter is meant to be the account of events in Jerusalem referred to, but not repeated, in the *Julian Romance*.[50]

The features of the Temple rebuilding story found in the letter are best explained by the fact that the Syriac author depended on Gregory and Philostorgius (as preserved by the *Artemii Passio*). This can be seen not only by the many similarities to these accounts, but also by the fact that he reproduced both Gregory's story of the fire proceeding from miraculously opened gates and Philostorgius' account of the fire in Jerusalem mentioned in the list of cities.[51]

In addition to including incidents recorded in Gregory and Philostorgius, the letter's author probably also used a letter sent by Jerusalem's bishop reporting Palestinian earthquakes in 419. The no longer extant letter can be reconstructed from references in Augustine, Hydatius, Marcellinus Comes, and the *Consularia Constantinopolitana*.[52] Like the Syriac letter, it was addressed to all the churches of the world, it reported the collapse of many Palestinian cities in an earthquake, and it contained an account of the conversion and baptism of Jews and pagans followed by the appearance of the sign of the cross on the garments of those baptized. It is also possible that the letter of 419 contained an account of a procession to the Mt. of

found in both MSS containing the letter]). *Pace* Wainwright, the problematic section twelve, with its report of Julian's death (in language close to that in the *Julian Romance*), its Syriac method of dating and its reference to Julian's love of the Jews because they killed Christ (paralleled only in the *Julian Romance*) seems to be an integral part of the letter. The clumsy way it is introduced is matched by several other awkward literary seams in the body of the letter. While this letter was probably inspired by Cyril's *Letter to Constantius*, with which it shares several significant features, its exceedingly plain narrative contrasts sharply with the highly polished rhetorical style of the *Letter to Constanius*, even taking into account a poor translator. (On the authenticity of the *Letter to Constantius*, see J. Vogt, "Berichte über Kreuzeserscheinungen aus dem 4. Jahrhundert n. Chr.," *AIPHO* 9 [1949] 596-97).

[50]Compare the ending of the letter ("All this that has been written to you took place in actual fact in this way" [trans. Brock, 276]) with the conclusion of the *Julian Romance*'s reference to the rebuilding project ("I should be doing something superfluous if I inserted into our narrative what has been outlined by another writer, who has described these events fittingly, as they actually took place" [trans. Brock, 286]).

[51]See below for the close connection between the list of cities in Philostorgius and the letter.

[52]Hydatius, *Chronicon* 71a (AD 419) (A. Tranoy, ed., *Hydace, Chronique* [SC 218; vols. 1- ; Paris: Cerf, 1974-] 1.124; *Consularia Constantinoplitana* AD 419 (T. Mommsen, ed., *Chronica minora* 1 [MGHaa 9; Berlin:Weidmanns, 1894] 246; Augustine, *Sermo* 19.6 (C. Lambot, ed., [CChr 41; Turnhout: Brepols, 1961] 258); Marcellinus Comes, *Chronica* (T. Mommsen, ed., *Chronica minora* 2 [MGHaa 11; Berlin: Weidmanns, 1893] 74).

Olives, like that awkwardly inserted into the Syriac letter, since Marcellinus Comes refers to a christophany on the Mt. of Olives in his report of the events of 419. It is unlikely that the letter of 419 is based on the letter attributed to Cyril, because the latter apparently depends on Philostorgius.

Byzantine Historiographical Literature

16. Theodoros Anagnostes, *H.E. Epitome* 145 (610-15 CE)[53]

The notice in the seventh-century epitome of Theodoros' *Tripartite History*, compiled ca. 518, is probably based on Sozomen, although it is too brief to be certain.[54]

17. Theophanes, *Chronographia* A.M. 5855 (ca. 813 CE)[55]

Although Bidez believed Theophanes preserved the account of an anonymous Arian historian,[56] more probably he simply conflated Philostorgius and Theodoret.

18. Georgios Monachos, *Chronicon* 9.3 (ca. 842 CE)[57] [Theodoret]

19. Georgios Kedrenos, *Chronicon* (ca. 1100 CE) [first notice from Theophanes, second from Georgios Monachos][58]

20. Johannes Zonaras, *Epitome Historiarum* 13.12 (ca. 1118 CE)[59] [Eunapius][60]

21. Michael Glykas, *Annales* 4 (mid twelfth cent. CE)[61] [apparently Georgios Monachos, Kedrenos and possibly Chrysostom]

---

[53]G. C. Hansen, *Theodoros, Anagnostes Kirchengeschichte* (GCS 54; Berlin: Akademie, 1971) 61.

[54]According to the note in his *apparatus fontium* ("Soz v.22 [Sokr iii.20]"), Hansen is not absolutely certain that Sozomen was Theodoros' source.

[55]C. de Boor, *Theophanis Chronographia* (2 vols.; Leipzig: Teubner, 1883-1885) 1.51-52.

[56]See above, n. 38 on Philostorgius' sources.

[57]C. de Boor, *Georgii Monachi Chronicon* (2 vols.; Leipzig: Teubner, 1904) 1.543-44.

[58]I. Bekker, ed., *Georgii Cedreni Historiarum Compendium* (CSHB 26-27; Bonn: Weber, 1838-1839) 1.525-26, 537-38.

[59]L. Dindorf, *Ioannis Zonarae Epitome Historiarum* (6 vols.; Leipzig: Teubner, 1870) 3.211.

[60]See above, n. 28.

[61]Ed. I. Bekker, *Michaelis Glycae Annales* (CSHB 2; Bonn: Weber, 1836) 470-71.

David Levenson

22. Nikephoros Kallistos, *H.E.* 10.32-33 (fourteenth cent. CE) [62] [Soc., Soz., Theodt., Philost.][63]

Syriac Chronicles
23. *Chronicon miscellaneum ad AD 724 pertinens* AD 674. (ca. 641 CE)[64]
   While the first section of this chronicle, which extends only to 641, does not report the events in Jerusalem, it does refer to Palestinian earthquakes which destroyed twenty-one cities on Iyyar 27, 363. This information is probably derived ultimately from Philostorgius, perhaps through John of Ephesus' sixth-century *Ecclesiastical History*, whose account of the fourth century is lost.
   24. *Chronicon anonymum pseudo-Dionysianum.*(775 CE)[65] [Soc., Julian Romance][66]
   25. *Chronicon anonymum ad AD 846 pertinens* (ca. 846 CE)[67] [Chrysostom, *Adv. Jud.*][68]
   26. Michael the Syrian, *Chronicon* 7.5 (ca. 1195 CE)[69]
   The first notice is taken from Socrates. The second combines Socrates' account with that of Theophanes, perhaps transmitted through Ignatius of Melitene.[70]

Arabic Historiographical Literature
27. Agapius, *Universal History* (ca. 942 CE)[71]

[62]PG 146.536-537, 540-541, 544

[63]For Nikephoros' sources for the Temple rebuilding story, see G. Gentz and F. Winkelmann, *Die Kirchengeschichte des Nicephorus Callistus Xanthopulus und ihre Quellen* (TU 98; Berlin: Akademie, 1966) 97-98.

[64]E. W. Brooks, ed., *Chronicon miscellaneum ad annum p. Chr. 724 pertinens. Chronica minora* 2 (CSCO 4, Scr. Syr., ser. 3, vol. 4; Louvain: Durbecq 1903) 133.

[65]J. B. Chabot, ed., *Incerti auctoris Chronicon Pseudo-Dionysianum vulgo dictum* (CSCO 121, Scr. Syr. 43, ser. 3, vol. 1; Louvain: Durbeocq, 1927) 178-79.

[66]See Brock, 284, for sources. His tentative suggestion that the introduction comes from the *Julian Romance* is certainly correct.

[67]E. W. Brooks, ed., *Chronicon anonymum ad a. p. Chr. 846 pertinens. Chronica minora* 2 (CSCO 4, Scr. Syr., ser. 3, vol. 4; Louvain: Durbeocq, 1903) 199-200.

[68]Brock suggests that the account is based on Theodoret, but, as he points out, that source does not contain the Jews' reply to Julian. The Syriac chronicle's account corresponds closely to that in *Adv. Jud.* 5.11, which the chronicle also used for its accounts of the revolts under Hadrian (183) and Constantine (193).

[69]J. B. Chabot, ed., *Chronique de Michel le syrien patriarche jacobite d'Antioch* (4 vols.; Paris: Leroux, 1899–1910) 4.141 (left col.) and 4.146 (right col.).

[70]Brock (285) notes the use of Socrates in the second account.

[71]A. Vasiliev, ed., *Kitab al-Unvan, Histoire universelle, écrite par Agapius (Mahboub) de Menbij* (PO 7; Paris: Firmin-Didot, 1910) 580-81.

28. *Nestorian History (The Chronicle of Se ʿert)* (ca. 1036 CE)[72]

Agapius' ultimate sources are the *Julian Romance*, Socrates, Theodoret, and Philostorgius. The *Nest. Hist.* includes features from Socrates, Theodoret, and Philostorgius. Since both works elsewhere in the Julianic period share much common material from theses same sources, both probably depend for the Temple story on a common Syriac source that had already combined the earlier accounts.

Alexandrian Tradition

29. John of Nikiu, *Chronicon* 80.1-2 (end of seventh cent. CE)[73]

30. Severus ibn al-Muqaffaʿ, *History of the Patriarchs of Alexandria*, pt. 1, chap. 8 (end of tenth cent. CE)[74]

31. *Arabic Synaxarium of the Coptic Church*, 2 Baounah (May, 27) (end of twelfth/beginning of thirteenth cent. CE)[75]

32. *Ethiopic Synaxarium*, 2 Sanē (May 27) (fourteenth/fifteenth cent. CE; translation of the *Arabic Synaxarium*)[76]

The Temple rebuilding narratives in the *History of the Patriarchs* and in the *Arabic Synaxarium* share several features. The most striking is the connection of the events in Jerusalem with the miraculous preservation of the bodies of John the Baptist and Elisha when Julian ordered them burned. In both accounts this serves as an introduction to the *translatio* of the bodies to Alexandria, celebrated annually on May 27. The fact that each one shares some different features of the ultimate sources (Theodoret and Socrates) demonstrates that they used a common Alexandrian Christian source rather than one depending on the other. A similar tradition probably lies behind John of Nikiu's brief notice as well.

Medieval Latin Literature

33. Cassiodorus-Epiphanius, *Historia Ecclesiastica Tripartita* 6.43 (540-80 CE)[77] [Theodoret]

---

[72]A. Scher, ed., *Histoire nestorienne*, trans. P. Dib (PO 5; Paris: Firmin-Didot, 1910) 229.

[73]H. Zotenberg, ed., *Chronique de Jean, évêque de Nikiou, texte éthiopien publié et traduit* (Paris: Imprimerie nationale, 1883) 317. Cf. R. H. Charles, *The Chronicle of John, Bishop of Nikiu* (Oxford: Williams & Norgate, 1916) 76 (Charles, ch. 79 = Zotenberg, ch. 80).

[74]B. Evetts, ed., *The History of the Patriarchs of Alexandria* (PO 1; Paris: Firmin-Didot, 1904) 416-20.

[75]R. Basset, ed., *Synaxaire arabe jacobite* (PO 17; Paris: Firmin-Didot, 1929) 531.

[76]I. Guidi, ed., *Synaxaire éthiopien* (PO 1; Paris: Firmin-Didot, 1907) 533.

[77]W. Jacob and R. Hanslik, eds., *Cassiodori-Epiphanii Historia Ecclesiastica Tripartita* (CSEL 71; Vienna: Hoelder-Pichler-Tempsky, 1952) 365-66.

David Levenson

34. Isidore of Seville, *Chronica Maiora* 345 (615 CE)[78] [Rufinus][79]

35. Amulo of Lyon, *Epistula seu Liber contra Judaeos ad Carolum Regem* 19 (846 CE)[80] [Isidore, *Hist. Trip.*][81]

36. Haymon of Auxerre, *Historia sacrae epitome sive de christianorum rerum memoria Libri Decem* 3.8 (mid ninth cent. CE)[82] [Isidore][83]

37. Ado of Vienne, *Chronicon in aetates sex divisum* AD 361 (ca. 869 CE) [84] [Isidore]

38. Flodoard of Rheims, *De Triumphis Christi Sanctorumque Palestinae* 2.2[85] (mid tenth cent. CE)[86] [Rufinus, *Hist. Trip.*]

39. Marianus Scotus, *Chronicon* AD 382 (1082 CE)[87] [Isidore]

40. John of Salisbury, *Policraticus* 8.21 (1159 CE)[88] [*Hist. Trip.*]

41. *Annales Magdeburgenses* AD 365 (1164 CE)[89] [*Hist. Trip.*]

42. Sicard of Cremona, *Chronica* AD 364 (1231 CE)[90] [Isidore, *Hist. Trip.*, Ruf. (?)]

43. Vincent of Beauvais, *Speculum Historiale* 10.42 (ca. 1244 CE)[91] [Rufinus]

44. Roger Wendover, *Flores Historiarum* (mid thirteenth cent. CE)

[78]T. Mommsen, ed., *Chronica maiora Isidori iunioris* (MGHaa 11; Berlin: Weidmanns, 1894) 467-68.

[79]Mommsen's edition (467) incorrectly identifies the *Hist. Trip.* as Isidore's source.

[80]PL 116.153.

[81]Amulo's account is taken verbatim from Isidore, with only one phrase reflecting the *Hist. Trip.* The Migne edition refers only to Rufinus (Isidore's source) and the *Hist. Trip.* B. Blumenkranz (*Juifs et chrétiens dans le monde occidental, 430-1096* [Paris: Mouton, 1960], 245, n. 143) mentions only the *Hist. Trip.* as Amulo's source.

[82]PL 118.868a.

[83]Following the Migne editor, Blumenkranz (245, n. 143) mistakenly takes the *Hist. Trip.* to be Haymon's source. In the same note he also identifies the *Hist. Trip.* rather than Isidore as the source for the account in Ado of Vienne (see below).

[84]PL 123.93d-94a.

[85]PL 135.513c-516a.

[86]P. C. Jacobsen, *Flodoard von Rheims: Seine Leben und seine Dichtung 'De triumphis Christi'* (Mittlelateinische Studien und Texte 10; Leiden: Brill, 1978) 105, 237.

[87]G. Waitz, ed., *Mariani Scotti Chronicon* (MGHss 5; Hanover: Hahn, 1844) 528.

[88]C. C. J. Webb, ed., *Ioannis Saresberiensis episcopi Carnotensis Policratici* (2 vols.; Oxford: Clarendon, 1909) 2.388 (798b-806c).

[89]G. H. Pertz, ed., *Annales Magdeburgenses* (MGHss 16; Hanover: Hahn, 1859) 124.

[90]O. Holder-Egger, ed., *Sicardi Episcopi Cremonensis Chronica* (MGHss 31; Hanover: Hahn, 1904) 123.

[91]*Speculum Historiale* (Duai ed.; 1624) 557.

45. Matthew Paris, *Flores Historiarum*,[92] *Chronica Majora* AD 364 (mid thirteenth cent. CE)[93]

The St. Albans chronicles of Roger Wendover and Matthew Paris are virtually identical for the period before 1066. Their exact interrelationship is uncertain,[94] but it is clear that the Temple rebuilding account ultimately derives from Ado.

46. Martin of Troppau, *Chronicon* AD 362 (1270's CE)[95] [Vincent]

47. Ranulph Higden, *Polychronicon* 4.28 (mid fourteenth cent. CE)[96] [Isidore, *Hist. Trip.*]

Medieval Hebrew Chronicles

48. Abraham Zacuto, *Sefer Yuḥasin* 6.9 (1504 CE)[97] (5.7 in Shulam's *editio princeps*[98]))

Zacuto translates into Hebrew the *Supplementum chronicorum* of the Augustinian monk Jacopo Filippo Foresta of Bergamo[99] (or another work with identical contents), as he did for many of his notices of world history, which he says he found in "Christian chronicles." He follows Foresta's distorted account which reports the destruction of the Temple built by Julian by an earthquake in the reign of Valentinian and concludes with an account of Valens giving the Jews permission to rebuild the Temple.

49. Gedaliah ibn Yaḥya, *Shalshelet ha-Qabbalah*, pt. 3 (ca. 1587 CE)[100]
   a. 106b;   b. 109b.

---

[92]H. R. Luard, *Flores Historiarum* (Rolls series 95; 3 vols.; London: Eyre and Spottiswoode, 1890) 1.190.

[93]H. R. Luard, *Matthaei Parisiensis, monachi sancti Albani, Chronica Majora* (Rolls Series 57; 7 vols.; London: Longman, 1872) 1.166.

[94]See R. Vaughan, *Matthew of Paris* (Cambridge: Cambridge University Press, 1958) 21-48, 92-109.

[95]L. Weiland, ed., *Martini Oppaviensis Chronicon Pontificum et Imperatorum* (MGHss 22; Hanover: Hahn, 1872) 452.

[96]C. Babington and J. R. Lumby, eds., *Polychronicon Ranulphi Higden, monachi Cestrensis* (Rolls Series 41; 9 vols.; London: Longman, 1874) 5.170-172.

[97]H. Filipowsky, ed., *Sefer Yuḥasin Ha--Shalem* (3d ed. by A. H. Freimann; Jerusalem, 1962/63) 246b.

[98]Constantinople, 1566 (no pagination). Shulam's edition represents a significantly different text type from that preserved in Filipowsky's Bodleian MS.

[99]*Supplementum chronicorum orbis ab initio mundi usque ad a. 1482*. The popular work appeared in six Latin editions (1483-1503) and two Italian translations (1488 and 1491) before Zacuto wrote the last section of *Sefer Yuḥasin*.

[100]*Shalshelet ha-Qabbalah* (Venice, 1587) 106b and 109b.

The first account, taken from Zacuto, is placed in the reign of Valentinian. The second, a translation of Foresta[101] (whose chronicle he mentions in his introduction [4b]), is strangely placed in AD 588 (AM 4349) in spite of the references to Julian and Valens. Evidently he confused the fourth-century earthquake with the one in AD 588.

50. David Gans, *Tzemah David* (1592 CE)

    a. AD 367;   b. AD 380;   c. AD 584.[102]

For the attempt to rebuild the Temple under Julian, Gans cites Bünting[103] and Caesius.[104] In fact, Gans used only Caesius' account and his translation was influenced by Zacuto's wording and possibly Ibn Yahya's. In addition to the rebuilding attempt under Julian, he reports two other attempts in an effort to harmonize his sources: under Valentinian (AD 380), for which he cites Zacuto, and under Maurice (ca. 584), for which he cites Ibn Yahya.

Dating the Event: The Jerusalem Fire and the Palestinian Earthquakes of May, 363

Three dates are associated with the incident:

    a. Iyyar (May) 19.[105] According to the Letter of Cyril, the date of the earthquake that stopped the work and destroyed twenty-one to twenty-three Palestinian cities.[106]

    b. Iyyar 27. According to the *Chron. misc.*, the date of the fall of twenty-one Palestinian cities as punishment of the pagan, Jewish and Samaritan cities which joined Julian.[107]

---

[101]A. David ("The Historical Work of Gedalyah Ibn Yahya, Author of *Shalshelet Ha-Kabbalah*" [Heb.; Diss., Hebrew University, 1976] 42) suggests that either Ibn Yahya depended on Zacuto or they both used a common source for their accounts of the attempt to rebuild the Temple.

[102]M. Breuer, ed., *Sefer Tzemah David le Rabbi David Ganz (Prague, 1592)* (Jerusalem: Magnes, 1983) 242, 244, 260.

[103]Heinrich Bünting, *Itinerarium Sacrae Scriptura: dass ist ein Reisebuch über die gantze heilige Schrifft* (Helmstadt: Siebenbürger, 1581).

[104]Georg Caesius, *Chronick oder ordentliche Verzeichnuss aller Cometen* (Nuremburg: Fuhrmann, 1579).

[105]In 363, the lunar and Julian Iyyar coincided exactly, leading Brock (268) to see a connection with Lag Baomer (Iyyar 18), the day the work was to have begun. The first reference to the festival that I have found comes from the twelfth century (R. Zecharia ha-Levi Gerondi, cited in *Tur, Orah Hayyim*, 493) and such a long silence in Rabbinic discussion counts greatly against an early origin for the festival.

[106]Textual corruption makes it impossible to determine the exact number of cities in the list.

[107]Although Agapius and Philostorgius (as abbreviated by the *Artemii Passio*) do not provide dates, they do contain information about the earthquake clearly related to that in the letter and the *Chron. Pasch.* Agapius reports the destruction of twenty-two Palestinian cities. The *Artemii Passio* lists four cities (three of which are at the

c. Baounah (May) 27. According to the *Arabic Synaxarium*, the date the bodies of John the Baptist and Elisha appeared in Alexandria after they had been rescued by Christians when Julian had ordered them burned.

Libanius (*Or.* 1.134) confirms that earthquakes destroyed many Palestinian cities just before Julian's death on June 26.[108] Ammianus, however, who is probably best informed about what stopped the work on the Temple, mentions only continuous fires coming from the foundations. If he (or Chrysostom in one of his eight references to the incident) had known about the earthquakes, they would almost certainly have mentioned them.[109] Two somewhat tenuous pieces of evidence from Julian's works relate to the question of dating: (1) John the Lydian's statement that Julian was on campaign in Persia (i.e., after March 5) when he wrote to the Jews claiming that he was in the process of rebuilding the Temple, and (2) Julian's comment in *Ep.* 89b (date uncertain) that he intended (διενοήθην) to rebuild the Temple. Many have taken the aorist to mean that Julian already knew the enterprise had failed.[110]

The following hypothesis would explain the evidence. Repeated fires stopped the attempt to rebuild the Temple in Spring 363. (May 19 is a bit late if *Ep.* 89b implies that Julian already knows the project has failed.) A number of Palestinian cities were destroyed by earthquake(s) in late May. Christians originally saw the

beginning of the letter's list), notes that many more were destroyed and, then, like the letter, mentions Jerusalem, with the note that fire broke out there. Neither the letter nor the *Artemii Passio* refers at this point to the dramatic account of the fire each had narrated earlier. This clear relationship between the accounts in Philostorgius and the letter of Cyril is best explained by assuming that Philostorgius' account originally contained a list of twenty-one or twenty-two cities which was abbreviated by the author of the *Artemii Passio*. The Philostorgian list made its way into Syriac, perhaps in the lost fourth-century section of John of Ephesus' *Ecclesiastical History*, and was then used by Agapius and the authors of the letter of Cyril and the *Chron. misc.*

[108]This is also consistent with the archaeological record. See Kenneth W. Russell, "The Earthquake of May 19, A.D. 363," *BASOR* 238 (1980) 47-64.

[109]Ammianus is particularly interested in earthquakes and refers to them frequently. Cf. 22.13.5; 23.1.7, and the famous excursus on the subject in 17.7.

[110]E.g., J. Bidez, *L'Empereur Julien, oevres complètes.* Vol. 1, *part 2: Lettres et fragments* (Paris: Les Belles lettres 1924) 102, n. 2; Vogt, *Kaiser Julian*, 47, 53; G. W. Bowersock, *Julian*, 121. Levi (226, n. 25), followed by Stern (557), argues that the aorist indicates only that "Julian discusses his intention from an historical perspective," and the passage does not, therefore, imply that the project had already failed. Bowersock (121) argues that Ammianus' placement of the incident with events at the beginning of the year (*isdem diebus*) and Julian's apparent reference to it as past in *Ep.* 89b prove that the enterprise failed while Julian was still in Antioch. Against this line of argument are John the Lydian's explicit statement and Ammianus' frequently imprecise use of *isdem diebus* (see T. D. Barnes' critique of Bowersock's position in *CR* n.s. 35 [1985] 48-50).

quakes as punishment of the pagan and Samaritan cities that had sided with Julian and had attacked their Christian inhabitants.[111] This explains why May 27 could be associated both with the *translatio* of the saints' bodies and the date of the earthquake. Very quickly (i.e., already before Ephrem and Gregory recorded the oral tradition about the event), the earthquakes that punished the Palestinian cities were associated with the fires that frustrated the Temple rebuilding project somewhat earlier.

[111]Cf. the Alexandrian tradition first cited by Rufinus (11.28) that the bones of John the Baptist (Philostorgius [7.4] mentions Elisha also) were burned by pagans in Sebaste and the ashes sent to Alexandria. See also the accounts of pagan attacks on the Christians elsewhere in Palestine (Gaza [Gregory 4.86; Soz. 5.9], Ascalon [Theodoret 3.7]; Scythopolis [*Chron. Pasch.* 546], Paneas [Philostorgius 7.3]).

ABBREVIATIONS

Ancient Sources

Biblical

Gen	Genesis
Exod	Exodus
Lev	Leviticus
Num	Numbers
Deut	Deuteronomy
Kgs	Kings
Isa	Isaiah
Hab	Habakkuk
Mal	Malachi
Ps	Psalm(s)
Prov	Proverbs
Eccl	Ecclesiastes
Esth	Esther
Dan	Daniel
Chr	Chronicles

Matt	Matthew
1 Pet	1 Peter
Rev	Revelation

Apocrypha

1, 2 Macc	1, 2 Maccabees
Sir	Sirach
Tob	Tobit

Pseudepigrapha and other Jewish Literature

Bib. Ant.	*Biblcal Antiquities*
Jos. and Asen.	*Joseph and Asenath*
Josephus	
Ant.	*Antiquities*
J.W.	*Jewish War*
Jub.	*Jubilees*
Par. Jer.	*Paralipomena Jeremiou*
TPL	*Testament of Levi* (in *Testaments of the Twelve Pastriarchs*)

Qumran

1QH	*Hôdāyôt* (*Thanksgiving Hymns*) from Qumran Cave 1
1QIsa	Copy of Isaiah from Qumran Cave 1
1QM	*Milḥāmāh (War Scroll)*

1QpHab	*Pesher on Habakkuk* from Qumran Cave 1
1QS	*Serek hayyaḥad (Rule of the Community, Manual of Discipline)*
4QDan	*Daniel* fragments from Qumran Cave 4
4QGen	*Genesis* fragments from Qumran Cave 4

Rabbinic Literature
Mishnah, Tosephta, and Talmud Tractates

ʾ*Abot* .	ʾ*Abot*
b.	Babylonian Talmud
Ber.	*Berakot*
B. Bat.	*Baba Batra*
Hor.	*Horayot*
m.	Mishnah
Meg.	*Megilla*
Moᶜed Qat.	*Mo ᶜed Qaṭan*
Nazir	*Nazir*
Sanh.	*Sanhedrin*
Yebam.	*Yemabot*

Other Literature

Mek.	*Mekilta*
Gen. Rab.	*Genesis Rabbah*
Sipre	*Sipre*
Tg. Neof.	*Targum Neofiti 1*
T. Onq.	*Targum Onqelos*
Tg. Ps.-J	*Targum Pseudo Jonathan*
Tg. Yer.	*Targum Yerushalmi*

Early Christian

ATh	Acts of Thomas
Apost. Const.	*Apostolic Constitutions*
Chron. misc.	*Chronicon miscellaneum*
Chron. pasch.	*Chronicon paschale*
Cyril	Cyril of Jerusalem
Catech.	*Catecheses Illuminandorum*
Ep.	*Epistle*
Ephrem	Ephrem of Nisibis
HNat.	*Hymni de Nativitate*
Exp. in Ps. 110	*Expositio in Psalmos 110*
H.E.	*Historia Ecclesiastica*
Hist. Trip.	*Historia Ecclesiastica Tripartita*
HNat.	*Hymni de Nativitate*

Abbreviations

Hom. in Acta Apost.	*Homiliae in Acta Apostolorum*
Hom. in Mt.	*Homiliae in Mattheum*
In Dan.	*In Danielem*

Modern Secondary Literature

AB	Anchor Bible
AcOr`	*Acta Orientalia*
ALD	*Aramaic Levi Document*
AnBib	Analecta Biblica
AnBoll.	*Analecta Bollandiana*
BASOR	*Bulletin of the American Schools of Oriental Research*
BDB	F. Brown, S. R. Driver, and C. A. Briggs, *Hebrew and English Lexicon of the Old Testament*
BETL	Bibliotheca Ephemeridum Theologicarum Lovaniensium
Bib	*Biblica*
BSOAS	*Bulletin of the School of Oriental and African Studies*
BZ	*Biblische Zeitschrift*
CBQ	*Catholic Biblical Quarterly*
CChr	Corpus Christianorum
CII	Corpus Inscriptionum Iudaicarum
CJ	*Classical Journal*
CP	*Classical Philology*
CPJ	Corpus Papyrorum Judaicarum
CR	*Classical Review*
CRINT	Compendia Rerum Iudaicarum ad Novum Testamentum
CSCO	Corpus Scriptorum Christianorum Orientalium
Scr. Syr.	Scriptores Syri
CSEL	Corpus Scriptorum Ecclesiasticorum Latinorum
CSHB	Corpus Scriptorum Historiae Byzantinae
DJD	Discoveries in the Judaean Desert
EBib	Etudes Bibliques
ET	English translation
GCS	Griechische christliche Schriftsteller
FOTL	Forms of Old Testament Literature
GKC	*Genesius' Hebrew Grammar*, ed. E. Kautzsch, tr. A. E. Cowley
GRBS	*Greek, Roman and Byzantine Studies*
HAT	Handbuch zum Alten Testament
HDR	Harvard Dissertations in Religion
HKAT	Handkommentar zum Neuen Testament
HSM	Harvard Semitic Monographs
HSS	Harvard Semitic Studies
HTR	*Harvard Theological Review*
HTS	Harvard Theological Studies

HUCA	*Hebrew Union College Annual*
ICC	International Critical Commentary
IG	Inscriptiones Graecae
Int	*Interpretation*
JBL	*Journal of Biblical Literature*
JJS	*Journal of Jewish Studies*
JQR	*Jewish Quarterly Review*
JSJ	*Journal for the Study of Judaism in the Persian, Hellinistic and Roman Period*
JSOTSup	Journal for the Study of the Old Testament—Supplement Series
JTS	*Journal of Theological Studies*
KB	L. Koehler and W. Baumgartner, *Lexicon in Veteris Testamenti libros*
LCL	Loeb Classical Library
LUÅ	Lunds Universitets Årsskrift
MGHaa	Monumenta Germaniae Historica auctorum antiquissimorum
MGHss	Monumenta Germaniae Historica scriptorum
MGWJ	*Monatsschrift für Geschichte und Wissenschaft des Judentums*
MS(S)	Manuscript(s)
MT	Masoretic text
NTS	New Testament Studies
OGI	Orientis Graeci Inscriptiones
Or.	*Oratio, Orationes*
OrChr	*Oriens christianus*
OTP	James H. Charlesworth, *Old Testament Pseudepigrapha*
OTS	*Oudtestamentische Studiën*
PG	J. Migne, Patrologia graeca
PL	J. Migne, Patrologia latina
PO	Patrologia Orientalis
PTS	Patristische Texte und Studien
PVTG	Pseudepigrapha Veteris Testamenti Graeca
PW	Pauly-Wissowa, *Real-Encyclopädie der classischen Altertunswissenschaft*
PWSup	Supplement to PW
RAC	*Reallexikon für Antike und Christentum*
RB	*Revue Biblique*
RevQ	*Revue de Qumran*
RTL	*Revue Théologique de Louvain*
SANT	Studien zum Alten und Neuen Testament
SBLASP	Society of Biblical Literature Abstracts and Seminar Papers

Abbreviations

SBLDS	SBL Dissertation Series
SBLTT	SBL Texts and Translations
SC	Sources chrétiennes
SCS	Septuagint and Cognate Studies
SD	Studies and Documents
SEG	Supplementum Epigraphicum Graecum
SJLA	Studies in Judaism in Late Antiquity
SNT	Studien zum Neuen Testament
SPB	Studia Postbiblica
Str-B	[H. Strack and] P. Billerbeck, *Kommentar zum Neuen Testament*
SUNT	Studien zur Umwelt des Neuen Testaments
TAPA	Transactions of the American Philological Association
TDNT	G. Kittel and G. Friedrich, eds., *Theological Dictionary of the New Testament*
TJA	Tiberius Julius Alexander
TU	Texte und Untersuchungen
VC	*Vigiliae Christianae*
VT	*Vetus Testamentum*
VTSup	Vetus Testamentum, Supplements
WUNT	Wissenschaftliche Untersuchungen zum Neuen Testament
ZAW	*Zeitschrift für die alttestamentliche Wissenschaft*

ABOUT THE CONTRIBUTORS

Harold W. Attridge completed his dissertation in 1975 under John Strugnell on the interpretation of scriptural traditions in the *Antiquities* of Josephus. He has subsequently made contributions in the areas of Hellenistic Judaism, Gnosticism, and New Testament Exegesis. He is currently on the faculty of the Department of Theology of the University of Notre Dame.

Bernadette Brooten completed her dissertation in 1982 at Harvard University on women leaders in ancient Jewish synagogues. She has pursued research on women in early Jewish and Christian communities and is on the faculty of Harvard Divinity School.

James H. Charlesworth, after studying under John Strugnell, completed a dissertation at Duke University in 1967. He has made significant contributions to the study of Judaism of the second temple period and to the study of the Jewish background to early Christianity. Well known as editor of the *Old Testament Pseudepigrapha*, he is currently the George L. Collord Professor of New Testament Language and Literature at Princeton Theological Seminary.

Adela Yarbro Collins completed her dissertation, on the combat myth in the book of Revelation, at Harvard University in 1975. She has made contributions to the study of Jewish and Christian apocalyptic traditions and is engaged in research on the historical Jesus and the Gospel of Mark. She is Professor of New Testament and Christian Origins at the University of Notre Dame.

John J. Collins completed his dissertation on the *Sibylline Oracles* under John Strugnell in 1972. He has made contributions to the study of apocalyptic literature of the intertestamental period and to the study of Hellenistic Judaism. He is currently Professor of Hebrew Bible and Director of Graduate Studies in the Department of Theology at the University of Notre Dame. He also serves as editor of the *Journal of Biblical Literature*.

Robert Doran completed a dissertation at Harvard University on 2 Maccabees under John Strugnell in 1981. He has continued to explore the history and historiography of Judaism in the Hellenistic period and is currently on the faculty of Amherst College.

James Davila completed a dissertation in 1988 under Frank Moore Cross and John Strugnell at Harvard University on the unpublished manuscripts from Cave 4 at Qumran. He is a visiting assistant professor at Tulane University.

Contributors

Russell Fuller completed his dissertation at Harvard University on the text of the minor prophets in 1988 under the direction of John Strugnell. He is currently on the faculty of Wellesley College.

John Gager completed his dissertation with John Strugnell in 1967 with a dissertation on Moses in Greco-Roman Paganism. He has subsequently done pioneering work on the use of social-scientific disciplines in biblical study. He is currently Professor of Christian Origins at Princeton University.

Jonas C. Greenfield specializes in Semitic philology and has collaborated with John Strugnell on a number of projects connected with the Dead Sea Scrolls and is currently on the faculty of the Hebrew University of Jerusalem.

Daniel J. Harrington, S.J. completed his dissertation in 1969 under John Strugnell at Harvard University on the text of Pseudo-Philo's *Biblical Antiquities*. He has made controbutions to the study of intertestamental Judaism and the New Testament. He is currently on the faculty of Weston Colllege School of Theology where he is also general editor of *New Testament Abstracts*.

Robert A. Kraft completed a Ph.D. degree at Harvard University in 1961 with a dissertation on the *Epistle of Barnabas*. His subsequent research has concentrated on Jewish and early Christian traditions, as well as on the use of the computer in biblical studies. He is currently on the faculty of the University of Pennsylvania.

David Levenson completed his Ph.D. in 1980 at Harvard University. His dissertation, under the direction of John Strugnell, examined the stories of the Emperor Julian's attempt to rebuild the Jerusalem Temple. He is currently on the faculty of Florida State University.

Kathleen McVey completed her dissertation in 1977 at Harvard University on Syriac traditions about George Bishop of the Arabs. She has subsequently been engaged in research on Syrian traditions, particularly the poetry of Ephrem, a translation of whose hymns she has recently published. She is currently on the faculty of Princeton Theological Seminary.

Frederick J. Murphy completed a dissertation under John Strugnell at Harvard University in 1984 on *2 Baruch*. He is currently on the faculty of Holy Cross College.

Carol Newsom completed her dissertation on the Songs of the Sabbath Sacrifice from Qumran under John Strugnell in 1982. She is currently on the faculty of the Candler School of Theology at Emory University.

George W. E. Nicklesburg completed his dissertation on Jewish traditions about immortality and eternal life at Harvard University in 1968. He has subsequently made contributions to the study of Jewish apocrypha and pseudepigrapha, particularly the Enochic tradition. He is currently on the faculty of the School of Religion at the University of Iowa.

Emile Puech, O.P., has collaborated with John Strugnell on projects connected with the Dead Sea Scrolls. He is currently on the faculty of the École Biblique et Archéologique Française in Jerusalem.

Eileen M. Schuller completed her disserration on the Dead Sea Scrolls under John Strugnell at Harvard University in 1984. She continues to work on Qumran material while teaching on the faculty of McMaster University, Ontario, Canada.

Michael Stone completed his dissertation at Harvard University in 1965. He has subsequently made major contributions to the study of Jewish literature and thought of the late Second Temple period as well as on Armenian literature. Most recently he has completed a commentary on *4 Ezra*. He is on the faculty of the Hebrew University of Jerusalem.

Thomas H. Tobin, S.J. completed his dissertation at Harvard University under John Srrugnell in 1980 on Philo of Alexandria's interfpretations of the creation stories in Genesis. He continues to publish in the areas of Hellenistic Judaism and Hellenistic philosophy. He is currently on the faculty of Loyola University of Chicago.

Emanuel Tov is a specialist on the history of the text of the Hebrew Bible and the Septuagint and has been engaged in research on the significance of Qumran materials for text criticism of the Hebrew Bible. He is on the faculty of the Hebrew University of Jerusalem.

Eugene Ulrich completed a dissertation in 1975 at Harvard University on the Septuagint text of the books of Samuel and Kings. Subsequently he has made contributions to the study of the Septuagint and to the text of the Hebrew Bible. At present he is a collabator of John Strugnell in the project of editing the remaining fragmentary Dead Sea scrolls. He is on the Faculty of the Department of Theololgy at the University of Notre Dame.

James VanderKam completed his dissertation on the Book of Jubilees, receiving his degree from Harvard University in 1976. He has subsequently made contributions to the study of apocrypha and pseudepigrapha, particularly Enochic traditions. He is now on the faculty of North Carolina State University.

Sidnie Ann White completed her Ph.D. at Harvard University in 1988 with a dissertation on the text criticism of Deuteronomy. She is collaborating with John Strugnell on the publication of Dead Sea Scroll manuscripts and is currently an assistant professor at Albright College in Reading, Pennsylvania.

Lawrence Wills received his Ph.D. from Harvard University in 1987 under John Strugnell with a dissertation on Jewish court legends. He is currently on the faculty of Harvard Divinity School with particular responsibility for language instruction.